Processual Sociology

Processual Sociology

Andrew Abbott

The University of Chicago Press   CHICAGO & LONDON

ANDREW ABBOTT is the Gustavus F. and Ann M. Swift Distinguished Service Professor at the University of Chicago. He edits the *American Journal of Sociology*.

The University of Chicago Press, Chicago 60637
The University of Chicago Press, Ltd., London
© 2016 by The University of Chicago
All rights reserved. Published 2016.
Printed in the United States of America

25 24 23 22 21 20 19 18 17 16   1 2 3 4 5

ISBN-13: 978-0-226-33659-6 (cloth)
ISBN-13: 978-0-226-33662-6 (paper)
ISBN-13: 978-0-226-33676-3 (e-book)
DOI: 10.7208/chicago/9780226336763.001.0001

Library of Congress Cataloging-in-Publication Data
Abbott, Andrew Delano, author.
  Processual sociology / Andrew Abbott.
      pages cm
  Includes bibliographical references and index.
  ISBN 978-0-226-33659-6 (cloth : alkaline paper) — ISBN 978-0-226-33662-6
(pbk. : alkaline paper) — ISBN 978-0-226-33676-3 (e-book) 1. Social sciences—
Philosophy. 2. Sociology—Philosophy. 3. Change—Social aspects. 4. Becoming
(Philosophy)—Social aspects. 5. Ontology—Social aspects. 6. Sociology—Moral and
ethical aspects. I. Title.
  HM585.A237 2016
  301.01—dc23

                                                                      2015031807

♾ This paper meets the requirements of ANSI/NISO Z39.48–1992
(Permanence of Paper).

In memory of my brother Frank

CONTENTS

PREFACE

This volume assembles nine theoretical papers written at various times in the last dozen years. Some have been previously published, some published in other languages or in obscure venues, some not published at all. Although on the surface they concern diverse topics, these papers share a common theme underneath: the elaboration of a processual approach to the social world.

By a processual approach, I mean an approach that presumes that everything in the social world is continuously in the process of making, remaking, and unmaking itself (and other things), instant by instant. The social world does not consist of atomic units whose interactions obey various rules, as in the thought of the economists. Nor does it consist of grand social entities that shape and determine the little lives of individuals, as in the sociology of Durkheim and his followers. Nor does it consist of conflict between given units, as in the work of Marx and his many imitators. Nor yet of symbolic structures that determine and shape our perception of the social world, as in the tradition following from Geertz and Schneider. These are all distinguished traditions, and each has its successes in the analysis of human affairs. But the approach here is different.

A processual approach begins by theorizing the making and unmaking of all these things—individuals, social entities, cultural structures, patterns of conflict—instant by instant as the social process unfolds in time. The world of the processual approach is a world of events. Individuals and social entities are not the elements of social life, but are patterns and regularities defined on lineages of successive events. They are moments in a lineage, moments that will themselves shape the next iteration of events even as they recede into the past. The processual approach, in short, is fundamentally, essentially historical. All the micro-elements with which the other approaches begin are themselves macrostructures in the processual approach. Their stability is something to be explained, not presumed.

The immediate ancestry of processualism lies in pragmatism and the Chicago School of sociology that grew up in dialogue with it. Unfortunately, no one in the Chicago School ever bothered to write systematic social theory. And the pragmatists themselves devoted more attention to psychology than to social theory. Moreover, the pragmatist encounter with rigorous processualism was truncated by George Herbert Mead's death when he had only begun to elaborate his reactions to Whitehead.

As one of the heirs of these various traditions, I have been working for many years on a systematic exposition of processual social theory. But so massive an endeavor inevitably produces subproblems and intermediate implications. Indeed, I have found that it is through careful work on such subproblems that I achieve the more general clarity that has so often eluded me when I approached my task deductively. Thus, for example, the processual approach requires a clear theorization of time, and so I gathered my work on various theoretical and methodological subproblems of social time into the book *Time Matters* over a decade ago. There I addressed theoretical topics like the nature of temporality, the problem of turning points, and the mechanisms of social entity formation, as well as methodological topics like how to imagine causality and social action, how to handle the many ambiguities of temporal order, and how to operationalize conceptions of events.

The present book brings together another generation of such papers, which investigate different aspects of the processual approach and in some cases challenge or extend arguments in that earlier collection. Part 1 begins by directly introducing some aspects of the processual ontology. Part 2 then moves to some methodological (chapter 4) and theoretical (chapter 5) implications of that ontology.

These first five chapters are a unit. They remain within the now-traditional view of social theory as an abstract approach to the social world—a view from the outside, in some sense. However, the processual view's focus on the everyday making of social reality inevitably confronts it with the empirical fact that social events are produced not only by causal mechanisms, but also by moral judgments and values. So the last four chapters confront some of the issues that are involved in the moral and value character of the social process and, therefore, of any scientific enterprise that studies it. The chapters of part 3 address the questions of personal outcome and social order, and those of part 4 address questions about normative practice within the social sciences.

In none of the four parts is the analysis more than suggestive. (By contrast, my current draft of the formal exposition of a processual social ontology alone—the subject of part 1—is longer than this entire book.) But these chapters capture important aspects of the problematics that processualism must address, and it may well be that in a world of shorter attention spans, pointed essays may more effectively convey a perspective than can a systematic exposition.

Let me now review the book's contents in a little more detail. As I said, the three papers of part 1 concern matters of social ontology. The first considers the endurance of social things in a processual world, their "historicality." Taken for granted in most approaches to social life, this is a central problem of processual thinking: if change is the normal state of things, how does anything ever stay the same? The second chapter considers the problem of human nature from the point of view of processualism: How can we talk about "human nature" if that nature is always changing? The third chapter generalizes the ecological arguments of my book *The System of Professions*, arguing that it is not enough to conceive of some particular social area as an ecology surrounded by powerful forces, as if one part of the social process were moving while its surroundings were fixed and enduring. No; all is change. Therefore, we must consider the whole social world as being constituted of such ecologies, linked together such that each changing ecology appears as "powerful external forces" to the others with which it is linked.

Each of these three chapters shows how different the social world appears when we approach it processually. Individuals and social entities are made dynamically through time, and, moreover, their relation to one another at a moment (ecology) constitutes a mutual conversation that is as important as is the over-time conversation of lineage, which attempts to bind the past, present, and future of some one particular social thing. Thus, context matters, not just through time but also across (social as well as physical) space. These chapters continue a line of analysis first explored in the third part of *Time Matters* and given empirical shape in my earlier book *Department and Discipline*. (All of my books are integrally related to the present one, and so for the sake of simplicity I shall cite them throughout by their titles, after their first appearance in the "author-year" format.)

The two chapters of part 2 take this processual focus to a new area, the premises of sociological theorizing. The first fleshes out the duality of time investigated in chapter 3. The concept of ecology originally emerged (for me, at least) in the empirically obvious fact that professions' histories at a given moment are in some ways determined more by the contemporaneous environment of other professions than by some internal logic of their own "narratives" over time. Historicality does matter, but it matters because it endows actors with current properties that may advantage or disadvantage them in living the present moment. But while an ecological perspective addresses this problem, it doesn't really address the philosophical question of how we should begin to think about "the present" as a moment, about process as evident in a single instant of the passage of time. Chapter 4 addresses this problem as both a methodological and a theoretical issue. It urges us to broaden our repertoire beyond the familiar narrative framework that sustains our usual methods, both quantitative and qualitative. We need also a lyrical sociology, by which I mean a sociology of moments and of emotional identification. The chapter underscores the dangers of a purely narrative approach to process, recovering the "momentary" approach to time so much decried by the Marxists and by the Manchester School's critique of the "ethnographic present." It also implicitly challenges some of the arguments in part 2 of my own *Time Matters* and extends the arguments in chapter 7 of that book. At the same time it raises the possibility of "humanist sociology," which will be taken up in the epilogue to the present book.

Becoming more processual in one's theoretical thinking has another important consequence besides obliging one to think consciously about the relation of the over-time and the across-space. It has also the consequence of vastly multiplying the number of social situations to be addressed. If sequence (location in time) matters, then A after B is different from B after A. If ecology (location in space) matters, then being A near B and C is different from being A near D and E. Thinking processually thus makes one ever more sensitive to particularity, and, more important, it defines particularity not only in terms of ego, but also in terms of those around ego. This locational complexity combinatorically increases the complexity of the social life we analyze. Chapter 5 confronts the implications of this fact of excess, made so evident in processual thinking. To be sure, the original motivation of the chapter is more abstract. It starts from the simple fact of social excess, on the one hand, and the obvious lack of any theoretical means to think about it, on the other. But the combinatoric complexity involved in thinking processually provides one motivation for the first of these, while processual theories provide accounts of both the origins of excess (in habituation and group dissolution, among other things) and the strategies by which we handle it (for example, by serialism—the sequential enjoyment of various different benefits in a world of excess goods).

As noted earlier, parts 3 and 4 embody a turn toward the normative. This turn is facilitated—perhaps even necessitated—by the processual approach. The processual view reminds us that only the present ever exists. All the causal effects of the past must work by affecting the shape of the present (by what I shall in chapter 1 call "encoding" themselves into the social structure). But this transition of all "causal" effects through a single moment creates an opening for moral activity. Causal effects are only one aspect of what determines things in the present. The present is also determined by our action, which we both undertake and judge under the sign of "oughtness," of morals. In these two parts I begin to analyze this realm of oughtness.

It is important to note that some other kinds of social theory treat moral behavior as an empirical fact: something to be causally explained. Durkheim's analysis of morality was of this kind, even though he himself was a man obsessed with moral duties that he did not at all regard as externally, socially caused, but as inwardly obligatory. (I shall analyze that contradiction—what I shall call "knowledge alienation"—in chapter 9.) And indeed, within the massivist Durkheimian approach to the social process, it can be difficult to see what is the place for morality, or indeed even for free will, which becomes a kind of "error variance" in Durkheim's probabilistic view of social causation. But processualism, by insisting that all "cause" flow through the present, inevitably creates a real opening for free action as a phenomenon. So within it, the analysis of moral activity becomes a special obligation.

Chapters 6 and 7 begin this investigation by turning to the classic question of our criteria for good social life. These questions have often been regarded as simply empirical questions, at least at the individual level. A good life is a wealthy life, or a happy life, or a sexually satisfied life, or whatever. Similarly, at the social level, we have the Parsonian concept of "the problem of social order." Chapters 6 and 7 question these simple arrogations of personal outcome and social order to the empirical realm. Chapter 6 considers the various possible criteria for individual lives—what it calls the problem of outcome. It argues that our usual common-sense conceptions of "how things turn out" are in fact strongly normative, particularly with respect to their thinking about time and process. The chapter therefore considers a much wider array of possible conceptions of outcome, noting their inevitably moral character. Chapter 7 undertakes the same analysis at the social level, considering the classic problem of social order as posed by Parsons, but extending that analysis to many other forms of order than the simple one he considered. Again, the central problems involve how we imagine value as located in time, a problem that has vexed philosophers since Aristotle. Both these chapters thus focus on processual accounts, of individual and social good respectively. Both are largely speculative, and like the two preceding chapters they add to their processual stance a theoretical commitment to broadening the repertoire of sociology.

Chapters 8 and 9 address the question of moral practice in sociology itself. They thus capture more particular consequences of the inevitably moral nature of social science. Like the analyses of personal outcome and social order that precede them, they grow out of the processual position's direct encounter with the moral shaping of events. Chapter 8 discusses the problem of inequality as it has been investigated empirically within the atemporal, aspatial approach of traditional sociology. The chapter shows first that what appear to be measurement decisions are actually normative decisions, continuing the critique of "normal empirical practice" that was made in chapter 6. It then turns to the ontological problems inherent in failing to think about inequality within a processual framework. Not only does the paper argue that most analyses of inequality inadvertently assume moral positions they may well not actually advocate; it also shows how most concepts of inequality have a temporal incoherence that can be rectified only by an openly normative analysis of preferable kinds of life courses.

Chapter 9 turns to a very specific question, that of the morality of the professions, not qua empirical issue, but qua moral issue: not so much how we understand the empirical phenomenon of professional morals, but rather how we ourselves live the moral practice that defines the lives of academic professionals. The analysis begins with the problem of knowledge alienation—theorizing about social life one way and living it another. It then analyzes the Durkheimian position on morality and eventually finds itself forced to theorize how best to marry empirical and normative analyses of social life, a marriage that I am persuaded is required by the processual approach to social ontology. The analysis moves inevitably towards a conception of the social process as simultaneously empirical and moral, and towards a social science that includes not only empirical and theoretical work, but also explicitly normative work of the kind currently found only in political theory, among the social sciences.

The book closes with a sketch of the humanistic sociology that seems to me to grow out of the processual vision. While humanism is most evident within certain methodological frameworks, I am persuaded that it embodies a stance viable across all methodologies. While this sketch originated as a comment on claims for "critical sociology" and similar political enterprises, it rests, in the last instance, on the conception of the social process that underlies this book. It grows directly from theory.

The book thus has a clear logic to it, and an underlying common thematics. But the pieces remain separate enough to be read individually. In editing, I have aimed to emphasize common themes, but have left within each chapter the independent motivating section that originally launched its argument. This creates occasional repetition and occasionally abrupt transitions from chapter to chapter. But seeming infelicities are the price of guaranteeing that while the book can be read in independent bits, it also has an underlying unity and indeed the sense of direction that I have emphasized in the preceding summary.

There is one further aspect of the texts that may be jarring to a straight-through reader. The chapters are not all written in the same rhetorical structure, nor do they all employ the same mode of theorizing. Perhaps most noticeable is that some are highly detailed formal expositions while others take a more conversational, oral form. The transition is particularly noticeable between chapters 2 and 3 and between chapters 6 and 7.

The explanation is a simple one. All of these chapters began life as formal lectures, but some have come further from that origin than have others. Editing for this volume has changed all of them considerably, to be sure, but the exigencies of prior publication have left a large mark. Chapters 3 through 6 were all published in settings where extensive scholarly machinery was required. Chapters 1, 2, and 7 through 9 are either unpublished or were published in settings where the machinery was unimportant. Chapters 3 through 6 thus have many footnotes, employ fixed and often stylized rhetorical structures, and contain as much or more evidence as they do theoretical argument. They also have more internal signposting. By contrast, the preceding and following chapters contain less evidence and make their arguments in a more loosely discursive form.

All these chapters range fairly widely across disciplines and methods. They move from quantitative to qualitative and back, and encourage readers to follow me into literatures with which they have no familiarity and in which I am not an expert. It is my belief, however, that the thread and focus of the theorizing successfully hold all this interdisciplinarity together. Indeed, such chapters seem to me to be interdisciplinary in the proper sense of that word.

As for the actual historical order, chapter 3 dates from the late 1990s, and chapters 1 and 6 date from the early 2000s. Despite their original publication dates, however, these three chapters were more or less produced together.

Chapters 4 and 7 came in the mid-2000s, again produced more or less together. Chapters 2 and 9 came in 2009 and 2011 respectively. Chapter 5 was first written in 2009, and evolved for five years into the version published here. Chapter 8 was written in 2014 and slid directly into this book.

I have dedicated the book to my late brother. He and I were unlike in many superficial ways, but curiously alike in a few deep ones. I write scholarly books. He built a sweat-equity ranchette. But we were both puzzled by life and by other people. We fought like animals as adolescents, and we saw each other seldom as adults. But his death made clear a buried bond of unsuspected strength. May he rest in the peace that he seldom knew while he was alive.

* Part 1 *

The three following chapters concern social ontology. They set forth a processual approach to the nature of both individuals and social entities. Indeed, the argument will be made that individuals are social entities, no different for many purposes from bureaucracies, social movements, and cohorts.

The first two chapters were originally written as conference lectures, and have been left in the informal tone characteristic of such lectures. The third, by contrast, is a lecture-become-article and has therefore more scholarly machinery: footnotes and references.

All three chapters stand in the same tradition of processuality, however. Responding to the essentially historical nature of social life, they start from the premise that the social world is one of constant change. Stability must therefore be explained. They take for granted that the social process is one of moments and, moreover, that those moments are local—"presents" in both the spatial and temporal senses of the word. Events are those local consummations of action and interaction that knot the contingencies of the present into new relations and structures that become the constraints and potentialities of the next moment—its past. Such assumptions require that we rethink the nature of the traditional units of social analysis: individuals and social structures. The results have startling implications.

Thus, the argument for the "historicality of individuals" in chapter 1 implies that the common theory of "levels" of the social process—biology, personality, social structure, culture or whatever other series we may use—is fundamentally mistaken. There are no levels. Social entities and forces are not larger than individuals. They are just a different kind of pattern defined on events, which are the true substrate of the social process. Similarly, the argument for a processual concept of human nature implies that the debate over the rationality of *Homo economicus* is a red herring. The important facts of human nature concern how personalities link past, present, and future, and because of the social nature of the personality these linkages can be expected to vary from culture to culture. Finally, the argument for linked ecologies underscores the fact that single actors—individuals or social entities—are never purely free but must always make their futures in conditions shaped by others; and not only by those others that are socially nearby, but also by those further off. This in turn implies that analysis of one social structure alone can never make sense. Structures are always involved with other social structures beyond them, and beyond that with legal systems and other actors that are themselves involved in yet further competitions and difficulties of their own. The social process unfolds through the alignments and disalignments of all these things "across the present," not in some local equilibrium.

The three chapters that follow thus present an introduction to thinking processually about social life. Most important, they start from the axiom of change. Change is not something that happens occasionally to stable social actors. Change is the natural state of social life. Stability is a creation or, more often, a linguistic mirage. There are no "social movements." There is nothing but social movement.

CHAPTER 1

The Historicality of Individuals[1]

I shall here argue that we should reinstate individuals as an important force in history. By this I do not mean a return to great-man history, or great-woman history for that matter. To be sure, social structure can and sometimes does confer on particular individuals extraordinary power to shape the future. But the crucial explanatory question in such cases is not the quality or actions of those individuals, interesting as these might be. Rather, it is the conditions under which such social structures emerge and stabilize. The real question, for example, is not why it was that Elizabeth Tudor chose not to marry, but rather how it came to be that there was a social structure in which her refusal to marry could have such enduring political consequences. In this sense, great-person history is merely an empirically defined subbranch of the history of social structures in general. It is not really about individuals qua individuals, or even about individuals taken as a group or type, but rather about the conditions that make particular individuals particularly important. So it is not to the great-person mode of thinking about individuals that I urge our return.

Nor will I urge us to turn to what we usually call "the life course perspective," although some of my own past work on careers is certainly cognate with that perspective, at least in methodological terms. In life course approaches,

1. This paper began as the presidential lecture of the Social Science History Association in 2003. It was subsequently published with minor revision in the association's journal, *Social Science History*. "The Historicality of Individuals," *Social Science History* 29, no 1: 1–13. Copyright 2005, Social Science History Association. All rights reserved. Reprinted by permission of Duke University Press. I have here edited it slightly, but have not altered its tone of informal speech.

as is well known, we do not seek the meaning of events by looking across cases, as we do in variables-based social science. Rather, we look along the cases, finding the meaning of this or that event by its relation to the unfolding of an individual's experience. This is the same whether we take a narrative approach and study the "story" of an individual life with textual methods, or take an analytic approach and study an ordered sequence of some variable's values over an individual life course using time series methods, sequence analysis, or some other such formal approach. Either way, we are interested in the sequential unfolding of the outcomes of a person's life.[2]

This relatively strong focus on outcomes seriously limits the life course approach. The social process doesn't have outcomes. It just keeps on going. Individuals don't have outcomes either, except the invariant one that we must all expect in Keynes's long run. So the implicit analytic focus of life course studies on individual outcomes creates important problems, which we can see by looking at the concept of careers—the central life course concept of my own substantive field, the study of work and occupations. In our study of careers, we often see the individual as a kind of final slate on which the outcomes of social processes are written. Analytically, that is, most studies of careers presuppose a world in which large social forces push little individuals around, placing successive marks on individuals' work experience, which is then taken as the final explanandum. Translating this presupposition into more substantive language, we might say that big exogenous changes in technology, division of labor, markets, and legal institutions dictate the successive experience of the working individuals caught within them.

But of course the individuals who experience the various intermediate outcomes that make up a career take action in the meantime, while their careers are still in process. And these actions constitute further outcomes of those experiences. One way out of the analytical cul-de-sac implicit in the life course approach is therefore to focus our attention on those further outcomes—the interpretations and actions through which workers come to respond (usually collectively) to the larger social forces pressing on them. There is of course a literature that does this: our long and distinguished inquiry into the social movements through which workers respond to the changes of capitalism. These social movements are precisely the social structures that have emerged among workers to respond to the individual pressures placed on them by the social structures of the capitalists and, indeed, by aspects of the general social

---

2. I shall consider an alternative to such sequentiality in chapter 4. For a longer analysis of the idea of outcome, see chapter 6.

structure that are beyond the capitalists' control—by what we might call the conjuncture.

But, like the social movement literature, this literature too ignores a central fact about individuals. That fact is what I shall call the historicality of individuals. And I will insist that this historicality of individuals is a central force in determining most historical processes. In brief, I shall argue that the sheer mass of the experience that individuals carry forward in time—what we might imagine in demographic terms as the present residue of past cohort experience—is an immense social force. It is all too easy to ignore this easily invisible force, for we fall into that ignorance almost inevitably when we take up periodized historical thinking, as we so often do when we work at the group level. In fact, the vast continuity of individuals over time forbids such periodic analysis, however convenient it may be; most individuals alive in a given period were also alive in the period immediately preceding it. In short, individuals are central to history because it is they who are the prime reservoir of historical connection from past to present. This is what I mean by the historicality of individuals.

Let me start by saying in a little more detail what I mean by historicality. In the first instance, I mean continuity over time. And I argue that individuals have continuity over time to a degree that social structures do not. Note that we assume this relative dominance of individual continuity whenever we make the common remark that social change is getting faster and faster. This assertion involves the assumption that individuals last longer than social structures; for only then do they have to suffer the changes in the latter that force them to realize the extent of mutability. In a world of which it can be said that social change is happening faster and faster, it must be the historical continuity of individuals that provides the sinew linking past and present. It is the historicality of individuals that enables us—even forces us—to know social change.

Now the belief that social change is happening faster and faster also entails a belief that the imbalance between individual and social structural continuity used to be less than it is now. That is, while some might wish to take it as axiomatic that individuals have more continuity over time than do social structures, the actual relation between individual and social structural continuity is probably an empirical matter, varying with time and place. I agree wholeheartedly that we ought to think about degree of historical continuity as an empirical variable. But for convenience of exposition, I shall here somewhat arbitrarily ground my theory in a stylized understanding of contemporary society. In that stylized understanding, it seems to me, we take it for granted that individuals "last longer" than do most social structures.

This "lasting longer" can involve different kinds of things. There seem at first glance to be at least three principal dimensions to such historicality. The first of these is biological. Individuals have bodies that are in some sense physically continuous over time. Although the cells of our bodies are continuously renewed, this renewal is clearly something more precise than is the analogous renewal of, say, a formal organization by gradual replacement of its members. Bodies carry forward records of the past in quite literal ways. They retain disease organisms. They retain an implicit record of past nutrition. They retain the marks of past behavior—of occupation, of exercise, of drug abuse, of unprotected sex. Their immune systems retain a record of past exposure and nonexposure to various pathogens.

Few of these things are retained so exactly by any social structure. Marriage is perhaps the social structure that most closely resembles the individual in this biological sense of historicality, for the various practices of marriage—sexual, hygienic, residential, dietary, and so on—undoubtedly lead to a pooling of much of this biological heritage. In that literal sense, husband and wife do indeed become one flesh. And marriage, like any other dyadic social structure, also depends in a quite literal way on the biological life of the two individuals involved. It dies with either one, and hence, it, too, is always dead in the long run. So marriage is somewhat like individuals in its biological historicality.

But, beyond relations like marriage, most social structures have nothing like this physical continuity. Members change. Rules and practices come and go. Even the social structures that are more or less built around biological commonality or common biological history—genders, kinship structures, lobbying associations for various diseases, and so on—do not have the relatively extensive but nonetheless focused biological continuity that characterizes an individual.

Thus the historicality of the individual is in its first sense biological. Biological individuals carry forward with themselves a huge mass of historical experience, written quite literally in and on their bodies. The historicality of individuals is in its second sense memorial. It arises in the peculiar concentration of memory in biological individuals. By this I don't necessarily mean that social structures can't remember anything. I have no problem with thinking that my memories of past meetings of the Social Science History Association (SSHA) are the organization's memories as well as mine.[3] What is different is that the memory of individual humans is concentrated in their

---

3. As noted earlier, this lecture was originally given at the Social Science History Association's annual meeting—hence the choice of example.

biological selves in a way that the memory of social structures is not. A sizable plurality—perhaps even a majority—of the world's existing memories of Andrew Abbott are concentrated in my head. To be sure, hundreds of thousands of such memories exist elsewhere—in the minds of my teachers, classmates, colleagues, friends, students, relatives, insurance salesmen, and even perhaps in the mind of the conductor who punched my ticket on the train last Thursday. It is crucial for social theory to remember that the self, in this sense, is strewn all over the social landscape, not absolutely concentrated in one biological locale.

But even so, the individual memorial self is less diaphanous than are the memorial selves of social structures. As I have just said, a fairly sizable fraction of the total body of memory relating to Andrew Abbott is in my one head. By contrast, the memories of social structures like SSHA are fairly uniformly scattered in the brains of thousands of members and former members and readers of our journal, of workers in the hotels where we have our annual meetings, and so on. There is no one sensorium where anything like a majority or even a sizable plurality of this memory is located. Even our executive officer commands only a miniscule fraction of the world's total recollection of SSHA. This distribution of memory, let me repeat, does not mean that SSHA doesn't have a memory. Quite the contrary. As an organization's president discovers each time there arises some policy issue that involves organizational precedents, there is a very extensive organizational memory—sometimes mutually supportive, sometimes mutually contradictory, sometimes brighter, sometimes fainter, but always distributed to many different people. But this memory, although extensive, is quite widely and relatively uniformly distributed. Memories of individuals, by contrast, are relatively highly concentrated. This makes the impact of their continuity much greater.

One might note that the memory of an organization is widely distributed also in the sense that it is contained in a widespread body of records. These records constitute a third vector of historicality, for their whole purpose is the literal recording—and thereby the historicizing—of a social or individual entity. Unlike in the case of biological and memorial historicality, it may seem difficult to make the case that the recorded historicality of individuals exceeds that of social structures. However, persons as legal beings have roughly the same historical endurance as do corporations, which are after all *personae fictae*. Thus, there is a legal being who is me, loosely constructed from documents that record my birth, marriage, property, liabilities, contractual obligations, military service, credit record, citizenship rights and obligations, and so on. This legal being is roughly equivalent to a corporation's legal being, recorded in similar documents concerning foundation, merger, property, liabilities, contractual obligations, and so on. But while corporations thus have a legal historicality similar to that of individuals to some extent, the legal historicality of corporations can be truncated and limited in arbitrary ways that a natural person's legal historicality cannot. So even corporations lack the legal historicality of natural individuals, although like all truly social entities, they may outlast individuals in time.

Moreover, the vast majority of social structures are not corporations or even formal organizations. They are things like neighborhoods, occupations, newspaper readerships, church congregations, social classes, ethnicities, technological communities, and consumption groups: often disorganized or unorganized but nonetheless consequential as social structures. These often do not have formal records. If they do, the records are often of diverse kinds, changing rapidly over time. And even their nonrecorded memories are scattered through diverse people having diverse relations to them. Only a few members of these groups have more than a miniscule connection with the whole body of those memories.

Such social structures have quite diaphanous historicality. Their vast riot of memories is embodied in neither a few persons nor a legal being. Because their memories are widely distributed and their records often weak, such structures can change quickly and easily. There is little to keep them coherent over time. The discipline of sociology, for example, has been something like a social reality for about a century. In that period it has drifted quite rapidly from being a progressive and explicitly religious common interest group of do-gooders, reformers, and political academics to being a group of highly professionalized social scientists with an exclusive disciplinary association that aims to produce college teachers. Much of the reason for this change lies in the sheer ease with which the discipline can forget its past—a past that is expiring today in decent silence in the minds of emeritus colleagues.

To a first approximation, then, historicality consists in biological, memorial, and recorded continuity. There is at least a possible case to be made that the total mass of this historicality of individuals, at present, is greater than that of all but a fairly small handful of social structures. What are the consequences of this? The first consequence is that "larger social forces" no longer tower over the individual in the social process. They tower over particular individuals, as we all know at first hand. But they do not tower over the great mass of individual historicality. For while a single individual is easily erased by death, the large mass of individuals is not. And that mass contains an enormous reservoir of continuity with the past. This continuity confronts the "large social

forces" of our arguments—the division of labor, the technological conjuncture, the coming of capitalism—with a huge, recalcitrant weight of quite particular human material that severely limits what those large forces can in fact
accomplish.

This continuity means, for example, that we cannot write a history of periods. We customarily write the history of a population in terms of periods: the
Jazz Age, the Depression, the 1960s, the Reagan years, and so on. This makes
the historical "selves" of a social structure like "The United States" seem to
be a succession of snapshots. But most of the people involved in the adjacent
snapshots of this sequence are of course the same. Of the population who experienced the depths of Depression as workers—the people who were at least
fifteen years old in 1930—about three-quarters were at least fifteen years old in
1920. That is, most people who lived and worked in the Depression had also
lived and worked in the Jazz Age. (In fact, by this definition about half of them
had been workers by 1910, although not necessarily in the United States, to be
sure.) The Depression, that is, largely fell on people who had experienced periods of real prosperity. This fact is obvious but nonetheless important. The
experience of the Depression cannot be understood without it.

As the population ages, this reservoir of memory grows deeper and deeper.
The US median age has risen from twenty-three to thirty-six over the last century, and the 75th age percentile has risen from about thirty-nine to fifty-one.
The implications for social memory are very great. In 2003, we were thirty
years past the great turning point of 1973—the year that saw the end of the
Vietnam War, the end of the Bretton Woods agreements, the first oil shock,
and the Watergate hearings. But 43 percent of the population in 2003 had
been at least ten years old by 1973 and could therefore remember the prior
era, the moment the French call *les trentes glorieuses*, the thirty glorious years
of economic growth and egalitarianism after the war. By contrast, thirty years
after the American Civil War, only 24 percent of those alive had been at least
ten years old when the war ended. Thus, the reservoir of memory at thirty
years is now almost twice as large. As a result, the historical continuity of
closed groups like the population is very much a function of their vital statistics. And the reason we now think social change is so much faster is that more
of us live longer, and hence experience more social change.

This may seem like a trivial example, something we all know. But we do
not write as if we knew this. For instance, my argument about the importance
of historicality also implies that there really is no such thing as a population
survey with independent waves. All surveys repeated at regular intervals are
to a large extent surveys of implicit panels. It was this that Paul Lazarsfeld had

in mind when he argued that "the population votes in the same election but not on it," meaning that many voters were using their current votes to respond to political concerns that arose much earlier, and that may have driven their votes in several prior elections. This statement is worth quoting at length:

> For example, the tendencies operating in 1948 electoral decisions not only were built up in the New Deal and Fair Deal era but also dated back to parental and grandparental loyalties, to religious and ethnic cleavages of a past era, and to moribund sectional and community conflicts. Thus in a very real sense any particular election is a composite of various elections and various political and social events. People vote for a President on a given November day, but their choice is made not simply on the basis of what has happened in the preceding months or even four years; in 1948 some people were in effect voting on the internationalism issue of 1940, others on the depression issues of 1932 and some, indeed, on the slavery issues of 1860.
>
> (BERELSON, LAZARSFELD, AND MCPHEE 1954:315–16)[4]

Note that these compositional implications will be straightforward only on the assumption of perfect memory. This in turn suggests that we ought to devote serious research to the question of when, how, and why the depth and accuracy of this kind of memory changes. In practice, to be sure, this is not how election research developed. Most election research was driven by the pragmatic aim to elect particular candidates, and focused therefore on one particular implication of the historicality of individuals: the fact that a relatively small number of people change position from election to election. These "floating voters" were—from a pragmatic point of view—far more important than the immensely stable average voter and the historicality that produced his or her stability.

Note also that the impact of this memory and continuity—of this historicality—can vary greatly, and particularly for those events that occur only rarely in the typical life course. Votes occur with great regularity, so the impact of historicality—although massive—is relatively continuous in time. But for events that occur rarely in life, it turns out that the later in life a given event typically occurs, the shorter the shadow it casts in the overall population memory, and the more it is affected by the shifting age of the population. The American population quickly forgot about a world without Medicare,

---

4. Lazarsfeld's own social theories are discussed in chapter 6.

because only 9 percent of the population was in its mid-sixties by 1964 and hence had experienced old age without Medicare. These few disappeared quickly, and so Medicare became an assumed entitlement very quickly. By contrast, the draft, which ended only ten years later (in 1973), was still clear in the minds of 28 percent of America's male population thirty years later, because the draft is something that affects young people, and so 28 percent of men still alive thirty years later had been subject to it at some point. So reinstating the draft might be easier than eradicating Medicare, because more people who can remember the draft are still alive and so might see a precedent for it. Of course, as this particular example makes clear, they could also more strongly oppose it because they had had a bad experience with it. The direction of historicality's impact is not given *ex ante*. What is given is simply the fact that memory will play a much bigger role in any discussion of a draft than it will in a discussion of Medicare.

My examples of voting and political positions involve the memory of individuals quite literally. But the labor force provides us examples of a much more general form of historicality. This is not the descriptive historicality of memories and records, but a general substantive historicality, like that of the body.

Let me begin with an example. The workers retiring in the period 2000–2005 are not just an arbitrary group who happen to be retiring. On the contrary, they bring with them to the moment of the retirement decision quite specific historical baggage. Some of this baggage they can shed, like their educational level; it is not particularly consequential that they are on average considerably less educated than the current labor force. But some of their historical baggage is very consequential. For example, it matters very much that about half of the male workers in this retiring cohort are veterans, with a variety of special benefits available to them. It matters very much that while the union wage and benefit premium was at a peak during their early work life (a peak value from which those who were senior union workers at that time did very well), that premium then declined rapidly at precisely the point in the careers of today's retirees when they should have been stockpiling retirement money. The financial and practical resources that this cohort brings to retirement are thus decisively shaped by their historical labor experience; their past is "encoded" into their present, in the guise of a lack of the retirement resources their parents had at a similar point in their own lives. And of course period changes in medicine mean that today's retirees can expect to live more than a decade longer in retirement than did their parents, with costs to match. Because of this encoding, these fourteen million people (the retiring segment of the fifty-five to sixty-four cohort in the American labor force, about 55 percent of them men) provide an enormous reservoir of continuity, of process and structure, underneath the changing surfaces of the work world of the United States in the last forty years. That continuity comprises personal memory, common social and political experiences and attitudes, common patterns of material resources, and a substantial amount of common labor force experience.[5]

This mass of personal attributes and experience carried forward through time can be thought of as a fourth kind of historicality, which I shall call substantive. A familiar concept embodying substantive historicality is the lifetime income concept, which has seen fitful use as a measure of inequality. But to see it as a measure of inequality is to see it simply as an outcome, a thing without further consequences, which we use simply to rate one life course by comparison with another. While the comparison is important enough, as chapters 6 and 8 will argue, the processual interest of lifetime income also lies in its own further causal consequences at any given point in the life course. That is, we are interested in lifetime income up to a given point in part because of the things it then enables or prevents at that later point—an easy or difficult retirement, for example. Every such asset (like every liability) is carried forward through time and presents its possessor at any moment with a variety of possibilities and restrictions.

Taken across a whole cohort, the mass of this substantive historicality is at any moment a central determinant not only of that cohort's experience, but of the whole society around it. For example, the substantive historicality of retiring cohorts means that we cannot envision "retirement" in some abstract sense, even if we allow our sense of it to change across the historical epochs we analyze. Every cohort will bring to retirement a varying set of assets and liabilities piled up by the history that it has both made and endured. Moreover, since retirement at any given moment involves several cohorts of potential retirees, even a period approach cannot capture the fact that the various cohorts involved in retirement at any given moment bring a systematically diverse set of encoded experiences to it, a diversity that will itself determine the politics of retirement in that instant.

What is true at the moment of retirement is true more generally. At any given moment, events and period changes are marking the experience of the various cohorts. Long trends, local fluctuations, idiosyncratic changes:

5. The example in this paragraph (and the encoding argument more generally) were developed at much greater length in my chapter on work and occupations in the second edition of the *Handbook of Economic Sociology* (Abbott 2005).

all these mark cohorts indelibly—with characteristic work trajectories, with skill and experience sets, with financial resources, with occupational and employment-specific advantage and disadvantage—and all of these marks are carried forward into the future by the simple historicality of individuals.

At any given moment, the sum total of these marks, of this encoded historical experience, constitutes a set of possibilities and constraints within which various actors must work in the present. Major period events—the "larger forces" of most models of the work world—are not exogenous to this system of historical structures. They are themselves enacted as part of it. For example, employers with new technical designs or bureaucratic conceptions can't hire specific kinds of highly educated workers if those kinds of workers don't exist. That is, the encoded historicality of individuals at any given moment forces employers to live within its constraints. Employers may have to make do with nonoptimal workers in the short run. And in the long run they may have to respond to such constraints in various ways. They may need to transform the labor process to make use of existing labor and skill supply. They may need to force or facilitate migration, or to move production to new labor markets. They may need to support institutions to produce particular skills. But they have to respond somehow. Their history is not merely of their own making, nor is it merely of their making through their contest with the social movements of working classes. The encoded mass of historicality is in fact their greatest single constraint.[6]

To this point, my argument—if I can paraphrase it brutally—may seem simply that historical demography is too important to be left to the demographers. But I would like to show at least the beginnings of two other arguments that are related to this one progenitor, one of them a direct blood descendant, the other a marriage connection who brings with her a vast and imposing dowry.

The blood-descendant argument involves moving beyond thinking about the historicality of individuals to thinking about the historicality of intermediate kinds of groups. I have talked about substantive historicality in the context of groups like the whole population and the labor force. These are large, inclusive groups from which exit is generally by some straightforward and relatively uniform means—death in the first case, and retirement or other departure from the labor force on the other. But when we start to invoke my concept of historicality in the case of, say, individual occupations, we enter

6. See Brint and Karabel 1989 for a discussion of changes forced on community colleges by the needs of employers.

a whole new realm. To conceive of the historicality of an individual occupation over time is obviously the first step in any general theory of the history
of occupations, but it is extremely difficult. Such a concept must involve all
the threads of individual substantive historicality weaving in and out of the
occupation through the normal demographic processes of occupational entry,
internal mobility, and exit. At the same time, such a concept must also involve
the more traditional "history" of occupations—the internal story of the succession of occupational tasks and occupational organizations over time. And
it must also involve the contextual history of an occupation's often radically
changing position in a division of labor, the ecological level that was the focus
of my own first work on professions.[7] It is this reinsertion of the individual
historicality of individuals into the macro- and ecological-level analysis of
occupations—analyses that we already possess, to a large extent—that is un-
derlined by my first cadet argument.

My second related argument—the argument "related by marriage"—is a
little more elusive. It is this. Once we have used the concept of encoding to
recognize the ways in which large amounts of past history are brought into the
present—as assets and liabilities and constraints in the present that arise when
we remember the historicality of individuals en masse—we must then make
yet another step, to see how it is that structural rearrangement takes place in
the present moment. That is, we must see how encoding moves forward from
one moment to the next, in the process potentially rearranging the whole of
social structure.

There is a crucial premise hidden here. The utility of the idea of encoding
is that it gets us out of the trap presented by the fact that the past is well and
truly gone, the fact that there can be no effect at a historical distance. The
concepts of historicality and encoding get us out of that trap by reminding
us that certain parts of the past are continuously (re)encoded into the present
synchronic social structure, in the sense of thereby acquiring historicality—
the appearance of endurance in time. In that moment-to-moment succession
of presents, however, everything in the social structure is at risk, and everything can change—even the "big structures." At the same time, something
about the process and nature of encoding produces the illusion that there

7. On the professions, see Abbott 1988a. (As noted in the preface, I shall hereafter refer to
this book simply by its title *System of Professions*. This convention—title alone—will be followed here for all of my own books.) The theoretical argument of this paragraph is specified
in greater detail in a chapter on the theory of mobility (Abbott 2006) in a collection edited by
Steven Morgan, David Grusky, and Gary Fields.

are "big historical structures" that somehow reach over long periods, producing the further illusion of long, enduring historicality for certain kinds of social structures, like our old friends "modern capitalism" and "the relations of production." We need to figure out how this illusioning process works. Undoubtedly it involves not only direct synchronic determination of the "causal" sort, but also conceptual reorganization of the kind usually called "cultural." This is the dowry that my argument-by-marriage brings. By recognizing that encoding involves a synchronic phase of rearrangement of things, we open the process of encoding to cognitive and, more broadly, cultural reorganization.[8]

In summary, then, I have one big point and two cadets. The main point is that historical demography is indeed too important to leave to the demographers, because none of us can ignore the implications of the historicality of individuals. The enduring mass of biological individuals is one of the largest "social" forces that exists. The first cadet argument is that taking historicality seriously gets even harder when we look at intermediate social groups like occupations, social movements, and so on. The second cadet argument is that figuring out how the historicality of individuals and social groups is actually encoded from moment to moment will inevitably involve us in thinking about cultural as well as behavioral determination. In these three arguments are implicit the main lines of theorizing and research within the processual approach.

8. My argument is thus somewhat more dynamic than that of Norman Ryder, whose classic paper on cohorts and social change focuses mainly on the impact of encoded differences on lives in cohorts ("intercohort temporal differentiation in the various parameters that may be used to characterize these aggregate histories"; Ryder 1965:861). The structural consequences envisioned by Ryder are principally stable or statically dynamic ones: for example, static conflict between generations or simple articulation of social change by cohort turnover. He does, however, recognize the more dynamic implications of cohorts that are emphasized here. His remark that "although the stimulus for innovation is most likely to come from the employers, the feasibility of new directions depends in part on how well they have been anticipated by the educational system" (Ryder 1965:848) clearly indicates a recognition of the macrostructural implications of past cohort experience when taken as a present historical reality.

CHAPTER 2

Human Nature in Processual Thinking[1]

Of the three lines of potential development mentioned at the close of the preceding chapter, the most easily pursued is the issue of individual historicality itself. The chapter noted a number of forces conducing to the maintenance of continuity "along the lineage of an individual": physical or biological objects, memory, and deliberate record retention. And it seems quite obvious that these forces are essential for understanding the actual continuity over time—the "thingness"—of social groups like occupations or social classes or ethnic groups. But with respect to individuals, we might think, there's little need to account for continuity; the body provides that. Moreover, associated with the body and, more broadly, with the notion that atomic individuals are the main units of the social process (a notion common to both economics and psychology among the social and behavioral sciences), is the idea that there are certain universal qualities of human individuals as beings. This concept of "human nature" is indeed an essential constituent of several of the approaches alternative to the processual one, all of which take the continuity of individuals over time to be nonproblematic. Therefore, for a processual view that begins with problematizing that continuity, an important first step is to address the concept of human nature, asking what kind of concept of human nature

1. This chapter was originally written as a paper for the conference "Tracking Concepts of Human Nature" at Villa Garbald, Castasegna, Switzerland, in July 2009. I thank the Collegium Helveticum for its kind invitation and support. A German translation was published as Abbott 2011. The paper has been slightly revised here although, as in the preceding chapter, I have not changed the relatively informal tone of a spoken talk.

is possible under processual assumptions. This chapter's encounter with that problem thus makes a logical next step in the book's argument. But, as in most of these chapters, I retain the original motivating arguments from the original paper, making the shift into explicit processualism only after a review of the human nature concept in general.

In the course of an academic life, a working social scientist inevitably encounters many concepts of human nature. One gets used to shifting between them: from *Homo economicus* to the oversocialized dope, from egos and ids to genetically-founded temperaments, from the infinite plasticities of Geertz to the universal emotions of Ekman. It is not possible to understand colleagues in other disciplines without making such shifts; even a social encounter often requires constant adjustment to whatever human nature concepts are invoked in the course of the conversation.

In my own work, however, I have not employed a concept of human nature—at least under that name—for thirty-five years. When I first began my studies of sociology, I believed in human nature. I expected that I would sample the many theories about it and ultimately decide which one was correct. But sometime in graduate school I seem to have given up on the notion of human nature altogether.

This is not to say that I haven't made generalizing assumptions about humans. I have indeed done so. But I am not sure of the mutual consistency of those assumptions, and I have done my best to make them as minimal as possible in any case. For sociology as a discipline is premised on the assumption that humans are far more modifiable than they look in the eyes of psychologists and economists. Or, to put it in a less contentious way, the things that interest sociologists in the social process arise more from the differences between humans than from the similarities between them. Whether the concept "human nature" refers to a reality of the lifeworld or to an a priori assumption of disciplinary discourse, sociologists tend to focus on difference more than similarity among human beings, and thus make little use of human nature concepts per se.

But at sociology's borders with other disciplines, one is always interacting with colleagues who believe in human nature. And so we argue with economists (and with some political scientists) about *Homo economicus*. But that is not a serious debate about human nature. Economists themselves are the first to say that *Homo economicus* is just an assumption, and probably an incorrect one; Milton Friedman's most famous paper concerns that issue, after all. But recently, the renascence of psychology in its new biological guise has begun to remind us social scientists that we have whole disciplines of colleagues whose first inclination in thinking about the human project is to create a concept of human nature or to seek one in empirical data. These colleagues genuinely believe that the best way to figure out human life is to discover the universals of human nature and its development, a project that seems to me doomed from the start.[2]

Clearly, then we must begin at the beginning, by characterizing what is at issue in the conversations we have about this matter. One says "about this matter" rather than "about human nature" because the latter phraseology assumes that there exists in the lifeworld such a thing as human nature, and that that thing exists substantially rather than definitionally (as a reality rather than as something we invent). That is, our first problem is that the term could be a mere nominalist convenience, denoting some set of things defined relatively and therefore definitionally existent, as in "human nature consists of those aspects of the person common to all individual humans." This "human nature" cannot be the null set, obviously, since the category "human" exists. But that fact does not guarantee that the contents of the set are of any real importance in explaining social life, which is really what is meant when we use the concept "human nature" in the social sciences. We all have five fingers, but social scientists don't think of that as part of human nature. We all have consciousness, but consciousness is not usually considered part of human nature. Human nature in its modern sense is used to denote a particular set of dispositions—toward particular kinds of actions rather than other kinds of actions.

But second, the term human nature could be a *misleading* nominalist convenience (i.e., a labeling of something that is specifically not there in the lifeworld). Or, more extreme still, it could be a performative, intending to make us enact as realities the things contained in a particular human nature concept, following W. I. Thomas's famous dictum that "if men define situations as real, they are real in their consequences." This is indeed one of the possible critiques of *Homo economicus. Homo economicus* might appear to be the reality of human nature simply because *Homo economicus* is an understanding of human nature that is taught as scientific truth in tens of thousands of classrooms to millions of students every day. Given the time and money spent teaching modern people that this is how they behave, it is little surprising that they do so.

2. The Friedman paper mentioned is "The Methodology of Positive Economics," Friedman 1953.

Thus, I shall attempt in what follows to avoid language that precommits me to any particular substantive concept of human nature, but shall try nonetheless to canvass the various concepts that have been deployed in its general intellectual vicinity. More specifically, I here reflect on two major topics: first, the various dimensions implicit in discussions of human nature; and second, the human-nature-like assumptions that are employed in processual theories of social life.

DIMENSIONS OF HUMAN NATURE

I begin with what I take a concept of human nature to be. As a thinker in the pragmatist tradition, I take human nature to be the set of assumptions about humanity we use in practice to found our various inquiries into the human condition. I wish to underscore three things about this rough definition. First, I say "humanity," rather than "human beings," to emphasize my unwillingness to prejudge whether these are assumptions about the human body and the personality (which are the most common sites for "human nature" in the wake of the Enlightenment and Darwinism) or about some other unit of human life or lives. Second, I say "assumptions we use in practice" rather than "a priori concepts" because I think the latter are a chimera, and I do not think that there is or could be a correct or "true" set of assumptions about human nature. In my view, there is at a given locality in the social process a set of working ideas about what we might call the foundational qualities of humanity. They constitute whatever idea of human nature applies in that locality. But they are only working ideas, not Platonic ones.

Third, I say "to found"—rather than "to serve as a logical basis for"— because I don't want to worry about whether such concepts are conscious or unconscious, mutually consistent or inconsistent, and so on. It suffices for me that they are concepts which are at the basis—explicitly or implicitly—of a certain set of local arguments about human experience. Note that this position does entail the belief that it is very nearly impossible to make a coherent argument about humanity without human nature assumptions of some kind. An argument has to have bases somewhere if it is not to be tautological or purely performative.

To be sure, assuming that all coherent arguments about humanity must involve human nature assumptions is assuming something that is true only in knowledge systems like ours, systems with universalizing pretensions. There have been many knowledge systems that have restricted the quality of "humanity" (the group to which the concept human nature applies) to a

certain kind or color or status of what we today would regard as human beings. But I think we can take it for granted at present that employing putatively
universal conceptions about humans is a requisite of any acceptable type of
knowledge. By this I don't necessarily mean that all human organisms will be
conceived as the same in any acceptable type of knowledge, but simply that
they will all in some way be conceived as human, and that that "way" is what
we mean by the governing concept of "human nature." All members of the
species must be understood to be human.

To repeat, then, "human nature" is that set of assumptions about humanity that someone uses in practice to found his or her inquiries into various
aspects of the human condition. On this definition, there are of course many
different concepts of human nature. Such concepts can be categorized in a
number of different ways.

First, there is the question of the site of "human nature." While the majority of concepts conceive of human nature as inhering in individual human
beings, a sizable minority believes that human nature inheres in groups of individuals, or even in the whole species. Examples of individual-based human
nature concepts are familiar enough. Here are the various instinct theories:
Freud with his Eros and Thanatos, W. I. Thomas with his four wishes, and so
on. Indeed, one can see "instinct" as simply a term used to label any quality
of persons that is (1) constant, (2) embodied in each instantiation of a species,
and (3) profoundly important, but (4) underivable from other things. One
wonders if such a view might not be behind Veblen's "instinct of workman-
ship" and the more implicit faith in man as maker (*Homo faber*) that pervades
Marx's writing. But instinct theories are not the only ones locating human
nature in the individual. Utilitarianism also does so, as do a whole range of
positions identifying human nature with rationality.

Conversely, there are also various concepts of an "instinct" for sociability,
which in effect take socializing, and hence social life itself, as central to human
nature. In sociology we often cite this view to Simmel, but one could equally
trace it to Adam Smith's "sympathy" and "propensity for truck and barter."
Those who see sociability as a part of human nature nonetheless usually root
that sociability in a self construed as independent and autarkic.

By contrast, a more radical group simply thinks that the nature of humans
is inherently social. Aristotle leans this way, and Dewey commits to it wholeheartedly. Implicitly in this camp are those who focus their thinking on imitation and emulation—people like Tarde, with his laws of imitation, and Veblen,
with his notions of relative striving and conspicuous consumption. The many
explicitly and implicitly essentialist theories of races, ethnicities, genders, and

so on lie in this group as well. For all these, human nature is fundamentally a group nature.

Thus, a first way of categorizing concepts of human nature is in terms of their unit: some think human nature is a property located in individuals, others that it leads inevitably to groups, and still others that it is located principally in particular social groups, each of which indeed has its own "human nature."

A second categorization classifies human nature concepts by whether they involve emotions, actions, or meanings, three basic zones of human experience. There are some approaches to human nature—Freud's is the most obvious—that are primarily concerned with emotions. Freud's presuppositions about human nature concern psychic energy, structures of impulse control, and desires for sex, peace, and other forms of emotional gratification. To be sure, there are several different Freuds over the course of his life, and interestingly his unit for human nature drifts to some extent from the individual, in his early and middle work, to the social group, in his later work. But these changes in unit notwithstanding, Freud is always primarily concerned with emotional experience, an experience that provides both the "human nature" premises for his argument and the theater in which those premises work themselves out.

By contrast, Marx is much more preoccupied with action. His unit for human nature is social class, and he is less interested in the emotional experience of social classes than in what they do, and secondarily in what they think. For Marx, emotion and meaning arise from social class, which is itself the congealed framework of prior action. Marx's toolbox of human nature concepts—labor, labor power, alienated labor, surplus product, class interest, and so on—are all fundamentally action concepts. He tells us point-blank that men make their own history (albeit subject to "larger" constraints). Indeed, this focus on action is something Marx shares with the whole *Homo economicus* tradition against which he argues.

Unlike Freud or Marx, the Malinowski of *Argonauts of the Western Pacific* (1961) is interested in how Trobrianders make meaning of their world. He spends pages on activities, to be sure (building boats, for example). But the general aim of the book is to understand how those activities make sense of life, thereby assigning it the meanings through which Trobrianders can carry on in their daily lives. Inevitably, this project involves Malinowski in assumptions about the symbolical aspects of human nature and, indeed, about the dangers of meaninglessness. These are also central in other anthropological works, like Evans-Pritchard's *Witchcraft, Oracles, and Magic among the*

Azande (1976), where the assumptions about the necessity of meaning-making are the heart of the book.

So my second categorization of human nature concepts is in terms of the zones of experience on which they focus. There are those that focus on emotion, those that focus on action, and those that focus on symbols. These each in turn provide different frameworks for the others, creating a complex array of possibilities.

My third categorization is a distinction between human nature concepts that are purely formal and those that have content. *Homo economicus* exemplifies the purely formal approach. Hobbes, Locke, Mandeville, Bentham, and company do not tell us what humans want, but merely that it is the nature of humans to want things. The same is true for Kant's categorical imperative, which lacks any actual content but merely demands that we should always act as if our maxim of action establishes a universal law.

By contrast, Freud tells us that we want particular things: mother, or sex, or sex with mother, or whatever. Freud, that is, has a content to his wants. And of course Freud is not the only content-based human nature theorist. Aristotle's idea of man as political animal is another such concept, and a long list of writers has believed that humans have a religious nature or a sense of wonder. Midway between contentless and contentful ideas of human nature are things like Maslow's hierarchy of needs and the functional anthropology of the later Malinowski, in which a list of basic needs is supplemented by a list of somewhat optional further needs. Indeed, all varieties of strong functionalism fall into this midway position.

A final dimension of human nature concepts is that of mutability. Some concepts treat human nature as an unchanging given. *Homo economicus* is of this type, as was the Hobbesian "nature of man," with its "three principles of quarrel." Others follow Aristotle in believing that man, like all other things, has a "nature"—an entelechy—which lies within him and which is inevitably realized in his life. In such a view there is change, but not really mutability; for although there are surface transformations, they are merely the signs of man becoming himself, becoming something that was in him from the beginning. In Hegel this transformation becomes the union of possibility and necessity in man in-and-for-himself, a union that results in the subjection of becoming to the contingency of reality.

One could take another step, in which human nature is relativistically defined. In this view, human nature is simply those aspects of individual humans, in any given society, that are changing more slowly than the others, and that hence become forces of constraint on those others. Human nature in such a conception becomes analogous to tradition, which can be defined in analogous fashion as the most slowly changing aspects of the cultural system. This relativistic definition of human nature brings us, however, to a whole new approach to social life. For it entails—or at least suggests—the idea that everything in social life is changing all the time. Human nature, in such a scheme, is simply the slowest thing in a perpetually changing world. This is a processual argument, one that requires its own full inquiry.

Before we move on to that inquiry, however, it is useful to summarize my argument so far. I have noted four dimensions that differentiate concepts of human nature:

1. Whether they principally concern human individuals or social groups;
2. Whether they principally concern emotion, action, or meaning;
3. Whether they are formal or substantive;
4. Whether they admit change or insist on constancy.

One could imagine an investigation of concepts of human nature that considered how and when these various dimensions of a society's human nature conceptions might change. Or one could look at the logical constraints and facilities that these various dimensions present to one another. But while those things might be interesting, they are not my own most immediate concern. For it is with the fourth difference that I am principally concerned: the form of a human nature concept compatible with a social ontology that is based completely on processual principles. If one considers the world to be perpetually in process, what becomes of the idea of human nature?

HUMAN NATURE IN PROCESSUAL THINKING

I have elsewhere sketched the outlines of a processual ontology.[3] A processual ontology begins from the problem of explaining social change, which

3. This processual ontology is stated to some extent in the epilogues to *Department and Discipline* (Abbott 1999) and *Time Matters* (Abbott 2001b), although neither of those is a systematic exposition. (Both books are hereafter cited simply by title.) At the time I wrote the paper on which this chapter is based, I expected my full statement of this ontology—already then embodied in the much-revised chapters of a book on the matter—to be in print shortly. Unfortunately, that has not happened. Important parts of this ontology—encoding, for example—are discussed in the preceding chapter and in the related pieces mentioned in its footnotes 5 and 7.

it resolves by assuming that change—not stability—is the natural state of social life. Such a move makes explaining stability the central question of social theory. In the processual view, we speak of stability when we observe lineages of events that keep recurring more or less similarly over time. That is, the social process consists of a flow of events. In this flow, various events are linked together, nonexclusively, into lineages, which in our eyes constitute the things that we recognize as being at the micro level in most social theories: personalities and social groupings.

Such lineages have all the haziness and boundary complexity of the kinship lineages with which we are familiar. They are continuously remade in social life, and although they have certain kinds of interior continuities, they are not Aristotelian entelechies simply realizing an inner nature. We are personalities not because we have some inner compass, set by biology or even by infantile sexuality; we are personalities because we continuously remake ourselves given the experiences, memories, possibilities, connections, and so on that we have created in our lives heretofore. Moreover, our personalities are not under our full control, since others react to what they imagine is our personality, not to what it is or what we imagine it to be. Therefore, our sensorium is not a sole proprietor, but merely a majority stockholder in our personalities, with fractious "outsiders" conducting proxy fights from time to time. In addition, our sensorium is stuck in a body that is only partly under the sensorium's control but that constrains that sensorium in important ways: by becoming sick, lustful, tired, or any of the many other things that bodies become.

In such a world, the normal elements of human nature are disassembled. Social groups and individuals are not fully separated, since both are simply lineages defined on events. That a particular event is part of one lineage doesn't preempt it from being part of another, any more than my being in the Abbott lineage prevents my being in the Orne, Delano, Deedee, O'Shea, O'Mahoney, Lynch, and Kelliher lineages. Any event is in many social "things" at once. Moreover, such an ontology also disassembles the Cartesian individual into at least three parts—the body, the sensorium or consciousness, and the personality. Therefore, the normal first choice of human nature concepts—whether to locate human nature in individuals or in groups—no longer makes much sense.

As for the next dimension—emotion/action/meaning—I have no particular brief in this chapter. However, my inclination is to treat emotion as the mode of experience that arises as we make lineages on the body/sensorium/ personality border: to treat action as the mode of experience having to do with the borders between personalities or between social entities or between personalities and social entities; and to treat meaning as the mode of experience related to the use of cultural materials to articulate relations among all of the other kinds of lineages and, indeed, often within them. On these assumptions, human nature is again disassembled, for it is by no means clear that there are permanent stabilities of one or another kind in one or another of these modes of experience. Moreover, if such stabilities do exist, they may well be indistinguishable, because all three modes are simply aspects of a single process.

But the third (formal/substantive) and the fourth (changing/unchanging) dimensions are clearly central to any human nature concept that could be based on a process ontology. Since my ontology rests on change, so also must my human nature concept rest on change. Moreover, since I wish any such concept to be general, I must of necessity make my human nature concept largely formal. The relativistic concept given above begins this move. Under that concept, we call something "human nature" if it is the part of the lineages of discrete individuals that changes most slowly. It is, in that sense, the "tradition" of each given individual, and its generalizable patterns are the common individual "traditions" that we might call human nature(s).

Note that as a consequence of this argument, human nature would play a larger and larger part in the solidarity of the world as individual bodies live longer and longer. (We saw this argument in chapter 1.) "Traditions"— in the specific sense of durable *social* things—loom smaller in a world where individuals expect to live seventy to ninety years. Few social structures last half that long, other than as forms; their practices, beliefs, commitments, membership, and organization change at a staggering pace, by comparison with individuals.

More important, in a world where all micro-entities in the social process are built out of lineages of events, the "nature" that matters lies not in something about the lineages, but rather in the regularities of the process of lineage-making itself. "Human nature," therefore, consists of those things that control the "solidity" of social lineages, that shape the process by which lineages stabilize into personalities and social groups.

I have written in chapter 1 about one aspect of this process, which I have called historicality. By historicality I mean the sum of those processes by which events contrive to leave relatively permanent traces of themselves in the ongoing present. At any given instant, the past as such does not exist. Only those parts of it can influence the present which have somehow encoded themselves into the ongoing present, leaving traces that can continuously reproduce themselves as the present makes its perpetual way into the oblivion of pastness. So the vectors of historicality are central aspects to any account of social life whatever. (This is, in fact, just as true in nonprocessual accounts of the social world as in processual ones.)

I have distinguished four aspects of historicality. The first of these is corporeal historicality. For social things, corporeal historicality refers to buildings, roads, cities, physical infrastructures, and so on—the built environment in the broadest sense. For individuals, of course, the core of corporeal historicality is the body itself, with its record of past exposure to disease, past use and misuse, and so on. It is part of human nature—at least at present—to have such a physical body, with all that such "having" entails, not the least of those entailments being death. That the social process transpires in part via the regular death of human individuals is extremely consequential, as we have found out from the postponing of death nearly twenty years in the last century.[4]

The second aspect of historicality is memorial—the presence of memories in minds. We are familiar with this in biological individuals, but as I have argued in the preceding chapter, a given individual sensorium contains only a portion of the total memories associated with that biological individual: the rest are in the "other minds" of former boyfriends, repairmen, colleagues, and so on. Social groups have such memories, of course, but they are much more evenly dispersed. There is no one sensorium that has most of them, and for this reason, although social groups can change in the short run much faster than can individuals, they are not affected as drastically by death in the long run.

The third aspect of historicality is recorded historicality—the creation of records embodying the past in the form of writing, film, digitization, or some other form of long-term storage. Records matter because they are invulnerable to the inevitable processes of biological succession. Interestingly, social entities produce many more records than do individuals, who conduct much of their social business within their minds or viva voce with others. (Note how this is changing because of social media, however.) Therefore, in most eras, biography is a much more difficult art than institutional history. It is no doubt in part for this reason that social entities are usually considered "bigger" than individuals, even though, as we have seen, that statement is in many ways untrue (particularly in terms of temporal endurance).

---

4. In chapter 1, since I was talking only about individuals, I used the term "biological historicality" for what I am here calling the corporeal historicality (of individuals). The corporeal historicality of social groups is not purely in bodies, but is also "corporealized" in physical infrastructures like buildings, cities, highways, and the like.

Taken together, the various contents of these three modalities of historicality can be called substantive historicality. Substantive historicality comprises the mass of memories, qualities, experiences, interrelations, and resources that is common to a particular cohort, for example. Even so corporeal a "memory" as the simple size of my own generation—the American baby boom—has enormous consequences for current reality, as the looming bankruptcy of the American social insurance system shows.[5]

Thus, a first crucial part of "human nature" is the quality of historicality. We do not start social life de novo in each moment, but rather do so within the confines of that portion of the past which is encoded into the social process we experience. Human nature is fundamentally historical.

A second part of "human nature" is the simple sequentiality of experience, the fact that we experience the world in a particular order, one event after another. There are a number of indicators of this quality. The first is the relative dominance in our present of the experiences of the recent past. I would not want to assume some regular functional form to this dominance, although obviously one is tempted to do so by analogy with prospective discounting vis-à-vis the future. For even if there were such a form, it clearly must shift with age. As individuals grow older, the deeper past can assume a greater prominence in their lives. (I will return to this topic in chapter 6.)

A second indicator of this sequential quality of experience is the enormous collection of what we may call "narrative verbs," by analogy with Arthur Danto's concept of narrative sentences.[6] These are verbs that presuppose two moments in time. Examples are all English verbs starting with "re-," like "rewrite" and "remarry," since these presuppose that earlier episodes (of writing and marriage respectively) took place at some time in the past. But there are more pointed cases; "to regret," for example. One cannot regret something that has no past. Regret inevitably involves a past event (which could of course be the "not-happening" of a desired event, as well as the happening of an undesired event). So also with the verbs "debunk," "betray," "remember," and "forget." Each of these labels an action in the present vis-à-vis an action or situation in the past. All evince the sequentiality of experience. All describe

5. Chapter 1 treated substantive historicality as a fourth type. In this chapter, I have broadened the definitions of the first three types and redefined their total content as substantive historicality. It is, of course, the particular arrangements of this content across millions of people that constitutes the means by which encoding produces the appearance of "larger forces" and historical action at a distance. The details of that arrangement are not considered here.

6. Danto 1985, ch. 8. This reference will recur several times in later chapters.

precisely that binding of events into or out of a lineage that I have earlier noted as the basis of the microsocial world we see. In a world of events and process, these processes of binding are the heart of "human nature."

But there is an abiding assumption about this sequentiality that is more specific, and that seems to me to run through most process approaches to the social world. That is the notion of habituation. Most process approaches to social thought seem to take it for granted that humans (and, indeed, probably social groupings) develop habits over time. There is disagreement whether these habits are good (Dewey) or bad (Weber). But the assumption that habituation is universal seems to be the main substantive belief of processual thinking about human nature.

It is not impossible that the habituation assumption might be an ideology, and in particular a human nature ideology of the nineteenth century, with its restless desire for achievement, novelty, and progress. One can well imagine that most cultures would involve a concept of habit; the emergence of habits seems an obvious attribute of experience in the lifeworld. But the existence of habits does not necessarily imply that habit—and in particular the dangers and the evils of habit—should be one of the ruling ideas of a culture. Yet these beliefs are clearly central to the personality ideology—and more broadly the cultural ideologies—of the modern world. Indeed, through much of modernity runs the theme that not only is habituation universal, but that habit is bad, and indeed that the past in general is to be rejected and transcended. That is, the obverse of our focus on habit is the idea of progress.

A less ideological way of putting this is to say that my earlier focus on memory—the presence of the past in the present—implies a correlative focus on anticipation—the presence of the future in the present. For if, as chapter 1 has argued, the past is in the present as encoded constraint—historicality shaped into substantive limitations—the future is in the present as (encoded?) possibility, as future narratives pulled back into possible plans.[7]

Here we can replicate the logic of my earlier argument, by considering the implications of that future possibility for human nature in the present. The most obvious of these implications is the quality of freedom to choose. For the alternative possibilities in the present leave us free to enact various futures. And if these are—to be sure—not free from all constraint, they are nonetheless open enough for us to need continually to choose plans of action or inaction.

---

7. The ideas of habit and progress are discussed more extensively in chapter 7. The reader may recognize this view of memory and anticipation as one of the central arguments of Saint Augustine's *Confessions*, book 11.

This too seems to me a fundamental concept of human nature in the processual framework: there is not only habit, but also choice. Chapter 9 and the epilogue will explore the implications of this fact for our moral experience.

Looking to the future, we find again the dominance of the near at hand. Just as the immediate past environs us most evidently, so too the immediate future is often the dominant ground of our choices. This issue is, of course, well studied in the literature on hyperbolic and exponential discounting, as well as in the broader literature on time preferences. Less studied is the question of when we want our outcomes—now or later or in eternity—for a focus on the present is built into the usual concept of discounting. Indeed, the notion that the present is quite literally the most important moment in history is built into the nineteenth-century mindset that still dominates our world, for all its computers, space travel, and radiation oncology.[8]

Thus, sequentiality is important in the future as well as in the past, and in the transition of the one to the other. Here, too, we find the same kinds of narrative verbs, referring both to a present moment and a future one: prophesy, foresee, promise, desire, expect, dread, anticipate. Such verbs characterize our choices of events as we go forward: what are the events we choose to make part of ourselves, and what events we reject. Thus, we see that individuals experience themselves narratively in the formal sense, as well as in the simple sense of telling stories about themselves to themselves. For they continuously enact their very selves in a flow of events, thereby making the unfolding lineage that is a self.

This is of course happening to social groups at the same time, although the use that social groups make of individual bodies in the process of enacting themselves is quite different from the use made by individuals. But it is nonetheless the same in general form, embedded in a flow of events and perpetually binding certain events into the lineage organization while separating off other events.

Sequentiality thus pervades human nature as we look forward in time, just as it does when we look backward. And as I have noted earlier, it is clear that just as habituation seems an assumption about human nature that becomes necessary as process theories look at the past, so too the correlative idea of progress and novelty dominates those conceptions as process theories look forward. Dewey is the clearest example here, with his thoroughgoing optimism, unbroken by two world wars, fascism, and the other horrors of the

---

8. The topics of progress and direction will be more extensively covered in chapters 6 and 7.

twentieth century. The idea of progress reaches well into other theoretical frameworks, to be sure, and probably qualifies as one of the general human nature ideologies of the modern age.

At the same time, just as habit is sometimes conceived not as a facilitating expertise (Dewey) but as a deadening routine (Weber), novelty is conceived sometimes as progress (Ogburn) and sometimes as mere fashion (Sorokin). Different kinds of human nature assumptions and different evaluations of them are clearly possible here, even within the process camp, depending on one's pessimism or optimism. That the future is going somewhere, however, is always assumed. In social science, at least, no one yet has taken the process position and at the same time argued for a random, directionless future.

Finally, I should note two aspects of a processual concept of human nature that are built into the ontological assumptions on which I have based my argument. First, I have throughout assumed a concept of locality. Lineages make themselves locally. They have easier access to some parts of the social process than to others. They have a "here and now" that is different from most other heres and nows across the process. It is human nature, that is, for each lineage to have a specific location in the process, to be something or someone in particular. Paradoxically, it is universal to be particular.

Second, although I have not analyzed the three zones of human experience—emotion, action, and meaning—these have, it seems to me, at least one fundamental property, arising from the constitutively social character of human living. Each of the three produces a notion that becomes a criterion for judging it. This is simply an empirical fact, obvious from the inspection of any society or culture of which we are aware. For emotion, the criterion is something we might call sympathy, a being-with-ness. For action, the criterion is oughtness. For meaning and symbolization, the criterion is truth. Of the content of these criteria I say nothing. That content has been diverse beyond all imagining. Sympathy, that is, does not necessarily mean feeling sorry for someone, as it often does in our culture. It simply means that any culture about which we know anything has a criterion for thinking about the rightness of relation between individuals, and, indeed, between social entities. Similarly, oughtness does not necessarily mean contemporary law and morality, nor does truth mean correspondence with the dictates of modern science. I mean merely that some version of these criteria emerges in all known forms of human living.

More important still, they emerge together. We often think of truth and oughtness as separate things: is and ought. We often say that thinkers like

Marx and the Progressives "ran is and ought together." It is more likely that they are naturally together, and that we moderns have decided to try to live as if they were apart. Thus, we often treat social behavior as purely material and caused (in social science) but then judge it separately as right or wrong (in the law). The tail-chasing character of this proceeding is quite clear. Stated more generally, the most common human way of relating "is" and "ought" is performativity—erecting a set of oughts which define a world that we then treat as true. In the modern world, we pretend that this is not the situation. We believe that we have contentless, formal social oughts (utility, justice, etc.), leaving the substance of those oughts to the individual, and focusing our attention on truth conceived in the narrowest, most materialist fashion. There has a resulted a civilization focused on such spiritual matters as the best tasting fermented grape juice and the chemicals most useful for helping people endure an existence defined *ex ante* as meaningless. But in most societies and cultures, the experience of a performed reality dominates. This is indeed what humans do as a species: they imagine sand castles in the air, and then live in them. The Epilogue will to some extent elaborate this argument.

CONCLUSION

I have discussed four dimensions of human nature concepts: where they locate human nature, what zones of social experience they include in it, whether they are formal or substantive, and whether they acknowledge change. As a processualist and a pragmatist, I reject a firm position on the first of these dimensions because I reject the normal sharp distinction of kind between individuals and social entities. On the second, I assume that human nature concepts have to deal with all zones of human experience (rather than just one among the three general realms of emotion, action, and meaning), because I mainly focus on the qualities imposed on such concepts by the flow of time. This forces me to a concept of human nature that focuses on the "nature" of the way humans (and social groups) change over time: what the Chicago School used to call "natural history."

As for the details of my own concept of human nature: Human nature, first, is rooted in the three modes of historicality—corporeal, memorial, and recorded—and the complex of substantive historicality that they enable. It concerns the means by which those modes interact and shape the developing lineage that is a person or social entity. It is also rooted in what we might call optativity, the human capacity to envision alternative futures and indeed alternative future units to the social process. (Optativity relative to the future would be analogous to historicality relative to the past, but I am not investigating its particular details here.)

Human nature, second, is rooted in the sequentiality of experience, its constant reference to events past and future, and its constant construction of a lineage, in the moment, by binding together different events. This is evident in the huge array of verbs embodying formally narrative conceptions of the self, defining the self by defining directional action in time.

Human nature, third, is rooted in a perpetual dialogue of habituation and novelty. Both of these can be substantively meaningful as well as trivial and vacuous. I don't have a particular position on them at this moment, although my personal character is clearly that of a substantive habituator who sees most novelty as vacuous.

Finally, human nature is organized around ideals that guide us as we live from day to day, simultaneously making our selves and the social entities in which we participate. These can loosely be called sympathy, oughtness, and truth, but they have a substantive content and even a form that is itself always built in particular localities in the social process. They are a basic unity, but cultures can—and ours does—decide to separate them in various ways. To explore the bounds of their possibilities seems to be the human project.

CHAPTER 3

Linked Ecologies[1]

INTRODUCTION

Among their other themes, the preceding two chapters have begun to clarify the important duality of temporality in the processual approach. On the one hand, all is changing, and therefore all is diachronic, even the entities of the social process itself. Entities emerge only because historicality enables them to do so. And they emerge as lineages of events that tend to recur, and that tend thus to become the seemingly stable individuals of the traditional ontologies. In particular, corporeal, memorial, and substantive historicality provide the basis for links that are employed by ongoing activity to create the lineage that we will identify as "a person" or "a group." But, on the other hand, since everything is changing, everything is contingent. The present is all that exists, and all effects of the past must work through encoding that—combined with moment-to-moment action—has preserved those effects across the succession of contingent presents to the one present of now. In that synchronic present, those encoded aspects of the past must have their effects, not by any means automatically, but with the same risk of revision and redirection that faces all aspects of the present.

What we have not considered yet is how these effects happen: how contingency, constraint, and action interact in the now to knot the various momen-

---

1. This chapter began life as a lecture for the meetings of the Association française de sociologie in October 1999. A French version was published in 2003 and, after talks at various universities and professional associations, the English version here was published in *Sociological Theory* in 2005. As I have noted in the preface, this chapter begins a sequence of four chapters in a much more academic genre than the preceding two.

tary events into another secured present-become-past that can in turn shape a succeeding present. This is the moment of action and the logically succeeding moment of encoding—a pairing that George Herbert Mead called "passage." A crucial theoretical fact about passage is that it occurs in a complicated network of social relationships. The temporal present is huge "horizontally," as it were; it has many subparts, substructures, and subspaces. It is not the economists' equilibrium world in which everyone is simultaneously interacting with everyone else via a fixed price that all face. (We can create such worlds—we call them markets—but they are not the natural state of affairs.) This complex social-structure-in-the-moment contains all the information of the deep past that can influence the present, either as records or some other form of encoded historicality or—more importantly—as the present system of adjacencies and relationships that is the momentary social structure, providing the locales, facilities, and constraints that shape the possible actions of the moment.

A generic word for this structure-in-the-moment is an ecology. By using that word, I am of course invoking a long tradition of work that has not explicitly identified itself as processualist. It has identified itself more as "contextual in space" than "contextual in time." But, as I have suggested elsewhere (Abbott 1997), these two contextualities are in practice logical correlatives. The processualist approach to social time entails the ecological approach to social structure at a moment, because the idea that encoded social structure contains all effective information about the causal past is the only way to account for apparent historical action at a distance in a social world that exists, ontologically, moment-to-moment. Thus, the philosophical foundations of the idea of ecology lie in processualism, as those of processualism lie in ecology. The two ideas are conjugate parts of a single approach to social time and space.

That said, however, ecology is also often understood as one of several ways to reconcile the apparently divergent accounts of social life generated by the two traditional ontologies—individualism and social emergentism. So we can also motivate the present chapter in that way. A long-standing debate pits individualist against emergentist accounts of social systems. For the individualists, social systems are the additive results of individual phenomena, aggregated through simple structures like markets. For the emergentists, social systems constitute an independent level, whose fully social structures coerce individual phenomena "below them." Between these radically opposed accounts have long existed a number of intermediate views. In these intermediate accounts, individuals make their own histories, but—to change the Marxian dictum into a processualist one—in that making they produce extended structures that in turn render them unable to make those histories under conditions of their own choosing.

Thus, another way of stating my task in this chapter is that I here extend what is perhaps the best known of those intermediate conceptions, the idea of ecology. Ecological argument is familiar in sociology. The Chicago School applied it everywhere—in the study of occupations, of interaction, and, most famously, of urban phenomena from mental illness to marketing. Ecological thinking remains important in urban studies, where the repeated announcements of its death bear unwilling witness to its vitality, as does the recent emergence of hierarchical models of community effects. Ecological arguments have also been extended from physical urban spaces to abstract social spaces. Wallerstein's celebrated "world system" is essentially an ecological conception, and Hannan and Freeman's population ecology approach to organizational analysis relies on explicit ecological arguments, as does McPherson's similar approach to organizations and occupations.[2]

Ecological theory, however, has usually been particular rather than truly general. The usual ecological account in the social sciences considers a system of actors in a set of locations—countries in the world system, for example. But ecological accounts usually make strong assumptions about what is outside these systems. In world systems theory, for example, religion figures as an unstudied external actor; the various states are bound into a patterned ecology of interaction, but the various religions are not. Only one part of the social world is conceived as subject to the constraints we call "ecological;" the rest is fixed. The same critique has been made for many years with respect to the Chicago School's unwillingness to study the external linkages, financial structure, and political economy of the city.[3]

I here answer this critique with the concept of linked ecologies. Instead of envisioning a particular ecology as having a set of fixed surrounds, I reconceptualize the social world in terms of linked ecologies, each of which acts as a

2. Ecological argument has often arisen in the context of comparative history, where it provides a middle way between case-based narrative and formal causal comparison. It embraces a broader range of facts than does individual case analysis, but retains the contingent interplay that is narrative's great attraction. The classical citations in human ecology are Park, Burgess, and McKenzie 1925 and Hawley 1950. See also Hughes 1971 on occupations, and Goffman 1963 on interaction. On the "death" of the Chicago School, see Alihan 1938, Castells 1967, and Dear 2002. On hierarchical models, see Bryk and Raudenbush 1992. Abstract ecological arguments include Wallerstein 1976, Hannan and Freeman 1977, and Rotolo and McPherson 2001.

3. See Wallerstein 1976:151–56. For this kind of criticism of the Chicago School, see, e.g., Castells 1967 and Logan and Molotch 1987.

flexible surround for others. The overall conception is thus fully general. For expository convenience, however, it is easiest to develop the argument around a particular ecology. I shall here use that of the professions.

Thus, the professions constitute an ecology like those among nation-states, ethnic groups, and so on. Professions wish to aggrandize themselves in competition, taking over this or that area of work, which they constitute into "jurisdictions" by means of professional knowledge systems. A variety of forces—both internal and external—perpetually create potentialities for gains and losses of jurisdiction. Professions act and react by seizing openings and reinforcing or casting off their earlier jurisdictions. Alongside this symbolic constituting of tasks into construed, identified jurisdictions, the various structural apparatuses of professionalization—growing sometimes stronger, sometimes weaker—provide a structural anchoring for professions. Most important, each jurisdictional event that happens to one profession leads adjacent professions into new openings or new defeats.[4]

Such an argument captures the intensely ecological, contingent character of professions' histories and provides a theoretical alternative to a teleological historiography in which professions grow like independent units, dictated by internal entelechies, as if the professions had an equivalent of the "human nature" discussed (and rejected) in the preceding chapter. But the concept of openings and defeats presupposes a criterion of success, and that criterion is, in fact, external. In the original exposition (*System of Professions*, ch. 3) the several professions' claims for legitimate control were judged by various "audiences": the state, the public, coworkers in the workplace. These external judgments ratified professions' claims and thereby made them efficacious against competitors. But these external referees of jurisdiction drew their own legitimacy from outside the system of professions. By uncritically recognizing that external power, we make the mistake noted above, conceiving these environing worlds of state, public, or workplace to be mere audiences: fixed and unproblematic entities in a position to judge claims of professional authority.

But the state, for example, is not such a simple and unified entity. Quite the contrary. It is itself an ecology, a complex interactional structure filled with competing subgroups and dominated by ecological forces quite similar to those driving the system of professions. It follows that state recognition of a profession's jurisdictional claims is more complicated than we had thought. Not only does a jurisdictional tactic like licensing have to succeed in the system of professions, it has also to succeed in the ecology of the state, usually

4. This paragraph summarizes the argument of *System of Professions*.

for quite different reasons. To transpire, any such project must work in two ecologies at once.

A similar pattern obtains in the urban process. On the simple ecological model, real estate patterns in a city or region derive from the locational competition of firms acting in this market. But in fact those patterns result not simply from the ecological competition of real estate firms and developers, but also from other ecologies: those of the general commercial sector, the nonprofit sector, and the government sector. Any successful development project must bring together some combination of actors across all these ecologies at once. As a result, the actor who competes in the spatial ecology of regions is not really a single actor, but rather a coalition that links one group of firms, government agencies, and voluntary associations into an alliance against other alliances linking other companies, agencies, and nonprofits. Individual alliance members compete in individual ecologies, but the alliance wins because the results of those local contests can be assembled into an overall achievement. Note that in such a system, the history of this or that member of an alliance, as well as the history of this or that particular ecology, derives ultimately from the history of alliances. Thus, the most important variables in the system are those that facilitate or constrain alliances and those that determine the various strategies of alliance. For example, differences in the relative size of actors in adjacent ecologies might constrain the possibilities of alliance, as also might the diversity of local arrangements of the members of the ecologies and differences in the speed of competition between the ecologies being linked.[5]

These examples illustrate the potential of a linked ecologies argument to sustain a more general analysis of the social process without losing the initial advantages provided by ecological theory. In its simple form, ecological theory allows us to escape the false historiography produced by assuming immanent development (in the case of professions, the development implicit in the idea of "professionalization"). A linked ecologies argument moves beyond this first form of ecological thinking by taking into account the simultaneous existence of numerous adjacent ecologies, all of whose actors seek alliances,

5. This alliance argument is implicit in Suttles's *The Man-Made City* (1990). A somewhat similar argument is made for abstract networks by Abell (1989) and for cities by Long (1958), who described the city as an "ecology of games": the political game, the banking game, the civic organization game, the ecclesiastical game, and so on. But for Long, alliances were occasional linkages between relatively distinct, well-defined games. In the present argument, they are by contrast the defining units of the system of ecologies taken as a whole. Nonetheless, the two arguments have strong affinities.

resources, and support across ecological boundaries. A further layer of contingency is thus identified. The viewpoint of linked ecologies provides a first model for how the continuous trajectories of past social action, encoded into the relations of present social structure, become the localities, facilities, and constraints of the next round of action.

This chapter thus makes a doubly complex argument, and it should be no surprise that it turns from the easy, flowing essay format of the previous two chapters toward a much more detailed exposition, completed by full scholarly machinery. The processual view is not simply a draft sketch; it is a fully developed approach to social life, and can sustain extended and detailed empirical argument. This chapter begins a series of four chapters embodying such arguments.

The chapter has two major sections, the first theoretical, the second empirical. We have first to clarify and formalize our existing concepts of ecology. The theoretical section therefore begins with the definitions necessary to ecological analysis, and then moves on to a brief discussion of the varying properties of ecologies. It concludes with a theoretical analysis of the specific advance proposed here, the notion of linkage between ecologies. There then follow two very extended sets of examples to illustrate the power of the argument. The first pair of examples shows the importance of inter-ecology linkage as a contingent phenomenon. The second set of four more brief examples shows the near impossibility of creating institutionalized linkages between ecologies, and provides further evidence of the kinds of forces that keep ecologies separate from one another.

This chapter is thus far more elaborated and detailed than its two immediate predecessors. Most of that elaboration takes the form of extended examples. A reader interested in theory alone can skip them. But the final section of this chapter (on overdetermination and on the conditions producing ecologies) does take up the main theoretical thread again. In particular, it considers the idea of ecology as a potentially general concept, of which things like markets, hierarchies, and so on can be considered special cases.

THE FORMAL STRUCTURE OF ECOLOGIES
AND LINKED ECOLOGIES

Definitions

When we call a set of social relations an ecology, we mean that it is best understood in terms of interactions between multiple elements that are neither fully constrained nor fully independent. We thus contrast ecology with mechanism and organism on the one hand, and with atomism and reduction on the other. The latter contrast is straightforward and general: ecology involves some kind of relation between units, whereas atomism and reduction involve only qualities of units themselves or of their aggregates. With mechanism and organism, the contrast is more specific. When we encounter complete and routine integration in the social world, we employ the metaphor of mechanics, as in the "rule governed systems" of role theory, for example. When we encounter systems whose elements move together in flexible homeostasis, we use the metaphor of organism, as in structural-functionalism. By contrast with these two, in ecological thinking the elements are not thought to move together at all; rather, they constrain or contest each other. "Ecology" thus names a social structure that is less unified than a machine or an organism, but that is considerably more unified than is a social world made up of the autonomous, atomic beings of classical liberalism or the probabilistically interacting rational actors of microeconomics.

This language suggests that the concept of ecology is analytic and metaphorical rather than ontological. But in this chapter I shall speak of ecologies as things—that is, ontologically. I will, for example, discuss "the ecology of professions" or "the university ecology" as particular social structures, rather than as metaphoric understandings of structures demarcated by some other means. By doing so, I bracket the question—important but much too large to be analyzed here—of whether the word "ecology" denotes an actual species of social structure or merely a theoretical framework with which we can interpret any of a number of types of social structures.

Analytically, the concept of ecology involves three components: actors, locations, and a relation associating the one with the other. In the ecology of the professions, these three components are the professions, a set of controlled tasks, and the links between professions and tasks. The basic structure of this ecology thus seems clear. But we should not proceed to the seemingly "obvious" assumption that tasks come first, then professions, then links. This is the ordering that is implied—indeed, assumed—by functionalism. But it is not correct, either as an empirical assertion or as an analytic presupposition. The locations of an ecology (e.g., tasks in the professional ecology) are not preexisting positions, except in a sense too abstract to be relevant to social theory. It is the process of constructing the relations between actors and locations that in fact constitutes and delimits both actors and locations. Analytically and empirically, the relational process is prior. I shall call this relational process ligation. By avoiding the available ordinary language word ("linkage"), I hope to remind the reader that ligation constitutes at one and the same time an actor, a location, and a relation between them. Creating a psychiatric approach to shell shock in the First World War, for example, redefined who psychiatrists were and what shell shock was, more than it defined a relation between a preexisting group and a given task.[6]

Because of the empirical and analytic priority of ligation, it is essential to remember that actors and locations are purely endogenous to social interaction. This is especially difficult with the concept of location. Our education in Cartesian coordinate systems makes us always imagine space as an empty continuum in which locations are defined by a regular coordinate system that we impose from outside, without reference to any internally produced topology. But social space is not like this. It has no empty locations. Its topology is defined relationally in the process of interaction and is therefore completely endogenous. Thus, a professional "location"—a task like obesity or alcoholism—is not a location by virtue of having a set of abstract properties that position it in some abstract social or cultural space in advance of social interaction, but by virtue of the fact that various professions have constituted certain sets of social, psychological, and biological phenomena as obesity or alcoholism in the process of fighting over the vast array of potential expert work in the society. The position of alcoholism "between" medicine, psychotherapy, law, and so on follows from the activity of those professions, not from variable properties discernable ahead of time within "the phenomenon of alcoholism." Indeed, this is as true for the very definition of alcoholism as it is for its position in the system of professions.

That there are no empty locations in social space does not mean that all of social space is equally "constituted." For example, there are areas of "potentially professionalizable work" that are currently constituted under loose, common-sense understandings, as was "getting dotty" before it became "senile dementia," "organic brain syndrome," and eventually "Alzheimer's disease." It is useful to have a formal name for general zones of experience that are not yet constituted into particular locations vis-à-vis a particular ecology. I shall call such zones "arenas," it being understood that by using such a term

6. The term "linkage" will later be used to refer exclusively to connections between actors in different ecologies. With the exception of this terminological change, this section on the professional ecology itself directly summarizes the argument of *System of Professions*. The shell shock example is discussed in Abbott 1982:266–75, 459–61.

I do not invoke any notion that arenas are somehow predefined by social functions.[7]

The utility of careful attention to such conceptual details is made clear by looking at a second ecological system, the university system. In the United States, higher education is organized into several thousand institutions, each of which makes up an organizational turf where various disciplines, professions, and other expert groupings fight for control of material resources for research and instruction, on the one hand, and of areas of knowledge and intellectual endeavor, on the other. The actors in this ecology are not a fixed, exclusively demarcated group, as are the professions. Their endogeneity is much more evident. But they are fairly definite social things. Some of them are professions themselves, others are well-defined academic disciplines, and still others are the many would-be professions, disciplines, and interdisciplines that are perpetually condensing out of specializations and interdisciplinary space. Change among these actors is much more rapid than among the professions, and individuals move between them much more fluidly than they do between professions.

The locations in this ecology—the things that these groups are attempting to control—are in most cases not as familiar as those of the professions, largely because they are not—with the exception of disciplinary knowledges—so easily reified. Like its actors, the university ecology's locations are emphatically endogenous. These locations are constituted as sites within the universe of instruction and research, and various kinds of resources—material (financial, infrastructural), demographic (e.g., students), and even symbolic (i.e., paradigmatic dominance of certain intellectual problems)—are expected to adhere to them. In this constituting of academic control, locations can be assembled

---

7. There is, of course, an infinite regress argument possible on the term "arena," since I have given no means for defining or demarcating arenas, but have refused to allow them to be defined functionally. Although resolving this infinite regress requires arguments beyond the immediate discussion, here I simply state the rough answer: we can legitimately speak of arenas because they are defined by the past states of the social process, as they are—in the examples given—by prior common-sense classifications. No social world ever exists without a preexisting topology of some sort. Hence, it is legitimate to imagine "locations" being newly defined in "arenas" that are shaped neither by currently forming location definitions nor by universal functions. I regret what may seem like an arbitrary multiplication of terminology, but only rigorous definition can tame the multivocality of common-sense terms. The following terms have specific senses in this chapter: arena, audience, avatar, bundle, ecology, hinge, jurisdiction, linkage, ligation, location, position, setting, and settlement.

in many different ways—in far more ways and with far more overlap than occurs in the ecology of professions. Since they are quite different from the well
defined and relatively stable jurisdictions of professions, I shall use the term
"settlements" to refer to these locations constituted within the university ecology. Academic settlements can take the form of a special faculty, a major or
concentration, a set of courses, a body of more or less controlled knowledge,
or any combination of these. They may involve research practices, evidentiary
conventions, and perhaps systems of knowledge application, as well as all the
structural apparatus of journals, degrees, conferences, and so on. Settlements
lack the strongly exclusive character of professional jurisdictions. There is no
sharp separation between academic disciplines, which often overlap in methods, theories, and subject matter, and which sometimes differ more in style
and heritage than in substance.

The other settlements of the university ecology are even more indefinite.
Liberal education, extracurricular life, and technology transfer, for example,
are examples of nondisciplinary settlements, each of them being a location
in the university ecology associated with particular faculty members, and
each possibly having its own special practices and forms of knowledge, and
its own social structures, supports, and resources. That these "settlements"
could also be seen as organizational functions is precisely the point. Viewing
them ecologically enables us to see them—correctly—as more dynamic; it also
makes the university world less machine-like and more contingent. Note that
these other settlements often crosscut disciplinary settlements.[8]

Since the present paper replaces the concept of "audience" (from the
analysis of professions given at the outset) with the notion of "linked ecologies," it is important to say something about the audiences for the university
ecology. In the professional ecology, it is fairly clear who are the actors and
who are the audiences for actors' claims: the professions as actors on the one
hand, and the workplace, public, and state as audiences on the other. But in
the university ecology it is not clear exactly where the ecology ends and the
audiences of the various claims within it begin. We might think of trustees and

---

8. I avoid reusing the term "jurisdiction" precisely because the locations of the university
ecology do not have the sharp separation implicit in that word. I am using the term "settlement" here in the sense used in *Chaos of Disciplines* (Abbott 2001a:136–44), on which I have
drawn for this analysis. (*Chaos of Disciplines* is hereafter cited simply by its title.) In *System
of Professions* (pp. 69–79), I used "settlement" in a different fashion, denoting by it the exact
quality of the link between profession and work: exclusive control, division of labor, client differentiation, or whatever.

state legislators as fully external audiences, but students, administrators, and in many cases external clients constitute not merely audiences—analogous to the workplace, public, and legal audiences of the professional ecology—but also endogenous actors. For example, many types of university administrators have their own associations, degrees, and supposed knowledge. Indeed, they have their own ways of thinking about the shaping of academic settlements. They "bend" the whole ecology, in the sense that the very dimensions along which the disciplines and professions cut up the world of knowledge—intellectual dimensions first and foremost—are not important to administrators, who would rather constitute the different settlements of the university ecology around, say, types of students, types of resources used, or types of education. A cognate argument can be made for the students themselves. In the terms used here, then, the university ecology may be a place where the audiences are merging into the ecology as actors, or, to put it in the terms developed here, a place where two formerly linked ecologies are merging into a single ecology.

The university ecology thus requires that we generalize the image of ecology implicit in the "system of professions." It forces us to see that professional jurisdiction is only one type of location and that the topologies of other ecologies may be more overlapping and crosscutting. It forces us also to see the boundaries of ecologies as newly problematic. Yet at root it still relies on the fundamental concept of an ecology as a set of actors, a set of locations, and a set of links between the two.

An even more extreme example of an ecology is the political system. Although it may seem counterintuitive to call the state an ecology, any government consists of dozens of competing units and parts. In the United States, dozens of "governments" have authority over any given place: towns, counties, states, and the federal government, to mention only the standard concentric series, to which are often added various overlapping and crosscutting partial governments: school boards, water commissions, sewage districts, regional authorities, planning boards, and so on. Even in statist France, one speaks of governments, plural, and departments, plural; the Conseil d'Etat exists precisely so that the administrative state will not break out into competing factions. In short, "the state" is in practice neither a single unified thing, nor a complex machine with many parts, nor an aggregate of many individual wills. It is yet another ecology of competitors, albeit one in which some members have their hands directly on the machinery of government.

But if we seek within politics the basic units of an ecology—actors, locations, ligation—things get quite difficult. To be sure, politics has a "visible" ecology that is quite simple. Political systems are deliberately designed to have settings in which conflict is supposed to occur between formally constituted political actors. These settings—the legislatures, administrative councils, and electoral committees of democratic political systems, for example—might be viewed as a set of visible locations for the political system, within which are supposed to act representatives, administrative appointees, electors, and other duly constituted social actors, who aim to control these places in the same way that a profession controls a jurisdiction or an academic discipline controls its settlement. Other political activity is considered "informal," if not illegitimate. There is thus at least the appearance of a stably organized, fully domesticated "ecology" of politics.

But just as the university ecology reaches well beyond the disciplines, so too the ecology of politics always includes far more than these formally consti-tuted actors and their formal settings of action, which in fact become a subsys-tem that determines only the intermediate stakes in a political process that ac-tually evolves far more broadly.[9] In this broader political ecology are actors of many, many different kinds: parties, civil servants, administrative departments, pressure groups, journalists, substantive experts, and so on. More important, the "locations" in this ecology are not the previously mentioned formal legis-latures, administrative councils, and electoral committees; these latter are bet-ter viewed as simple settings of competition. They are not locations at all, in the ecological sense of being endogenously created positions in a competitive space. The real locations in the political ecology are the analogues of jurisdic-tions in the professional one; they are themselves constructed out of matters of political concern, just as the jurisdictions of professions are constructed by the professions out of the continuum of potential tasks, and the settlements of academia out of the continua of things to be known, ways of knowing, and students to be taught. Another way of putting this is to say that no political group is interested in dominating a legislature simply for the sake of dominat-ing a legislature; what it really wants to dominate is some set of political issues, decisions, and outcomes.

To denote these sets of political decisions, actions, and outcomes that are the real locations of the political ecology, I shall speak henceforth of political

---

9. It was the classical theorists of the liberal state—above all, the Rousseau of *The Social Contract*—who envisioned a realm of political equality insulated from a civil society in which there could be inequality. But even Rousseau was acutely aware that politics in practice in-volved far more than the formal institutions of government. These matters will become central in chapters 8 and 9.

"bundles." These are the analogues of professional jurisdictions and academic settlements. Examples might be "social policy," "interventionist economic policy," or "deregulation." As with jurisdictions, there is no fixed or given shape to political bundles, no preexisting topology of politics. To see politics as unified *ex ante* into coherent issue bundles is to make precisely the same mistake as did the functionalist theory of professions when it thought that the shape of professional work was determined by abstract functional requirements rather than by a relentless process of interaction and competition. Issues, policies, and outcomes are tied to one another by social action, not by functional necessity.[10]

Bundles differ from settlements and jurisdictions in important ways. First, the three clearly represent a range of stability. Professional jurisdictions tend to be stable for considerable periods. Academic settlements turn over somewhat more quickly, while rebundling of political issues takes place at a rapid rate. The issue of deregulation, for example, went from being part of populist left politics to being a staple of conservative politics in less than a decade in the United States. Similar rebundlings are commonplace in the United States, in part because the two-party system makes bundling so draconian a simplification of politics. Second, the three types of locations differ in their levels of separation. Jurisdiction takes exclusive relationship as its model, whereas settlement and bundling take overlap and coincidence much more for granted. Medicine's control of expert treatment of bodily health and law's monopoly of courtroom and judiciary remain the professional ideal, while interdisciplinarity is a recurrent ideal in universities, and coalition-building a recurrent ideal in politics.

Underneath all three of these examples, however, is the basic concept of an ecology made up of a set of actors, a set of locations, and a set of links between them. The character of these three elements may change, but the fundamentals of the concept are the same. An ecology comprises actors, locations, and ligation. The last is the primary process, producing as it unfolds in

10. The aim of any given political actor is not necessarily the mastery of this or that political issue or even this or that political bundle, but to see the success of the greater part of the political issues with which that actor is concerned. Laumann and Knoke (1987) have shown, in their study of the national political field in the United States, the diverse strategies of actors in such an ecology. Some actors concern themselves entirely with a few issues, but follow them profoundly and in all settings. Others concern themselves with everything they can, exchanging quantity for quality. Note that for the specialists an optimal strategy is to impose on others their own bundling of policies, while the generalists aim to succeed on the backs of others' bundling of the issues.

interaction the pattern of constituted actors and locations that can sometimes look like a reified, *ex ante* structure. As we have seen, ligation takes different forms—jurisdiction, settlement, bundling—in different ecologies, varying by temporal duration and degree of exclusion, among many other things.

The Properties of Ecologies

I argued earlier that when ecologies come into contact with each other, we see the emergence of alliances between subgroups in one ecology and subgroups in another. These alliances and the points of contact that enable them are the determining factors in a system of linked ecologies. But the possibilities for such contact and alliance are shaped by the internal character of the ecologies being linked. So we must first discuss the many ways in which those internal characters can differ.

We begin with the forms of the actors and of their associated locations: the dimensions, numbers, and covering pattern of actors and locations. Some ecologies have actors all of one common size. In others, size varies. In terms of distribution, some ecologies have one or two major actors surrounded by lesser groups and perhaps some isolates. Others have a more uniform packing. Finally, some ecologies have purely exclusive actors; professions are generally disjunct, for example. By contrast, political actors are often overlapping in complex and irreducible ways, because single individuals and subgroups can be members of several different "larger" political actors.

When adjacent ecologies are of the same material form in terms of actor size, distribution, and exclusiveness, the linkages between them will unfold in a way quite different from the way those linkages unfold when the adjacent ecologies are of differing forms. Thus, when linked ecologies each contain a small number of exclusive actors, we can expect the creation of simple correspondences between the two sets of actors. When they are both of a complex and diaphanous form, as with the political ecology discussed above, we will more likely see ephemeral alliances, and homomorphism will matter less. In the third case (the case of considerable difference in the material and structure of the two ecologies that may become linked), the situation seems quite unpredictable, as we shall see below in the case of medical licensing.

We must also consider the pattern of created locations: the jurisdictions of the professions, the settlements of the disciplines, the bundles of politics, and so on. Some locational systems are highly exclusive—like professional jurisdictions. Others mix overlap in some dimensions with sharp separation in others, like the disciplinary settlements in academics. Sometimes, as in the political ecology, it is hard to find real exclusiveness anywhere. Indeed, as we shall see, the exact pattern of overlap for various political bundles is one of the important stakes of the political ecology. Beside this variation in degree of overlap, there are many other important dimensions on which linked locational systems can vary. Locations can be large or small, packed in or loosely covering, and so on. Given all these various dimensions of difference, it follows that the degree of homomorphism between the locational structure of two ecologies will influence very strongly the kinds of alliances that can be made between them, just as does the degree of homomorphism between their actor structures.

Finally, we must consider the kinds of links between actors and locations, the varieties of ligation. These too can vary considerably between ecologies. Even within the realm of professions, we see various kinds of jurisdictions: not only exclusive control, but also division of labor, client differentiation, and so on. In universities, the typically extensive substantive overlap between disciplines is often accompanied by sharp differentiation in methodologies, yet in some cases there is little substantive overlap and settlements are indeed fully exclusive. Looser settlements—liberal education or technology transfer, for example—can also range from exclusive to interpenetrating. In the ecology of politics, bundles of issues and policies can be tied together in myriad ways of unimaginable complexity, and, as I have noted, these bundlings tend to change steadily. In general, then, there is a long list of variables in ligation: exclusivity, intensity, types of division, legal standing, external recognition, and so on. As with actors and locations, ligation must be compared in detail across ecologies, above all in order to understand the possibilities it affords for alliances between them.

Analysis of the interior forms of neighboring ecologies and the homology between them must be supplemented by analysis of their differing temporal structures, for these too affect the possibilities of linkage between ecologies. Just as there is a question of the numbers, patterns, and ligations of actors and locations in the synchronic competitive space of an ecology, there is also a question of the grain of an ecology in time. There can be rhythms and cycles of actors, or of locations, or of the links between the two. One of the most important tendencies of the ecology of professions, as well as that of occupations more broadly, is the historical acceleration of the rhythms of the actors. In the nineteenth century, professionals made their studies in youth and needed no further education for a lifetime. But by the turn of the twentieth century, engineers, for example, had come to see their knowledge obsolesce before their careers were finished. Other professions quickly followed suit. Today, nearly all the professions face such a rapid rhythm. Yet when knowledge doesn't last to the end of a career, the very idea of career is questioned, which in turn begins to challenge the underlying demographic constitution of the professions themselves, which originally arose as groups of individuals with a common career pattern. We see this clearly in the failure of the "information profession" to emerge as a stable and effective actor in the ecology of professions, despite the massive importance of information work in the current economy. The blunt fact is that knowledge turns over too fast for a real information profession to emerge, unless the very design of the profession were to reorganize itself around a life-stage concept.[11]

Since a given ecology has its own characteristic rhythms, connection between two ecologies can depend on the parallels and disparities between those rhythms. As we shall see below, medical licensing was a continuously important concern for nineteenth-century doctors. But for the political systems they faced, it was only of occasional importance, with the consequence that the doctors' allies changed often over the years as they sought friends in a political ecology largely disinterested in them. Thus, not only do the synchronic structures of adjacent ecologies make a difference in linkage between them, but so do their temporal ones.

Having set forth the various types of differences that can affect the possibilities for linkage between ecologies, we can finally return to the original question and theorize the inter-ecology links themselves. To recapitulate, the concept of linked ecologies recognizes that events within any particular ecology— changes in jurisdictional claims, settlement patterns, and political efficacy— are hostage in some sense to events in adjacent ecologies. In the "ecology/ audience" model in *The System of Professions*, this hostage relationship was conceived as a kind of external judgment. The state or public made a judgment of professional jurisdictional claims, and accepted or rejected them on external grounds. In the linked ecologies argument, however, this hostage relationship is more mutual. Both sides are ecologies and both sides look for something out of the transaction. To succeed in one ecology, a particular competitive strategy must therefore provide results to allies in an adjacent one. To restate an earlier example, medical licensing passes (or is struck down) only because doing so provides a payoff not only for either the doctors or their "irregular" competi-

---

11. There are such life-stage occupations (short-order cook, for example), but they often have difficulty organizing for collective activity. See Abbott 2005 and also the examples given in chapter 1. On information professions, see *System of Professions*, ch. 8.

tors, but also for some political group against its political competitors. For example, licensing might help out civil servants in their conflicts with legislators by giving the civil servants reason to demand a bigger budget.

Issues that provide these kinds of dual rewards, differing in the two ecologies, I shall call *hinges*. Synchronic and diachronic patterns within and between ecologies create possibilities for alliances between actors and locations across the borders of ecologies. Exploring these possibilities are various interecology contacts, the whisperings and the negotiations from which come the alliances of the future. Out of those explorations come in turn the hinges, the strategies that work as well in one ecology as in the other. Note that a hinge can not only provide different rewards, but can actually be of a fundamentally different type in the two ecologies that it links. To take again the example of medical licensure, we shall see that in the medical world it was a characteristic of ligation, while in the political world it was a contested location.

Indeed, this difference of what we might call the axes of hinges may well be what keeps ecologies separate. If two adjacent ecologies were squabbling over the same resources, and issues occupied similar axes in both of them, there would be little keeping the ecologies from merging. It is precisely because politics is organized differently from the professions—around different issues, with different kinds and qualities of actors, with different concepts of location and ligation, and with different rhythms—that the world of the professions does not simply merge into the more general world of politics.

A good example of this separation is the emergence of sociology itself, which first began as part of a much larger entity—the progressive reform movement—whose basic arena of activity was not the university, but that of politics. As the university system gradually condensed into its new form in the late nineteenth century, the reformers who happened to be located in universities formed, among other things, a local version of reform—sociology—which did not shed its last direct connections with the political world until the 1930s and 1940s. But the expansion of the university system after 1900 that created the opportunity for academic sociology also created a whole new type of competition. And that new competition defined the terms in which sociology competed with the other (new) disciplines that emerged around it: anthropology, political science, and the slightly older economics and history. Ultimately, these terms of competition—the concept of the undergraduate major and the idea of disciplinary specialization, for example—meant that academic sociology had to separate from reform or merge into the academic teaching of social work. But the terms of this academic competition were not given *ex ante*. They were produced by the internecine conflict of the disciplines themselves in the academic setting.[12]

It is this ability of new arenas of competition sometimes to constitute themselves as separate ecologies that makes ecological analysis worthwhile as a general strategy. Otherwise, the social process would simply consist of an undifferentiated flow (as it is in purely contingent theories of history) or a systematically proliferating and differentiating system (as it is in the evolutionary functionalism of Parsons, for example). But by viewing ecologies as current arenas of competition that can be linked together and even in some cases amalgamated or divided, we can reduce the contingent complexity of the social process without assuming any fixed or functional structure to it.

To evaluate this argument, we need to consider some examples of linked ecologies. I shall therefore take the system of professions as my core ecology and examine some cases of linkage between it and the ecologies around it.

LINKED ECOLOGIES: EXAMPLES

Professional and Political Ecologies

To illustrate linked ecological analysis, I begin with two examples of medical licensing, an issue that brings together the professional and political ecologies. In the first of these examples—nineteenth-century medical licensing in New York—action succeeds because striking down licensing becomes a successful hinge action, with both political and medical payoffs. In the second—medical licensing in the same period in England—action fails because despite its success in the political ecology, it fails to provide enough payoff in the professional ecology to mobilize a sufficient supportive coalition.

Taking the New York case first, I begin with the actors, locations, and ligation history of the medical ecology.[13] The actors in the New York medical ecology in the nineteenth century included three different medical sects: the

12. On the early history of sociology, see Turner and Turner (1990) and *Department and Discipline*, (Abbott 1999: ch. 3). Note that the concept of "hinge" is to some extent cognate with Padgett and Ansell's (1993) "robust action." Both involve the importance in action of brokerage points between different structures.

13. The most important sources on the medical history of New York are Walsh 1907; Duffy 1968, 1974; and Van Ingen 1949. For medical licensure generally throughout the United States, Rothstein 1972 remains the most important source. A detailed study is Rosenfeld 1984. For the legal history, I have followed the account of Walsh 1907, filled out by my own reading of the journals of the legislature.

allopaths, who were the inheritors of earlier British and continental medicine; the homeopaths, a new sect arriving from Germany in the 1840s; and the eclectics, who tried to embrace all methods. There were also Thomsonian botanical doctors and a large miscellany of midwives, pharmacists, chemists, and others. Unlike these latter, who were unorganized or disorganized, the three medical sects pursued the structural road to professionalization: journals, societies, university-based schools, and so on. A crucial part of that program was licensure, generally conceived as state-authorized penalties against those who practiced medicine without the imprimatur of the sect. But since the three sects could not bring themselves to recognize each other, coordinated action was impossible.

The work at issue among these various actors was that of curing human physical problems, which was itself constituted, by means of these jurisdictional battles, into what we now would think is the jurisdiction of health. But what was and was not part of this health jurisdiction was very unclear in the nineteenth century. Delivering babies, for example, was only "medicalized" in the course of the century, and even then not very completely; it was principally a family event, not a health one.

In terms of ligation, all of the various actor-groups spent most of the nineteenth century jockeying for control of various areas of medical work, the higher-status professions aiming at exclusive jurisdiction, the lower-status ones at retaining a free field with openings for all. Exclusive jurisdiction was won and lost several times by the allopaths during the early years of the century, but around midcentury a Jacksonian free-for-all opened medical work to all comers. In the last third of the century there were roughly parallel establishments for the three major sects, coupled with a variety of restrictions on the others, although enforcement was often weak.

Finally, in 1907 a general reorganization of all this turf emerged. In teleological histories of professionalization, this was the goal towards which all the nineteenth-century comings and goings had tended. By contrast, in the linked ecological perspective, the 1907 licensing system meant the creation of an institutional system that provided an acceptable basis on which to terminate one form of jurisdictional competition while beginning others, both in medicine and in politics.[14]

14. See Rothstein 1972, and above all Rosenfeld 1984. On the homeopaths, see Kaufman 1971. Laws seeking to regulate the practice of medicine were proposed almost annually throughout the nineteenth century, but most disappeared in the public health committees of the assembly. I report here results from my own review of state documents. Any unreferenced

Throughout the nineteenth century there were nowhere near enough doctors in the three sects, much less in allopathy alone, to meet statewide health demand, and so in practice the jurisdictional pattern tended to be one of client differentiation, the sects serving the higher status clients, the others the lower. As we shall see when we consider links between the ecologies, however, there were a number of specific medical "locations" that were in fact constituted at the behest of the political system. There too, the aim of high-status healers was to create exclusive jurisdiction by a small group, and the aim of low-status healers was to destroy it.

By contrast with this relatively straightforward medical ecology, the political ecology was extremely complex. In the first place, the very arena of political activity was hard to define. The vagaries of American state formation had created three major settings for politics—city, state, and federal—without really deciding which issues were to be resolved where and why. National issues—slavery until the Civil War and reconstruction afterwards—gave form to some political parties, but not to others, which were purely local. As for city and state politics, their relation was transformed several times during the century (there were four new constitutions) as different sides prevailed in the debate over home rule for the city of New York. Moreover, the boundary between government and private activity was quite hazy. Nineteenth-century city governments typically acted as coordinating and pass-through agents aiding landholders in local infrastructural improvements, rather than as general redistributors of income and creators of public infrastructure.[15]

All this implied that the identity of "the government of New York," and indeed even of what it meant to speak of "governing New York," was quite hazy. For example, in 1866 the state legislature directed the taxes, debts, building codes, and public health of the city. The state governor named the commissioners of police, of health, of fire, and of immigration, while the city's mayor named the commissioners of streets and of the aqueduct, and the electorate

primary assertions on New York politics come from that review. From 1792 to 1907, there were eight successful projects that aimed at increasing the regulation of medicine. For these, there were perhaps twenty or thirty failures. There were also four or five successful proposals to reverse or overturn regulation, and a considerably larger number of failed attempts to do this.

15. The sources on state and city politics in New York in the nineteenth century are numerous and diverse. There is no definitive and complete account. Hammond 1844 and Jenkins 1846 remain important sources. Simple summaries are Brown 1922 and Johnson 1922. Recent studies of importance are Spann 1981, Hammack 1982, and McCormick 1981. On the role of cities in particular, see Sam Bass Warner's classic *The Private City* (1968). See also Teaford 1984, McDonald 1986, Einhorn 1991, and Monkkonen 1995.

chose the mayor, the council, the aldermen, the commissioners of education, and the controller, who in turn named the commissioners of the city's hospitals and of the city's prisons.

As this recitation makes clear, the actors in the New York political ecology were numerous and diverse. These actors included political parties, which were in turn constituted of clubs, firefighting companies, commercial interests, and "patronage swamps"—specific areas of government work under party control. There was also an extensive administrative corps (actually, several competing administrative corps, some of them in Albany, some in New York). There were also the legislative bodies in Albany, sometimes dominated by the city's Tammany Hall, sometimes by the upstate Republican machine.[16] There was the Board of Regents, a council of notables named for life (by whatever political party controlled the state at the moment of vacancy) and charged with supervising all the public and private educational establishments in New York. Throughout the century there were also recognized groups representing private interests: for example, the elite reformers who governed the state behind the scenes in the 1870s and 1880s.

The locations at stake among the many and widely divergent actors in this ecology of politics were very diverse. They included decisions about public policy, about public expenditure, and above all about what was to be considered public in the first place. They involved agriculture, manufacture, health, transportation, retailing, education, crime, slavery, and dozens of other things. As a result, the competing activities by means of which the professions aimed to establish and control the jurisdiction that we would eventually call 'medicine' took place in the context of political actors who themselves were competing in an ecology of agents—governmental as well as private—of which the central question was the manner in which a vast and indefinite array of goods and services would be distributed and paid for. The state was indeed yet another ecology of little groups fighting their own little wars for their own little reasons. Indeed, the locational and actor complexity of this ecology was so great that it is difficult to descry any real structure of policy "bundles." There were major issues, to be sure, but they were combined and recombined in dizzying varieties of ways.

16. Histories of Boss Tweed, Tammany Hall, and the Tammany Society are numerous, but for the most part they aim more at shock value than serious analysis. Werner 1928 remains important. Mandelbaum (1965) was the earliest to see Tweed as the politician who first resolved—despite himself—the coordination problem that had theretofore stymied politics in the large American cities.

Between these two ecologies ran an extensive variety of ties and claims. Medicine was mixed up in many problems and social establishments of which the identity—political or technocratic, statist or medical—was very much in play. Public general hospitals, quarantine hospitals, mental hospitals, and asylums for the retarded not only employed many doctors, but also provided targets for medical lobbying about "public health," public morality, and employment. Medical people served in many of the offices and councils concerned with what we would now call public health: a city health department, a council on contagious illnesses, a bureau of "summer physicians" and, of course, the vast system of quarantine and immigrant inspection on Ellis and Staten Islands. Here too, doctors played several roles: employee, reformer, and political agent. Doctors of all types were also involved in public debates on medico-legal questions: abortion, the legal status of the insane, professional malpractice, the functions of the coroner, and insurance and pension issues. And of course they spoke publicly on various topics in areas that they claimed concerned "public health" (which was not yet a common locution): clean water, sewers, street cleaning. Doctors took these political activities seriously, perceiving them as technocratic matters of public health. But other political actors often viewed their interventions as partisan or self-interested. As a result, doctors' pretensions to be recognized as experts were to a large extent hostage to their political activities.[17]

On the linked-ecologies argument, the political system interested itself in the internal affairs of the healers—the fight between homeopaths and allopaths, for example—only when the allopaths and homeopaths could be allied with different political positions in the political ecology. For only then would the fight between homeopaths and allopaths as professions provide anyone in the political ecology with helpful political resources. This might explain the general stalling on the medical licensing issue in the late nineteenth century, which has usually been attributed to obscure conflicts between medical sects. Rather, since the allopaths and homeopaths were not adversaries in the many politico-medical arenas in which doctors were active, no political actors had any incentive to offer either of them licensure in exchange for partisan

17. On the subject of public health in New York, see Duffy 1968, 1974. For a surprising and amusing story of medical influence, see the history of the Croton aqueduct and the sewers in Goldman 1997. Doctors favoring wet sewers found themselves opposing the many parties interested in the for-profit nightsoil industry that was fertilizing New Jersey fields with New York excrement. The political role of the New York Academy of Medicine has been well studied. See Van Ingen 1949 and also Duffy 1968, 1974.

support. For example, there was a great debate over the origins of the cholera epidemics—whether they came from human contact or from "miasmas."
These two theories implied different policies with different political costs,
supporters, and detractors—in the one case, quarantine (with costly specialty
hospitals, not-in-my-backyard problems, and delay of expensive business
shipments); in the other, a program for general public health (with expensive
pure water, wet sewers that harmed the nightsoil industry, housing inspection
that hurt landlords, and so on). But since allopathy and homeopathy both
included supporters of both theories, competitive issues within the realm of
healing offered no turf for political profit-taking.[18]

The early nineteenth century provides at least one clear example of this
fact: that changes in medical licensing happened only when those changes
could succeed in the interprofessional arena and at the same time could serve
the interests of some actor in the ecology of politics. In 1843 a crescendo of
complaints bombarded the legislature demanding the abrogation of all penalties for unauthorized healing. On 2 May 1844, the Assembly did indeed strike
down the existing penalties by a vote of 61 to 40 (NYAJ 1844:1042).[19]

This success was not the result of party politics, even though the Whigs
and Democrats were at each others' throats and the Democrats themselves
had divided into radicals and "hunkers" over the issue of passive versus active government. Indeed, the numbers absent from the vote indicate that this
was not really an essential question for either party. But the geography of the
votes shows that votes for the continuation of regulation came from three

18. For an extended discussion of allopathic views of cholera, on both sides of the miasma/
germ divide, see Rosenberg 1962, ch. 4, 9, and 12. Among homeopaths, the miasma theory can
be found in various sources (e.g., Warner 1858:106ff; Small 1876:236). By contrast, the germ
theory, with its contagion/quarantine implications, can be found in Comstock 1868:43–44.
Most homeopaths, like most allopaths, sat on the fence (see the excellent review of the homeopathic approach in Paine 1867, which starts by announcing the germ theory and then moves
without hesitation into a miasma model). Thus, the two schools did become less differentiable
across the broad front of political issues that involved doctors, and other actors in the political
ecology probably no longer cared about resolving their conflict in the professional ecology. As
a result, the homeopathic medical association was recognized by the state from 1865, and there
was a homeopathic state mental hospital from 1874.

19. The two houses of the state legislature, Assembly and Senate, both published *Journals*
and *Documents*. I have denoted these NYAJ, NYAD, NYSJ, NYSD respectively. For the *Journals*, it suffices to say the year and the page. For the *Documents*, one must add the number of
the document. Thus NYSD 1844, 31:3 means the third page of Senate Document 31 for the
year 1844.

regions whose counties had large populations and large numbers of already-authorized doctors: New York and its immediate environs, the populous counties from Albany westward, and the counties of the southern tier along the border with Pennsylvania. Votes to strike down regulation came from the rural and mountainous areas of New York: the counties along Lake Ontario, the Adirondack counties in the extreme north, and the Catskill and Taconic counties between Albany and New York. The vote was thus overwhelmingly a vote of urban regions against rural ones, and the key to the situation was the importance of herbal medicine in the rural regions.

But this is not what was discussed in the legislative debates about medical licensing. Rather, the debates were about the partisan issue dividing Whigs, radicals, and hunkers—that of activist government—and they invoked all the highest stakes of that debate—democracy, liberty, equality, and science. For example:

> Your committee have yet to learn that science, and a long established profession have anything to lose from open and fair competition or to fear from error and quackery, when free to combat them with the power of light and truth. (NYAD 1843 62:6)

> A people accustomed to govern themselves and boasting of their intelligence, are impatient of restraint; they want no protection but freedom of inquiry and freedom of action. (NYSD 1844, 31: 3, 5.)

This grandiloquent language shows us that medical licensure fell in 1844 because the demands of the empirical healers (above all, the botanical doctors known as Thomsonians) in their competition with allopathic doctors provided the democratic radicals with a chance to shout about their faith in liberty, competition, and the reason of the average man. The project of abrogation didn't succeed because the Thomsonians persuaded members of the legislature of their various arguments about medicine; rather, it succeeded because some members of that legislature saw that the question of abrogation would give them a chance to shoot rhetorical arrows at their enemies, the hunkers and Whigs. There was medical action because medicine could be an occasion for political action.

Thus, an event like deregulation of doctors in New York became a hinge event. It was situated not solely in the system of professions, but also in the political system. It should be obvious that the rule that a hinge event must "succeed" in two ecologies at once obtains just as powerfully if the impetus comes from the other side, the political ecology. The contrasting case of nineteenth-century British medical licensure—a case of failure of action— makes that clear.

Again, we review the actors, locations, and ligations of the ecologies in-volved. In the early nineteenth century, England had more or less four of-ficial types of healers, plus the usual range of empirics, botanicals, midwives, and so on. First, there were perhaps 1,500 physicians, who were university-educated, high-status, and long since organized into the Royal College of Physicians. Second, there were several thousand surgeons, descended from the old barber-surgeons' guild and organized into the Royal College of Sur-geons in 1800. Although qualifications and an examination existed for sur-geons, neither was stringent, and one could enter the profession easily from military surgery. Third, there were the apothecaries: tradesmen selling drugs and dispensing advice with them. Apothecaries made the first moves in the nineteenth-century licensing game, acquiring an act in 1815 that licensed them, allowed professional examinations, and trademarked the term "apoth-ecary." Lower in status than surgeons, apothecaries were considerably more numerous, numbering perhaps ten thousand in the kingdom in the 1820s. Competition from apothecaries in the early nineteenth century led the sur-geons to tighten their examinations, and many men entering general practice passed both sets of examinations.[20]

In addition to these three groups were the chemists and druggists, a less organized group who simply sold drugs (without any advice), and whom the apothecaries saw as their opponents and inferiors. The chemists also were governed by Parliamentary acts, although these mainly focused not on prac-tice but on purity of medicines. Beyond the chemists were still more heal-ers. The general lack of medical care throughout the society meant that many people set up in various forms of general practice under still other names, without any form of qualification or label. All of these practiced various pieces of what we would now consider general medicine, including such tasks as at-tending at childbirth. The name "doctor," of course, was not protected. And, as in America, the actual extent of "medicalization" was by no means clear.

20. General sources on the British medical professions in this period include Reader 1966 and Loudon 1986, the former placing the medical men in a broader context, the latter a first-rate, extraordinarily detailed study of actual medical practice. On chemists, see Russell et al. 1977, which well describes the complex alliance of pharmacists and analytical chemists, two groups that are wholly separate in the United States. See also the discussion in Erickson 1952:243ff.

The continuous jockeying in this professional ecology is evident in the many attempts at legal control of it: the apothecaries act in 1815, attempts to amend that act in 1825 and 1833; bills to regulate medical practice in 1816, 1818, 1841, 1844, 1845, 1846, 1847, 1850, 1854, 1856, 1857, and 1858; select committees on medical education in 1834 and on the medical profession in 1847; and a long and complex history of attempts to regulate doctors in civil service and military positions. As in America, there were many tries for few successes. But since homeopaths were not in England the force that they were in America, the actual dynamics of competition in the English professional ecology were different. In America the competition was more or less between equal schools, at least after the retreat of the botanicals. In England, the competition was, characteristically, a status competition between groups jostling in a vertical hierarchy. (And it came to an end when the three top groups allied against the rest in 1858.)[21]

The political ecology facing this vertically fluctuating professional ecology was itself vertically organized. Much more than in America, the political realm was constituted around a single formally democratic structure— Parliament—in and through which most political actors had to channel their efforts. Although there was an extraparliamentary politics of considerable importance, and although much of nineteenth-century British politics concerned political actors' access to Parliament, what matters for medical licensing is that the core of the Parliamentary political ecology was tiny indeed. There were about six hundred seats in the Commons, and the total parliamentarily active group cannot have been numbered much more than perhaps two or three thousand people. Shaping the politics of the country in the great London political clubs—Brooks, the Carlton, the Reform—political coalitions controlled not only Parliament but also the patronage-filled bureaucracies.[22]

21. The list of parliamentary activities comes from my own survey of the indexes of the *Journals of the House of Commons, Hansard's Parliamentary Debates,* and *Sessional Papers,* as well as the massive *Subject Catalogue* (Cockton 1988) for the relevant years. On the various negotiations and complexities among the medical groups themselves, see Berlant 1975, Loudon 1986, and above all Newman 1957. The last of these describes the legal situation in excellent detail, but only from the point of view of the medical personnel.

22. British politics in the middle third of the nineteenth century are usually regarded as having been in transition from the unreformed aristocratic politics of the eighteenth century to the populist, party-dominated politics of the late Victorian era. The foremost exponent of this view was Norman Gash (1953, 1965, 1972), but it continues to be standard (see, e.g,, Jenkins 1996). For a general study of the emergence of liberalism, see Parry 1993, and for an alternative view of reform, see Newbould 1990.

The actual actors in this tiny arena were shifting alliances shaped by personal friendships, inherited political allegiances, and rapidly changing personal fortunes. The location they aimed to control was "office," that is, the holding of the monarch's authority to make a government, with which went the ability to initiate major legislation and to exercise a patronage power of some considerable use in maintaining family and alliance fortunes. As in many democratic systems, holding office was far more important than was maintaining a consistent politics, and throughout the century we have examples of prime ministers proposing and passing—merely in order to stay in office—bills to which they were in private completely opposed. Disraeli's passage of the 1867 Reform Bill is only the most celebrated example. This organization of the political ecology around personal matters rather than political bundles grew out of the unified interest of the political class in shedding its political power as slowly as was compatible with social stability. In such a world, party conflict involved family political traditions more than it did contested political bundles, and in fact, the parties were by no means strongly attached to particular political locations. The Tories tended to be interested in conserving the past and anchored the old landed interest, to be sure, but they also included technocrats like Sir Robert Peel who would prove willing to strike down the Corn Laws that bankrolled the principal (landed) constituency of the Tories. But the Whigs (later, Liberals) were great landholders quite as much as the Tories, if not more so.[23]

As in New York, the area of activities we now call public health created an important link between the medical and political ecologies. But the driving force in that emerging arena was not medical or political. It was largely

---

23. On the patronage system of office, see Lewis (1952:32), who remarks that "a large proportion of Government offices was directed to the outdoor relief of the upper classes." Note that despite the overwhelmingly common class interests across parties, the tiny disagreements between the protectionist Tories, the technocratic Peelites, and the "reforming" Whig/Liberals embodied enough "difference" to provide the leverage whereby larger public differences pressured Parliament into a vast overhauling of British life. Indeed, one might say that in order to fight purely internal squabbles over minor matters of status and precedence, the great English aristocrats used the larger differences of the public as their weapons, with the indirect consequence of abolishing the foundations of their power. This is an example of the deliberately self-similar character of democratic political institutions, whereby slight self-interest differences in the political class are harnessed to larger differences of the whole society in such a way that internecine warfare in the political class produces policies dictated by broader constellations of interests. See *Chaos of Disciplines*, pp. 173ff. This self-similarity is the hidden foundation of classical pluralism as described by Dahl (1961).

administrative, and came mostly from the remarkable Edwin Chadwick. From his position as secretary to the national Poor Law Commissioners and later to the General Health Council, Chadwick's enormous energy took him and his investigators—sometimes doctors, sometimes engineers, sometimes middle-class reformers—into dozens of areas: clean water, burial grounds, housing sanitation, and so on. One of those many areas was medical licensing, for Chadwick's tidy administrative mind was outraged by the fact that a sizable minority of Poor Law medical officers (one in every parish in the kingdom) were not in any way qualified to practice medicine. Strangely, the Poor Law medical officers ended up competing with the regular medical profession by providing cheaper services, and the regular profession often attacked the Poor Law system for this reason (see Lewis 1952:76). At the same time, Chadwick's vision of public health involved engineers and chemists as well as physicians, surgeons, and apothecaries. It was not merely medical, but broadly scientific. (Chadwick was a doctrinaire Benthamite.) This was one of several reasons why the British medical professions were nowhere near as deeply involved in the politics of "public health" as were those in New York. They were much less dependent on state largesse—the workhouses and poorhouses did not sustain employment among those groups of doctors most active for licensure. Even worse, they did sustain employment for lower-status practitioners despised by those very "licensers." Thus, the state was effectively a competitor in the professional ecology itself.[24]

The story of medical licensing in the 1840s—the period of greatest licensing activity—was that no version of licensing could be found that would produce payoffs in both ecologies. In 1840, the Whigs introduced a licensing bill at the behest of a partisan group of surgeons whose real aim was to attack the governing bodies of the Physicians, Surgeons, and Apothecaries. But this strategy from the professional ecology failed to prove of much political use to anyone. The Home Office (in charge of England's internal affairs) more or less took the point of view of the existing corporations (*Hansard* 3rd series, 56:362–63 [1841]) and indeed there were no real political enthusiasts for the

24. On the emergence of a genuine state bureaucracy in this period, see Parris 1969. The classic study of Chadwick is Finer 1952, and that of Chadwick's impact on public health is Lewis 1952. A more recent and detailed study of the public health area as eventually constituted is Hamlin 1998, which in particular portrays the competition provided by Poor Law medical personnel (Hamlin 1998:93ff.) On the daily life and practice of the Poor Law Medical Officers, see Loudon 1986 (ch. 11).

bill, but rather skepticism from all quarters. The fact was that there was no political profit to be made from supporting or opposing the bill (cf. Newman 1957:154ff).

After the general election of 1841 brought in the Tory ministry of Sir Robert Peel, however, Sir James Graham, the new home secretary, brought in a major medical reform bill in 1844. Graham's action was partly a response to the steady prodding of opposition (Whig) politicians. Most of these had little prior connection with the subject. Rather, medical reform seems to have become a useful issue with which they could twit the government, so Graham sought to disarm it preemptively. Indeed, even Graham's logical allies—like Chadwick at the Poor Law Commission—seem to have been dangerous friends.[25] Graham's bill had a long and tortuous history, but ended in failure after his many unsuccessful attempts to arbitrate between the conflicting interests of the various healing groups. In the end, they all unified around hatred of the bill's creation of a strong, central, governmentally-appointed board that would have supervised professional licensing. This time, licensing worked in the political ecology but not in the medical one.

More generally, medical licensing was seen too many different ways by too many actors; no single version of it could be found to work in both ecologies. In the Peel government's somewhat authoritarian and technocratic approach, licensing was part of a broader program (bundle) of institution creation in government, a program of bureaucratization and social control that had taken shape in the new Poor Law, the Factory Acts, and the creation of the metropolitan police. Other parties treated it as a handy tool for various ephemeral political uses. The medical professions, on the other hand, treated it as a burning issue of monopoly, a fact shown clearly by the opposition to the Graham bill as first proposed, which strongly protected the two royal colleges to the great resentment of apothecaries and other general practitioners. Once

25. The standard work on Sir James Graham is Erickson 1952, and the standard biography of Sir Robert Peel is Gash 1972. A study of the Peel administration specifically is Crosby 1976. Chadwick was playing his own political games with doctors (cf. Hamlin 1998: 182–83). He was also playing games with Graham, whose brother had been appointed registrar general over Chadwick's evident disapproval (Lewis 1952:32). Chadwick's *Sanitary Report* was one of the most revolutionary documents of the age, and Graham of political necessity "maintained a wary reserve" (Lewis 1952:62). Graham may have been looking to the medical world for weapons with which to fight his state-internal battles with Chadwick, whose position as secretary of a freestanding board (the Poor Law Commissioners) allowed him to intervene at will in matters of great import to the political classes, whose outlook he did not fully share.

Graham conciliated the GPs, he had lost the elites, who attacked him for loss of their vested interests.[26]

Yet the very failure of licensure to succeed as a hinge had enduring importance within the medical ecology itself. In Great Britain the National Association of General Medical Practitioners emerged in specific opposition to the activities of the three professional corporations vis-à-vis the 1841 and 1844–45 medical bills. The licensing debate thus not only led to complex alliances but also resulted in new structures within the professional ecology itself.

These first examples underscore the importance of the varying properties of ecologies discussed earlier. First, they show the importance of studying the relative comparability of size and other qualities across actors in the linked ecologies. In New York, allopathic physicians were about as numerous as the homeopaths, but were more numerous than the eclectics. The nonmedical healers probably outnumbered all three medical groups taken together. Yet all of these groups were tiny by comparison with the major political groups and organizations of the state. The doctors of New York numbered perhaps three thousand in 1840, and perhaps six or seven thousand in 1900, while Tammany Hall—but one of many political clubs in but one city—numbered fifteen thousand in 1892 (Blake 1901:150). To be sure, the political actors closely involved in medical licensure—the legislature, the regents, and the health commissions of the state and city of New York—were much fewer, but still the political world was overall a vastly more numerous world than was the medical world in New York in the nineteenth century. The doctors were but one of the numberless pressure groups drifting around in the political ecology. By contrast, in England it was the political ecology that was small and tightly focused.

Equally important are general differences in ligation. Medical actors aimed at exclusivity or were already largely exclusive. To be an allopath was to not be a homeopath or an eclectic or a botanical healer, and so on. The same was true for the others. But in the political world there was no such exclusiveness anywhere. Members of Tammany might also be members of the Assembly, bureaucrats or other administrators in state or city government, members of

---

26. Hamlin (1998:157) remarks: "Chadwick offered Peel and Sir James Graham an innocuous yet viable way for moderate governments to respond to the polarized condition-of-England question." That is, public health more broadly was the proposed hinge issue. But because the medical professions presented a relatively united front against government-sponsored reform, rather than presenting a variety of views differentiated by subprofession, no joint action was possible. Things might have turned out quite differently had the apothecaries broken ranks. For a medical-side view of the constitution of this politics, see Berman 2002.

governmental commissions, democratic party officeholders, and so on without losing their identities as members of Tammany Hall and—something that matters considerably vis-à-vis the ecology of professions—without losing their identities as members of this or that occupation. Political actors were not exclusive actors. Indeed, the exact overlaps of various actors were very much stakes of the entire political ecology.

This leads to a second point. It is essential to realize that what is location in one ecology can be ligation quality in another. For the New York doctors, medical licensing concerned a crucial property of the linkages of actors and locations, the quality of exclusive jurisdiction. For the English doctors, licensing was not only such a quality of ligation, but also the defining boundary of a social actor; ultimately, all three regulated medical professions made common cause against all the others. For the political ecology, by contrast, licensing was not a characteristic of the links between actors and locations. It was, rather, a policy—that is, a location. In the political ecology, therefore, medical licensure was a tiny question bundled among many other things as a way of consolidating and dominating political terrains that were much larger. In New York, licensing was bundled with other issues of liberty and freedom, in this case the liberty to pursue health in one's own way. In England, by contrast, it was bundled with public health and social control, as a precondition of good government.

A third crucial issue, mentioned earlier, is temporal grain. For the doctors, licensure was a perpetual question, but a question which, when one had voted some laws and created some administrative structures to embody them in practice, could in their view be regulated once for all. By contrast, political affairs, of the city as of the state, were far more hasty things. They were not envisaged in any long run, but only in the short. Only rarely did the political ecology concern itself with matters of regulation looking even ten years into the future. Much less did the political ecology envision definitive regulation, and indeed medical licensing in the late twentieth century was effectively disemboweled by the expansion of nursing, the appearance of physicians' assistants, and the supervision of managed care. This mismatch of the rhythms of interests in licensing between the two ecologies surely implied that the allies of the doctors—of the allopaths as well as of the homeopaths—necessarily varied during the decades of battle over the question of licensure. As the political kaleidoscope turned up new openings within the political system, the doctors found now one group, now another to be their principal allies in the pursuit of licensure. This rhythmic discord perhaps also implied that the doctors ultimately succeeded in getting "permanent" licensing only when other medical issues—chiefly the cost of medical care and the problem of specialization (Stevens 1971)—began to provide straw from which political bricks could be made on the more rapid time scale of the political ecology. Permanent licensing came, quite literally, because licensing was no longer a politically useful controversy.

The Professional and University Ecologies

Rather than seeking an alliance with some particular unit of an adjacent ecology, a profession could attempt to create an avatar of itself within that ecology. This would be the creation, in some sense, of an institutionalized hinge. We have just seen an example of this—although in the reverse direction—in the case of the Poor Law medical officers, who were a governmental creation in the professional ecology. Such a strategy commonly results in conflict between original and avatar, since the two face fundamentally different competitive situations. This reshaping of avatars shows well the powerful internal dynamics of ecologies, the ways in which those internal conditions of competition tend to keep ecologies separate. To illustrate these dynamics, I shall consider four short examples here of attempted avatars between the professional and university ecologies: two originating in the professional ecology and two originating in the academic one.

The avatar process is to some extent already visible in the cross-sectional fact that there are three basic kinds of actors or disciplines in the American academic ecology, loosely defined by whether they give graduate degrees, undergraduate degrees, or both. First, there are the thirty or so "heartland" disciplines that give both kinds of degrees—math, economics, English, and so on. Heartland departments hire faculty almost exclusively from their disciplines' PhDs, and are always associated with undergraduate liberal arts majors. Beside these heartland disciplines are the purely research-based disciplines like cognitive neuroscience, development studies, and Renaissance studies, which sometimes generate their own PhDs but typically do not have undergraduate majors. These are often linked to research worlds outside the university, in government and industry. Finally, there are what I shall call the undergraduate disciplines, like criminal justice, occupational therapy, film studies, and Puerto-Rican studies, which are undergraduate fields typically based on an occupation, an identity, or some other undergraduate demand factor, and which for the most part do not generate and hire their own PhDs.[27]

27. For an extensive discussion, see *Chaos of Disciplines*, ch. 5.

Undergraduate disciplines are often avatars created by large practice professions seeking a place in the academic ecology and catering to the practical side of the student mind. Although American community colleges originally aimed to bring liberal-arts education to the masses, by the 1970s the entire movement had turned occupational. Many practice occupations entered the tertiary education system in this period, the most conspicuous example being nursing, which was almost completely hospital-based in 1950 and almost completely college-based by 1990.[28]

But the shaping power of the academic ecology transforms the academic avatars of practice professions. A first example is computer science. The original roots of computer science lay in applied mathematics and electrical engineering. The major associations predated the full development of the first generation of electronic computers: the Association for Computing Machinery appeared in 1947, and the Society for Industrial and Applied Mathematics in 1952. By the time third-generation computers arrived in the 1960s, both computer programming and systems analysis had emerged as widespread forms of work. But they lacked formal academic foundation. The needs for rapid and mass training, for systematic evolution of computer knowledge, and for legitimation of what appeared to be ad hoc, recipe-based knowledge, acquirable by anyone smart enough to master it: all these things gradually called an academic discipline into existence.

In terms of training, that discipline was wildly successful. After expanding moderately in the 1970s, the number of schools with computer science (CS) programs exploded in the 1980s and 1990s. The number of CS BAs grew from 7,200 in 1978 to 35,000 in 1989. Although this figure has since flattened out as programming jobs leave the United States for India, it remains about 3 percent of all bachelors degrees in America. The CS field has also begun to approach heartland levels of PhD production and is now nearly self-sufficient in PhD-level faculty.[29]

28. In fact, 87 percent of nursing students were in the 1,070 hospital schools in 1949 (West and Hawkins 1950:10,19). Small hospitals drew much of their care staff from students, who provided 80 percent of home front nursing services during World War II (Haase 1990:2). By 1983, however, there were only 281 hospital schools left, and they were graduating only 14.9 percent of the nurses. (*Facts about Nursing* 1984–85:138, 126). Recalling the core themes of chapter 1, however, we should note that the immense existing mass of hospital-school-trained nurses meant that the profession as a whole was still 50 percent hospital-trained at that time (*Facts* 1984–85:27). On the transformation of the community college system, see Brint and Karabel 1989.

29. Throughout this section (all four examples), data on programs in colleges comes from volume 4 of the *College Blue Book* for the relevant years. Similarly, all figures on degrees come

But the practice profession and the academic discipline have largely de-coupled. While the demand for current basic-level programming skills is large, those skills turn over very quickly. Even so, the theoretical issues of comput-ing are largely independent of changes in programming, and even in program-ming level. As a result, CS departments have difficulty finding faculty willing to teach highly demanded skills, because those skills are themselves of little interest or importance to the academic faculty. Essentially, a separate training faculty is hired. In summary, the academic competition of CS with applied mathematics and related disciplines has necessitated a level of abstraction for the academic field that rapidly distances it from the applied field. And, unlike the situation in medicine, the applied field does not in practice live directly off academically generated innovations. At the same time, the practice discipline remains dominant. As late as 2004 there did not exist a separate society for purely academic computer science.[30]

Criminology is another case where the impetus for the academic discipline came from the practice profession. To be sure, the heartland disciplines did study crime, but practice associations grew up in parallel. The American Cor-rectional Association dates from 1870 and the National Probation Association from 1907. Police training emerged in the university context in the 1930s, and "police science" became a separate section in the major heartland crime jour-nal in 1934. By 1941, college faculty engaged in training police—most of them former policemen themselves—had created the National Association of Col-lege Police Training Officials, which in 1947 renamed itself the Society for the Advancement of Criminology, and in 1957, once that "advancement" seemed to have reached its goal, once again renamed itself as the American Society for Criminology (ASC).

Thus, the principal academic society in the criminology area emerged as an "academicizing" of faculty whose original aim was to train policemen.

---

from the relevant volumes of the *Digest of Education Statistics*, produced by the National Cen-ter for Educational Statistics and available from the Government Printing Office. Data on the founding dates of organizations come from the *Encyclopedia of Associations*. For sources on the development of computer science education in early years, see the comprehensive Austing et al. 1977.

30. On the divergence between academic CS education and industry needs by the year 2000, see the special issue of *Computer Science Education* in March 2002 on "Software En-gineering Education and Training," and in particular editor Hossein Saiedian's introduction (2002). In fact the ACM, SIAM, and the IEEE-based Computer Society remain the most im-portant academic professional societies for CS.

But the academic ecology's immense pressure for abstraction did not stop. Although the heartland academics working on crime published in the same places as did the newly academicized "police scientists," they had no interdisciplinary society pulling them together, and inevitably they oozed into the police trainers' SAC/ASC. More of the heartlanders began to work in emerging criminology departments and schools. By 1953 a heartland social scientist was president of the ASC, and since 1963 nearly all its presidents have been heartland social scientists. At present, 30 percent of members are academics in sociology or other heartland departments, 35 percent are in criminology departments, and 15 percent in other "undergraduate discipline" departments, for a total of 80 percent pure academics. This takeover of the ASC by the academics—half of them from heartland departments and more than half with PhDs from those departments—has in turn created an opening for (and indeed has almost required the creation of) another practice-based academicizing group, the International Association of Police Professors, founded in 1963 and renamed in 1971 the Academy of Criminal Justice Scientists.[31]

This pattern—academicizing, followed by capture from the academic side and a new academicizing from the practice side—was driven in part by an immense success: the very rapid expansion of criminal justice study in American colleges, from a handful of colleges in the 1960s to many hundreds today, reflected in an expansion from seventeen thousand criminology and law enforcement BAs by 1978 to twenty-seven thousand in 2000, about 2 percent of all bachelor's degrees granted in the United States. But it was also driven by the utility of the ASC for heartland academics themselves. As competition intensifies in the core of the old heartland disciplines, substantive specialization provides in some ways a shelter from that competition, both in career terms for individuals and in resource terms for the subspecialty. The history of the ASC is thus driven by its performing different functions in the two ecologies: legitimation in the professional one, respite from competition in the academic one.[32]

31. A general history of the ASC is Morris 1975. These membership percentages come from my own random sample from the ASC's current directory (www.asc41/director/title.htm, accessed December 2003). The shape of the heartland criminologists can be traced through the history of their interdisciplinary society's journal, the *Journal of the American Institute of Criminal Law and Criminology*, which had a "Police Science" section by 1934, and which in 1951 added "*and Police Science*" to its title.

32. On early criminology education, see Piven and Alcabes 1968.

The situation of new avatars is somewhat different when the expansion that creates them is an expansion into the professional ecology from the academic one. I consider two examples: psychology and economics. Both have the degree pattern that characterizes established heartland disciplines, producing a doctorate for about every twenty bachelor's. Both have developed large presences outside academia over the course of the twentieth century. Yet they have decisively different patterns of development.

Psychology began as an academic discipline, and the APA (in 1870) as an organization of academic researchers. Applied—or, as it later became known, "clinical"—psychology began on two fronts. The first of these was work with delinquency in child guidance clinics, schools, and criminal courts, where psychologists usually became members of psychiatrist-headed treatment teams. The second was the fully autonomous jurisdiction of intelligence and personality testing, introduced to a wide public by the extraordinary impact of the Army Alpha test in the First World War. In the 1920s, testing gradually spread throughout American society, from business to school, from hospital to court.[33]

The applied psychologists were often women, and applied psychology had difficulty getting recognition in the APA. (Before 1945, full membership required postgraduate publication.) An abortive applied psychology association flickered into and out of existence in the late teens, succeeded by a clinical section within the APA (1919–37). In 1937 the clinicians again separated from the APA, creating the American Association of Applied Psychology. This was reabsorbed into the APA in 1945. By then, the war—in which about a quarter of American psychologists served—had confirmed clinical psychologists firmly as the legitimate testers of the intelligence, vocational aims, and personality quirks of soldiers, students, workers, and employees. After the war, the brand-new NIMH devoted substantial funds to the training of clinical psychologists, and the field ballooned. The first moves of clinical psychology into psychotherapy date from the postwar period as well.

In the 1970s, certification and licensure for clinical psychologists marched rapidly across the United States, covering virtually all states by 1980. By this point, clinicians were dominant in the APA, and reimbursement for not only testing but also psychotherapy had been won from various third-party payers, a signal victory in the professional ecology over the arch-rival psychiatrists. So dominant were the clinicians that the academics seceded from the APA,

33. Basic sources on the history of psychology as a discipline include Riesman 1976, Napoli 1981, Routh 1994, and Capshew 1999.

creating the Psychonomic Society as early as 1959 and the more successful American Psychological Society in 1988. The latter is now the basic professional association of academic nonclinical psychologists.

Psychology thus provides an example in which the academic discipline spawned a practice wing that over about sixty years became so powerful as to drive the academics themselves to secession. Reincarnation of an academic discipline in the professional ecology failed because the pressures of professional practice drove the APA in directions unacceptable to academics dedicated to general theory and experiment in psychology. In the process, clinical psychology eventually built its own separate academic system—the schools of "professional psychology"—complete with separate journals and bodies of knowledge. Faculties at such schools include very few researchers in foundational psychology; the schools' researchers work mainly on applied problems like therapy efficacy, test construction, and so on.

The practice wing of psychology originated from techniques invented by the field itself and readily accepted—aside from some conflicts with psychiatrists—outside it. By contrast, economists who ventured into the policy and advice arena—a venture that dates from the earliest years of the discipline—found themselves surrounded by businessmen, bureaucrats, volunteer leaders, and others who claimed equal expertise about the same things. In the discipline's early years—the AEA was founded in 1885—there was a fairly seamless gradation from applied economists working in business and government through to the professors in universities. A sign of this was the success of the discipline's independent foundation for peddling economic expertise—the National Bureau of Economic Research, which dates from 1920.

But the 1930s and 1940s saw a major change. The war years brought operations research (OR), whose cost/benefit analysis rapidly became a basic tool for applied economists. OR was rather like psychological testing—straightforward, doable only by experts, but not requiring much truly academic expertise. It was desired by clients, but controllable and ownable by the profession. At the same time, the war period also brought Keynesian economics, a comprehensive and quite academic system that dominated national economic policy for thirty years after the war. More important, the period brought a level of statistical and mathematical sophistication to academic economics that began to deeply divide the academic and applied fields. By the 1950s, Arrow and Debreu were doing their Nobel Prize–winning work on general equilibrium: a transformatively brilliant theory, but one with somewhat otherwordly assumptions. Such work was utterly irrelevant to applied economics, other than as a legitimating totem.

Thus, abstracting developments—driven by the mathematicization that seized academic economics after the war—began to push the academic and practice wings of the discipline apart. All the same, the applied economists have never left the American Economic Association. And the AEA continues to be dominated by academic economists, even though those academic economists have had their own society for statistical and mathematical economics (the Econometric Society) since 1930. This alliance continues because the applied economists generally believe that the mathematical dreaming of the academics provides the legitimation for their own considerably more home-spun work. Most applied economics involves little more than the first two semesters of microeconomics and the first semester of macroeconomics. Economists both applied and academic report that this is what they really share, and, indeed, that this is all they really know. But the vast mathematical daydreams of the academic economists—which have been the subject of internal jeremiads for many years—provide the incomprehensible proof that applied economics rests ultimately on "science."[34]

This holds true even when academic and applied economists enter the same policy arena and fight over it. A good example is the conflict between academic and applied economists in the analysis of federal manpower programs. The debate pitted applied economists, who wanted to measure the programs by doing randomized experiments, against academic economists who wanted to use "scientific" statistics, the latter group being led by James Heckman, who had in fact won the Nobel Prize for just those statistics. But although long, hard, and unresolved, the fight has not produced anything like the schism in psychology. It seems clear that applied economics remains tied to academic economics in part because the professional competitions in which it is engaged are so severe, as I have already noted. So academic legitimation proves a crucial resource for applied economics and keeps it closely tied to the academic ecology.[35]

These four cases show, then, that attempts to make avatars across ecology lines inevitably run into the problem that the internal forces of competition in the avatar's ecology tend to drive the avatar in directions unforeseen ahead of time. There is, in that sense, no way to build a perfect hinge. No structure can be built that can completely escape the differing pressures of interaction within two different ecologies.

34. On the knowledge of economists, see Reay 2004.
35. The manpower example comes from the work of Daniel Breslau (1997a,b).

OVERDETERMINATION AND THE
EMERGENCE OF ECOLOGIES

Despite the generality of the linked ecologies approach, there are clearly cases in which analysis in terms of linked ecologies is impossible. The most important such case occurs when ecologies lose their separation because of the overwhelming number of linkages binding them.

A good example of this is the arena of military activity. The theme of interservice rivalry is an old one, and the military arena would seem well described by an ecological analysis. The basic actors in this ecology would be the services and their subunits—Army, Navy, Air Force, and Marines, together with their various specialized subsections of Special Forces, Submarine Force, and so on. In the traditional interservice rivalry model, these actors compete for resources of men and money, but in an ecological model we would conceive of the "locations" to be monopolized as bundles of work: specific tactical tasks and, beyond those, bundles of tactical tasks that add up to strategic bundles. Command of resources should flow from control of such strategic bundles, as, for example, command of resources slipped from Air Force to Navy when the American nuclear deterrent moved underwater in the 1960s.

Certainly for long stretches of American military history, a linked ecologies model works well. The military was a small area of competing groups controlling widely divergent tactical tasks and facing a fairly straightforward political ecology in Washington. State governments were occasionally involved because of the extensive use of the military in the suppression of civil disorder, although most such work fell to the hermaphroditic (state/federal) National Guard units.

But the strategic world of the post–Cold War period makes such a model quite inappropriate. In the current imperial situation, the American military must maintain a complex set of strategic outputs ranging from nuclear deterrence to preparedness for major conventional war to the long list of quasiwarfare activities characteristic of imperial militaries: counterterrorism and reprisals against terrorism, police actions involving conflicts over race, property, and the like in places where policy makers decide America has interests, protection of American nationals working worldwide, guaranteeing the free trade that keeps America hegemonic, and so on. Such tasks call for officers with as many political skills as military ones and involve extensive collaboration with other agencies both American and non-American, governmental and private. The network of production involved in these outputs is much too dense to conceptualize in terms of subsegments of the military competing for control of this or that strategic service.[36]

In effect, the military is enmeshed in too many ecologies for it to move in any direction. Imagining it as a set of professions involved in jurisdictional adventures over who controls traditional combat, unconventional warfare, and operations other than war can capture only a tiny portion of the systems of environing relations that govern it. It is for this reason that the great books about the bureaucratic politics of the military—Morton Halperin's *Bureaucratic Politics and Foreign Policy* (1974), for example—spend most of their time first elaborating an enormous cast of characters and their interests: the branches of the service, the civilian and military bureaucracies, the NSC, the CIA, the congressmen with their worries about base closure and military business, the manufacturers with their desire for military profits. Only then do they trace the various settings and rituals through which these characters and interests shape a decision before, during, and after it is made. Such books portray a system far too clogged with influence, alliance, and opposition to be seen as a relatively open system of ecological relations or competitions. In such a congested world of influence and overdetermination, ecological models are less useful.

This argument about overdetermination implies that whether a zone of the social process takes on a specifically ecological nature is an empirical question. An important further question is therefore that of the conditions under which such ecologies emerge. If we could answer that question in future work, we might also understand why in some cases we see overdetermined, congested zones of social structure that are not ecological in character.

36. The literature on the military "ecology" is mostly normative. Both sides agree on a loosely ecological perspective on interservice relations. They differ on whether that rivalry is a good or a bad thing. Those who believe that interservice rivalry produces better security through competition think the historical record demonstrates the dangers of the massive intervention by outside (civilian) policy bureaucracies (themselves enmeshed in other competitions, although this is not emphasized in the defense literature). An example is Hoffman 1999. Those who believe that interservice rivalry produces dangerous coordination failures think the historical record underscores the dangers of ecological competition between the services. Davis 1985 exemplifies this "dangerous rivalry" conception, even making a linked ecologies argument in which civilian political combatants (Congress and the executive branch) make use of rivalries in the Pentagon to achieve civilian political aims (pp155ff.) Halperin and Halperin (1985) also provide some noteworthy examples. In summary, a linked ecologies approach may be applicable to the military case, but only if used with extreme care. My own analysis of the military case is Abbott 2002.

But the recognition of overdetermination also returns us to my remark early in this chapter that one could contrast ecology with mechanism and organism (the two great emergentist theories of structure) on the one hand, and with atomism and reduction (the two pillars of individualist theories of structure) on the other. I suggested that it might be possible to regard ecology as a general model of which the others might be limiting cases. It is useful to sketch such a possible organization of social ontologies.

All of these views attempt to give general ontological models for social life. A first dimension of difference among them is the "level" of entities in such an ontology. For the atomists—microeconomics, for example—the entities are biological individuals. Social entities are mere appearance. For the emergentists, whether they use mechanical or organic metaphors, social entities are real, while individual behavior displays only random variation around socially determined averages. Ecological views however are agnostic about entities, which can be individual or social. Indeed, as a processual view, ecological thinking tends to take the nature of entities as endogenous. Entities can appear or disappear. They are not fixed *ex ante*, even in their "level." In fact, consistent levels are not a required concept in such an ontology.

A second dimension of difference is degree of interrelation. In the atomic view of microeconomics, actors/entities have no relations. They act independently in the face of the market realities established by aggregate supply and demand. There are newer, network conceptions of atomic social structure that do conceive of such relations, but these have had some difficulty capturing networks' variation over time. In the emergentist perspective there are typically quite strong views about interrelation of units. These can be more or less rigid or mechanical, or they can reflect a fixed or varying (and therefore "organic") division of labor. Again, the ecological view is centrally located. It recognizes interrelations but does not make strong assumptions about them, and particularly not about their fixed nature. On the contrary, because ecological thinking is processual, relations are continuously made and remade in time. And I have just noted the extreme case in which there are so many interrelations present that the flexible competition frequently found in ecologies proper is not possible.

Under the processual ontology, we regard the social process as consisting of events occurring to a current array of individuals and social entities, events which are then knotted into lineages with historicality (perhaps changing them distinctly in the process) and then perhaps encoded into the social structure instant by instant, either through one of the forms of historicality earlier discussed or as newly current relations between different entities in the process. These relations define a system of adjacency on the various parts of the synchronic social structure. In moments when *individual* historicality has stronger results than *social*, the individual lineages may provide the most appropriate ontological model for the process. Under the reverse situation, the social lineages may predominate. The appropriate model (microeconomics or Durkheim) will thus be an empirical matter. Similarly, the interrelations of entities in the present can vary; they may be unrelated, or competitively related in a dynamic structure, or rigidly related into fixed structures or flexibly related into fluctuating divisions of labor, or even hyper-densely related into almost immovable structures. Again, this is an empirical matter. The word ecology represents the most endogenous version of these conceptions: the one most open to temporal fluctuation, the one most open to action, the one most open to change in levels or dynamics. It problematizes the very terms with which the other conceptions begin, and thus seems to provide a useful general concept, of which the others can indeed be regarded as special or limiting cases. When encoding produces relatively rigid and permanent structures, we might expect rigid bureaucratic systems. When it creates vast areas of interchangeability, we expect markets. Thus ecology proper is simply the version of these relations that embodies the most historically contingent version of encoded structure. The other ontologies can be regarded as simplifications of it, or as specifications appropriate in particular circumstances. One could go on to try to specify the conditions for these different specifications, but that would take us far beyond an already lengthy chapter.

* Part 2 *

Part 1 has established some of the basic parameters of the processual position. The world is a world of change, and stability must be explained. Stability arises in the form of lineage; individuals and social entities are in fact lineages of events, not enduring things. The process of lineage-making works through various forms of historicality, and the essence of historicality is "encoding," the process by which the past gets preserved, moment by moment, into the present, the only place where it can influence or shape events. Encoding is sometimes in bodies, sometimes in memories, sometimes in records, and sometimes simply in the shape of social interconnection in the moment. All of these form part of the localities, facilities, and constraints within which the various forces of the present—social and cultural action, various forms of social "causation"—shape the currently open events into a next round of "lineages and their connections."

The two chapters of part 2 start to move beyond this initial sketch of the processual position. Each is motivated by a simple theoretical inversion that appears, at first glance, to have little to do with processualism. The first asks what social analysis looks like when it is not organized around a narrative of either a case or a group of variables. The second asks what social analysis looks like when it does not focus on scarcity as the central problematic of human affairs. But while these initial questions seem unrelated to processualism—indeed the first almost looks antiprocessual—each rapidly spirals into direct engagement with the processual position. Thus, with respect to chapter 4, avoiding narrative simply means focusing on the present as a moment of passage, which means providing further philosophical and methodological foundations for the central processual duality: between the steadily passing time of lineages and the momentary time of mutual determination in the present. Similarly, with respect to chapter 5, excess turns out to be one of the main consequences of a processual view, because encoding writes the complexities of the past into the locational complexity of the social structure viewed in cross-section. Moreover, processes like habituation play a role in generating problematic excess, and processual strategies like serialism play a role in dealing with it. Thus each chapter—the one methodologically, the other substantively—provides an extension of the processual model.

Like chapter 3, chapters 4 and 5 are each in the heavily documented and precisely argued genre of standard academic publishing. And while each begins with a short introduction specifying its relation to the broader processual argument of the book, I have left each in its original rhetorical form, complete with the original motivation that sets up its main puzzles.

CHAPTER 4

Lyrical Sociology[1]

In the two phenomena of lineage on the one hand and ecology on the other, we have seen two aspects of temporality. In lineage we see the diachronic time of narratives, of careers, of "emergence." In ecology we see the synchronic time of mutual determination, the time of action, the time indeed of reality and experience. This chapter will extend the analysis of processualism by investigating in great depth this dual nature of temporality, focusing on the synchronic. The diachronic, narrative side of temporality has been well analyzed elsewhere. I have myself published extensive discussions of it, in *Time Matters* (chapters 1 and 4 through 7). By contrast, the temporality of the moment—within which all mutual determination takes place—is understood in a more limited way. To be sure, network analysis, equilibrium theory in microeconomics, cross-sectional regression, and similar approaches all examine social relations in a kind of timeless present. And as we have just seen, ecological analysis provides a rich route into this complex present. But even setting aside the complex nature of reciprocal determination in the present, the present is always pregnant with the changes possible in passage itself. Because encoding is moment-to-moment rather than permanent, the seemingly timeless present is always on the brink of change, an episode in a long succession of moments, permanently transitory. The present chapter emphasizes

---

1. This chapter was drafted for presentation at a seminar on 11 March 2004 sponsored by Intersections, a University of Michigan initiative bringing together the sciences and the humanities. I thank also the referees at *Sociological Theory* where the piece was published (25:67–99, 2007).

this embedding of the seemingly fixed present into passing time, exploring the phenomenon of passage itself.

It conducts this inquiry through an analysis of the concept of lyric, which is the poetic version of this appreciation of the transitional. The chapter is motivated by a straightforward theoretical inversion, considering the possible opposites of narrative in its broadest definition. It seeks the other way of knowing time. We usually assume that the correct way to understand the social world is to tell stories about it. These can be stories of actual people or institutions: histories, biographies, organizational case studies, world systems analyses. Or they can be "stories" of variables, as in the many forms of quantitative analysis. In the second chapter of *Time Matters*, I examined carefully the difference between these two kinds of stories, arguing that "stories" of variables have major disadvantages as ways of understanding the social world. But the present chapter lumps together both kinds of "stories"—of individuals and of variables—as narrative approaches to the social world, and asks what the alternative to such a narrative approach to that world might be. That alternative is a sociology founded on particular moments, on particular locations, and on a particular, committed emotional stance of writer towards material. It is a sociology of transition.

Like the preceding chapter, this one is long and detailed. The concept of a transitional present is not well studied in social science, and many different approaches are needed if we are to make it visible. The chapter thus takes detours through literary criticism and the history of ethnography, as well as analyzing several sociological texts in detail. It also raises general questions of temporality that will reappear in chapters 6 and 7. But its organizing questions involve the lyrical apperception of the social process.

The chapter unfolds as follows. It begins with an analysis of text, creating a basic first experience of lyrical sociology. It then looks to classical criticism and literary theory for formal definitions of the lyrical impulse. A long third section specifies the nature and dimensions of lyrical sociology, using a number of examples. The fourth section digs even more formally into important related literatures (contemporary literary theory and the history of ethnography) and into specific issues (location and emotion). It is here that the chapter's relation to the general thematics of processualism becomes clear: the problematic relation of linear time and momentary time, of lineage and moment, of location in time and location in social space. These are all central issues in processualism, and it is useful to investigate them within a specific and limited area. In the end, then, this chapter about moments captures a central aspect of the social process over time.

THE QUESTION OF LYRICAL SOCIOLOGY

The Chicago River, its waters stained by industry, flows back upon itself, branching to divide the city into the South Side, the North Side, and "the great West Side." In the river's southward bend lies the Loop, its skyline looming towards Lake Michigan. The Loop is the heart of Chicago, the knot in the steel arteries of elevated structure which pump in a ceaseless stream the three millions of population of the city into and out of its central business district. The canyon-like streets of the Loop rumble with the traffic of commerce. On its sidewalks throng people of every nation, pushing unseeingly past one another, into and out of office buildings, shops, theaters, hotels, and ultimately back to the north, south, and west "sides" from which they came. For miles over what once was prairie now sprawls in endless blocks the city. (Zorbaugh 1929:1)

During the 1970s and 1980s a word disappeared from the American vocabulary. It was not in the speeches of politicians decrying the multiple ills besetting American cities. It was not spoken by government officials responsible for administering the nation's social programs. It was not mentioned by journalists reporting on the rising tide of homelessness, drugs, and violence in urban America. It was not discussed by foundation executives and think-tank experts proposing new programs for unemployed parents and unwed mothers. It was not articulated by civil rights leaders speaking out against the persistence of inequality; and it was nowhere to be found in the thousands of pages written by social scientists on the urban underclass. The word was segregation. (Massey and Denton 1993:1)

While these two passages disprove the old canard—going back at least to *Fowler's Modern English Usage*—that sociologists can't write, their versions of good writing are nonetheless very different. Yet they have the same topic: Harvey Zorbaugh's paean to Chicago and Douglas Massey and Nancy Denton's jeremiad about segregation are both about the character and dynamics of cities. And they have similar politics; for if Massey and Denton flaunt their political message from the start, Zorbaugh's book soon reveals its roots in the progressive tradition. Moreover, both passages aim to evoke in the reader a certain frame of mind—for Zorbaugh a sense of excitement and intensity, for Massey and Denton a sense of surprise and outrage.

What differentiates these two passages is, rather, their language. Zorbaugh invokes not only simple metaphors like the "stained" river and the "looming" and "canyon-like" Loop, but also the Homeric simile of the el tracks as the blood system through which circulates the diurnal pulse of city life. Massey and Denton, by contrast, use no figures of speech beyond the dead metaphors "multiple ills" and "rising tide," and the equally tame synecdoche by which "speeches," "pages," and "word" concretize the American political consciousness from which the problem of segregation has disappeared.

The only strikingly figurative language on Massey and Denton's opening page is the chapter title: "The Missing Link." Having no obvious referent, this historic phrase propels the reader forward into the text: What link? Between what and what? Why is it missing? Yet we do not know, at the end of Massey and Denton's first paragraph, the answers to any of these questions, nor indeed do we know whether the book concerns segregation itself or the manner in which discussion of it disappeared. By contrast, Zorbaugh's chapter title— "The Shadow of the Skyscraper"—refers directly to the text that follows: literally, because that text concerns the part of the city that is immediately north of—and hence literally shadowed by—the Loop skyscrapers, and figuratively, because it concerns the social life that grows up because of, and hence "in the shadow of," the urban conditions whose most visible result is the Loop towers themselves. Indeed, the skyscraper synecdoche points to a puzzle even more focused than that of Massey and Denton: Is Zorbaugh the technological and ecological determinist that this shadow figure seems to imply?

The evident difference in figurative language presages a more subtle difference in subject matters. Zorbaugh writes of the city itself—its geography, its people, its places. Massey and Denton, by contrast, write of talk about the city—the talk of politicians, funders, social scientists, and others. One passage is about a thing, the other about ways of seeing (actually, not seeing) a thing. Indeed, this difference of subject partly drives the difference in figuration. It is because he finds the city fascinating and overwhelming that Zorbaugh can wax poetic, while Massey and Denton, who find nothing so romantic or vivid about the gradual forgetting of segregation, must simply hammer that forgetting into our consciousness with six repetitions of the same grammatical structure, taking their rhetorical cue from sermons and political speeches rather than from poetry.

Thus, the passages differ in both figuration and concreteness. But finally— and perhaps most strikingly—they differ in temporality: one passage is about something that is, while the other is about something that has happened. Every one of Zorbaugh's main verbs is in the present tense. The river "flows," the streets "rumble," the arteries "pump," the people "throng." Zorbaugh's only past tenses are a past participle used as an adjective ("stained"), an imperfect indicating the transition from earlier forms of society ("what once was prairie"), and a simple past indicating the origins of the daily commute in the suburbs ("from which they came.") In short, Zorbaugh writes about a state of being, a moment. By contrast, Massey and Denton write about an event. Every main verb in their passage is in the past tense (most of them the indefinite imperfect "was"), and indeed the passage starts with not just the past but the perfect tense—in the phrase "a word disappeared." The only present tenses are the participles indicating ongoing action in the past:"decrying," "administering," "reporting," "proposing," and "speaking."

In summary, then, both paragraphs concern the city. Both take an activist and passionate view. But Zorbaugh writes figuratively about the city itself as a current state of affairs, while Massey and Denton write unfiguratively about urban discourse as an unfolding history. Of the three differences—in figuration, concreteness, and momentaneity—I want to focus here on the last: that between writing about a state of affairs and writing about a happening. After all, we have a simple name for what Massey and Denton are doing, for telling a story; we call it narrative.

The idea of narrative has a cyclical history in modern scholarship.[2] In the great rout of teleological and Whig history by the social-scientific and bottom-up histories of the 1960s and 1970s, the idea of narrative shared the exile of the older generation that had perfected it. In the insurgent generation, the social science historians thought narrative was mere talk rather than rigorous quantitative analysis, while the bottom-up historians identified storytelling with "master narratives" that aimed to hide from our sight the "peoples without history." As for the sociologists, the sociological mainstream thought it had left narrative behind in the 1930s with W. I. Thomas and life history methods. Indeed, in the 1960s and 1970s narrative became a niche product in academia, written only by a few conservative historians and by a handful of social scientists rebelling against the causal orthodoxies of their disciplines.

Then in the 1980s the fashion changed. Newly particularized, narrative reemerged as a major mode of academic writing, from oral histories of individuals to grand chronicles of classes and ethnic groups and genders. Alongside the new narrative production came the equally new products of the cultural and linguistic turns, which indeed for many people were continuous with the narrative one. For such people, "narrative" meant all three things at

2. For sources on the history of narrative, see McDonald 1996.

once; following stories, investigating cultural symbols, and attending closely to language.

This narrative onslaught was not a return to the maligned teleologies of Whig history. Rather, it self-consciously opposed a social science thought to be excessively analytic. In particular, it attacked the preoccupation of analytic social science with causal stories about relations between reified constructs like "bureaucracy" or "southern attitudes," which were opposed to (admired) narratives that recounted real actions of real actors both social and individual. Indeed, the cultural turn followed logically from this opposition, via the argument that the very categories of causal analysis (bureaucracy, southern attitudes, and so on) were themselves the creations of real actions by real people.[3]

But the contrast between Massey/Denton and Zorbaugh is not one between a story of reified variables and a story of concrete actors. Rather, it is a contrast between telling a story and not telling a story at all. There is no story in Zorbaugh. Compared to *The Gold Coast and the Slum*, analytic social science and the new narratives of the 1990s are simply different versions of the same thing: stories of variables in the one case, and of actors in the other.[4] For telling a story is precisely what Zorbaugh does not do. He rather looks at a social situation, feels its overpowering excitement and its deeply affecting human complexity, and then writes a book trying to awaken those feelings in the minds—and even more the hearts—of his readers. This re-creation of an experience of social discovery is what I shall here call lyrical sociology. That is, I am going to oppose narrative not to causal analysis, as we typically have in the past, but to lyric. And I am going to argue that sociology—indeed, social science—ought to have lyricism among its available genres, and ought to think about lyricism as a general alternative to "story" thinking, broadly understood.

The rest of this chapter will make the case for such a lyrical sociology. I begin with a brief review of the literary theory of lyric and derive from it a set of basic dimensions for the lyrical impulse. I then discuss these dimensions at length, illustrating them with examples. A final section digs more deeply into

3. I have written extensively on the opposition of narrative and analysis, (see, e.g., *Time Matters* C. 2, 4), as well as on methodologies aiming to transcend it (see Abbott 1992, Abbott and Tsay 2000).

4. Thus the opposition of narrative and analysis is a fractal one, nesting narrower versions of itself (causal stories versus "narrative analysis" of the historical sociology type) within broader ones (narrative versus lyric). See *Chaos of Disciplines*, ch. 1. Note that Massey and Denton's book involves both causal analysis and a historical story.

the theoretical foundations of the lyrical mode and positions lyrical sociology in recent methodological and theoretical debates.[5]

I aim this chapter at the general sociological audience. I am not preaching to the antipositivist choir, although my earlier experience with such essays suggests that only that choir will listen.[6] Nor, although it applies literary theory and concepts, is this chapter goring the equally familiar ox of "smoothed-over," "monological," "nonreflexive" ethnography. I am, rather, pointing to a theme or emphasis already strong in many types of sociological work and urging us to develop that theme more strongly. I am thus writing in the tradition of Brown's *A Poetic for Sociology* (1977), a book that derives aesthetic canons for sociological thinking from the vocabularies of literary, dramatic, and artistic analysis.[7]

THE CONCEPT OF LYRIC

To oppose narrative to lyric is to invoke an older body of literary theory than did the narrative turn, with its opposition between narrative and analysis.[8] The literary warrant for the concept of narrative came from the high structuralist tradition: Propp's (1968) analysis of Babi Yaga, Todorov's (1969) of the *Decameron*, Barthes's (1974) of Balzac's *Sarrasine*, and Genette's (1980) of Proust's *A la recherche*. The urtext of this tradition was Barthes's *Analyse structurale du récit* (1966), a detailed exposition of narrative as a branching succession of events and possibilities. Implicit in Aristotle's discussion of nar-

---

5. The examples used in this chapter are somewhat arbitrary. I have made no attempt to find "best" examples, although I have chosen a wide range of examples in order to emphasize the breadth of lyric. I should note that Brown (1977:63–4) specifically uses Zorbaugh as an example of bad aesthetics, because of his lack of distance on his subject. I disagree.

6. As of the original writing of this paper (2004), there had been 246 citations to the three theoretical pieces on "narrative positivism" that I had published in the early 1990s. Exactly two appeared in the *American Sociological Review*. That twenty-nine such citations had appeared by then in the *American Journal of Sociology* says more about my affiliation with that journal than about the impact of my work on the quantitative mainstream.

7. Oddly, Brown speaks little of emotion and of lyric, which will be central concepts in my analysis. On "nonreflexive" ethnography, see Clifford 1986:7. Obviously, the argument here implies that Clifford's analysis was fatally flawed.

8. Actually, the narrative turn in social science seldom made formal use of literary theory. Most often, its invocation of narrative simply legitimated a general preference for the subjective, the symbolic, and the personal. For further discussion of some of the sources mentioned in this paragraph, see Abbott 1983b.

rative in the *Poetics*, this concept of a branching sequence of events is at the heart not only of the narrative turn, but also—indeed even more so—of the analytic social science against which the narrative turn defined itself. Both are in this sense utterly narrative in conception, treating reality as a story with a beginning, a middle, and an end, or as a model with independent, intervening, and dependent variables, as the case might be.

As this lineage suggests, the theorists of high structuralism were not concerned with the lyrical sensibility. The *récit* was focused on codes of heuristic and action; symbols and emotions were merely attached here and there to the flowing structure of the core narrative mystery. We must therefore look further afield for conceptual help.[9] An emblematic source is the famous "Preface" to *Lyrical Ballads* by William Wordsworth. Wordsworth's text provides striking evidence of how appropriate and useful it is to invoke the concept of "lyrical" with respect to sociology. I quote here one of the most celebrated passages of that text, but with two very slight changes; I have changed "poems" into "studies" in the first sentence, and I have changed "humble and rustic" into "urban" a little later on. Other than that, this is a verbatim quote:

> The principal object, then, proposed in these [studies] was to choose incidents and situations from common life, and to relate or describe them, throughout, as far as was possible, in a selection of language really used by men, and, at the same time, to throw over them a certain coloring of imagination, whereby ordinary things should be presented to the

9. There is no general history of lyrical poetry in Western culture or even in English literature, so far as I can tell. On the relative absence of theories of lyric poetry among the ancients, see W. R. Johnson 1982. On the theory of English lyrical poetry from Chaucer to Coleridge, see MacLean 1940. On French lyrics, see Levrault 1902, Huot 1987, and Maulpoix 2000. Lyric as a genre did not really exist for the Greeks. The Romans made lyric the lowest of genres, largely because it had the least claims as a vehicle of moral improvement and instruction. Following the classical tradition, the Renaissance also thought that lyric concerned nonserious topics (as opposed to gods and heroes) and hence should be seen as occasional and unimportant. Such early modern poets as Donne and Herbert wrote superb lyrics, but Herbert's greatness lay in bringing a lyrical stance to higher (in his case, sacred) topics, and Donne's progression from secular to sacred lyrics clearly bespoke the classical allegiance to higher things. A similar development took place in France. The history of genres in poetry is thus surprisingly like the history of genres within sociology itself. There is a hankering after work that is instructive, a suppression of the emotional (at least other than the moralistic), an insistence on high, important topics, and—when the old high topics get boring—the definition of a new set of supposedly low things (e.g., deviance in sociology, quotidian human affairs in poetry) as important and worthy of inquiry.

mind in an unusual aspect; and further, and above all, to make these incidents and situations interesting by tracing in them, truly though not ostentatiously, the primary laws of our nature. . . . [Urban] life was generally chosen, because in that condition the essential passions of the heart find a better soil in which they can attain their maturity, are under less restraint, and speak a plainer and more emphatic language. (Wordsworth [1801]1965:446–47. Interpolations as noted in text)

This passage sounds exactly like Robert Park's essay "The City."[10] Yet changing "humble and rustic" into "primitive" instead of "urban" would have produced the credo that sent Malinowski to the Trobriands and Leach to highland Burma. Moreover, Wordsworth's criteria for lyricism have their echo in modern polemics about sociology. Wordsworth wanted lyric to be about common life, and its subjects to be simple folk rather than the heroes and gods of Augustan poetry. So too did C. Wright Mills (1959) condemn sociology for its preoccupation with grand social forces and causal abstraction. Wordsworth wanted lyric to be expressed in common language. So too do we now say that sociology should be written in simple terms, not in jargon. Wordsworth wanted lyric to discern in simple things the "primary laws of our nature." So too do we want sociology to find the laws of social life. To be sure, Wordsworth believed these laws to be most visible in rural life, whereas sociologists as dissimilar as Max Weber and Robert Park have argued that the laws of human nature and society are nowhere more evident than in the city. But nonetheless they all agree that there are places in the social world where the laws of human behavior rise very near the surface.

Only in his recommendation that we "throw over [our investigations] a certain coloring of imagination," whereby ordinary things take on some "unusual aspect," does Wordsworth go beyond the familiar bounds of sociological polemics. The main imagination we consider in sociology is the theoretical imagination, whereas it is clear that Wordsworth has in mind here an emotional imagination that can juxtapose strong images and powerful feelings to awaken in a reader the emotion that the poet has himself felt, but that is now—in the famous phrase from later in the "Preface"—"recollected in

10. Cf. Park 1925:2–3. For an interesting reading of Chicago School sociology in particular as intensely literary in conception, see Capetti 1993. See also Lindner (1996), who elegantly documents the connection of Parkian sociology with journalism. Taking its title from Wordsworth, this chapter originally appeared in print as "Against Narrative: A Preface to Lyrical Sociology."

tranquillity" (Wordsworth [1801]1965:460) Yet even here, we sociologists are not necessarily agreed on how we differ from Wordsworth. For we do not always insist on the theoretical imagination. At work in the Massey and Denton passage above is not so much a theoretical or an emotional imagination as a moral one. Indeed, neither of my opening passages really believes in theory for theory's sake. But where Zorbaugh wanted to bring us the sheer excitement and "Pindaric" grandeur of the city, Massey and Denton want to engage our moral sense.[11]

And perhaps a want of Wordsworth's "coloring of imagination" is what has really led to the much discussed decline in influential public sociology. Perhaps it is not so much our moral timidity and our obsession with professionalism, as Burawoy (2005) has argued, but rather our colorless imaginations and our plodding moralism that have driven sociology from the public stage. Perhaps the great sociological classics of the postwar years were popular less for their often deep moral passions than for their always powerful evocation of their writers' emotional reactions to topics as disparate as the organization man, the street corner, and the melting pot. It is striking indeed that of the eleven top titles on Gans's (1997) sociological bestseller list, seven telegraph emotional themes in their titles (*The Lonely Crowd, The Pursuit of Loneliness, Blaming the Victim, Habits of the Heart, Worlds of Pain, Intimate Strangers,* and *The Hidden Injuries of Class*).[12]

In summary, it seems worthwhile to undertake a conceptualization of lyrical sociology. Perhaps there is a kind of emotional involvement with our topics that we can rediscover through detailed analysis. As my approach so far suggests, I shall derive the various parts of a conception of lyrical sociology from the critical literature on lyrical poetry. I must therefore make the usual disclaimer of the analogizer. My aim is to make old things look new and per-

11. "Pindaric" became a synonym for "heroic" or "excessive" in English lyrical theory following Cowley, who in the late seventeenth century rediscovered Pindar—the one explicitly lyrical voice in Greek poetry. Cowley and his contemporaries also rediscovered Longinus, who thought poetry was less for instruction than for simple communication of emotion from poet to reader. In the long history of lyric poetry this lack of instructional content has always been seen as its chief fault. As Samuel Johnson famously wrote, "The end of writing is to instruct. The end of poetry is to instruct by pleasing" (1958:245). Among the many current writers who believe with Johnson that narrative cannot be other than moralizing, see White 1987. Note that I have largely ignored the issue of the audience for lyrics, poetical or sociological. I thank David Wray and Jeff Morenoff for pointing this out.

12. I will analyze Burawoy's argument in more detail in the epilogue.

haps provide us with a new way of reading the work of some of our colleagues, if not a new way of writing our own. There may be some jarring moments, but one hopes they are worth the price.

I undertake a relatively formal translation of concepts in part to avoid facile equivalences (of the form "Lyrical sociology is really *x*") that could short-circuit the inquiry and lead to mere recapitulation of earlier debates. For example, one could jump to the conclusion that lyrical sociology is the same as ethnographic sociology. But we should not accept that argument without having first tried to imagine—on the basis of theoretical argument—how a lyrical impulse might express itself in historical sociology or quantitative sociology as well. One could also jump to the conclusion that lyrical sociology is merely popular writing or merely descriptive writing. These too would short-circuit a more serious consideration.

Our general guide must always be the aim to imagine a kind of sociology—really a kind of social science—that is in some profound sense not narrative. This doesn't mean that it can't contain narrative elements—Zorbaugh's book is full of little stories. But it means that its ultimate, framing structure should not be the telling of a story—recounting, explaining, comprehending—but rather the use of a single image to communicate a mood, an emotional sense of social reality.

Since explanation—which is almost inevitably narrative in character—has been so strong a theme in social science methodology, we shall find that few books are explicitly lyrical.[13] I shall use a variety of examples below, but they were almost never conceived as wholly lyrical works. Rather, we have to look for whatever pieces of lyrical sociology we can find. And of course, many analyses that are conceived narratively have strongly lyrical subsections. But lyrical sociology must be more than wonderful writing and literary bravura. We are looking for an assertion of lyricism against narrative, and in particular against narrative's most familiar avatar in the social sciences—explanation.

---

13. Functionalism is a possible exception to my assumption that all explanation is inherently narrative in structure. Functional explanation presupposes maintenance of something in the present by an arrangement of forces that will "correct" any deviation from some functional goal (Stinchcombe 1968). Functionalism and related equilibrium arguments do not really require narrative explanations that move through real time; they exist in abstract, contentless time. I discuss such arguments further in chapter 7.

LYRICAL SOCIOLOGY

I consider the concept of lyrical sociology under two headings. The first and more important is stance, by which I mean an author's attitude towards what he writes and towards his audience. The second is mechanics, by which I mean the devices an author uses in constructing his text.[14]

Stance

The heart of the lyrical impulse is a stance of the writer toward the studied object on the one hand, and toward readers on the other. (Richards [1925] calls these "feeling" and "tone," respectively.) That stance is engaged rather than distant, and the engagement is an emotional one, an intense participation in the object studied, which the writer wants to recreate for the reader. Moreover, this engagement is not ironic; the lyrical writer does not place himself outside the situation but in it. If there is an irony to his lyricism, it is an irony shared with the object and the reader, not an irony that positions the writer outside the experience of investigation and report.

There is a temptation here—in the word "irony"—to fall into a facile but misleading equivalence. Hayden White, among others, has invoked the tropology of Northrop Frye to analyze social scientific writing (in his case, history). He notes metaphor, metonymy, synecdoche, and irony as four basic tropes, loosely associated with the four genres of romance, tragedy, comedy, and satire. And at first blush, the lyrical seems to fit well under romance. But these are all narrative categories, straight from the Aristotelian canon; all concern the aims and outcomes of a plot. There is no necessary reason to think that the lyrical impulse is romantic, and indeed in Japanese poetry—which is almost entirely lyrical in conception—it often is not so, however romantic that poetry may seem to narratively conditioned Western eyes.[15] We shall have

---

14. Referees of this piece asked why I used terms like "stance" and "mechanics," which are not "lyrical" themselves. But there is no more reason to write lyrically about lyric than to write absurdly about the absurd, pace Samuel Beckett. Lyrical writing is as disciplined and formalized—perhaps more so—than other kinds of writing.

15. Oddly, Frye himself (1957:41) saw irony as an evolution from the "low mimetic," believing that a direct logic led from writing about those of our own stature (low mimetic or basic realism) to writing about those "inferior in power or intelligence to ourselves" (1957:34)—for him, the very definition of irony. At the same time, Frye believed in a direct connection of lyric and irony, because for him "the [lyric] poet, like the ironic writer, turns his back on audience" (1957:271). This seems very implausible until one recalls Frye's special definition of "irony" as

occasion below to recall this confusion, for it is a commonplace of sociology today that engagement with one's topic is not "scientific," as if distance and irony were the only legitimate stance for sociological writing.

Returning to my two opening examples, we can see that Zorbaugh is indeed lyrical in his stance. He is engaged, and quite unironically engaged, with the city he describes. At the same time, however, he is rigorous and disciplined in his engagement. Indeed, it is to some extent the rigor of his book— its multiple roots in interviews, document search, and observation—that allows him to see what is so exciting about the new North Side. But this rigorous engagement remains immediate, almost apperceptive, unlike the moral engagement of Massey and Denton. The latter are distanced and judgmental. In their passage we see the social world only through the writing about it that makes them so angry. In Zorbaugh, we see both the city and the author's astonishment at it. He is social with the Gold Coasters, lonely with the rooming house dwellers, wistful with the Bohemians, cosmopolitan but listless with the slum-dwelling immigrants.

After engagement, the next quality of the lyrical stance is location. The lyrical impulse is located in a particular consciousness, that of a particular writer who is in a particular place. In discussing poetry, we often phrase this by simply saying that lyric involves the subjectivity of the writer. And indeed, the psychological criticism of the early twentieth century attributed various aspects of lyric poetry to various personal (often Freudian) concerns. But more broadly, the lyrical writer is acutely conscious of himself not just as author but as the person whose emotional experience of a social world is at the heart of his writing.[16]

For an example of these aspects of stance, consider a classical sociological text with an explicit lyrical emphasis, Malinowski's *Argonauts of the Western Pacific*. With its extraordinary descriptive passages and its elaborately choreographed digressions (e.g., the long catalogue of villages in chapter 2, the entire chapters on canoebuilding [5] and on words in magic [18]), this book openly mimics the Greek epics from which it takes its title. Larded as it is

---

writing about those below us. White's analysis is found in White 1973. I shall invoke Japanese lyrical aesthetics in more detail below.

16. Of course, subjectivity is explicitly invoked in much contemporary writing about social life; for a time in the 1990s we wondered whether our colleagues' books were about their purported topics or about themselves. But while we may differ about whether this shift was desirable or lamentable, seeing it as right or wrong, scientific or unscientific, is a mistake. The proper question is whether it is aesthetically successful. The problem with the new subjectivity may be less that it is bad social science than that it is bad poetry.

with information and careful investigation, it is nonetheless an overwhelmingly personal book, dominated by the personality Malinowski has chosen to project. To be sure, the Malinowski of *Argonauts* is no more the Malinowski of the diaries than the Wordsworth of *The Prelude* was the Wordsworth of the Annette Vallon affair. But for all Malinowski's rhetoric about the "science of man," the book is extraordinarily lyrical in conception. Malinowski wants us to see the Trobrianders as he saw and felt them. He falls out of his scientific pose again and again, not because he's a Westerner or a colonialist or a Pole or a man, but because he's too good a lyricist not to.[17]

There is no necessity that a highly subjective book be lyrical. *The Lonely Crowd* (1950), for example, is a highly subjective book. One comes away from it with a very strong sense indeed of David Riesman as a person: a reflective moralizer located somewhere between bemused geniality, conservative reaction, and visionary critique. But if Riesman never ascends to jeremiad, seldom does he relax into lyricism. His emotions never overmaster him nor create in him a stabbing sense of the humane. Nor is he intent on reproducing in us his emotion about modern, other-directed society. Indeed, we never quite know whether that emotion is amazement or disgust or hesitancy or delight. Rather, Riesman is the model other-directed social critic: careful, detached, a little ironic, vigilant of others' views and potential critiques.

After engagement and personal location, the third element of the lyrical stance is location in time. The lyrical is momentary. This above all is what makes it nonnarrative. It is not about something happening. It is not about an outcome. It is about something that is, a state of being. This is true even of *Argonauts*, which is not really about a particular kula trip (although it tells stories of several of them), but rather an evocation of the Trobriands at a moment in time, in which the kula is cyclical and endless. Malinowski knew perfectly well that the world he studied was passing—witness his continuous remarks about war, cannibalism, and other precolonial practices, and his portentous closing line: "Alas, the time is short for Ethnology, and will this truth of its real meaning and importance dawn before it is too late?" (1961:518). But he consciously created the image of a world in a moment, a snapshot of another world in being, even as that world changed.

17. Other detailed descriptions can be found throughout—the stylized boat trip, for example (Malinowski [1922] 1961:33–48). That Malinowski aimed to emulate his countryman Joseph Conrad is well known. Ginzburg, however, thinks that the key literary influence on *Argonauts* was rather Robert Louis Stevenson (Ginzburg 2000). See also Malinowski's diary (1989). The example of Malinowski recurs often in this book.

A contemporary book that well illustrates all three aspects of the lyrical stance is Michael Bell's ethnography of the "natural conscience" of an English village, *Childerly*. Bell is engaged throughout, a distinct subjectivity. Unlike Riesman, he is not unwilling to be seen wrestling with his data, to be seen confused and hesitant. He wants us to know the complexity of his own reaction to the residents' debates about fox hunting, scenic views, and "country people." He captures his village at a particular moment of transition, after the beginning of rural gentrification but before the genetic modification and mad cow affairs. He gives us a sense of residents' aching search for a "natural morality" that can be a legitimate alternative to the shifting and increasingly illegitimate class system, a search that is at once partly successful and partly doomed. In short, *Childerly* is a deeply lyrical book, filled with an almost Japanese sense of the transitory. It helps, of course, that it is about beautiful things—about farms, aviaries, and gardens, about thatched houses, honest labor, and homey pubs. But the book's lyricism lies in its approach to these things, not the things themselves.

Mechanics

The chief mechanical differences between a lyrical and a narrative sociology stem from the differing intent of the writers. A narrative writer seeks to tell us what happened and perhaps to explain it. A lyrical writer aims to tell us of his intense reaction to some portion of the social process seen in a moment. This means that the first will tell us about sequences of events while the second will give us congeries of images. It means that the first will try to show reality by abstract mimesis while the second will try to make us feel reality through concrete emotions. It means that the first will emphasize the artifice through which his mimetic model is made, while the second will emphasize the vividness of his passion towards the world he studies. These larger differences will be reflected in the details of writing. The lyricist will use more figurative language and more personification.

The most important of these differences is the first, that between story and image. Narrative writing centers on a sequence of events or, in the quantitative version, a sequence of variables. This sequence of events or variables explains the phenomenon of interest. By contrast, lyrical writing centers on an image or images. These are viewed in different ways, through different lenses, to evoke the sources of the writer's emotional reaction.[18]

18. We cannot require that lyrical images always be unique and subtle, just as we cannot require that all scientific models be elegant and parsimonious. Lyrical traditions often rely on

For example, Nicholas Christakis's *Death Foretold* considers medical prognostication in serious illness. An MD-PhD, Christakis did several large-scale surveys of physicians' prognostic responses to medical vignettes as well as several questionnaire-based surveys on doctors' attitudes about prognosis. He also did dozens of interviews and gathered hundreds of documents.[19] In the narrative framework, one would expect such a book to be organized around a sequence of variables that determine which kinds of physicians prognosticated when, and to whom, about what. One would expect a narrative of chapters, starting with patients and their illnesses, then turning to doctors and their qualities, and finally to the flow of prognostic information throughout the disease course: What do doctors tell patients at the start, how does this change as cases unfold, and how does it end up when death or survival ends the story? But in fact the book simply circles around the image of the doctors telling (more often, not telling) patients about the future. There are chapters on error in prognostication, on norms about it, on how it is done, on rituals about it, and on prognosis as self-fulfilling prophecy, but there is no simple narrative of prognosis. The reader in narrative mode finds this organization of the argument repetitive and undirected: Where is the causal story? Moreover, the author seems preoccupied and hard to pin down. He isn't an abstracted sociologist outside the situation, nor is he a consistent advocate for one or another position within the ranks of medicine itself.

But if we read the book as a lyric, it makes much more sense. There is no real narrative at all. There is only the image of a situation: the doctor, the unknown and unknowable future of illness, and the patient; the corpus of general medical knowledge on the one hand and the individual peculiarities of this disease and this patient on the other, and always the imponderability of an outcome that will be probabilistic for the doctor, but deterministic for the patient, who will either live or die. Seen this way, as an asymmetric situation that opposes probability and determination, the prognostic situation far transcends medicine. It is the same as advising a friend about marriage, assess-

stock, standard metaphors, despite our usual belief in the importance of new and arresting images. (I thus differ from Bachelard [1957: see especially the introductory chapter], who insists on the radical individuality of lyrical images.) So we should not be surprised that lyrical sociology, like lyrical poetry, may be full of hackneyed images: individual images like "the city-dweller," "the worker," and "the delinquent," and abstract images like "father-son social mobility" and "urban poverty."

19. Interestingly, Christakis's book, like Massey and Denton's, concerns an act of forgetting: the forgetting of prognosis in modern medicine. Despite the topical similarity, however, the books' structures are strikingly different.

ing a dissertation topic for a student, or proposing a legal strategy to a client charged with a felony. The medical setting merely makes it more universal, more penetrating, precisely as a strong lyrical image should.

On this line of argument, Christakis's real aim is to make us feel the damnable ambivalence doctors face about prognosis—indeed, the damnable ambivalence he himself feels as a practicing physician. And he has chosen to do this not by writing in the familiar "let me tell me a few of my perplexing cases and what they teach us about life" genre that has produced so many facile medical best sellers. There we would have again the Riesman persona: the careful, detached, somewhat ironic expert telling us a few delectably ironic stories, admitting us behind the veil. Rather, Christakis has written real sociology—hard-core quantitative analysis combined with endless, almost obsessional interviewing—to try to bring this one terrifyingly important situation to life for us, to show us how it makes him and other physicians feel: confused, tentative, and threatened, but also curiously and almost magically powerful. This overarching lyrical stance is struck on the dedication page, where we read that Christakis was six years old when his mother was given a 10-percent chance of living as much as three more weeks.[20]

Christakis's book shows that lyrical writing in my sense—writing whose chief intent is to convey a particular author's emotional relation to a certain kind of social moment—is quite possible even in predominantly quantitative work. The book thus illustrates not only the antinarrative character of lyrical sociology, but also its insistence on the communication of passion, even at the possible expense of abstract representation of reality. We can see the importance of the latter choice by considering a book that from exactly the same starting position makes the reverse choice; Scott Snook's *Friendly Fire* (2000), a book we expect to be passionate and naturalistic, but which is in fact relentlessly mimetic and artificial. *Friendly Fire* is a riveting account of how American warplanes at 1030 hours on 14 April 1994 shot down two American helicopters in Iraq carrying twenty-six officers and civilians: American, Kurdish, Turkish, British, and French. We expect an impassioned analysis, for not only is Snook, like Christakis, both a professional and a sociologist, but he is also personally touched by his topic, having himself been wounded by friendly fire in the Grenada engagement in 1983.

Snook's theory is distilled into an unforgettable full-page diagram of all the

20. As Christakis happily notes, this prognosis was incorrect: in fact, his mother died many years later. Note that despite its generally lyrical stance, the book ends on a tone of moralism; the last chapter is titled "A Duty to Prognosticate."

forces, issues, and events leading to the shootdown, here reproduced in figure 1 (Snook 2000:21). The diagram is precisely dimensional: narrative time goes to the right and proximity to the accident goes down the page. So in the upper left-hand corner we have things like "fall of the Soviet Union" and "long history of interservice rivalry," and through the middle we have things like "aging airframes," and "USAF and US Army units live apart," down to more proximate things like "ad hoc seating configuration in AWACS," "helicopter MSNS not on ATO," on to "ambiguous radio calls" and "IFF failed," and finally, about fifty balloons and eighty or ninety connecting arrows later, in the lower right-hand corner we come to the shootdown.

But even this extraordinary representation of narrative flow is not enough for Snook, who spent years poring through safety reports, military documents, court-martial trial documents, and even video records. He does give a simple text version of the story in the book's second chapter, "The Shootdown: A Thin Description." It is exactly that: a careful, detailed, and—in a restrained, military way—somewhat passionate story. But the next three chapters are re-tellings of the entire story from the points of view of three of the four principal actors: the fighter pilots, the flying combat airspace control crew (AWACS), and the command organizations that should have integrated the Army service helicopters (which were shot down) into the interservice theater organization (which did the shooting). The fourth actors—the dead helicopter crews—left only faint traces, a few conversations and standard operating procedures discussed in the thin description. Unlike Akira Kurosawa in *Rashomon*, Snook has no medium to bring them back to life.

But while Snook gives a virtuosic, multilevel, and multistranded organizational narrative in the tradition of Perrow's *Normal Accidents* (1984), his analysis is almost without emotion. One senses Snook as narrator. One senses his military personality (by its obsession with a level of organizational detail unthinkable elsewhere). But beyond his remark that he himself was shot ten years before, there is little hint of his emotional reaction to, or even his judgment of, the various actors. The agonizing side of this event—the remorse of the pilots, the shamefacedness of the Air Force, the "what happened to everyone after the fact"—none of this is analyzed, nor, beyond a few adjectives ("a visibly shaken TIGER 01"; Snook 2000:71), even mentioned. We never even find out how the shootdown was identified as a friendly one, how the news spread within a day to the secretary of defense, or what the initial reactions were. Only the story of how the rare event occurred is of interest, because of Snook's remorselessly narrative (i.e., theoretical) focus on the causal question at hand: How did this happen? In a setting that is an invitation to lyricism, this author

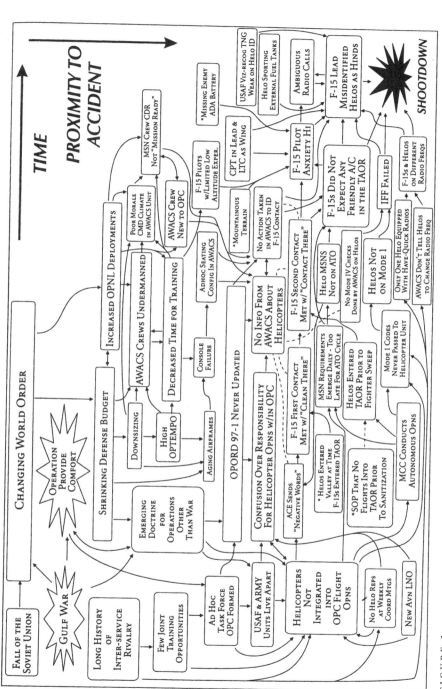

FIGURE 1.

with every right to wax lyrical about how humans experience chance and intention and meaning simply refuses to deviate from his narrative path.

Snook's book illustrates not only the dominance of mimesis over emotion in narrative social science, but also the dominance of narrative artificiality, which has its origins in narrative's Aristotelian imperative to instruct the reader. (Indeed, the book ends with an appendix entitled "Friendly Fire Applied: Lessons for Your Organization?") Narrative artifice is, in the first instance, evident in the very intention of explaining what is, after all, an extremely rare event, one that we would have attributed immediately to simple chance had it not been for its human consequence of twenty-six unexpected deaths. (Equally rare but less freighted events go undiscussed every day.)

Also undiscussed are the many results, other than the shootdown, of the various causes in Snook's master diagram. Those results are, of course, important reasons why the causes were lined up in the way that led to the shootdown. Interservice rivalry not only leads to the shootdown, for example; it is often thought to provide competition, which leads the services to self-improvement, as we saw in chapter three. That is, it is believed to have important positive outcomes, which may be what keep it in existence despite such occasional disastrous results as the shootdown. But in Snook's explicitly didactic narrative form, we focus only on certain results of a set of causes: an approach slightly different from the Barthesian succession of "kernels" and "links," but nonetheless standard in narrative social science. This form leads to a hierarchically structured story flow—what I have elsewhere called the "ancestors plot"—which looks at all the causes of a particular event, from the most immediate to the most general. It is an extremely artificial story form. Not only does it select out of the inchoate social process a funnel of things focusing on one particular result, ignoring the other "descendants" of those "ancestor" events; it also puts abstractions like "new world order" and "emerging doctrine for operations other than war" into the same story with empirical details like "helicopters not on mode I" and "F-15 pilot anxiety high." (I shall later return to this problem of mixing "large" and "small" things.) Narrative stylization is thus quite extreme, although one should repeat that Snook is by no means unusual in this stylization. It is the standard form for all narrative social science, quantitative and qualitative.[21]

21. Cf. the discussion of the military at the end of the preceding chapter. "Kernels" and "links" are found in Barthes (1966)1981. On the "ancestors plot," see chapter 6 in this volume. The similar "funnel of causation" model was set forth in the celebrated book by Campbell et al. on the 1952 and 1956 elections, *The American Voter*, and is also discussed in chapter 6 of

So far we have considered the major emphases of lyrical versus narrative "mechanics": image rather than story, concrete emotion rather than abstracting mimesis, and naturalism rather than artificiality. Let me turn briefly to two more focused aspects of lyrical technique: personification and figurative language.

Personification is in fact common throughout sociology, and indeed through social science more generally. Treating collectivities as persons is a commonplace of social analysis, as it is of common language and of both Roman and common law. But when we think of personification in lyric poetry, we mean the personification of things not normally personified: nonhuman animals, inanimate objects, even concepts. Wordsworth's celebrated "Ode: Intimations of Immortality" begins with four full stanzas personifying the earth, the moon, flowers, animals, and so on. Classical Japanese lyrics personify mountains and trees, cloaks and sleeves, and even houses and gates, often using long-standing symbolic conventions to do so. Oddly enough, this extreme personification is quite characteristic of narrative sociology, and in particular of its quantitative version. The personification of variables like "bureaucracy" and "gender" is customary usage in quantitative sociology, as when we say, "Gender does nothing here" to mean that the coefficient of the gender variable in an estimated model is insignificant. Personification is also customary throughout the narrative analysis of organizations and communities exemplified by Snook's *Friendly Fire*. Indeed, many would argue that the refusal to apply personification to abstractions is one mark that distinguishes narrative sociology proper from the variables-based sociology that it seeks to replace.

But we are here concerned with the lyrical use of these devices as opposed to the use characteristic of narrative in the broad sense (that is, the sense that includes both mainstream variables sociology and narrative sociology proper). And in lyrical social science, these devices are used deliberately to achieve that "certain coloring of imagination" of which Wordsworth spoke, "whereby ordinary things should be presented to the mind in an unusual aspect." To see this, we require an emphatically lyrical text, and I shall take as

---

this volume. Note that it is possible to write in a strongly narrative mode without such a funnel design. Fleck's celebrated book on syphilis (1979) takes a largely narrative form, but insists on a network of narrative forces. Oddly, this results in a book that presents science as always momentary, always in transit; that is, it presents science as being in the lyrical mode. But Fleck does not aim mainly to convey his emotional reaction to science, so his book cannot be considered fully lyrical in my sense.

example E. P. Thompson's *The Making of the English Working Class* (1963), a book as explicitly lyrical as exists in social science. Completely unreadable as a story, *Making* is a narrative only in name. The "emergence" plot promised in the title exists only as a loose framework holding together disparate images of the working class that merge into a ghostly vision of a class whose coming into being was at the same time its passing away. This intensely lyrical tone is set in the much-quoted opening passage and never falters:

> I am seeking to rescue the poor stockinger, the Luddite cropper, the "obsolete" hand-loom weaver, the "utopian" artisan, and even the deluded follower of Joanna Southcott, from the enormous condescension of posterity. Their crafts and traditions may have been dying. Their hostility to the new industrialism may have been backward-looking. Their communitarian ideals may have been fantasies. Their insurrectionary conspiracies may have been foolhardy. But they lived through these times of acute social disturbance, and we did not. Their aspirations were valid in terms of their own experience, and, if they were casualties of history, they remain, condemned in their own lives, as casualties. (Thompson 1963:12–13.)

With its almost Biblical phraseology (cf. Revelations 7:14–17), this passage promises to resurrect those who are ignored, to give them that "coloring of imagination" heretofore reserved for "great" figures of the period like William Pitt and Arthur Wellesley. It promises the "personification" of people not before seen as persons. And indeed, the book that follows does precisely that in language that is powerful indeed. Here is a typical passage from the opening of the chapter entitled "The Liberty Tree."

> We must now return to Thomas Hardy and his companions who met in "The Bell" in Exeter Street in January 1792. We have gone round this long way in order to break down the Chinese walls which divide the 18th from the 19th century, and the history of working-class agitation from the cultural and intellectual history of the rest of the nation. Too often events in England in the 1790s are seen only as a reflected glow from the storming of the Bastille. But the elements precipitated by the French example—the Dissenting and libertarian traditions—reach far back into English history. [. . .] Constitutionalism was the flood-gate which the French example broke down. But the year was 1792, not 1789, and the waters which flowed through were those of Tom Paine (102).

Here we have extremely metaphorical language. And while those metaphors do involve abstractions (e.g., Chinese walls for historiographical barriers) as in variables-based narrativism, this is done only as part of the framing for the much more closely wrought lyrical text. Here, for example, thirty pages later (135–36), is the description of the same Thomas Hardy's trial for high treason:

> On the final day—as the jury retired for three hours—the streets around the Old Bailey were packed with excited crowds: a verdict of "Guilty" would undoubtedly have provoked a riot. A delegate from the Norwich patriotic society, named Davey, was in London to watch the trials. On the news of the acquittal, he posted back to Norwich, travelling all night, and arriving on the Sunday morning in the hours of divine service. He went directly to the Baptist meeting-house in St. Paul's, whose minister was an ardent reformer, Mark Wilks—one of the old style Baptist ministers who combined an occupation (as a farmer) with his unpaid ministry. Wilks was in the pulpit when Davey entered, and he broke off to enquire: "What news, brother?" "Not Guilty!" "Then let us sing, 'Praise God from whom all blessings flow'" (135–36).

Here are Davey and Wilks, who make no other appearance in this eight-hundred-page book, and whose entire discursive purpose is to replace with an unforgettable image what would have been in another writer the simple narrative summary sentence, "News of the acquittal traveled rapidly and caused much happiness among reformers." But Thompson's rendition is not really a narrative passage, although it tells a story. It exists to give us a striking image and to convey to us both the emotional tenor of working-class radicalism itself and Thompson's powerful reaction to it.

This personal intensity is often very strong. Bell's *Childerly*, discussed earlier, ends with a chapter using the village's peal of bells—and Bell's own participation as a ringer—to develop a metaphor of resonance that captures how the various aspects of village life resound upon each other. In such a chapter, personification and figuration ring out indeed.

MOMENT, LOCATION, AND EMOTION

I have so far examined the lyrical stance and the mechanics by which it shapes texts. But to show that lyric is not simply an elegant style that we throw over narrative and explanatory sociology to make them more attractive and pleasing, I shall now explore more deeply the three crucial theoretical properties that I have assigned to lyric: momentaneity, location, and the expression of nonmoral emotion. I can best do this by digging deeper into the literary and philosophical foundations of lyric, and by clarifying the relation of the lyrical to other modes of comprehension that might be thought to subsume it.

Lyric and Narrative in Contemporary Literary Theory

I need first of all to defend our ability to separate lyrical from narrative writing. If we cannot separate the two, then the lyric focus on moments is just part of the larger enterprise of telling a story, whether of causes or of actions. As it happens, the problem of separating lyric and narrative has arisen in the theory of poetry itself. That debate parallels the debate over lyrical sociology, and the same skepticisms arise for the same reasons. The literary debate will lead us to the philosophical one, from which we return to the main theoretical analysis.

An important strand of modern criticism denies the distinction between narrative and lyric altogether, implicitly claiming that all lyric is historical—narrative in intent as well as by the accident of having been written at a particular moment. Thus, we hear of Wordsworth's "symbolic narratives" in *The Prelude* (de Man 1984:57). We hear how "objective historical forces rouse themselves in the [lyric] poem" (Adorno 1989:160). We hear of "models of historical change" in Shelley's "Ode to the Western Wind" (Chandler 1998:545). Indeed, one could take Chandler's attempt to understand fifty years of England's history through the literature of one year as precisely an attempt to assert the identity of narrative and lyric, of historical time and particular moment.

But while Chandler correctly reads the "Ode" to say that prophetic poetry can shape the future by uttering statements in the present, this reading does not make the "Ode" a narrative or give it a "model of historical change" other than its implicit assertion that action is possible in a radically free present.[22] And while Shelley certainly wrote poetry that was explicitly narrative

22. Chandler also ignores the paradoxical yoking of circular, seasonal time in the first three stanzas of the "Ode" to linear, historical time in the last two, as well as the more important fact that circularity is where Shelley ends ("If Winter comes, can Spring be far behind?" ll. 69–70). As we shall see below, circular time is linked to the lyrical stance. A definitional problem needs to be underscored here. Several readers of this essay have insisted that the word "lyric" denotes, in effect, all types of poetry. This is probably true in modern, nontechnical usage, but not in serious literary theory. It reflects the fact that contemporary poets have largely stopped writing epics, odes, and the other formal subgenres of poetry. But while "The Mask of Anarchy" may have "impressive lyricism" for Chandler, he knows he is using the word metaphorically

and prophetic (e.g., "Queen Mab" and "The Mask of Anarchy"), and was obviously obsessed with the passing of time (as in the widely anthologized "Ozymandias"), most of his narrative and prophetic poetry is allegorical and didactic rather than lyrical in any sense other than the lay one of using a great deal of figurative language.

De Man's work on Wordsworth is a test case here, since I have taken my concept of lyric from Wordsworth's early prose. And in the vast majority of his many readings of Wordsworth, de Man explicitly separates narrative and lyric, a separation he makes by insisting on the roots of Wordsworthian lyric in the moment. Past and future—the very stuff of narrative—are brought into the present by imagination. Indeed, they are seen only from that imaginative present, defined by the poet's present concerns and self. Because imagination is always interpretative, it necessarily breaks the continuity of action (and thus of narrative), making a new, "commentative" (Weinrich 1973) present in which the lyrical stance has its being, off to the side, as it were, of the story.

> The moment of active projection into the future (which is also the moment of the loss of self in the intoxication of the instant) lies for the imagination in a past from which it is separated by the experience of a failure [i.e., failure to understand one's action without reflection] (1984:58).

> The future is present in history only as the remembering of a failed project that has become a menace. For Wordsworth, there is no historical eschatology, but rather only a never-ending reflection upon an eschatological moment that has failed through the excess of its own interiority. (1984:59)

Narrative, in de Man's Wordsworth, dissolves into lyric (rather than the other way around, as happens in the eyes of some sociologists). De Man repeatedly underscores the metaphors Wordsworth uses (in *The Prelude*) for this intense and disturbing sense of the passage of time in the present: "the immeasurable height / Of woods decaying, never to be decay'd, / The stationary blasts of waterfalls" (de Man 1984:56, quoting *The Prelude* VI, 556–58). Indeed, he argues that narrative itself is transcended in Wordsworth:

---

and that the poem is actually an allegory with lyrical elements, just as Wordsworth's *Prelude* is an autobiographical narrative impregnated with long lyrical sections.

The narrative order, in the short as well as in the longer poems, is no longer linear; the natural movement of his rivers has to be reversed as well as transcended if they are to remain usable as metaphors (de Man 1993:92).

Moreover, de Man explicitly distinguishes lyric ("the instance of represented voice"; 1984:261) from "the materiality of actual history" (1984:262). In the essay "Literary History and Literary Modernity," he makes the radical claim that all literature is fundamentally antihistorical and notes that Baudelaire— the very paradigm of modern lyric poetry in the standard account—is completely focused on the present, to the exclusion of other times.

In each case, however, the "subject" Baudelaire chose for a theme is preferred because it exists in the facticity, in the modernity, of a present that is ruled by experiences that lie outside language and escape from the successive temporality, the duration involved in writing (1993:159).

The entire process [of writing] tries to outrun time, to achieve a swiftness that would transcend the latent opposition between action and form (1983:158).

In de Man's view, Baudelaire—and indeed all lyricists or even all literature—is always caught in the movement between act and interpretation:

The ambivalence of writing is such that it can be considered both an act and an interpretative process that follows an act with which it cannot coincide (1983:152).

Interestingly, this separation of act and comment on act, of narration and interpretation, echoes the linguistic analysis of tenses, which has shown the existence in most European languages of two different sets of tenses, one of which is used to tell ordered stories (narrative) and the other of which is used to provide personal commentary on things (discourse).[23]

23. I am indebted to Susan Gal for insisting on this point. The classic source on the two systems of tenses is Benveniste 1971. See also the monumental Weinrich 1973. Barthes (1972:25ff) differs slightly, arguing for the separation of the two systems, but emphasizing the temporal precision of the narrative tenses rather than their impersonality. (And note that the act/ interpretation distinction is more or less Mead's I/me distinction.) I have concentrated on de

To see a moment as complete in itself, yet absolutely transitory, is thus the foundation of the lyric sensibility. This view is seen at its most extreme in Japanese literary aesthetics, which derives from a tradition whose major extended works—the imperial poetry collections and even the enormous *Tale of Genji*—are lyrical rather than narrative in overall conception. Indeed, the single most debated term in classical Japanese criticism is the term for the transitory quality of things, *mono no aware*. Nor is such a concept absent from Western aesthetics. As de Man notes in his analysis of Wordsworth's concepts of time and history, the acute sense of time's passage in Romantic poetry ultimately arrives at that notion of perpetual dissolution which is known in the Western poetic tradition as "mutability," a subject that has exercised English poets from Chaucer to Spenser, and on to Wordsworth and Shelley.[24]

Literary theory thus seems in the last analysis to accept a fairly strong sep-

---

Man here both because he wrote extensively about Wordsworth and because he is an important enough figure to serve as paradigmatic contemporary critic. It is notable that Eliot's *Four Quartets*, one of the great monuments of twentieth-century lyric poetry, are explicitly concerned with the infolding of past and future into a nonnarrative present, from the opening section of "Burnt Norton" ("Time past and time future / What might have been and what has been / Point to one end, which is always present"; ll. 44–46) to the last lines of "Little Gidding," ("A people without history / Is not redeemed from time, for history is a pattern / Of timeless moments"; ll. 233–35). Wordsworth's "stationary blasts of waterfalls" find their exact counterpart in Eliot's "still point of the turning world" ("Burnt Norton," l. 62). The structuralists, not surprisingly, had much less to say about lyric than the deconstructionists like de Man; their criticism (e.g., Barthes's tour de force on Balzac and Genette's on Proust) focused largely on narrative.

24. I am following here the argument of Miner at al. 1985, especially the section "Development of Poetics," pp. 3–17:

> Yet in China, in Korea, and especially in Japan, prose narrative was not soon enough encountered by great critical minds as the normative genre for it to provide the basis for a systematic poetics. That honor went to lyricism (Miner et al. 1985:5) .

The locus classicus of Japanese writing on *mono no aware* is the analysis of the Genji by Motoori Norinaga (1730–1801). I have found inspiration also in the detailed analysis of the theories of Fujiwara no Teika (1162–1241)—Japan's first systematic critic and also one of her greatest poets—provided by Vieillard-Baron (2001). For an introduction to the tradition itself, see the Kokinshu (ca. 905), whose introduction by Ki no Tsurayuki is the most famous single statement of the Japanese lyrical aesthetic. Kokinshu also shows how compilers managed to develop short (thirty-one-syllable) lyrical poetry into a larger comprehensive form. It is striking that Adorno explicitly ruled out the Japanese lyrical tradition as irrelevant to modern lyric poetry because it was not produced by the same social formation (1989:158). On dissolution and mutability, see de Man (1993:94). The classic treatment is Williamson (1935). Shelley's poem on mutability ends: "For, be it joy or sorrow, / The path of its departure still is free: / Man's yester-

aration between narrative and lyric as modes of comprehension. Insistence on the moment is the heart of the lyrical impulse, while narrative involves the actual passing of time, marked by events. To be sure, the lyrical moment need not be literally instantaneous. To take my own earlier examples, both Zorbaugh and Malinowski describe "presents" that last for months, if not years. Moreover, this present often exists within clear bookends of historical transition; Zorbaugh reaches from time to time into the historical past of Chicago, for example, as does Malinowski into the past of the Trobriand and D'Entrecasteaux islanders. Indeed, this framing of the moment with transitions on both sides intensifies our sense of it as a moment, precisely because it is embedded in a continuous and inevitable flow of time and change.

Once we acknowledge the separation between narrative and lyric, it becomes possible to see why historical sociology—which is sometimes beautifully written and hence "lyrical" in the lay sense—is not lyrical in the technical sense, but rather the reverse. Most of historical sociology is concerned with causes and typical sequences of events, matters that are inherently narrative. More important, the rhetorical form of narrative is so powerful that we have grave difficulty not automatically formatting any selected period of history into a narrative structure with a beginning, a middle, and an end. Even catastrophic, final events like the Armistice of 11 November 1918 or the dropping of the atomic bombs in 1945 can be made the middles of stories with a mere modicum of narrative ingenuity.[25]

There is a more formal reason for this problem of the multiple narrativity of human experience, one that has to do with the nature of temporality itself. A long philosophical tradition has argued that there is an inherent inconsistency between the view that time is tensed (time as past, present, and future)

---

day may ne'er be like his morrow; / Nought may endure but Mutability" (ll. 13–16). That is an explicit denial of the possibility of coherent narrative or even history.

25. This is as good a place as any to note that there is little lyricism in the first great historical sociologist, Karl Marx. Even the long passages of *Capital* that are about poverty—the "Illustrations of the General Law of Capitalist Accumulation" late in volume 1, for example—exist to support the intellectual and moral argument of the book, not to tell us Marx's feelings towards the poor. "The Irish famine of 1846 killed more than 1,000,000 people, but it killed poor devils only," he tells us. "To the wealth of the country it did not the slightest damage" (Marx 1887; vol. 1:704). The importance of the famine dead is for Marx's argument, not for themselves as human beings; the contrast with Thompson could not be stronger. The same attitude shows in the magnificently figurative *Eighteenth Brumaire*. While Marx is at considerable pains to give us his emotions, they comprise a seething anger and a thoroughgoing contempt. These are moralizing emotions, not lyrical ones.

and the view that time is an ordered sequence (of dates).[26] The first view captures the idea of temporal direction, but has no account for why particular events change their quality from future to present to past in the order that they do. The second view captures the idea of the sequence of events, but has no account of direction. Historical narrative, as customarily understood, is a version of the second view, tracing events from beginning to end via the succession of events in the middle. What such narrative loses, of course, is the fact that each one of the intermediate events was a present at one point, and hence was once open to all sorts of realizations, not just the one that obtained in actuality. But this intermediate present disappears in narrative history because we know ahead of time where the historical story ends: that Elizabeth I does not marry Robert Dudley, that the South lost the Civil War, that Truman defeated Dewey, and so on. To be sure, the middling events may lead us further off the "main road" of narrative than we thought. To make us feel this extra deviation is the highest art of the narrative historian: to make us somehow think for a moment that Amy Robsart's suspicious death was overlooked, that Dick Ewell did take Culp's Hill on the first day at Gettysburg, that the *Tribune* did get the election right. But all historical narratives do ultimately lead to "what did happen in the end." The longer the narrative we tell, the heavier is this weight of teleology, the less our story can be an unfolding of unknowns, and the more we feel ahead of time the inevitable emergence of whatever end did in fact close that particular narrative. By implication, then, the indeterminate character of historical passage from moment to moment is actually clearest in the shortest possible narratives: that is, in purely momentary "stories," or—in another word—in lyrics.

Moment and Narrative in Ethnography

The literary and philosophical traditions are thus united in making distinctions that justify the separation of lyric and narrative as modes of comprehension. For both, the focus of the lyrical mode is the moment of the present.

26. Note the imperfect parallel to the two tense systems discussed in note 23. The classical citation for the two temporalities is McTaggart 1908, although a similar argument is implicit in Bergson 1910. See also the independent rediscovery of this problem by Shackle (1961), who worked out its implications for economics. I will discuss this problem at more length in chapter 6. I should also note that the philosopher Galen Strawson's 2004 paper "Against Narrativity," despite its similar title, actually concerns a topic different from mine: whether people actually do or ought to live their lives as narratives.

Moreover, they both imply that—paradoxically—the best representations of historical passage as a phenomenon are not plots—sequences of events—but rather the momentary Bergsonian durations of tensed time, which are always centered on a particular, indexical present. This conclusion suggests that perhaps lyrical sociology is linked directly to ethnography, which has such a momentary quality. Indeed, ethnography has several characteristics in common with lyric. It is written by a particular person. Since it involves being somewhere, it is usually about a moment. And it often embodies intense personal engagement. So it meets the three basic requisites of the lyrical stance by its very nature. And we have seen some clear examples of lyrical ethnographies—Bell and Malinowski, for example—and could add many more, from Young and Willmott's (1957) famous examination of families in East London to the extraordinary *Tristes Tropiques* of Lévi-Strauss (1955).

But there are qualifications to this argument. The engagement of an ethnographer need not be a direct and emotional one. Leach's *Political Systems of Highland Burma* (1954) synthesizes an enormous amount of published material and ethnographic experience, after all, but lacks any authorial emotion other than a withering sarcasm directed at structural-functional colleagues.[27] But more important, modern ethnography is not necessarily about moments or places. It often deliberately embeds field work in a larger historical flow, as does Katherine Verdery's *Transylvanian Villagers* (1983), for example, or in a larger regional or social structure, as does Michael Burawoy's *Manufacturing Consent* (1979).

This embedding of a local present in "larger" things (larger temporally or socially) echoes the similar argument we saw in the Chandlerian strand of literary criticism: that the lyrical moment is ultimately in the service of (larger) narrative. In his essay on lyrical poetry, for example, Adorno (1989) argued explicitly that even in this most individual of forms, social forces are clearly evident. (Indeed, he argued that the individualism of the form is precisely what is socially formed about it.) This position—that the apparently individual or isolated moment is the best place to see larger social forces (rather than

---

27. Examples of both lyrical and nonlyrical ethnographies are legion. Even when the topic of an ethnography is transition and change, it is possible to be lyrical or nonlyrical about it. Gans (1962, 1967) wrote about the planned destruction of an old slum and the de novo creation of a complete suburb without much lyricism, yet Rieder (1982) describes the racial transition of Canarsie in Brooklyn with an intense emotional involvement. In *Manufacturing Consent* (1979), Michael Burawoy utters hardly a word of lyricism. He shows some strong emotional cards in the preface, but not about his field situation.

the best place to see transition and particularity)—is much the same as that implicit in the works just cited by Verdery and Burawoy. And indeed, Burawoy (1998) makes such an argument explicitly in his call for an "extended case method" that aims to descry large forces in particular spatial and temporal localities. Discussion of that method can thus further specify lyrical sociology by locating it with relation to existing sociological genres.

The extended case method (or, as Van Velsen [1967] preferred to call it, "situational analysis") was elaborated after 1935 by Max Gluckman and colleague Africanists who became identified as the Manchester School of Anthropology. It was an attack on Radcliffe-Brownian structuralism for theoretical abstraction and ahistoricism. In rereading this tradition, Burawoy took up the second of these criticisms by reversing the first: his solution for ahistoricism was the (quite abstract) Marxist theory of history.

> The extended case method applies reflexive science to ethnography in order to extract the general from the unique, to move from the "micro" to the "macro," and to connect the present to the past in anticipation of the future, all by building on preexisting theory (1998:5).[28]

Yet although he shared Burawoy's commitment to theory, Gluckman was in practice an inductivist whose theories emerged from an eclectic mix of fieldwork, document examination, historical analysis, and theoretical argument. He lamented (1947a:121) that—unlike Marxism—anthropology lacked a cohesive theoretical framework, giving as his own candidate for a general theory the idea of a dominant cleavage in society (1956:63). This idea seems quite timid beside the sweeping succession of modes of production in Burawoy's Marxism, and Gluckman's inductive shuttling between historical understanding and ethnography seems equally pale beside the almost deductive deri-

---

28. Burawoy's restatement of the Manchester credo (Burawoy was a student of Jaap Van Velsen at the University of Zambia) emphasizes some aspects of it at the expense of others. His advocacy of active intervention reverses Gluckman's (1947a) castigation of Malinowski for late-career do-goodism, although his insistence on history and change exactly echoes Gluckman's position. His omission of the tradition's obsession with reporting actual events misses an essential part of Gluckman's 1958[1940]) original work, but his insistence on the importance of historical contextualization follows Gluckman exactly. The data-heavy ethnographies of the Manchester School look quite different from the sometimes slender ethnographies of today's extended case practitioners. Indeed, a common critique of Van Velsen 1964 (as of Richards 1939) was that their works contained too much data (see Gluckman 1967:xvi).

vation of ethnographic interpretation from preexisting theory in Burawoy.[29]
For not only does Burawoy think that the larger theory drives ethnographic
interpretation, he also thinks—far more strongly than did Gluckman—that
larger forces in fact determine ethnographic situations. It is in fact precisely
the presumption of this determination that allows Burawoy to claim that ethnography can sustain inferences about larger forces.

Such a belief in the determination of the present (both spatial and temporal) by larger forces is completely absent from lyrical sociology as I am proposing it. This disattention is to some extent simply willful. The determination
of a present situation by something outside it is no reason not to celebrate or
investigate or understand it in and of itself. As one writer comments, "Imagine
what anthropology would look like today . . . if Radcliffe-Brown had written *Three Tribes in Western Australia's Concentration Camps*" (i.e., instead of
The Social Organization of Australian Tribes 1931; the quote is from Sanjek
1991:613). That Radcliffe-Brown tried to imagine from his data the tribes as
they would have been outside the larger, controlling enterprise of colonialism
is a good thing, not a bad one, even though it should not blind us to the fact
that the barbed wire no doubt transformed tribal life in dozens of ways.

But the willful disattention of lyrical sociology to larger forces also rests on
a deeper argument, one that rejects the whole micro/macro ontology implicit
in Burawoy's understanding of the extended case method. For that ontology
falls apart when we get serious about temporality, as became clear during the
original debates on the extended case method.

Gluckman and his followers argued that Radcliffe-Brownian structuralism
had turned ethnography into a description of society not as it actually was,
but as it "ought" to be if it were a perfectly realized version of itself. Similarly,
they felt, although Malinowski's ethnographies were data-grounded to a fault,
those data were often interpreted within a functional framework that seemed
outside real time (e.g., Malinowski 1935). This critique reflected different conceptions of the present: was it a simple tensed interval, as in the first theory

29. The theory of those larger forces is in Burawoy's case a theory of domination and in
particular a Marxist theory. Although it happens that this is a draconian specification of Gluckman's extended case method, that fact is not important in the sequel. While it is clear that
Burawoy's brilliant paper conflates the extended case method, reflexive inquiry, and Marxist
politics, the tradition flowing from the paper has mainly focused on only one part of his argument, the move from the ethnographic foreground to contextual forces on the largely deductive
assumption of the determination of "small" by "large." This line of reasoning dates from Burawoy's earliest work (1979:xiv–xv). The problems with the idea of "smaller" and "larger" forces
have already been raised in chapters 1 and 2.

of time given above, or was it a point in a larger ordered sequence of events, as in the second? Structuralist and functionalist accounts of societies created an "ethnographic present"[30] in which relationships and activities ramified in what seemed an endless (because timeless) present tense: "Nuer tribes are split into segments" (Evans-Pritchard 1940:139); "[Magic] aims at forestalling unaccountable mishaps and procuring undeserved good luck" (Malinowski 1935:77). By contrast, Gluckman's famous "Social Situation in Modern Zulu-land" began with the story of a bridge-opening told as a simple past narrative: "On January 7th I awoke at sunrise . . ." (1958 [1940]:2). Thus, in one case the present was an indefinite duration in which many kinds of things occurred in a routine manner, while in the other it was a specific instant in which a specific person did one particular thing. The two views thus capture exactly the classical philosophical dichotomy of tense versus order.

But they also invoked very different sizes of time units, and thereby invoked different layers of temporality. In Braudelian terms, the first present is that of *structure*, the deep (and supposedly unchanging) givens of a society, while the second is that of *événement*, the little events that float on that sea of structural stability. It was by their implicit assertion that "the present" was big (long in duration; i.e., "structural" in Braudel's sense) that the structural/functional anthropologists came to seem opposed to the idea of social change.[31]

But if one parses time into layers, as the extended case method must because of its belief in larger forces, what pieces of social life are to be put at what level? More important, which layer drives the others? Even though Malinowski and Gluckman shared the "circular" concept of repetitive equilibria (Gluckman 1958[1940]:46ff; Malinowski 1938), Malinowski's ideas attributed those equilibria to synchronic mechanisms observable in short intervals. By contrast, Gluckman's writings often centered quite specifically on what we would today call "larger mechanisms" of division and cohesion (e.g., 1955) and "extraneous forces" (1947a:111), which impinged on—indeed, more or less determined—the local situation. The bridge-opening just mentioned was employed by Gluckman to illustrate and articulate a social organizational

30. The term dates from the early 1940s. For a history, see Burton 1988. Two important sources on it are Fabian 1983, which argues on linguistic grounds that the ethnographic present is inevitably "othering," and Sanjek 1991, which provides a sophisticated argument against Fabian.

31. The Braudelian model is laid out *in The Mediterranean and the Mediterranean World in the Age of Philip II* (Braudel 1972) vol. 2, pp. 892–903. It has three layers: unchanging structure, varying conjuncture, and flickering events, the "ephemera of history" that "pass across its stage like fireflies, hardly glimpsed before they settle back into darkness . . ." (901).

analysis whose data and conclusions actually derived far more from the historical analysis of past events than from ethnography. In rejecting Gluckman's approach, Malinowski had argued (1938) that such moves to historical antecedents involved an attempt to reconstruct a "zero-point" of culture before contact with the West. Culture was better understood synchronically, he thought; the past was utterly gone.[32]

Behind this debate, the unanswered question is how "large" historical forces can act "at a distance" or—more generally—how historical forces of different periodicities and purviews interact causally during a sequence of successive presents. (This is the most pointed way of posing in sociological terms the contradiction between the two temporalities discussed above.)[33] There is no generally accepted ontology of social life that addresses these questions. Because we lack such an accepted account, analyses inevitably choose a level of temporality whose duration is their "present." More important, they also make a choice about whether to view that present narratively or instantaneously: whether it is to be a step in a longer story or a moment in itself. Neither step absolutely denies the other, and each has its own pathology, as McTaggart's (1908) century-old paper argues. Those who believe in "larger forces" have their "structure and agency" problem (which, in effect, is about the present's independence to be for itself and not simply an instantiation

---

32. The Malinowski-Gluckman debate started with Malinowski's introduction to a volume of seven studies of change by young Africanists (Malinowski 1938) to which Gluckman's response was his work on "a social situation in modern Zululand" (1958, originally published in 1940). Malinowski's next response—at least as Gluckman saw it—was the posthumous collection on social change (1945), which in fact included much of the earlier material. Gluckman's savage review (1947a) was mitigated by a more fair appraisal of Malinowski's overall contribution (1947b). Gluckman perhaps thought he had the last laugh when his student Uberoi reanalyzed Malinowksi's data using a Gluckmanian approach (Uberoi 1962, with a foreword by Gluckman). On the other hand, Malinowski's classic was cited more times in 2005 alone—eighty-four years after its publication—than Uberoi's book has been cited in its forty-four-year lifetime.

33. The various substantive philosophies of history have various answers to these questions. In the Marxist model, for example, large forces drive lesser events, which become mere workings out of an inevitable larger pattern. In Braudel's layered model, by contrast, epochal changes in "big" structure (i.e., the long-duration present) come from the chance alignment of smaller duration changes at shorter temporal levels. My own views are evident in the discussion of encoding in chapter 1. There is no historical action at a distance; it is merely apparent, not real. One must therefore explain it. This can be accomplished only by analyzing the details of this "chance alignment." There is not space for that in the present chapter. However, as chapter 3 argues, the idea of ecology is central to such an analysis.

of some larger process) while the "presentists" have the problem of explaining social change and pattern in a world they have deliberately conceived as merely instantaneous.[34] Ernest Gellner (1988) argues that Malinowski chose the second of these paths deliberately to attack the unthinking evolutionism of his time (as well as "the so-called materialist conception of history"; 1961:516). Just as the move to narrative contextualization was for Gluckman a response to the structural/functional school's inherent tendency to ahistoricism, structural/functionalism had itself emerged to attack the diachronic inevitabilism of a previous generation of evolutionists and historicists.[35]

This historical discussion makes the lyrical position much clearer. Lyrical sociology embodies one of the two possible approaches to temporality in social analysis. It tends to arise as a deliberate response to the pathologies of the other approach, but of course has its own pathologies. But at its best, it provides a far more effective sense of passing time than does the inevitable tramp of narrative analysis. In lyric, we hear the whisper of possibility and the sigh of passage.[36]

34. The difference parallels exactly the two conceptions of time in Bergson (1910), who emphasized the subjective quality of experienced time (along with its tensedness), as opposed to the objective, external character of cartesian, dated time. In the one case, the pathology is solipsistic reverie, in the other the mechanical clank of causality. The McTaggart paper is discussed at greater length in chapter 6.

35. The whole debate is thus an example of the fractal return of a supposedly rejected argument—see *Chaos of Disciplines*, pp. 21ff. The present book embodies my own answer to this conundrum—that historical action at a distance is a mirage produced by moment-to-moment encoding, which replicates much of the immediate past, but leaves it open to action and change—even radical change—in the present.

36. A lyrical approach is, however, not the only way to attack teleology. Leach's *Highland Burma* was clearly an attack on both structural/functionalism and historical analysis of the Gluckman type. While Leach remarks in the introductory note to the 1964 reprint of his quite unclassifiable book (1964:x) that "it is the thesis of this book that this appearance [of equilibrium] is an illusion," three pages later he says with equal candor, "I do not believe in historical determinism in any shape or form. . . ." Indeed, Leach takes Gluckman as his principal theoretical antagonist, seeing him as a kind of watered-down functionalist (1964:ix–x). Leach's own position on temporality was an odd one. While his book demonstrates the incoherence of then-traditional anthropology as practiced by either the structural/functionalists or the historicists, it does so by moving the whole debate to the language (more broadly, culture) through which social structure is experienced and modified. But it then gives us no account of the historicality of symbol systems themselves, which is after all subject to the same "two-times" problem as is the traditional analysis of social structure against which Leach inveighed so noisily.

Location

This analysis of how lyric embodies passage in time can be transferred with only slight modification to lyric's embodiment of location in social space. Just as the transitory, mutable quality of a particular present moment is made most vivid by a lyrical approach, so too is the peculiarly local quality of a particular place. But since social space lacks the unidimensionality of time, we must adapt the argument somewhat.

Recall the distinction between two types of time: tensed time and mere order. Tensed time is what we live; ordered time what we narrate. The one is subjective and indexical; the other is objective and iconic. A similar distinction can be made in social space.[37] On the one hand, there is clearly an indexical notion of social space, a notion founded on what social space "looks like" from the point of view of the actors at any particular location in it: which parts of it are close or far, which are invisible or visible, which are reachable or unreachable. There is no necessary reason why these various "views" of social space, each from a particular point, should be reconcilable into some single system with universal dimensions that can itself contain all the information contained in the constitutive local views. For there is no reason why actor a should agree with actor b about whether they are close or connected or visible to one another, and if relations are not symmetric, it is by definition impossible to embody their information in a metric space of any kind. So we are stuck, on this first view, with an idea of social space as having a strong quality of indexical locality that cannot be merged into a general topology.

But we can—on the other hand—create a best possible "objective" model of the social space given all of this indexical information. We do that whenever we reason about the social forces behind elections and other events, and we have methodologies like multidimensional scaling to construct such models for us in a formal manner. Indeed, a long literature argues that we routinely act "as if" there were an objective social structure of this kind.

There are thus two different relations between point a and point b in social space: one of them the indexical relation that is composed of the interactional coming together (or confrontation) of the view of a from b and of b from a, and the other the "objective" relation that is produced by symmetrizing these

---

37. I am here explicitly rejecting the Bergsonian analysis of space. Bergson (1910) founded his analysis of the two-times problem on an explicit contrast between space, which is ordered in a Cartesian (i.e., objective) fashion, and time, which is inevitably indexical and thus cannot be analogized to space. McTaggart did not consider space at all.

views subject to a larger set of structures (the analogue of narratives in the temporal case) that we take to govern social space as a whole. We can think of these as the "positioned" (cf. "tensed") view and the "dimensioned" (cf. ordered) view, respectively. The former emphasizes the "disposition" of a given location—that is, its emplacement relative to its own view of its own contexts—while the latter locates each social "place" in a set of larger-scale and "unplaced" dimensions or structures, just as a narrative locates each event in a larger chain of events linked by an overarching logic.[38]

Just as the lyric stance rests on the indexical concept of the present moment, so too does it rest on the indexical concept—the disposition—of the present location. Just as it avoids the narrative temptation to embed particular moments in a teleological string of events, the lyrical stance also avoids the descriptive temptation to embed its subject in larger social formations that will define it. Lyrical sociology's sense of disposition is its spatial analogue of temporal passage. To the evanescent quality of "nowness" in time it adds an equivalent sense of the changing quality of "hereness" as we move in social space, of what we might call not evanescence but "intervanescence."

This interest in disposition marks lyrical sociology as different not only from the extended case method with its larger emplacements, but also from the new ethnography that arose out of the analysis of textuality and subject position that was inaugurated by Clifford and Marcus's (1986) celebrated collection in the mid-1980s. That collection aimed to contextualize both anthropological work and its objects. Authors were concerned with how anthropology's location in the colonial project affected the knowledge it produced at the same time as they were concerned with how colonialism had modified the cultures anthropologists observed. Both of these lines of questioning led authors to define local realities (the ethnographies and the things reported in them) by their location within "larger" social phenomena (the narratives and social structures of colonialism). That is, although this literature aimed to abolish the "view from nowhere" (by which term it understood the social scientific canon of objectivity), it did so by "emplacing" both viewer and viewed in specific places in a larger narrative and in a larger structural map, which narrative and map were themselves viewed dimensionally rather than indexically. Paradoxically, then, this literature itself produced a view from

---

38. Note that I am not arguing that the dimensional view, the "view from nowhere" of an abstracted social structure, is the creation only of a foolishly objective social science. Quite the contrary, views from nowhere are produced in the life-world itself routinely, as I have suggested. Vernacular views of social structure are more commonly dimensional than indexical.

nowhere, though a different one from that of the objectivists. But from a lyrical point of view, embedding a present in a narrative (objective or colonialist) replaces its quality of passage with a quality of teleology, and embedding a place in a larger social structure replaces its quality of disposition—locational indexicality—with a quality of dimensional fixedness in "larger" social entities. Lyrical sociology should rather be concerned with maintaining the dispositional quality of the object of analysis, its position in the social world as it—the object—sees that world.[39]

Lyric and Emotion

Having now specified the nature of temporal and (social) spatial location—the two types of "presentness"—in lyrical sociology, let me turn in closing to the third aspect of the lyrical stance, that of emotional engagement. I have argued that lyrical sociology is passionately engaged in its topic, that its authors take up emotional stances both toward topic (feeling) and audience (tone). Here lyrical sociology seems to come closer to the new ethnography, with its concern for the subjectivity of authors. But while the new ethnography is open to a wide variety of subjectivities—being mainly concerned with the acknowledgement of subjectivity rather than its content—I shall argue that the lyrical feeling and tone embody a specific emotional relation toward both audience and material.

Authorial emotion is by no means foreign to sociological writing. Quite the contrary. Consider the most famous basic list of emotions, that of Ekman (1972): anger, sadness, surprise, fear, disgust, and happiness.[40] Fear and dis-

39. Indexicality of location (that is, disposition) thus is more important here to lyrical sociology than is location per se. It is possible to stress the latter without stressing the former. For an example discussing location without indexicality, see my discussion of the importance of location in the writings of the Chicago School (Abbott 1997). One way of maintaining indexicality of disposition is to enlist those who are studied to be the privileged reporters of their own world. And certainly this has been characteristic of the new ethnography, as it often was of the old. In sociology, enlisting informants as investigators is a long tradition from Nels Anderson the hobo and Stanley the Jackroller to Ralph Orlandella the corner boy and Tamotsu Shibutani and Richard Nishimoto the interned Japanese-American students. And we have seen it in lyrical sociology in the (quantitative) case of Christakis, a doctor writing about his own profession.

40. Another celebrated psychologist, Lazarus (1991), lists anger, fright, guilt, sadness, envy, and disgust as negative emotions, and joy, pride, love, relief, hope, compassion, and aesthetic emotions as positive. The philosopher Solomon's famous (and long) list (1976) is anger,

gust are rare in sociology, as is happiness (perhaps it seems insufficiently professional). But surprise is common, being a stock-in-trade of literatures so disparate as the ethnography of exotic groups on the one hand, and game theory and simulation modeling on the other. Both these literatures aim to some degree to rub the reader's nose in unexpected things. But the reader, not the writer, is meant to feel the surprise, and this sometimes considerable authorial hostility makes it clear that such work is not lyrical sociology by my definition.

The remaining two emotions on Ekman's list seem very common in sociology and are perhaps better candidates for producing lyrical sociology: sadness in the guise of nostalgia, and anger in the guise of moral outrage. Nostalgia has pervaded writing about society for at least a hundred years. The "eclipse of community" literature is steeped in nostalgia, from *Middletown* to *The Life and Death of American Cities* to *Habits of the Heart*. Indeed the whole modernization paradigm, from Maine to Tönnies to Durkheim, has a strong element of nostalgia in it. The same emotion inhabits much of the mass society literature of the postwar period—such books as *The Organization Man* and *The Cultural Contradictions of Capitalism*—as it does such elite studies as *The Protestant Establishment*. Most of these works were not explicitly lyrical in intent, but a strongly elegiac mood pervades them. Nor is nostalgia the sole province of the communitarians and the elitists. The new labor history evinces a nostalgia that is almost cloying at times, and the various literatures on the decline of the "public sphere" embody a left nostalgia quite equivalent to that of the mass society literature.

Outrage is the other familiar emotion in social science writing. Massey and Denton's *American Apartheid* is an example, as I have argued, but the reader can no doubt supply dozens more; outrage is inevitably a dominant emotion in a discipline that has made inequality its most important single topic for many decades. Unlike nostalgia, outrage is seldom allied to lyrical writing in the lay sense, but sociological pieces animated by outrage certainly aim to communicate authorial feelings (condemnation of some lifeworld situation) and authorial tone (the reader is expected to join the author in his or her outrage). They thus clearly fit the engagement part of my definition of the lyrical stance. Yet while such work often makes use of strong images and figurative language, and while its aim is often to communicate its outrage from author to

---

anxiety, contempt, contentment, depression, despair, dread, duty, embarrassment, envy, faith, fear, friendship, frustration, gratitude, guilt, hate, hope, indifference, indignation, innocence, jealousy, joy, love, pity, pride, regret, resentment, respect, sadness, shame, vanity, and worship.

reader, it aims to awaken in the reader not an emotional state, but a desire for action. The literature of outrage is thus a weaker candidate for lyricism than is that of nostalgia.

But there is a more important quality, characteristic of both nostalgia and outrage, that militates against lyricism in the formal sense I am developing here. As the lyric stance requires, both nostalgia and outrage are rooted in a location that is defined indexically—that is, seen from the inside. Nostalgia is anchored in the now, and outrage is anchored in the here. So they begin with the proper "locational" quality of lyrical writing. But each evaluates that position by comparison with an external point that is neither now nor here. For nostalgia, the point of comparison is the golden imagined past; for outrage, the point of comparison is the equally idealized (and equally otherwise) state of equality. Each of these emotions, at least as communicated by sociologists, thus involves not one location but two. One of these locations is real and identified indexically as "here," while the other is unreal and not located other than as "elsewhere." And both nostalgia and outrage, far from finding something magical and special in the indexical here and now, judge the here and now to be wanting by comparison with this other idealized state. In nostalgia, the judgment is temporal—it embodies a narrative of decline—and so we can call it a narrative emotion. In outrage, the judgment is synchronic (although of course there will be a narrative about its origins), and so we can call it a comparative emotion.

Nostalgia and outrage thus exemplify larger families of narrative and comparative emotions. On the narrative side is not only nostalgia but also its reverse: progressivism. The early years of the *American Journal of Sociology* are filled with a complacent reformism that is strongly emotional in its hopeful view of the world. But there are also negatively anticipatory narrative emotions, as when futurologists aim to panic their readers over coming changes from now to later (e.g., the technomessiahs predicting the end of books and libraries). All these "narrative emotions" move us out of the lyrical mode and into the flow of story and event.[41] A similar analysis could be made of com-

---

41. I am here making a parallel with Arthur Danto's formal definition of "narrative sentences" as sentences that inherently involve two points in time (Danto 1985: ch. 8). We have already seen this notion in chapter 2's discussion of narrative verbs as a way of thinking about the sequentiality of human life. Danto's arguments will be revisited in chapter 6 as well. Note that I am not following the account of all emotions as inherently narrative (or as being necessarily embodied in narratives) that is given in the "narrative emotions" essay of Nussbaum (1988), whose core argument (pp. 234–35) strikes me as specious. The topics of conservative nostalgia and progressivism will return as conceptions of social order in chapter 7.

parative emotions, whose positive versions pervade the worship of markets in economics (although often with a fairly hostile tone towards the audience, which doesn't sufficiently understand the "truth" of markets) and of functional adaptations in certain schools of sociology.

But if we rule out narrative and comparative emotions, what is left for lyrical sociology? What would we mean by an "indexical emotion," an emotion rooted completely in the here and now about which the author is writing? Consider the examples of lyrical sociology given above, which show a variety of emotions: an "oh, brave new world" excitement in Zorbaugh, a profound amazement and even admiration in Malinowski (far indeed from the exasperations and rages of his diaries), a sense of agonized confusion in Christakis, a boundless but often exasperated sympathy in Thompson. Despite this variety, what these works have in common is the intense engagement of their authors—and, by extension, their readers—in precisely their indexical, located quality, the transitory and particular nature of their present heres and nows. At its best, this feeling is curious without exoticism, sympathetic without presumption, and thoughtful without judgment. It is always aware that confusion can come as easily from authorial misunderstanding as from subjects' experience. In fact, in seeking to see the world from the indexical time and place of their subjects, these authors become all the more self-conscious about their own. Indeed, the effect of their work is precisely to make us aware of our own mutability and particularity by presenting to us in careful detail the emotions and particularity of others, at a different time and place.[42]

It is striking that with few exceptions this emotion—let me call it humane sympathy—is not on the lists of psychologists and philosophers who write about emotion (see note 40 above). Compassion and pity are as close as they get, but both of these lack the reciprocal quality of humane sympathy as I envision it. They have a directional quality: from the emotionally secure self

---

42. I should note that none of the lyrical works mentioned overtly tells us the emotions of its author. Indeed the shift from telling these emotions (as writings in the social reform tradition usually did) to merely showing them (as these writers did) is probably one of the key ingredients of "science" as early-twentieth-century sociologists understood it. Like so many other things, this transition evinces a close parallel to lyric poetry, which moved sharply against "telling" emotion in the modern period. Eliot's famous "objective correlative" essay ([1919]:1975a) is the classic citation on this topic (but see Miles 1942 for an interesting quantitative study). In "The Perfect Critic" ([1920]1975b:57), Eliot went further, arguing that "the end of the enjoyment of poetry is a pure contemplation from which all accidents of personal emotion are removed: thus we aim to see the object as it really is. . . ." Such a statement could as easily have come from Robert Park in exactly the same year, with the word "poetry" replaced by "sociology."

to the emotionally troubled other. But the nature of humane sympathy reads both ways; it heightens our awareness of our own limitation in time and space by showing us, in all its intensity, that of others. In their mutability and particularity, we see our own.[43]

To be sure, this is a function of audience participation. If one reads only to find the narrative or structural account of a temporal and social present, the lyrical text will read as a disappointment, as I have noted above. This is clear in reviews of lyrical works.[44] Reviewers of *Argonauts of the Western Pacific* were to some extent bewildered by Malinowski's unwillingness to make causal arguments or to provide an origination narrative for the kula, although they were overwhelmed by his detail and impressed by his vividness. Reviewers of *The Making of the English Working Class* divided into those who saw it as biased, ideologically nostalgic, and lacking in causal or even narrative argument and those who appreciated its extraordinary passion and vividness but thought they saw an insufficiently coherent narrative or argument. Of the latter, Bendix (1965:605) says "The reader may in the end complain of a lack of guidance . . . . For all the hazards of conceptualization, without it history is trackless—and very long." Best (1965:276–77) at least admires Thompson's attempt at lyricism: "Now it can be said that he does his advocate's work very well and that some of his most memorable passages occur when he is doing it. He delights in making that seem sensible which has usually been accounted idiotic and in conjuring swans out of conventional geese." But ultimately, Best dissents from Thompson's interpretation. Far more hostile, Smelser (1966) reads what I am calling Thompson's lyricism as "radical historical specificity," and condemns it as unsatisfactory historiographically because it is not oriented to explanation and narrative causality. Zorbaugh's reviewers were more sympathetic, all commending the book for its vivid, literary quality and, in one case at least, strongly praising it for what Smelser would no doubt have called its atheoreticality ("It has benefited from the fact that its author has not

43. The notion of humanism will be revisited in the epilogue.

44. To save space I shall simply list here all the reviews considered, reserving formal citation for those quoted in text. Malinowski reviews: E. W. Gifford (*American Anthropologist* 25:101–2, 1923), M. Ginsberg (*Economica* 11:239–41, 1924), E. Schweidland (*Economic Journal* 33:558–60, 1923), F. R. Barton (*Man* 29:189–90, 1922). Thompson reviews: B. Semmel (*American Historical Review* 70:123–24, 1964), R. Bendix (*American Sociological Review* 30:605–6, 1965), N. J. Smelser (*History and Theory* 5:213–17, 1966), G. Best (*History Journal* 8:271–81, 1965). Zorbaugh reviews: R. D. McKenzie (*American Journal of Sociology* 35:486–87, 1929), J. W. Withers (*Journal of Educational Sociology* 3:313, 1930), R. P. Vance (*Social Forces* 8:320–21, 1929).

compressed too harshly his human materials, alive and often untractable, into predetermined categories" (Vance 1929:321).

Readers are thus often unwilling to read the lyrical text as anything but a failed narrative. But for the reader who is open to it, the lyrical text provides a representation of human mutability and particularity in their most vivid form. This encounter forces us to face two things: first, that we too are mutable and particular, and second, that our here and now are radically different from those of which we read. To be sure, these are things that we can know cognitively. But we easily forget them and consequently forget to experience them, rather than simply to know them. As these reviews show, while we commonly read texts in the nonindexical mode, looking for narratives or structural accounts that explain other people's lives by contextualizing them in various ways, we tend quietly to reserve to ourselves the privilege of living in the (only) "real" here and now, in the inexplicable, indexical present. But of course if the meaning of other people's lives can be explained not in terms of how they experience it, but in terms of some larger narrative or social structure in which they are embedded, so too can the meaning of our own. It is the merit of the lyrical text to avoid this trap by avoiding the move to narrative or structural embedding altogether. The lyrical text directly confronts us with the radical chasm between our own here and now and that of its subjects. Yet while the lyrical text shows us this chasm clearly, the chasm itself is crossed by our moral recognition of the common humanity we share with those we read about. The central emotion aroused by lyrical sociology is precisely this tense yoking of the vertigo of indexical difference with the comfort of human sympathy.[45]

The idea that aesthetic emotion arises in a confrontation between cognition and morality is longstanding in our aesthetic canon. Kant and Schiller wrote specifically of the situation in which something that we know to be potentially uncontrollable and frightening is tamed by the recognition that human morality remains unthreatened by it. They called this feeling the sublime, and saw it as one of the cornerstones of aesthetics. It seems to me that the fundamental emotion of the lyricism I have here analyzed is just such a "sublime." On the one hand, it confronts us with the disturbing fact of human difference; on the other, it reminds us of the moral (and paradoxical) fact that difference—in

45. Chapter 9 will investigate in more detail the "narrative trap" discussed in this paragraph and to some extent avoided by the lyrical move: taking one view of our objects of study and another of ourselves.

the guises of mutability in time and particularity in (social) space—is something we share.

With that conclusion I come less to the end of the present argument than the beginning of another, one that concerns the role of difference in social life and the meaning of its study. Human life is about the positing and exploration of differences. Our ability to see and enact so many and such variegated differences is what makes us unique among life forms, even though those differences reify and ramify and trap us in our own nets. But while I have no time to advance into the theory of difference, I do think it is established that the heart of lyrical sociology is precisely the evocation of this tension about difference: it confronts us with our temporal and social spatial particularities in the very process of showing us those of others. In doing so, it produces the unique emotion that I have called humane sympathy.

Other genres have sustained this feeling in other times. Rolf Lindner finds it in "the unprejudiced and yet passionate interest in 'real life'" of the journalists of a century ago (Lindner 1996:202). George Levine finds it in the attempt of the nineteenth-century realists "to rediscover moral order after their primary energies have been devoted to disrupting conventions of moral judgment" (Levine 1981:20). And humane sympathy is always under threat. Its favored genres can easily degenerate into voyeurism or exoticism or routinism or disillusionment, as many have noted. But that there are pathologies is no reason not to try here and now to cherish and develop the lyrical voice. It is our best hope for a humanist sociology, one that can be profoundly moral without being political.

I shall return to this theme of the moral versus the political in part 4 and in the epilogue to this book. But here I wish to underscore the close relation of this chapter to the processual position. This chapter has tried to create a view of the complex nature of the present that corresponds to the highly theorized complexity of narratives over time. I have attempted to show that even in a "freeze-frame" approach, the present is inevitably marked by passage and transition. An important part of that demonstration lies in the recognition, once again, of the centrality of encoding. Much of the variation and arbitrary interdependences of the past social process—what we normally write as "history"—is in fact written onto the present by some form of encoding.

But the variation that encoding leaves on the present—the million particularities we observe in any part of the social process—seems to us different from the narrative interdepencies we often impose on the lineage making that is the social process's own creation of its narrative character. Narration in social science is often the creation of a story that permits moral judgment and blame, that creates new particularities or decries old ones. It is in that sense generally a prelude to action. By contrast, the astounding cross-sectional variation of human possibilities tends to push use not towards action but, as I have just noted, towards the emotion of humane sympathy. To see truly "in the present" is to bracket one's potential for action and to attempt the great if doomed act of understanding the other in terms of the whole palette of particularities in the world. The present simply is. It is for that reason that the lyrical mode, with its commitment to the stationary waterfalls of the present, is a matter of emotion, of humane sympathy. This may be a prelude to action. But it remains apart from it.

CONCLUSION

I hope in this chapter to have established the existence of a lyrical impulse in sociological and social scientific writing. There is a place in social science for writing that conveys an author's emotional apprehension of social moments, and that does this within the framework of rigor and investigative detachment that we all consider the precondition of our work as social scientists. As researchers, we find the social world not only complicated and interesting, not only functional or disturbing, but also amazing and overwhelming and joyous in its very variety and passage. Our readers should know not only society's causes and consequences, not only its merits and demerits, but also, in the words of Kawabata Yasunari, its beauty and sadness.

CHAPTER 5

The Problem of Excess[1]

The preceding chapter expanded the processualist account by fleshing out the nature of the present, the transitioning space in which action and determination take place. This was fundamentally a methodological investigation, which nonetheless, as we have just seen, also involves the stance of the analyst towards the material analyzed. In the present chapter, the intervention is more theoretical. This chapter proposes a fundamental change in the theoretical problematic of social science: from scarcity to excess. This change could be pursued without any reference to the processual view, but, as I have noted earlier, processualism has important affinities with this shift of theoretical problematic. Processualism inevitably emphasizes the multiplicity—both diachronic and synchronic—of the social process. We have just seen this in lyrical sociology's recognition of the astounding variability of the social process over time and across space. Moreover, processual factors provide several of the reasons why excess is a problem. And process provides several models for our strategies for addressing excess. All the same, as in all chapters in this book, I have retained the original motivating section of the paper from which the chapter was derived, which did not make specific associations with

1. This chapter benefited from comments and audience reactions at the London School of Economics and university audiences at Oxford, Yale, Versailles-St. Quentin, Oslo, Michigan, and Northwestern. I thank Linsey McGoey for insisting on the importance of Georges Bataille. Since this is among the most recently written chapters in this book, it does involve some ideas from chapters that appear later in the arrangement here adopted. The original published version is "The Problem of Excess," *Sociological Theory* 32:1–26, 2014.

processualism. But the argument's affiliations with the processual view are pervasive and self-evident.

Like its predecessor, this chapter is rhetorically organized around the inversion of a customary assumption, in this case the assumption that the main problems in social life involve having too little of something: money (poverty), education (illiteracy), wellness (health disparities), and so on. I argue, by contrast, that in the modern world excess and overabundance are the main problems, or at least that excess and overabundance are common enough problems that we ought to try—for once—to theorize the social process in terms of excess.

The chapter opens with some simple theory and disclaimers before moving on to a history of the centrality of scarcity in social science thinking. It then considers Georges Bataille as an explicit theorist of excess, and examines (and rejects) the argument that excess of one thing is always simply scarcity of another. This demonstration that excess is an independent problem subject to independent forms of inquiry leads into a theoretical analysis of types of excess (too much versus too many) and levels of excess (individual and social). The chapter then considers five possible mechanisms of excess: overload, habituation, value contextuality, group disruption, and socialization overload. Finally, the chapter gives an extensive catalog of strategies for handling the problem of excess, ranging from denial through reduction to acceptance and embrace. Many of these are shown to be alternative motivations of social structures like markets and hierarchies that are customarily seen as means of handling problems of scarcity.

It should be noted that this chapter seems to accept as an analytical convenience the strong individual/social distinction that other chapters (and the processual view in general) have explicitly attacked. This is simply a convenience for exposition. The problematics of excess are to a large extent the same for individual and social entities, and the specifically social mechanisms are related to specifically social types of lineage making. So the chapter is in fact quite conformable with the processual view employed throughout this book.

Many great problems of our era are problems of excess: massive pollution, sprawling suburbs, a glut of information. Yet our social theories and normative arguments focus mostly on scarcity. Budget constraints, tradeoffs, impoverishment: these are concepts of scarcity. Confronted with excess, we nevertheless make scarcity the center of our attention.[2]

---

2. The problem of suburban sprawl was first argued in Britain in the interwar period (e.g., Williams-Ellis 1928), and then reached a crescendo of debate between writers like Whyte

There are various possible responses to this paradox. One could ask why it arises, which is an interesting question in the sociology of knowledge. One could turn to the empirical side of it, discussing the origin of problematic excess itself. I make here a third response, turning rather to the theoretical side of the paradox, our focus on scarcity. I want to sketch the foundations of a social theory based on the premise that the central problematic of human affairs is not dealing with scarcity, but dealing with excess.

Such an approach would resolve numerous problems in social theory. First, it recognizes—indeed grows from—the extraordinary variety and difference in the social world, problems that also drive us toward the process ontology that can analyze them more effectively than can ontologies making the presumption of stability. Second, focusing on excess would be *ex ante* conformable with the many empirical problems of excess that confront us. Third, it would enable us to see how our scarcity theories might constrain effective analysis of crucial social problems. By rethinking in terms of excess those problems that we usually conceive as problems of scarcity—poverty, domination, and so on—we might find completely new approaches to old questions. In this chapter, to be sure, I shall not fully achieve these desirable goals. Given limited space, I can only undertake the preliminary task of sketching the necessity, the lineage, and the basic internal logic of a sociological theory that rests on a problematic of excess rather than scarcity.

It is useful to begin with definitions. I shall use the words "scarcity," "abundance," and "excess" to refer respectively to having too little of something, having an unproblematically sufficient amount of something, and having too much of something. These are all relative judgments, of course; the phrases "too little," "enough," and "too much" identify not absolute amounts, but amounts relative to a standard. I shall therefore employ other words—"rare," "common," and "countless"—when I need words for absolute levels of avail-

_____

(1958), Gans (1967), and Venturi et al. (1972). The 1960s and 1970s brought concern over the glut of human beings; serious works predicted population catastrophe by 2000 (e.g., National Academy of Sciences 1971). They were right about the population prediction, but wrong about the catastrophe: GDP grew even more than population (Demeny and McNicoll 2006)! In the 1970s and 1980s, pollution of the environment became the focal glut, starting with Rachel Carson's best-selling discussion of DDT (1963) and broadening into a concern for emission-induced global warming. (Curiously, the chief author of the NAS population report—Roger Revelle—was also, in his earlier incarnation as an oceanographer, coauthor of the central modern paper on global warming.) By the turn of the century came the glut of "information." This concern had been launched by much earlier by Alvin Toffler's "information overload" concept, now made into a more evident reality by the Internet avalanche (Toffler 1970:311–15).

ability. I shall omit all consideration of whether countlessness is good or bad ("copious" versus "superfluous"), rareness is good or bad ("unique" versus "meager"), or even commonness is good or bad ("ample" versus "adequate"). But it is important to notice that we have such evaluative vocabularies, and, more broadly, that our vocabularies for scarcity, abundance, and excess are both immense and, in general, evaluative. (Note in particular that we have such vocabularies for emotions ["severe," "placid," "ardent"] and for action ["restrained," "measured," "manic"], as well as for cognition ["bare," "comprehensible," "complex"]). In this chapter, however, I shall use only the main trichotomy ("scarcity," "abundance," and "excess") for relative difference and, when necessary, the second trichotomy ("rare," "common," and "countless") for absolute amount. (Since "excessive" has considerably stronger negative connotations in English than "excess," I shall use "superabundant" as the adjectival form for "excess" when I wish to avoid those negative connotations.)

In this terminology, the task of the chapter is to reconceive social theory around the problem of excess: to argue that the central problematic of social life is not having too little of something, but having too much of it. The chapter has four main sections. The first reviews the role of excess in classical social theories, tracing the lineage of scarcity and excess as theoretical problems. The second considers the reasons why excess is not simply the obverse of scarcity. The third traces the mechanisms by which excess creates problems. The fourth examines the strategies we use to deal with excess, in the process reinterpreting—as excess-control strategies—such phenomena as markets, hierarchies, and divisions of labor. A brief conclusion mentions how some traditional "scarcity" problems might be recast as "excess" problems.

Any such argument must make disclaimers. For the most part, these respond to questions that have emerged regularly in prior reactions to the position argued here. The most important disclaimer is that the chapter aims to sketch a possibility, not to sweep all theories employing scarcity into the dustbin. Indeed, one of my main points is that scarcity and excess are not necessarily conceptual contraries, and therefore that studying the one does not reject studying the other. Second, the chapter is not about modernity. I do not take excess to be a problem particular to modern societies, although one could make an argument, following Keynes (1930), that excess has become a particularly urgent problem in modern economic life. But in fact, excess has long been characteristic of human existence, as has been maintained by authors as diverse as Marshall Sahlins (1972) and Georges Bataille (1991). Third, the chapter is not principally about subjectivity or cultural definitions of excess. There are, of course, wonderful papers to be written about the subjective sense of excess, as well as about the culture of excess. Inevitably, I mention some of the classics on these topics. But subjectivity is not my focus. I am here mainly concerned with how people and groups deal with the sense of excess, not with whether that sense has objective or subjective origins. Finally, I myself have no moral or ethical arguments to make about excess. The ethics of excess are of course an endless topic, from the ancients to the present. And important social theorists (e.g., Durkheim) have recognized that excess can create moral problems that require attention. But while I shall discuss the impact of excess on moral action as on other forms of action, I myself have no brief for this or that moral interpretation of excess.

Given these disclaimers, then, let us begin with a short history of the concepts of scarcity and excess in social theory.

SCARCITY AND EXCESS IN SOCIAL THEORY

It is no secret that scarcity has played a central role in classical theories of society. Western philosophy has long puzzled over whether excess is good or bad. Aristotle thought that abundance gave citizens the freedom to discern the true public interest, while the authors of Deuteronomy thought that only scarcity would keep the Children of Israel on the path to righteousness. Plato's concept of a divine and positive plenitude descended to Leibniz, Schelling, and Bergson, but Kant and Schiller, by contrast, noted in their work on "the sublime" the perilous quality of our emotional reaction to the excessive force of nature. Novelists also have divided on the issue of excess. In *The Sorrows of Young Werther* and *René*, Goethe and Chateaubriand respectively began that praise of emotional excess which would dominate much of the nineteenth century. Yet this very insatiability of human emotions became one of the core problematics of modern fiction in figures like Marianne Dashwood and Emma Bovary.[3]

In social theory, our focus on scarcity has more immediate roots in the literature of political economy. As we read the political economists from the eighteenth century forward, we can see excess recede into the background as scarcity takes center stage. To be sure, excess—or at least abundance—was

---

3. On the idea of plenitude, see Lovejoy 1936. The problem of excess arose even in mathematics. In 1874 Georg Cantor proved that the set of transcendental numbers could not be "counted" in the formal sense of being put into a bijective relationship with the natural numbers. Given the relatively small number of transcendentals with which mathematicians were familiar at the time, this was a profoundly disturbing result.

always the desired end of an economic system throughout that period. But the motor forces of the system began very early to be located in scarcity.

In Mandeville, excess is in the first instance personal. Mandevillians seek individual luxury. Social abundance—whether of goods, of employment, or, as Mandeville implies, of happiness—can arise only from personal vice, dishonest appetite, and striving after excess: "Bare Vertue can't make nations live in Splendor" (Mandeville [1724]1989:76). Although Mandeville's main argument concerns personal luxury and excess, he shows clearly that societal abundance itself (he does not discuss social excess) requires as its motive power the unworthy pursuit of personal excess above all else.

By contrast, in Adam Smith, "wealth" (which denotes a seemly abundance rather than Mandevillian excess) has become a mere result rather than an individual motivator. For Smith, personal motivation lies in truck and barter on the one hand and a rather timid "self-love" on the other. Smithian individuals are not Mandevillian sybarites but sober businessmen, not consumers but investors. And the most important abundance is not at the individual but at the social level, since Smith's purpose is to confute the mercantilists' beliefs about the wealth of nations. (He was not particularly interested in personal abundance or excess.) Glut and overproduction—the social level excesses—do not seem as apparent to Smith as they do to Mandeville, and of course Smith doesn't imagine the Victorian industry that will soon make such overproduction a reality, if a rather badly distributed one.

But Smith makes another important change. At the level of the individual, he emphasizes the division of labor, which is occasioned by differences of talents as realized through the propensity to truck and barter. Despite his overall focus on abundance as a necessary and desirable product at the social level, Smith's attention to division of labor opens the possibility—almost impossible for Smith's successors to avoid reading back into him—of conceiving an individual-level mechanism through which not individual excess but individual scarcity and competition will produce social abundance. The Mandevillian appetite for personal excess disappears in Smith, replaced by sober division of labor and seemly self-love. But the next step on this path seems inevitable.

It is Malthus who takes that step. The first excess in Malthus is the social superabundance of human bodies, and on the surface, Malthus's argument runs from the social fact of excessive population to the individual experience of scarcity and starvation. But in fact his argument centers on scarcity from the first chapter with its famous contrast of the arithmetic increase of subsistence with the geometric increase of population. Unlike Smith and the mercantilists, Malthus has no interest in the many good things that excess population can bring to a nation: military strength, cheap labor, and so on. The wealth of nations does not concern him. Indeed, nothing substantive about excess concerns him. What concerns him is only the disproportion of population and subsistence, and the consequent scarcity experienced by individuals. The social excess of population is merely a condition of this larger, foregrounded situation of individual scarcity. Malthus thus turns excess into a literal obverse of scarcity, which it is not in either Mandeville or Smith.

Malthus made this inversion quite deliberately, pitching his argument against what he saw as the overly optimistic social theory of the Enlightenment. The *philosophes* had expected society to be positively transformed by excess, in particular by abundant—even superabundant—knowledge. But on his first page, Malthus mocks Enlightenment notions like "the great and unlooked-for discoveries," "the increasing diffusion of general knowledge," and "the ardent and unshackled spirit of inquiry" (Malthus [1798]2008:9). He thinks these will amount to little.

Malthus thus turns on its head Mandeville's optimistic view of the substantive excess that will be produced by personal vice. In Malthus, luxurious desire produces not plenty but want. The only restraints on the negative excess of population are the immediate forces of scarcity and destruction (hunger, pestilence, war, and great [i.e., pestilence-ridden] cities), to which are added those enjoyments which for Malthus inevitably if indirectly lead to scarcity and want (luxury, "unwholesome manufactures," and "vicious customs with respect to women"; Malthus [1798]2008:45).[4] In his concluding chapter, Malthus tells us in no uncertain terms that "the general tendency of a uniform course of prosperity is rather to degrade than exalt the character" (Malthus [1798] 2008:150). For him, as for the authors of Deuteronomy, scarcity is morally desirable.

Formalizing Malthus, Ricardo produces the theory of scarcity that has sustained subsequent economics. On his first page, he notes scarcity as one of the two sources of value (quantity of labor is the other). Moreover, the Ricardian analysis of rent—probably the most influential section of the theory in the long run—is rooted in scarcity. That which is excessive—or even merely

4. This list is a standard excess list and, particularly in its latter section, it contains many of the things that Mandeville covertly or overtly admired. Malthus was made of sterner stuff. He summarizes the list with the remark that "All these checks may be fairly resolved [i.e., categorized] into misery and vice."

abundant—is worthless, however useful it may be. Ricardo is uninterested in the actual use of things; all that matters is their exchange value.

From the other side of the political fence, Marx too focuses on scarcity. *Capital* is one long meditation on scarcity; declining wages and class conflict are all about scarcity, even though an overwhelming fact of British history from 1750 to 1850 was the rapid expansion of economic production. By focusing on distribution alone, Marx upends the Malthusian arguments that the basic problem of society can be logically derived and that it concerns the theoretical disproportion between the growth potentials of agriculture and of population. In Marx the basic problem of society is empirically discoverable and concerns a political matter, the unjust allocation of socially superabundant production, which imposes personal scarcity on the majority of the population. Personal scarcity is still central, but it arises differently. Marx manages thereby to avoid comment on the central reality of nineteenth-century British economics: the sudden excess of production in both agriculture and manufacturing, an excess so large that not even all of India could absorb it.[5]

Even empirical economics managed to ignore excess. To be sure, the emergence of fully developed capitalism made the business cycle into a well-formed problem by the end of the nineteenth century, and in the business cycle, excess was fully as problematic as scarcity. But in the usual argument about business cycles, the problem of glut was really a problem of scarcity: glut of products meant not only low prices, but—more important—scarcity of employment. Thus the main line of empirical economics, growing out of liberal political economy, retained Ricardo's and Malthus's focus on scarcity as the central conceptual aspect of the economic problem, even when excess might be a central empirical one.[6]

Outside the mainstream of economics, there did arise a line of scholarship that treated excess of goods simply as a distribution problem, continuing the socialist argument that scarcity was artificially maintained, but taking a more optimistic view about the possibilities of ending that artificial maintenance. Excess of goods meant a lack of livelihood only if the excess could not be

5. British industrial production expanded by a factor of ten between 1750 and 1850, and population by a factor of about three (Hoffmann 1955, table 55). Output per worker thus tripled. But of course, only so much cotton can be worn at home. Fully 75 percent of British cotton textile production was exported by the 1870s (Hoffmann 1955:83).

6. In empirical economics, the word "glut" has been the usual word for excess. I have generally avoided it in this chapter because "glut" carries connotations about the impact and consequences of excess that "excess" itself does not. "Glut" is a much more strongly evaluative word.

accessed without wages. This line of upbeat mainstream economics began with Simon Patten, who published *The Theory of Prosperity* in 1902. John R. Commons followed Patten's lead in *The Legal Foundations of Capitalism* and *Institutional Econom*ics, and by 1930 Keynes was asking what humans would do with themselves in a few years, when productivity would mean that they would need to work only two or three hours per day.[7]

Keynes meant to be optimistic, but later writers turned his message negative. In 1958 John Kenneth Galbraith warned of the dangers of *The Affluent Society* in terms reminiscent of Malthus and Deuteronomy. And despite overwhelming evidence of economic growth, the mainstream managed to retain its focus on scarcity. Even overwhelming excess of goods could be turned into scarcity for purposes of analysis. The brilliant Gary Becker trumped Keynes by incorporating time itself as a scarce resource in utility-maximizing behavior; excess of leisure goods thereby disappeared behind the scarcity of time in which to enjoy them.[8]

As the conjuncture turned, however, so also did the role of excess, at least in some parts of economics. In extreme supply-side thinking, Mandevillian excess would arise at the top of the income distribution and trickle down, creating a well-regulated Smithian plenty for the middle classes. (The poor could either pull themselves up by their Malthusian bootstraps or simply struggle in Ricardian squalor; there was nothing in supply-side thinking that had not already appeared in the economic tradition.) Thus the concept of social-level excess disappeared behind a neo-Mandevillian economy of individual-level excess. Interestingly, one of the most criticized aspects of supply-side thinking was precisely its disattention to scarcity: the notion that America could "grow itself out of recession" seemed ridiculous to the mainstream.[9]

In summary, excess has seldom been a focal topic for formal economic thinking for the last two centuries. Mainstream economic theorists quickly translate most problems of excess into those problems of scarcity for which their intellectual machinery has come to be so well designed. Indeed, the

7. Keynes's argument appears in Keynes (1930) 1963. On the earlier optimist line of economics, see Fox 1967.

8. See Becker 1965. We shall turn to this argument in the next section.

9. On supply-side economics, see Krugman 1994. This example illustrates well an important distinction in my argument. Economics has talked a good deal about empirical phenomena of excess. As noted earlier, that topic is central to the business cycle literature. But what concerns me here is not empirical excess, but rather the habit of not using concepts of excess as central parts of theoretical logic. Underneath modern economic thinking is always a theoretical model about scarcity and limits, not about excess.

commitment of economic thought to the concept of scarcity was made definitionally absolute in what is arguably the foundational statement of modern economics: Carl Menger's *Principles of Economics*. Menger defines economics as the study of only those behaviors that involve "economizing," which is itself required only for "economic goods," which Menger in turn defines as those goods for which "requirements are larger than the available quantity" (Menger [1871] 1976: 94). To be sure, Menger conceived of goods that could be available in excessive quantities; his conceptualizations of value and utility recognize that possibility clearly. But he was simply uninterested in such excess goods ("non-economic goods," in his terms), and placed them definitionally outside economics.

The study of excess in economics provides a pattern to some extent repeated in other social sciences: occasional interest in excess among the unorthodox, but a main focus on scarcity. American sociology, to be sure, began with a fairly strong interest in abundance and excess. Simon Patten's main interlocutors included sociologists like Albion Small, Franklin Giddings, and E. A. Ross. John Commons was well known in sociology, and the discipline continued the optimistic anticapitalist themes of excess economics well after they had been extirpated in economics itself.[10]

But continental sociology looked quite different. Durkheim famously took excess as deeply problematic. In *Suicide*, he speaks of "the disease of the infinite."[11] He argues that human desire is inherently insatiable and hence inherently dangerous unless limited by social norms:

10. For details of that extirpation, see Furner 1975.

11. The phrase quoted is at Durkheim (1897)1951:287. The ultimate origins of the phrase "disease of the infinite" (*mal de l'infini*) are not clear. At first hand, Chateaubriand was Durkheim's source; the passage Durkheim cites (Chateaubriand [1802] 1926:116–17) would have been known to every lycée student. But Chateaubriand generally used the phrase "call of the infinite" (*appel de l'infini*). The "disease" version may have been a back-formation from the widespread later phrase *mal du siècle* for the broader version of the same phenomenon—disinterest in reality induced in part by satiation. The ur-text of this disinterest argument, Goethe's *Sorrows of Young Werther* (1774), often stresses the theme of sheer excess itself. See, for example, the letters of 3 and 8 November. But Werther's last formal letter (6 December) closes with the lines that became the watchword of the *Sturm und Drang*:

And when [man] soars with joy, or sinks into sufferings, is he not
in both cases held back and restored to dull, cold consciousness at the
very moment when he longs to lose himself in the fullness of the
Infinite (Goethe [1774] 1984: 124–25)?

Irrespective of any external regulatory force, our capacity for feeling is in itself an insatiable and bottomless abyss. But if nothing external can restrain this capacity it can only be a source of torment to itself (Durkheim [1897]1951:247).

Poverty, he tells us, "protects against suicide because it is a restraint in itself" (p. 254). It is the rich who are most in danger:

At least the horizon of the lower classes is limited by those above them. Those who have only empty space above them are almost inevitably lost in it, if no force restrains them (Durkheim [1897]1951:257).

Excess is thus both excess of desires—an emotional excess—and excess of things. The unstable relationship that produces suicide arises in the positive feedback between the two: the more you have, the more you desire. This argument had been familiar since the Old Testament prophets, whom Durkheim—the son of a rabbi—no doubt knew by heart. But at the same time, Durkheim was also following a long tradition of secular psychologies; the insatiability of human emotions had been a staple of Western psychological theory since at least the seventeenth century. Indeed, in his id concept, Freud was even then making excess the foundation stone of modern theories of the self. Thus, excess in post-Durkheimian sociology tended to take on the problematic, dangerous quality of Old Testament excess.

In political theory, many of the issues were the same. The incurable excess of and inevitable conflict between human desires has been a mainstay of Western political thinking since Hobbes. In the Federalists, and to some extent in their follower Tocqueville, a new obsession emerged: worry about the excessive and dangerous emotions of the common voters. Here too, excess was problematic, and here especially, excess concerned not only the excess of bodies, but also the excessive differences of political ideologies and policies. The plurality and the conflictual excess of human desires were at the foundation of modern republican and democratic thinking.

We see, then, that while the modern economists knew well about the empirical facts of excess, they developed a strong preference for theories attending to scarcity. The other major traditions of social thinking have more often been concerned with excess as a theoretical question, but they have mainly seen it as dangerous to individual character or morality. Their positions have rested less on a specific argument about how excess presents a challenge to moral activity itself than on a (moral) disapproval of a certain kind of character—one that lacks moral controls. In sum, the social science tradition has seldom tried to theorize society from the point of view of excess. It has seldom begun from the premise that the general problem of social life—whether of knowing or feeling or acting—is having too much rather than too little.

Suppose, then, that we try to formalize that approach. Suppose we insist on thinking about society principally in terms of problematic excess, as is suggested occasionally in the line of socialist and progressive economics and by many of the practical problems we face today. This would mean a thoroughgoing reconstruction of long-standing habits of thought that we have inherited from the past. For example, we would need to see poverty as a case of too much of something rather than too little, and conversely to start seeing privilege as a case of being able to minimize some problematic form of excess, rather than of being able to maximize something else whose excess is definitionally regarded as unproblematic.

Outside the social sciences, there has occasionally been serious reflection about excess (in Nietzsche, Wagner, and Foucault, for example). But most of these writers have been apostles rather than social analysts, morally committed to excess in the same way that the Federalists, Freud, and Durkheim were morally committed against excess. Perhaps the only general theory of excess—itself not very well specified—has come from Georges Bataille (1991). To be sure, Bataille was more concerned with reinterpreting cases than with providing a rigorous theory, and to be sure, he too was ultimately an apostle rather than a theorist. But his argument is nonetheless interesting.

Bataille begins from an almost cosmic assumption of excess: more solar energy comes into the world than is necessary simply to maintain life in that world. This leaves an inevitable excess, which can be used only for growth. (Growth for Bataille includes extension, in the sense of extending life processes to new spaces or zones, as well as simple multiplication of current life-forms in size or endurance.) If for some reason growth is impossible, then the excess of energy—and of the things produced with it—must simply be dissipated. Bataille's argument can be scaled down to the group or individual level, although it is originally framed quite generally. At these lower—and more real—social levels, dissipation of excess in effect means destruction and waste. The real aim of war is thus to waste excess resources. The real aim of love and sexual activity is to squander energy, resources, and time. Indeed, the real aim of all animal life—the eating of plants—is simply necessary waste and luxury: the world would otherwise be overfilled with decaying plants. Bataille's examples range from Aztec human sacrifice to Islamic expansion to the Marshall Plan, all of which he treats simply as variants of potlatch (which is also analyzed). It is no surprise that Mauss's famous essay on the gift was Bataille's starting point.

There are aspects of this argument that are surprisingly compelling. Bataille's reinterpretations of familiar cases are always interesting, and he is right to recognize that the particularism inherent in marginalist economics led to assumptions about individuals that inevitably could not deal effectively with general, system-level constraints. But he does not address the question of precisely why waste is necessary, a question which might have been resolved by pursuing more closely his analogy with the laws of thermodynamics. More important, he doesn't realize that "growth" and "extension" can take forms that undercut the need for waste (for example, the infinite extension of consumption needs and the fractal subdivision of the spaces of desire). Thus, in the end Bataille's general theoretical argument leaves more questions than it answers, thereby directing us to theorize the precise means by which excess creates problems. But at least Bataille sets the example of taking excess seriously as a subject for social theory.[12]

THE IDENTITY ARGUMENT

Before we can develop that theory, however, there is an important preliminary step. That is the rejection of the argument—clever, attractive, but in the last analysis unhelpful or even wrong—that excess of one thing is simply scarcity of another. Thus, as previously noted, Becker (1965) has argued that excess of possible consumer goods is simply lack of time in which to enjoy them all. I shall call this the identity argument. As I have noted, the identity argument has provided the economists with their formal justification for ignoring excess as a separate question from that of scarcity. It is therefore important to consider it at length. Only once it is set aside can we begin to set forth the mechanisms by which excess actually creates problems.

The notion that excess of one thing is scarcity of another arises in a simple intuition. Suppose we have a set with two kinds of elements and consequently two exclusive subsets, each of which has an internally consistent type (right- and left-handed people, for example). If these two subsets are of vastly different cardinality, it is simply a matter of convention whether we speak of the scarcity of the one type of element in the overarching set or the excess

---

12. Bataille's work exemplifies his own theory quite well, no doubt quite deliberately. It is mainly taken up with an excess of examples. *The Accursed Share* has two volumes, totaling almost five hundred pages, of which explicit theorizing takes up a scant thirty.

of the other; "most people are right-handed" is the same statement as "left-handed people are uncommon". But while this convention is obvious, it does not cover most situations. For example, suppose by contrast that we have a set with many kinds of elements, all but one of whose exclusive kind-subsets have equal cardinality. And suppose that that one has much smaller cardinality than the others. (For example, suppose nine exclusive subsets, each of which contains 11 percent of the larger set, plus one exclusive subset containing 1 percent.) We might in this case still speak of the scarcity of that one element in the overarching set. But we would not speak of excess among the others. Indeed, if there were enough types such that even the largest exclusive subset contained a maximum of 7 percent of the total of the overarching set (say, fourteen subsets of 7 percent each, and one of 2 percent), we would speak of the rarity of any particular type, and the "extreme rarity" of the one "truly unusual" type.

We can think about scarcity, that is, without having a conscious concept of excess opposed to it. Our concept of the alternative to scarcity is thus a residual one, and we adjust it to the situation. Only if there are very few types (and particularly in the case of only two types), do we really see excess of a particular thing as immediately equivalent to the scarcity of another.

It should be noted that we have similar concepts of excess that in the same way lack an "opposite" that is scarcity. These are perhaps less intuitive. For example, there are infinitely many rational numbers, but they are many fewer than the irrational numbers because the former are countable while the latter are not.[13] So we can speak of countable and uncountable infinities, and of the rationals as dense (there is a rational number between any two rational numbers), but of the reals as complete (they contain the limit of any possible sequence of rationals, even if that limit is not rational). But despite this difference, we would certainly not think the rational numbers are scarce. After all, they are infinitely many. Thus, just as in the case of scarcity we can imagine levels of scarcity without envisioning excesses as opposites to them, we can also think of levels of excess without inevitably thinking about any particular kind of scarcity as their opposite.

In general, then, there is no reason to think that scarcity and excess are symmetrically contrary concepts. But the Becker version of the identity argument does not actually work by simply exchanging excess of goods for scarcity of time in which to enjoy them. Rather, time is a factor of production; households produce utility by combining time and income. They do this in

---

13. See note 3.

two ways, for not only must time be directly used up to produce utility (in the process of consuming leisure); it must also be spent working in order to acquire the income with which to purchase the consumption goods that, when combined with (leisure) time, will produce consumed utility. There is thus not only a direct constraint (one has to "spend" time to enjoy leisure) but also an indirect one (time spent on leisure is time spent not earning income, and therefore not producing the wherewithal to buy the goods and services whose enjoyment is leisure). Long before the average household confronts the pure time constraint on leisure, its leisure is already limited by want of income to purchase the goods and services necessary to leisure.

By this argument, the only people for whom excess of consumption possibilities is simply equivalent to the scarcity of time in which to enjoy them are those without any income constraint. More specifically, such people are those whose income is unaffected by whether or not they work. They include the unemployable, those supported purely by transfer payments, and, most obviously, those with inherited wealth. For those people in particular, time is involved only in the direct production of (leisure) utility, and Becker's argument does reduce to a simple equivalence between abundance of potentially consumable goods and services and scarcity of time in which to enjoy them.

In this limited case, therefore, lack of time can serve as a budget constraint: a criterion of scarcity. But even in such a setting, there are some problems with treating time as a budget constraint. Income must purchase one thing; buying one good forbids purchase of another with the same income. However, it is not clear that time behaves in this way. We can certainly enjoy two pleasures at once. We can read a book while listening to music or sitting with a loved one, and so on. Although multitasking is no doubt overrated, one cannot deny that time can be multiply enjoyed in a way that purchased goods and services cannot. There is even a case to be made that multiple simultaneous enjoyment of utilities might enhance their individual value—watching a sports event with a friend with whom one can discuss it, for example.

This multiplicity of time's uses suggests a further problem. The classical choice situation in microeconomics involves two distinguishable goods, between which we choose on the basis of two things: first, convex isoquants that map utility-equivalent mixes of the two goods and, second, a budget constraint whose slope is determined by relative price. But in situations of excess we are generally making choices among not two but many alternatives. The researcher in a medium-size research library must decide which of a million books to read. Indeed, most such researchers must choose not one individual book but some combination of books, of which there are not one million but, roughly speaking, one million to the nth power, where n is the number of books chosen.

It is obviously silly to address this problem with the classical choice model. Even if we must choose only two books, the number of possibilities is half a trillion in a one-million-volume library. The classical choice model might approach the book choice situation by considering the choice of one book against a million possible alternatives, but the assumptions necessary to produce the properly convex isoquants would be heroic. Herbert Simon's concept of bounded rationality was long ago developed to deal with this situation, of course, but it did so by assuming that the chooser decided not to optimize but to employ heuristics that would produce some threshold level of utility. That's a more viable strategy than specific choice in so huge a space of alternatives: one simply picks books off the shelf until a book turns up that is minimally useful.

But of course that is not what researchers do. They have complicated research algorithms telling them which books to ignore, which indexes to use (and to ignore), and so on. Rather than classical choosers, they are probabilists and indeed enthusiastic Bayesians, relying very heavily on the choices of prior scholars. More generally, most modern algorithms for optimization in combinatorically generated spaces pursue Monte Carlo strategies. Typically, these strategies consider the value of some point in the combinatoric space in terms of an objective function. They then perturb the chosen combination following certain rules (and possibly integrating Bayesian priors), and see whether the objective function improves or not. If it improves, they accept the perturbation and try another. If it does not, then they accept the perturbation, but with a probability that declines as the iterations continue. (This is the Metropolis-Hastings algorithm for simulated annealing.)

Such algorithms for excessive spaces differ radically from the classical microeconomic model of choice between alternatives. In the first place, they are iterative, whereas the classic model produces an analytic solution, at least in principle. In the second place, they make few assumptions about the surface of the objective function in n-space, it being assumed that the surface looks more like the topography of Switzerland than like a smooth, everywhere convex surface.

But most important, they do not assume a unique and fixed measurability of the contribution of any one item to the objective function, but only the measurability of the value of a combination of items as a whole. They thus allow for the value of an individual item to vary depending on what else in present in the combination. The value of a particular book in a bibliography, for example, is obviously a function of what is already in the bibliography. This very broad assumption about measurability allows anything from absolutely distinguishable goods to close substitutes, indeed allowing substitutability itself to vary. In what follows, I shall refer to this property as "respecting value contextuality." It will play an important part later in this chapter. Here, the important point is what while value contextuality is respected in most modern optimization methods, it is not admissible in the classical choice model.

Note, however, that even modern optimization algorithms do assume the existence of some sort of objective function, which is in effect a measure, a *numéraire*. Although that *numéraire* respects value contextuality, it is still subject to a wide variety of other problems. The iterative strategy does not escape completely from a notion of "measuring" quality, but simply employs a far more general and realistic type of measure than does the choice model. Thus, to return to the scholar/library case, for example, most scholars employ Simonian bounded rationality with respect to this *numéraire*; they search for a threshold level of excellence in sources, perhaps continuing beyond that to some level determined by personal preference. But they do not—and cannot—iterate to the extent that optimization algorithms do.

But even if we turn from computer algorithms to simple human procedures for optimization under conditions of excess, we find that they do not set excess of one thing equal to scarcity of another. Thus, Gigerenzer's celebrated "take the best" algorithm implements choice by creating a hierarchy of properties for any two items (Gigerenzer 2000:171–97). One then proceeds down the hierarchy until one finds a property that distinguishes them. For example, we usually assume that if we have heard of only one of two cities, the one we have heard of is larger, but if we have heard of both, then the one that is a political capital is larger; if they're both political capitals, then we will believe that the one that is the capital of a larger state is larger, and so on. In practice, this rough-and-ready heuristic outperforms many formal models. But scarcity plays no role in it. Quite the contrary, the algorithm proceeds from the well known to the sparse, and stops at the first sign of differential result.

In summary, treating excess of one thing as scarcity of another seems dubious. Even within the classical choice framework, while one good may have the distinguishable and linear qualities necessary for the scarcity reasoning to work, the other may not have them, as we see in the case of Becker's switching of excess of goods for scarcity of time. More broadly, the excess situation typically involves choice of combinations of goods or utilities, often under conditions where information about them is incomplete and where prior knowledge about the value of a particular utility may be invalidated by other utilities included in the ensemble (that is, by value contextuality). Finally, it seems that none of the major approaches—combinatoric or heuristic—to the problem of choice in spaces of excess employs any kind of flip of one kind of excess for another kind of scarcity. All of them take iterative approaches, typically taking extensive advantage of prior information, however discontinuous it may be.

In short, there seems to be no real case for the identity argument. Excess is something fundamentally different from scarcity. It is only in the simplest circumstances that we are justified in simply recasting excess of one thing as scarcity of another.

EXCESS AS PROBLEM

Having dealt with the identity argument, we can now turn to the problem of how and why excess is problematic. As we saw in rehearsing the history of excess among political economists, excess can take place at two levels: individual and social. Since mechanisms of excess may differ at the two levels, it will behoove us to retain that separation here. It is also important that excess seems to be of two kinds. One of them is excess of one thing. I shall call this "surfeit." The other is excess that comes through the "manyness" of things; not through "too much" but through "too many." I shall call this "welter."

This twofold distinction gives us four kinds of excess to consider: individual surfeit, individual welter, social surfeit, and social welter. Examples of individual surfeit might be having too much money or too much knowledge or too much inspiration. But individual surfeit might also be emotional (as in depression or mania) or conative. (I use the philosophers' word "conative" to denote "having to do with purposive action." Examples of conative surfeit might be excessive ambition or obsession-compulsion.) Examples of individual welter are also familiar: too many possible friends, too many passions, too many possible topics for research, too many jobs to do well, too many moral obligations, and so on. Like individual surfeit, individual welter can range from the cognitive to the emotional and the conative.

So also at the social level. Modern theorists of knowledge have spoken much of the surfeit of things to know and the consequent specialization. Similarly, they write of the welter of socially constructed ways to know the world: ideologies, sciences, pseudo-sciences, popular impressions, and so on. Correlatively, social theorists from LeBon forward have seen a surfeit of dangerous emotions in crowds, as well as a welter of dangerously conflicting emotions between different crowds. Still other writers have seen a paralyzing welter of alternatives for social action (for example, Tocqueville on the near impossibility of concerted action in democracies), as well as conflict between these endlessly many alternatives, as we see in the complex party politics of those European democracies that follow proportional representation. Thus we see both surfeit and welter at the social level, just as at the individual one. However, while these examples show us that excess is a problem at both individual and social levels, and that it permeates not only the cognitive but also the conative and emotional realms, they do not show how it is that excess in fact creates problems for humans.

Showing how excess affects individuals and groups is particularly important because we are so familiar with how scarcity has its effects. The mechanism of scarcity is very simple. We assume humans or groups to be entities that can feel, act, and symbolize. Following the economists, we usually think of those processes as modes of production: each of them requires certain inputs to succeed, and scarcity means that some input is present in insufficient quantity. Therefore, production cannot succeed. That is, the mechanism of scarcity works through the first of Aristotle's four causes: material cause. Production fails for want of material. But in the case of excess, want of material should not produce problems; for any given resource, excess necessarily implies sufficiency. So production cannot fail for lack of something. Even with multiple resources, if all are sufficient and one or more is in excess, then that excess should not be problematic.

Excess must therefore be problematic for some other reason. As the reference to Aristotle suggests, the most likely reasons are structural (no clear plan for production) or final (no clear purpose for production). Thus, an obvious possibility is that sufficient inputs must not only be present, but must also be specifically selected or assembled to be effective in production. To be sure, we could choose inputs at random. But there could be constraints on which combinations of inputs are jointly sufficient. It could be that for sufficient resources A, B, and C, each of which has four different portions, only the partial combinations A1-B2-C1 and A2-B1-C4 will work. That is, we might have to coordinate particular subsets of the sufficient inputs. In that case, random selection will not necessarily succeed.

Thus stated, the excess problem sounds like a coordination problem. And indeed there are long familiar models for solving coordination problems, whether within the self or beyond it: markets, leviathans, hierarchies, and so on. This chain of association suggests the surprising view that leviathans, hierarchies and so on might actually originate in problems of excess rather than in problems of scarcity, a suggestion to which we shall return in the next section. But for the moment, what matters is that markets, leviathans, hierarchies, and so on actually function as coordination devices only if the things to be coordinated are subject to some type of formal trade-off, a structuring of production.

The case of markets is clearest. Markets require prices, which cannot emerge without scarcity (which helps produce the necessary commensuration) and the absence of value contextuality. In the context of excess, there is no scarcity; hence, there can be no prices, no budget constraints, and no basis for choice. That is, the theory of markets arises because of a coordination problem that is indeed about excess in some sense (too many possible choices for an individual to decide what he wants), but then it resolves that problem by imposing a form of scarcity. (That is, by imposing relative evaluation of all items on a common *numéraire* [pricing] and presuming a budget constraint with respect to that *numéraire*.) A more general approach to excess problems cannot accept such assumptions. There may be value contextuality or some other failure of commensurability, and by assumption there is no budget constraint. Put another way, if markets in fact derive from an attempt to resolve excess problems, they do so by imposing a form of scarcity. But what interests us here is not whether that scarcity is itself real or imposed, but rather why, in the first instance, excess presents problems that must be resolved: not how the coordination problem is solved in the case of excess, but why excess is problematic in the first place.

Individual Level

I begin with individual surfeit. Emotionally, individual surfeit creates problems through overload and habituation. An excess of one pleasure at one time may overwhelm the self, while an excess of one pleasure over time reduces the ability of that pleasure to satisfy. Cognitively, surfeit creates problems chiefly through overload. A place, a person, or a discipline can be too big to know. Yet surfeit of knowledge can also create problems by isolating an individual (from others who know different things) and by strongly reducing his or her ability to know other things, and so on. (The latter might seem to assume scarcity [of means to know] but could also follow from cognitive habits developed to handle the original overload.) Conatively, surfeit creates problems through overload (some tasks can be too big or too complicated) and through habituation (routines can degenerate into meaningless habits).[14]

---

14. Habit and habituation are discussed several times in this book: in the context of human nature (chapter 2), of social order (chapter 7), and of moral activity (chapter 9).

To be sure, one could argue that surfeit is self-regulating because of negative feedback. Thus, in the case of emotions and tastes, excessive things might become less fulfilling, and so be less sought, and hence seem less excessive in experience, and so eventually regain their ability to fulfill. But in many examples, this argument seems not to hold: the favorite ice cream permanently loses its savor, the long-practiced politics becomes meaningless, and so on. Habituation does not seem to be necessarily self-regulating.

Thus, whether we look at emotion, cognition, or action, overload and habituation seem to be the two principal mechanisms through which surfeit creates problems at the individual level. Overload involves what we might call "technological" constraints on the production of emotion, action, and knowledge; one way or another overload leads to paralysis or failure of production. (We could think of this as a failure of final cause [purpose] or effective cause [actor].) Habituation works slightly differently, implying that the value of inputs to emotions, action, and knowledge changes with its amount, and does so in such a way as not to permit a stable negative feedback system with a simple equilibrium.

Similar avenues produce the effects of welter at the individual level. Here the technological constraint arises through numbers: too many things to know, too many emotions to experience, too many possible actions. In all three cases, the self is paralyzed; there is an overload, but an overload of alternatives. This overload not only creates a direct problem of choice but, more important, induces considerable value contextuality. The sheer number of available alternatives produces a combinatoric redefinition of the value of each, which depends on the context of others chosen. Value instability arises through this momentary value contextuality across combinatoric marketbaskets of choices. And that value instability produces a further technological constraint on emotion, action, and meaning.

Thus, in the case of individual welter we find again two principal mechanisms. The first—overload—is shared with individual surfeit. But the second (value contextuality) contrasts with the second surfeit mechanism of habituation. Value contextuality across current possibilities is not the same as habituation over time to a single reward in excess. At the individual level, then, we have three basic mechanisms: overload/paralysis, habituation, and value contextuality.

Social Level

The same mechanisms obtain to a certain extent at the social level. Social surfeit and welter work in the first instance through overload, habituation, and value contextuality, much as they do at the individual level. These effects are particularly obvious in those social entities that are "individuals" in the sense of being congeries of biological individuals concentric with one another: families, neighborhoods, communities, provinces, nations and so on. Thus, a long familiar sociological tradition has discussed the effects of an overload of emotion in crowds: effects on politics, religion, and so on (Le Bon, Freud). John Dewey's famous *The Public and Its Problems* (1927) is an extended meditation on the overloading of the public by new means of communication, which creates both surfeit of information and welter of possible publics and possible policies. And there are theories on social habituation, too: for example, the familiar argument of Georg Simmel and Robert Park that metropolitan life overwhelms city dwellers with a surfeit of stimulation, leading to superficiality and lack of commitment.[15]

Such effects are visible not only in "social individuals," however, but also in things like ethnic groups, voluntary associations, bureaucracies, and genders, which we usually view as being constituted of aspects of individuals rather than of whole individuals. So we can imagine habituation in political groups, which over time require more and more extreme politics to fan the faithful into action. Or we can imagine academic disciplines unable to deal with onslaughts of new information. Or we can imagine voluntary associations torn apart by excess of internal dissension. Finally, the problems of value contextuality are a byword to anyone who follows partisan politics, particularly in parliamentary systems, where the political worth of a particular policy is completely at the mercy of other policies proposed alongside it.[16]

Thus we see overload, habituation, and value contextuality at the social level as at the individual one. The question remains whether there are at the social level new mechanisms by which excess creates problems.

A first possible new social-level mechanism for excess might be that excess produces conflict between individuals. Even in the supposedly excessive state of nature (Sahlins [1972] speaks of the Stone Age as possessing the first superabundant economy), there can be conflict, because of the attitude of universal possession created by an excessive world. But this new mechanism is more apparent than real. To be sure, it involves excess of individual desire. But in a world of excess, the sheer superfluity of satisfactions should make that excessive desire more easy of fulfilment. What actually creates these conflicts is not

15. See Park et al. 1925 (ch. 8, "Community Organization and the Romantic Temper") and Simmel, "The Metropolis and Mental Life" (Simmel [1903]1950:409–24).

16. See the discussion of "bundles" in chapter 3, for example.

the excess itself, but rather the mutually shared value schemes that lead actors to desire the same things. These in fact create scarcity, which in turn leads to conflict.

A familiar modern example of such an artificial scarcity is the marriage market. As any parent knows, when teenagers first pass puberty, they think that only a tiny fraction of the opposite sex could possibly be satisfactory as romantic or sexual partners. This is a traditional (and curiously reciprocal) situation of scarcity: too many of each side confronting too few of the other. Yet not too long afterwards, the vast majority of both genders will be married to one of those people whom they previously regarded as unsatisfactory partners. That is, what appears to be a conflict over supposed scarcity is actually created by a social regime of desirability that has in turn created a scarcity problem. For the fact is that the average individual could probably have a marriage of average success with thousands or tens of thousands of potential partners. The scarcity is induced precisely because of that staggering excess of possibilities. It thereby produces a belief in romantic specialness and in the idea of individual attraction, notions that are central to maintaining marriages over time.

Following the implicit suggestion of this case, I shall argue in the next section that these rating schemes create scarcity in order to deal with the first of my excess mechanisms—that of overload with its consequent paralysis of action. Many social institutions that we commonly understand in scarcity terms can be more productively construed as strategies for dealing with excess. The scarcity they involve is deliberately created to guide behavior. And it will be interesting to ask when in particular humans choose to do this, when it is that they turn what is in fact excess into apparent scarcity, which then drives their social and economic conceptions of their life processes. But for the moment what matters is that this does seem to be a choice, rather than a truly separate mechanism by which excess becomes problematic.[17]

Thus, in most cases excess does not produce effects through conflict. Rather, conflict is induced (deliberately or not) by the strategies used to handle excess. However, while conflict thus is not an additional social mechanism

17. Even Hobbes, in the celebrated chapter 13 of book 1 of *Leviathan*, recognizes that conflict arises between equal men only when they desire the same thing, and his supposed demonstration that this is the usual state of affairs is, in fact, only an empirical assumption, not a derivation from first principles. (Chapter 13 has surprisingly little connection with the dull recitation of mechanical psychology that precedes it.) It should be noted that modern advertising is essentially a system for training all people to want the same things.

for excess, there are two more realistic possibilities. Both of these follow from the nature of social entities. A brief note on that nature is thus useful.[18]

As just noted, social entities include not only things like cities and families that are often analogized to individuals, but also things like ethnic groups, social movements, and bureaucracies that consist of parts of individuals, rather than of whole persons. Because such entities involve continuous weaving or unweaving of new people and new parts of people, they can change much more rapidly than do individuals, who are burdened with a mass of memories and anticipations holding them together over the long run. In this sense, our constant names for social entities are a misnomer. We speak of "the civil rights movement" or "Irish-Americans," but these are not constant things in the ways that individuals are; rather, they are perpetually changing in membership, ideology, and structure. The specifically social mechanisms of excess are those which interfere with this process of continuous weaving and unweaving, thereby facilitating or destroying the coherence of the lineage over time. On this argument, for example, the civil rights movement of the mid-twentieth century held together as long as it had specific, straightforward objectives. Once the crucial court cases had been decided and the main civil rights legislation had been passed, the movement faced a plethora of possible future objectives and dissolved into subgroups with different interests. The opening of the broad realm of possibilities actually helped unmake the group. We may call this the disruptive mechanism.

In continuously self-reproducing social groups (as opposed to social movements), excess problems often arise in a slightly different way. The group's stability presupposes replacement of aging members by younger ones. But the excess of things necessary to be passed on to the new generation often leads to a habituation that undercuts the ability to generate new commitment. This process is quite evident in academic disciplines. Academic disciplines deal with the excess of things to know by creating canons: there have, after all, been many more sociological theorists than just Marx, Weber, and Durkheim. But the simplicity of the canon—as taught to those who have no idea what an immense reduction in complexity it represents—inevitably leads to habituation and consequent loss of respect. This in turn leads to effloration of new, noncanonical argument, which is most often merely the excess of the past, recreated in the present. Today's new theory is just rediscovered Mannheim

18. It is at this point that the process ontology becomes central to the chapter. Lineage issues create particular types of excess problems. The summary that follows restates arguments already made in more detail in chapters 1 and 2.

or Tarde or whomever. Only in truly progressive disciplines can this cycle be avoided, and those are few. As a result, most academic disciplines have no firmer definition of excellence than that something is "new," which in fact means only that it hasn't been observed in the canon in living professional memory (Abbott 2014b). In this case, excess produces meandering or cyclical patterns through its interaction with the problem of reproduction. I shall call this the mechanism of misinheritance.

In total, then, we have five different channels through which excess causes problems. Three are common to the individual and social levels: overload, habituation, and value contextuality. Two are specifically social: disruption and misinheritance. Of these five, overload leads to confusion and paralysis, and thus makes cognition, action, and emotion fundamentally impossible. Habituation and value contextuality both also paralyze through the inherent instability of their implications for action. All of these happen not only in the cognitive, but also in the emotional and conative realms, as I have noted. At the social level we see these mechanisms also; but in addition, we see the two mechanisms by which excess interacts with processes of lineage, either disrupting a group or unsettling its heritage through an overload of the processes of socialization.

STRATEGIES FOR EXCESS

Given that excess creates problems via these various mechanisms, there must then be strategies for dealing with those problems. There are indeed a variety of such strategies, both at the individual and at the social level. Broadly speaking, they fall into two types: reduction strategies and rescaling strategies. Reduction strategies are those strategies that cut down the amount of excess. There are two subtypes. A basic strategy simply ignores excess altogether. A more subtle and proactive strategy simplifies it and reduces it to tractable terms. I shall call these two versions of reduction the defensive and the reactive strategies respectively.

By contrast with these reduction strategies, rescaling strategies work by changing the definition of desirability. They don't reduce excess, but redefine it out of existence. These, too, come in a simple and a subtle version, and, as with reduction strategies, the simple version is the more extreme. It not only accepts existing excess but increases it, making excess and its enjoyment the core of life. This is the strategy urged by the apostles of excess earlier mentioned: Nietzsche, Foucault, Bataille, and so on. The more subtle version is a more judicious one, comprising strategies that somehow make a virtue of the inescapable fact of excess. I shall call these two the creative (the more extreme) and adaptive (the more subtle) strategies.

I have, then, four kinds of strategies: the two reduction strategies of defense and reaction and the two rescaling strategies of creativity and adaptation. They make a scale from the most conservative to the most radical approaches to excess—from defense to reaction to adaptation to creativity—and I shall review them in that order. We shall find that they make a pretty complete inventory of human behavior, which is quite important for my argument, since I wish to argue that we could in principle replace social theories based on scarcity with social theories based on excess.

Defensive Strategies

At the individual level, the easiest defensive strategy is simply to ignore excess. One can fall back on habits of mind and simply ignore novelty, difference, and the other makers of excess. In the sphere of action, such defensive modes of excess avoidance are standard. One can act habitually, simply choosing the same dish every time at the Chinese restaurant. One can choose randomly, as many people do when playing the lottery. One can imitate, choosing whatever is the popular thing in the environment or (what is logically equivalent) choosing the reverse of the popular thing in the environment. Often there are ideological tools to cover up these surrenders of will, as the ideology of romantic love covers up the quite random association of spouses in modern societies (a case mentioned earlier), or as elaborate fashion rules cover up for imitation.

At the social level, we see many of the same defensive mechanisms. The chief cognitive tools for social excess reduction are stereotypes and, more broadly, the traditions that constitute the "cognitive habits" of groups. Such stereotypes and traditions enable us to save the extraordinary time it would take actually to know others for themselves. On this argument, stereotypes are therefore not so much moral delicts as they are cognitive necessities, and getting rid of them is no more possible than getting rid of humans' dependence on air and food. It is, rather, the deleterious social consequences of certain kinds of stereotypes that must be the object of policy, because they are in fact the only possible object of such policies.

Randomness also is used to handle excess at the social level, although we don't tend to see it. For example, many social structures have positions that will function reasonably effectively no matter who is placed in them. That this or that particular person becomes a superstar in this or that academic or artistic field is relatively accidental. The narrowing of reputational rank-ings into steep hierarchies results from centralization of communications, not necessarily from better knowledge of the "actual" rankings of people, as Sher-win Rosen (1981) argued long ago. But if we impose artificially steep rankings on talent distributions that are in fact relatively flat, randomness inevitably increases. Luckily, it doesn't really matter who is the top soprano or the top swimmer or the top professor of sociology. Once created, social entities can survive despite relatively random and average inputs, something quite evident in the history of monarchy and aristocracy throughout the world. Random filling of elite positions probably makes very little difference to many social structures.[19]

As at the individual level, habit is again a dominant strategy for excess in the realm of social action. At the social level, we call habit "tradition." We solve the problem of what among many things to do simply by doing what we have always done. There is a strong case to be made that academic disciplines arise through just such a mechanism of tradition. Perhaps disciplines consti-tute desert islands of common concepts and methods in a vast sea of intellec-tual differences; the potential novelty of the world is after all far greater than we think. On this model, the disciplines grow by slow accretion, as wanderers in the huge ocean of possible knowledge wash up on the shore. They then tend to stick with tradition because no other island is visible. Canons may therefore be not so much fortresses of power as they are lonely atolls with at least the virtue of being above water.[20]

19. As an economist, Rosen of course assumes perfect rankability of all talents in a super-star market, noting that this implies imperfect substitutability (one article by a first-rate econo-mist may indeed be worth ten articles by mediocre economists), a phenomenon that partially explains the superstar incomes that are his object of study. However, I am here emphasizing Rosen's other mechanism, which is a technology that allows one actor to serve a larger and larger proportion of the market, as recordings concentrated classical music incomes into a fairly small elite of performers. But unlike Rosen, I am arguing that under such conditions of concentration, it doesn't really matter whether talent is well ranked, or (in the extreme case) whether it even exists (cf. Chambliss 1989). The ranking system produces the conditions of its own reproduction because it resolves the problem of excess. That is, up to a point, people will find reasons to think excellent the singing of whomever ends up being the top soprano (or top economist). The presence of George W. Bush in the White House is an obvious example of this phenomenon. The United States easily survived eight years of a president with mediocre abilities and limited experience, and substantial numbers of Americans thought Bush a distin-guished figure instead of a mediocrity.

20. Tradition will also be discussed in chapter 7. This mechanism for discipline formation was originally proposed in Abbott 2014b, which actually dates from 2009. The reader will

Fashion is of course another general strategy for excess, in which the defensive strategy of imitation plays a central role. For the individual, deciding one's clothes on a purely aesthetic basis is a burdensome task (Hsiung 2010). It is much easier to decide which clothes to wear because the system tells you the proper answer (in part by not even selling the things you might otherwise consider). At the social level, of course, fashion permits the endless replacement of perfectly useful clothing (or operating systems—I am writing this chapter in Wordstar 3.24 on a DOS computer) and hence the continued employment of millions of garment (or software) workers who might otherwise have the Keynesian problem of figuring out how to fill their leisure time with things to do. Fashion also facilitates other strategies for problems of excess, by providing material for ranking systems, which are, as I shall shortly argue, perhaps the most important of the reactive strategies for dealing with excess. As this analysis suggests, the phenomenon we call fashion is actually a compound mechanism combining several excess strategies: to defensive imitation at the individual level are added the reactive strategy of hierarchy and the adaptive strategy of serialism, the latter two of which I shall cover shortly. Note that fashion includes such intellectual mechanisms as the fractal mechanisms discussed in *Chaos of Disciplines* (ch. 1), whereby fractal intellectual fashions produce constant novelty (hence exploring excess creatively) and constant stability (hence preventing it from overwhelming us).

But there are two great defensive mechanisms for handling glut at the social level that are even more familiar to us than these. Markets and democracy are, in fact, means for handling excess. Logically, the two employ the same structure: truck and barter, in Adam Smith's famous phrase. To markets, the barterers bring differential amounts of resources according to their labor, productivity, capital, inheritance, and so on. To democratic polities, by contrast, the barterers bring, at least in theory, one voting unit of opinion or desire per person. In both cases, they then exchange what they bring. Both of these truck and barter strategies work the same way: they facilitate exchange under cer-

notice that this analysis of academics differs somewhat from that in chapter 3. More than ten years separate the two pieces, and in those ten years I spent much time studying (and defending) libraries and the research based in them. (See *Digital Paper*.) Inevitably, the excesses of books, of publication, and, indeed, of things to know changed my thinking about knowledge considerably, moving it even further in the direction chapter 3 had already taken in revising my original arguments about disciplines (formalized in *Chaos of Disciplines*, ch. 5). In many ways this excess argument is simply a new venture, and my concepts of disciplines and misinheritance in the present chapter are attempts to see the implications of excess for processual ontology in general.

tain rules (in particular an assumption of measure—the *numéraire* of cash or votes) in order to solve the problem that, as Hobbes put it so bluntly, "Naturally, every man has right to every thing," (*Leviathan*, book 1, ch. 14). The excess of choosers overwhelms the excess of the chosen, and makes it almost certain that excess will not be so great as to avoid all conflict. Markets and democracy solve this conflict (itself a question of excess of choosers) by enabling exchange under rules of commensuration.

Now as we have seen earlier, markets and democracy both operate by translating excess of one thing—economic and political aims and desires—into scarcity of another (a *numéraire* consisting of money or votes, distributed in various ways). In this sense, they follow the logic of the identity argument. But by recognizing that in fact markets and democracy are in the first instance mechanisms for dealing with excess, we can see that they are not in some sense necessary things, and that there are alternative ways of handling the same excess. One could, for example, reduce the excess of choosers by training people to different desires. About seven hundred dollars per person per year is spent on advertising in the United States, most of it training people to want the same things, which in turn produces the excess demand for a limited number of objects that—as Menger tells us—markets were invented to solve. In this case, that is, the use of rankings to solve the paralysis problem overshoots the mark. We can therefore simply transform Rosen's insight so as to see that such rankings create not superstar income, but superstar demand. If we believed that the purpose of advertising was to spread demand out through a relatively flat and quite superabundant space of alternatives in order to reduce the need for markets and the production of superstar demand, our advertisers would emphasize the importance of difference, variety, and multiplicity of alternatives.

It is in this sense that markets and democracies are defensive strategies. They simply deny the excess of things to be consumed, making it appear that modern consumers are limited by Malthusian scarcity when of course average modern American consumers enjoy levels of welfare and choice—in terms of health, well-being, transportation, knowledge, and services—beyond the dreams of even the richest consumers of a century ago. The apparent scarcity is produced by Veblenian conspicuous consumption and by a sales machinery (sales occupies 11 percent of the US labor force) designed to make people feel that they are lacking things. After all, one way to solve Hobbes's problem is simply to reduce desire, as Sahlins (1972:37) notes when he says, "The world's most primitive people have few possessions, but they are not poor," and as mystic ascetic religions have argued for millenia. Alternatively, one could assign goods and policies at random, or by tradition, or by using any of the other individual defensive mechanisms.

All these strategies in effect avoid dealing with excess altogether. They use randomness or habit to ignore the problem or they use exchange and manipulation to transform it into a problem of scarcity. Note that such methods are completely incapable of dealing with, say, the excess of ways to know the world or its more practical avatar, the problem of which books to read in the library. We could create a market in library books, as if they were scarce. Each faculty member and student could get five library chits a week and faculty could purchase their students' chits by teaching them. But it is obvious that such a market would not produce knowledge worth much. For such burning problems, we need a whole different range of strategies, much more drastic and much more proactive. These are the strategies I have called reactive.

Reactive Strategies

Like defensive strategies, reactive strategies for excess can be viewed at both the individual and the group levels. At the individual level we have cognitive strategies like abstraction, which reduce welter by turning multiplicities of diverse things into specific emanations of simpler but more abstract things. At its most drastic, abstraction can work by simply ignoring differences, thereby making an excessive collection of highly differentiated things look like a repetitive collection of identical things, among which random choice can easily suffice. This is science's way of thinking about laboratory rats or volcanic eruptions or supernovae. By contrast, contemporary humans typically resent being treated as mere representatives of this or that type, as "sex objects" or "tokens" or "men in the grey flannel suit" or "*Homo economicus*." They want to be (laboriously) understood as individuals. Abstraction does not work as well for human interaction.[21]

However, the dominant reactive strategy—whether for cognitive, active, or even affective excess—is hierarchizing and concentrating one's attention at the top end of the hierarchy. Restaurant reviews, college ratings in *US News and World Report*, university priority documents, Great Books lists: all these follow a simple of logic of "take the best, forget the rest." As I noted earlier, Gerd Gigerenzer (2000) has argued that this is one of the fundamental modes

---

21. D'Alembert's "Preliminary Discourse" in the *Encyclopédie*—so much derided by Malthus—is in fact a passionate statement of the importance of categorization, hierarchy, and division of labor as strategies for controlling excess.

of human cognition. But it is true of emotion to some extent as well: over-whelmed with a welter of conflicting emotional loads, one is likely to select a dominant few to experience. Hierarchy can work in reverse as well: a winnowing strategy can prune excess from the bottom, reducing a complex array of possibilities to a narrower group of serious alternatives. And the universal call to "set priorities" is nothing if not a command to ignore most things and concentrate on a few.

But there are other reactive excess-reduction strategies for individuals' feelings. The various psychotherapies and drug regimens for stress and panic are obvious examples, as is self-medication with alcohol. All of these aim to blunt feelings of excess and overload. At the same time, however, they begin to move into strategies for solving excess problems by modifying desirability (that is, rescaling). The extreme case here is hermitlike withdrawal from the world and from its concerns, already mentioned as among the defensive strategies. One removes oneself from excess simply by lowering one's level of desire to a point where a tiny and purely random amount of food or happiness or moral activity will suffice.

At the social level, we have many of the same reactive strategies, although they are further structured. Consider first reactive strategies for cognitive excess. Here we do not see the defensive strategies of stereotype and tradition, but rather division of labor and specialization. Both of these tame the vast array of possible things to know and skills to exercise. Division of labor is obvious in academia, for example, with its proliferation of specialists of many kinds. The inevitably excessive conflicts between these specialized disciplines and groups are themselves tamed by various systematically structured forms of reciprocal ignorance, which become noticeable only when they are violated, as in the humanists' invasion of the social sciences over the last two decades. As for the myriad amateur knowledges, the subsumption of such immediate everyday knowledge by expert, abstract knowledge also reduces the welter of things to be known. For example, there have been hundreds of careful histories and surveys of American communities. All these are subsumed into abstractions by academic articles on "typical patterns of urban development," in which the detailed prior work on community histories becomes "mere randomness" or "variation around the mean" or other kinds of unimportant things. The huge welter of amateur knowledge is thereby turned into mere experience: unimportant, given the abstraction of academia.

Hierarchy also permits other kinds of reductions. The failure of direct democracy in a group of any size is remedied by the fractal process of creating representative republican institutions, reproducing the mapping of individuals and their differences at a smaller, less excessive, more manageable level. (This is the theory of pluralism argued by Robert Dahl 1961, as I noted in chapter 3). Self-similarity of this sort is used throughout complex social systems as a modular and scalable strategy for reducing vast arrays of structural relations to instantiations of a few simple patterns (See *Chaos of Disciplines*, ch. 6). Immensely complicated social systems can thereby become easily navigable and manipulable. Specialization and self-similarity can thus be seen, with hierarchy, as the three fundamental reactive strategies for excess reduction at the social level.

Finally, there are a wide variety of strategies for dealing with excess social emotion. The most common of these are safety valves. The danger of excessive emotion is a long theme in social theory, from Le Bon onward. Clearly there are many social structures whose main purpose is the defusing or channeling of these emotional excesses: participatory and spectator sports, political rallies, and so on. Where excess male sexual energy has threatened social systems, we find quite elaborate brothel systems and pleasure quarters to keep the boys satiated and calm. And those who have read *Eros and Civilization* will recall that Marcuse saw the sexual revolution as in some ways repressive, because it stripped sublimated energy from social critique by simply indulging it. Another strategy for handling the excess of emotion in society is the forcing of emotion into private settings: churches, hospitals, homes, and so on. If excessive emotion threatens the social order, sequestering it proves an effective reactive strategy.

Adaptive Strategies

Defensive and reactive strategies deal with excess problems by taming them. It is therefore not surprising that we find many of the social institutions ranged in these strategies. Markets, hierarchies, republics, and so on are all ways of taming excess either by reducing or avoiding it. By contrast, there are many other aspects of social life that do not involve the reduction of excess but that, quite the contrary, involve adjusting to it, playing with it, even creating it where it did not exist. In order to continue our gradual move across this spectrum of strategies, I next turn to the more subtle form of positive excess strategy: adaptation.

As I have noted, adaptive strategies focus less on ignoring or reducing excess than on finding it more desirable and less disturbing. They rescale excess. Adaptation does this in a subtle and nuanced way. Again, the most familiar and obvious examples are the individual ones. A common example is surfing the web or, to give the equivalent for an earlier generation, reading encyclope-dias. To encounter a randomly ordered source and simply read through it is to wander arbitrarily through the enormous excess of knowledge, to choose randomness as a positive good. More sophisticated adaptive strategies take the form of seeing analogies, making translations, and yoking together areas of work that are often far apart. These are, of course, urged to the point of parody in the literature on interdisciplinarity. But they are nonetheless impor-tant strategies for adapting to excess. Translation is not an easy business, but the access it gives to new realms bespeaks the pleasures of excess.

In the realm of action, we see other strategies. Serialism is the most obvi-ous conative strategy for adaptation to excess. Over a life course, one moves through a sequence of jobs, of friends, of romantic partners, of interests, of hobbies. One moves at different rates in different areas, but few members of early twenty-first century societies remain in precisely one place for even twenty years on all these dimensions. It is true that we tend to tame this practice of serial adaptation to excess through narratives of odyssey or self-discovery or whatever. But narratives lie; we just keep on moving to the end. As a result, there is nothing as embarrassing as reading old pieces of autobi-ography, seeing photographs of oneself with forgotten friends, wearing dated clothes and hairstyles that one has come to find amusing.[22]

And just as we are different persons over time, most of us are different per-sons in the many social settings in which we live: dutiful mothers in one place, assertive academics in another, thoughtful friends in a third, clever manipula-tors in a fourth, and perhaps ardent musical performers in a fifth. Indeed, the excess of selves can be disconcerting at times, although perhaps less to us than to those who, knowing us in only one of these roles, are suddenly sur-prised to encounter us in another. But multiple selves in multiple contexts and multiple selves over time allow us to enjoy an excess of life possibilities that was not possible in societies with more rigid manners and structures.[23] It is, to be sure, true that these multiplicities themselves are sometimes organized into normative life-course trajectories: thus, academics who were once hot-headed

22. Serialism can thus be seen as a kind of reality underlying the retrospective discourse of self we encountered in chapter 1, on historicality, as well as the retrospective forms of outcome considered in chapter 6.

23. Note how such simultaneous multiplicity, like serialism, contributes to the solidar-ity of modern life, underscoring the contention in chapter 1 that the individual is in many ways a crucial vector of solidarity in modern life. Such an argument has its roots in Simmel ([1922]1955:58–84).

young radicals must inevitably become authoritative powerbrokers in middle age and generative facilitators in old age and retirement. But at least they get the chance to be all three things.

At the social level also, we find many adaptive strategies for excess. Some of these are structures that impose serialism. Term limits, compulsory retirement, and other such mechanisms are a means of generating turnover in order to embrace the vast excess of possibilities.[24] Another set of adaptive strategies are those which provide access to whole new realms of ideas, experiences, and people. Thus, cognitively, we see the emergence of complicated translation systems between the huge excess of different symbolic systems: pidgins, creoles, and dialect gradients arising between the already excessive languages of the world. The same kinds of things emerge in academic disciplines and interdisciplines, which have their own methodological creoles and theoretical pidgins. Yet by adapting to excess and difference, translation brings more and more experiences into our immediate world; it increases excess. As these examples suggest, translation systems themselves tend to stabilize and turn themselves into new differences (more excess) which in turn require intertranslation. In this sense, to adapt to excess means committing to perpetual change, both across social differences in a moment and across different successor societies over time. We do have academic disciplines that explicitly aim at this kind of translation: anthropology and history. And although it is in some quarters customary to condemn anthropology and history as politicized servants of empire, it is clear that their underlying projects aim—in ideal terms—at understanding the amazing excess of human society when taken on its own terms.[25]

There are other important forms of social structure that embody this adaptive approach to the excess of social life. Trusteeship, for example, is a conative social structure committed to balancing between past, present, and future.[26] We also have things like tourism, multiculturalism, and international exchange. These strategies—so often derided as political claptrap—are in fact of long standing and tradition. In earlier periods of European history, not only

24. Term limits and similar structures will be discussed in chapter 6. In the terms of that chapter, serialism is a strategy to be able oneself to enjoy multiple outcomes. Because this chapter was written late in the sequence of the book's composition, there are other anticipations in this passage of chapters yet to come, particularly of chapter 7 and the epilogue.

25. The concept of such humane sympathy was discussed in the preceding chapter, and will return in the epilogue.

26. Trusteeship will be considered in chapter 7.

elites but also middle-class families exchanged children across wide social and geographic spaces, precisely with the aim of creating truly multilingual and cosmopolitan adults. The monolingualism of modern nation-states—the United States being the most extreme example—is actually quite unusual in the history of human societies (Gal 2011). Multiculturalism may be a lifelong commitment and difficult practice rather than a facile teenage acquisition. But it is not any less important as a way of addressing the excess of human societies.

Creative Strategies

Finally, then, I come to creative strategies. The creative approach to excess is familiar enough, for it has been the subject of the great apostles of excess like Nietzsche, Foucault, and most particularly Bataille. But these writers have given the creative strategies for excess a bad name, having associated them with power, evil, and death. Interestingly, their theory of the individual is shared almost completely with the pessimistic lineage running from Deuteronomy through Hobbes to Malthus, Freud, and Durkheim: individuals have infinite desires which inevitably conflict. For the older lineage, however, this situation required the evolution of characterological controls, either internal (Freud) or external (Durkheim). By contrast, the apostles of excess celebrated lack of control, and inevitably appeared as prophets of evil by comparison with the mainstream theory of control.

Yet one could think about creating and celebrating excess not so much as an evasion of control, but as an answer to the Keynesian question of what to do with our free time. The modern world is astoundingly productive. Perhaps the extraordinary evolution of the arts of civilization, and their spread from the aristocracies to the middle and even lower classes, is not so much testimony to the evolution of new patterns of restraint and discipline with which to protect one's group interest, as Elias argued in *The Civilizing Process*. (For Elias, like all the rest, ultimately accepted the ideas of impulse and control that underlie the Deuteronomic lineage.) Perhaps that evolution rather reflects an attempt to fill leisure time with activity and creation, whether of conversation or thought or connoisseurship or artistic performance. In the modern world we have the luxury to eschew stereotypes, to know a spouse or friend in staggering detail, in ways impossible when families were mainly economic and reproductive units in desperate straits.

Bataille's theory seems clearly appropriate here. In a modern, hyperproductive world, every individual can live the complexities of Werther. Modern emotional subtlety may very well be a time-wasting strategy designed to fill the vast expanses of leisure that Keynes foresaw. In this sense, the Keynesian moment has already arrived. Everyday, average people enjoy on talk shows the detailed personal attention previously reserved for the highest of aristocrats, while Facebook allows every individual to curate a version of People magazine dedicated purely to herself. What is this, if not a staggering waste of time, effort, and resources, which an earlier generation might have dedicated to eradicating poverty, creating a general unified theory, or worshipping the gods?

One could similarly argue that the academic epidemic of radical juxtaposition, deconstruction, and hyribdizing, along with the valorization of previously unimportant differences, are all responses to the extraordinary effloration and power of scholarship in the nineteenth and early twentieth centuries. After all, there had been 33 American dissertations on Jane Austen by 1968 and a whopping 363 on William Shakespeare (McNamee 1968, 1969). By 1980 there had been 90 articles (in JSTOR) on Austen and 1,808 on Shakespeare. Small wonder that scholars began to write about race in *Mansfield Park* or colonialism in *The Tempest*!

In summary, the creative strategies for excess have acquired their bad reputation undeservedly. In fact, these are among the most familiar strategies in modern life, and in fact we have already arrived at the Keynesian moment of needing desperately to fill the time no longer required for subsistence or even for middle class production.[27]

CONCLUSION

In closing, I wish to turn briefly to recasting some classic problems of sociology in terms that make the problematic of excess central. Here are a few examples.

Consider the familiar problem of economists' perfect competition. We all know that perfect knowledge of a system is impossible. Indeed, those forms of

---

27. I have no space in this chapter to discuss the reciprocal dynamics of these mechanisms, although these are of obvious interest. For example, it may be inevitable that habits of scarcity will drive out those of excess. The aristocrat takes the attitude of excess, doesn't reflect about the future implications of his spending, doesn't think about depreciation, and so is eventually dispossessed by those who do care about such things and who count everything. But of course, those people's children live as aristocrats, waste their patrimony, and so on. Or again, similarly, lowering one's level of desire makes one prey for others in important ways. This has long been an account of the social implications of Indian religion, for example; it has often been argued that ascetic Hindus and Buddhists were ideal subjects for Asian despotism.

economics which attend to the costs of information recognize that quite well. But some people's imperfect knowledge is better than that of others. Indeed, an excess way of thinking about economic privilege is that the people at the center of, say, the stock market are people who are not swamped with bad information. Similarly, elite people who have been diagnosed with cancer are privileged precisely because they do not have to wander around the internet, being overwhelmed with the useless and often wrong information to be found there. They may have physician friends, and in any case they will know effective quality criteria for judging web pages (in this case, they know to look for things from the National Cancer Institute, and will quickly find the NCI Guidelines for Medical Professionals, which are reliable and current). Privilege, that is, lies in not being swamped with disinformation—whether about stocks or about cancer.

Or again, an excess way of thinking about wealth is that it saves you the problem of having to think about a lot of things. You don't have to worry about when cheap flights are available, when the clothing sales are, where you can go for vacation, which restaurants have which prices, when you can afford to retire. A whole set of burdensome information—prices, times, availabilities, future government policies, and so on—can simply be ignored. That is privilege indeed. Perhaps wealth is not so much about enjoying lots of utilities—goods and services—as it is about not having to spend time thinking about constraint, or regretting the inability to have experiences that you couldn't afford.

What about competition between disciplines? An excess theory suggests that disciplines don't actually compete at all. Rather, as I argued earlier, disciplines are lonely hearts clubs where people adrift in the huge sea of intellectual possibility are trying to find a few souls with similar preferences. New canons are lighthouses attracting the lonely survivors of prior intellectual wrecks and sinkings. To be sure, eventually a given canon may get powerful enough to dominate an island chain. But perhaps it is much more important to see the vastness of the ocean here than the politics of disciplinary defense and attack.

With respect to the theory of action, thinking in terms of excess provides a foundation for Eric Leifer's insight that skill means arranging your activity so that you never have to make a rational choice.[28] The problem with rational choice is that it is impossible, given the excess of information and the infinite

---

28. Leifer made this particular statement in the author's hearing at the Shaker Inn Conference in Enfield, New Hampshire, 18 August 1991. The argument, but not the pithy phrase itself, can be found in Leifer 1988.

excess of possible futures. Skill lies in keeping open many possibilities and options, indeed in retaining an excess of possibilities. And Padgett and Ansell's (1993) "robust action" is precisely a definition of power in terms of the creative retention of excessive possibilities of action. To decide is to concede one's freedom, to lose possibility.

One can even rethink poverty in excess terms. Broughton's study of women in a welfare-to-work program (2001:107–24) shows clearly that one of the central problems of poverty is the large cognitive burden it creates. Just to get to the program's classes, women had to make complex arrangements to ensure care for their children, to change doctors' appointments, to hide their valuables from predacious boyfriends, and so on. To be sure, they didn't have to have middle-class knowledge—of mortgages, for example. But the things they did need to know were not things with long-run future payoffs, like mortgages. On the contrary, the things they needed to know were things without long-run payoff, precisely because there would be intensive and continuous change in them: bus schedules, mothers' health problems, boyfriends' whereabouts. Indeed, one of the signs of impoverishment is precisely the move from long-run knowledge, with its continuous payoffs and lower cognitive load, to short-run knowledge that will be worthless or wrong after a brief interval. To take an example higher in the social pyramid, the status of scholars is being rapidly reduced because the continuous (and unnecessary) "improvement" in digital research tools forces them to learn new library tools all the time, just like the poor people who have to learn new bus routes, bureaucratic practices, and so on. The ability to lower your excess cognitive load by blocking needless change is a sign of privilege—in this case, one that scholars have lost.

These examples show that once we have recast social theory onto the basis of problematic excess rather than problematic scarcity, we find many new angles on old problems. A problematic of excess is not only a feasible foundation for social theory, but probably a very rich one as well. It is well worth exploring.

* Part 3 *

The next two chapters address one of the central questions of process: what is its result? Our usual answers to this question have been formulaic. Disciplines have conventions about the nature and timing of the dependent variables by which they capture outcome, and there is very little reflection about why we have chosen the particular forms and timings of "outcome" that we have in fact chosen. One thing, however, is clear. Most of the time when we think about outcome, we are concerned with whether it is good or bad. Predicting outcome is always important, to be sure. But what we care about is not the specific accuracy of prediction, but the moral quality of the actual result.

That is, thinking about results or ends inevitably involves us in matters of value and, in fact, of morals. Take the case of individual outcome, the topic of chapter 6. It turns out that sociologists think about outcome by considering the value of an independent variable at the end of some time interval, while economists evaluate the value of future time from its beginning (in the present), using the method of discounting to pull all future value back into the present as "total net present value." These concepts have radically different implications for both welfare and action. Under any appreciable discount rate, the economists' approach recommends that we ignore distant returns and enjoy ourselves in the present, while the sociologists' approach urges us to husband our resources now against the unknown dangers of an uncertain future. This is a purely normative choice, and one that very much influences how we interpret any research just as, indeed, it would influence how we live. Such differing outcome conceptions can also give quite different results in examining topics like inequality, for example.

With these two chapters on results, then, we turn towards the value-laden quality of the social process, and we begin to make that value-laden character central to our inquiry. Chapter 6 asks about individual outcome—mindful, as it must be, of the fact that individual outcome is always only temporary, a way station to a final outcome about which there is no doubt. Chapter 7 asks the equivalent question about social entities: the question not of outcome, but of "order," the state of a social system at a given time. Unlike individuals, social entities do not necessarily die, so the question of order has a quite different shape than that of outcome.

Taken together, these two chapters establish the general groundwork for an understanding of the role of values in the social process. And they do so in explicitly moral categories, for there can be no doubt that both "outcome" and "order" are thoroughly normative concepts.

Both chapters retain their original rhetorical forms, which have some complexities and so are usefully reviewed here. After a brief opening, chapter 6 employs the same opening as chapter 4: a detailed analysis of a particular case. The case is the concept of outcome within the work of a single well-known scholar, Paul Lazarsfeld. In the second section, concepts developed in this first analysis are applied more broadly to other exemplary work and further clarified. A third section then contrasts the various sociological outcome measures so far discovered with the outcome concepts of economics. The "two temporalities" argument of chapter 4 again proves useful in clarifying some of the ensuing difficulties. The chapter then turns to a long catalog of possible outcome concepts: point in time concepts; social and individual concepts; tensed versus untensed concepts; momentary, retrospective, and prospective concepts. The chapter does not come to any decision about a correct measure of outcome—indeed, it argues that such a choice is always an open, normative one. But it shows that the range of possibilities is wide.

Chapter 7 begins with a recapitulation of the complexities of outcome at various levels and of notions of social order and control. It then recasts the contractarians' "problem of social order" in the broader ontological framework of processualism. Like chapter 6, it gradually develops a set of categories for the evaluation of order concepts: substantive content, distribution of order in time, handling of social interweaving, relation of society and individual. With these categories in hand, it finally evaluates a broad list of order concepts: equilibrium concepts, equilibrium concepts under relaxed assumptions, empirical concepts, and normative concepts of order-in-process. Again, the aim of the chapter is not to come to any answer, but to survey the variety and conceptual diversity of the ways we can decide to think about social order. Both chapters 6 and 7 show that we are all moralists willy-nilly, and in ways we do not usually suspect. In the cases of outcome and order as in so many others, there is no value-free sociology. The social process is always a process of values.

CHAPTER 6

The Idea of Outcome[1]

Early in the movie *Saturday Night Fever*, Tony Manero (John Travolta) asks his hardware-store boss Mr. Fusco (Sam J. Copolla) for a pay advance with which to buy a pretty new shirt for Saturday night. Fusco refuses, saying Tony should plan for the future. "Fuck the future!!" says Tony. "No, Tony, you can't fuck the future," says Mr. Fusco. "The future fucks you."[2]

The issue between Tony and Fusco is the issue of now and later, of present and future, of moment and outcome. The plot of the movie, translated into simple economese, is that with the help of the marginally more rational

---

1. A version of the first part of this chapter was written at Peter Bearman's invitation for the Paul Lazarsfeld Centennial Conference held at Columbia University, 29 September 2001. Difficulties with air travel prevented my attendance. Bearman read the paper, and I received some comments afterward. I would like to thank not only that audience, but also audiences at Yale, Princeton, Michigan, Oxford, and Northwestern for comments on this chapter, as well as Michael Hout, David Meltzer, Ray Fitzpatrick, and Avner Offer for individual comments. Erin York gave research assistance. The paper was turned down by both *American Sociological Review* and *Social Forces*, and of course could not be submitted to the *American Journal of Sociology*, which I edit. It eventually appeared in 2005 as "The Idea of Outcome in U.S. Sociology," pp. 393–426 in *The Politics of Method in the Human Sciences*, edited by George Steinmetz. I have removed part of the second section of that version, and have edited the rest considerably. I dedicated the original version to the memory of my friend and colleague, the many-gifted Roger Gould, who died of a virulent leukemia at about the time I wrote it. Ironically, I didn't know that this careful reflection about outcome would all too soon prove useful in facing my own encounter with cancer.

2. The screenplay is Wexler 1977.

Stephanie Mangano (Karen Gurney), Tony becomes a little less of a hyperbolic discounter; he starts to take the distant future a little more seriously.

But he does not choose Fusco's outcome. Later in the movie, Fusco fires Tony over an irregular day off, but then rehires him, saying, "You've got a future here. Look at Harold [he points], with me eighteen years; [points again] Mike, fifteen years." The camera pans in on Mike—presented as a colorless, becalmed middle-aged man—and then back to Tony's look of panic. That's not a future Tony wants. His ultimate choice is a more open, undefined future, which begins with moving to Manhattan and thinking of Stephanie not merely as a sexual event but also as a friend. At the movie's end, he is still a young man in process.

The debate between Fusco and Tony captures something important about how we conceive our research. In the last analysis, much of sociology is about the ways things turn out. The typical dependent variable, both today and for many years past, is a result, an outcome, a Fusco thing. In Frank Kermode's phrase, sociology has "the sense of an ending."

Economists, by contrast, often seem to write about things without ends. "The balance of payments," "unemployment," "securities prices": these are things that fluctuate endlessly. There is no outcome, no final result. Rather, there is a loose equilibrium level (or possibly a steady trend) over the long run and various perturbations—sometimes quite large—around it in the short run.

That much of sociology is about ends rather than middles should not surprise us, because so much of sociology is about individuals: their social status, income, wealth, education, occupation, and so on—all the things Mr. Fusco has in mind. And, unlike balances of payments and unemployment, individuals do not go on fluctuating forever. There is only one true outcome variable for individuals, and it has no variance.[3] In a way, that's what Tony is saying; as he puts it shortly after the first exchange quoted above, "Tonight's the future, and I'm planning for it." For him, beyond tonight is death, either the actual death of his foolish friend Bobby, falling off the Verrazano Narrows Bridge, or the living death of middle-aged Mike in the hardware store. Those of us with flatter discount curves know that death is not so soon. There are many human variables with outcomes short-term enough to resemble continuously varying economic variables like unemployment: consumption patterns, dating habits,

---

3. The standard response to this bleak statement is of course to study the variation in the time till that outcome arrives. The full form of Keynes's famous epigram from the *Tract on Monetary Reform* is: "But this *long run* is a misleading guide to current affairs. *In the long run* we are all dead" (Keynes 1923:80, emphasis in the original). Note the strong presumption of discounting the future.

and so on. But the major foci of sociologists are not like that. They are bigger things, consequential outcomes like socioeconomic status, marriage duration, and education. And their consequence lies precisely in their irrevocability; we get only one or two chances.

In this chapter I analyze the concept of outcome. I shall begin by tracing the sociological concept of outcome, first as we find it in the midcentury corpus of one of sociology's founding methodologists, Paul Lazarsfeld. The second section broadens this discussion to some exemplary later work in sociology. A third section then contrasts this sociological approach with concepts of outcome in economics, turning to philosophical arguments to clarify those differences. The fourth and longest section then provides a catalogue of possible conceptions of outcome, organizing them along the theoretical dimensions that have emerged in the preceding discussions.

My conclusion is brief, for the chapter does not come to a final decision about the "right" concept of outcome. It concludes that there is no true, objective concept. Our choices of outcome concepts are irrevocably value-laden whether we follow convention or flout it. What we must do is choose our values consciously.

IDEAS OF OUTCOME IN PAUL LAZARSFELD

I would like first to consider the notion of outcome in several important works of Paul Lazarsfeld. This reflection will introduce my broader inquiry into the way we think about processes and their results in social science.

I begin with Lazarsfeld's much reprinted paper "The Analysis of Consumer Action" (coauthored with William Kornhauser), which lays out his analysis of purchase, for him the very prototype of human activity. An individual, Lazarsfeld argues, is subject to many influences. The process of purchase begins when one of these turns him into "a new person," one with "a favorable feeling toward Y make of car or a belief that X dentifrice will protect his teeth." After some weeks, "this changed person hears a friend comment enthusiastically about the product." This creates yet another person, who now "yields to a leisurely thought-encouraging situation, where he deliberates about the new car or the dentifrice and definitely decides to buy. . . ." But only when he finds himself "in a situation containing the precipitating influence to induce the purchase," does he finally succumb and buy the good.[4]

---

4. All quotes are from Kornhauser and Lazarsfeld 1955:397. This framework for action is surprisingly like the language Bergson uses to discuss choice, in which we have "not two

Lazarsfeld underscores the order of events, insisting on a strongly ordered list of experiences that culminates in purchase. Later in the paper he lists all the phenomena on this list in the case of "the simple matter of soap-buying." First, there are three things that lie "far back on the time-line":

a) Why the consumer buys soap at all
b) Why she likes soap of a particular color odor, hardness, etc.
c) Why she believes all soaps are equally good

And then there are seven things "somewhat nearer the purchase and more concrete":

d) Why she buys soap of the X-type and price
e) Why she buys X-soap specifically
f) Why she buys one cake instead of several
g) Why she buys at this particular time
h) Why she buys at this particular place
i) Why she buys as she does now (this month or this year) as contrasted with other months or years
j) Why *she* buys (i.e., why this kind of person does the family buying rather than others)
(Kornhauser and Lazarsfeld 1955:398)

Outcome here is a simple action: buying soap. The analysis follows what I have called "the ancestors plot" (*Time Matters*, pp. 144, 291), in which analysis means seeking all the (causal) ancestors of a particular event. Product choice is an outcome that lies at the current end of a long, backwards-proliferating net of causes. Its own consequences are not considered, nor is it embedded as one small part of some larger web of events. Only those parts of the larger web are relevant that affect this particular choice to buy.

This model might be expected to undergird Lazarsfeld's later studies of voting. Yet the reader of *Voting* (1954) will be astonished to discover that Bereleson, Lazarsfeld, and McPhee almost nowhere discuss the outcome of the election they studied, even though the 1948 election was and is by universal consent an extraordinary one. This lack of attention is strikingly evident in

---

tendencies, or even two directions, but a self which lives and develops by means of its very hesitations, until the free action drops from it like an over-ripe fruit" (Bergson 1910:176). See the discussion of Bergson in *Time Matters*, ch. 7.

the celebrated sixteenfold table (SFT) with which the authors seek to un-tangle the relationship between saliency of class issues and attitudes towards Truman. The SFT is essentially a two-period transition matrix for a standard fourfold crosstab of these two dichotomous variables. If we treat it as a regular Markov chain and square it until it converges, it predicts a swing to Truman invisible in either the before or the after marginals of the transition matrix, both of which have Truman's favorable rating at 54 percent. The limiting value of 68 percent indicates precisely the Truman swing that happened in fact, and so the SFT seems to a current reader like a secret weapon for pre-dicting electoral outcome.[5]

But Lazarsfeld ignored this implication about electoral outcome, insisting that reflection about particular transitions in this matrix would decide whether salience of class issues drove image of Truman or the other way around. So the book disattends to the "big outcome" and focuses its attention on the local shifting around, on the process. Indeed, its major theme is that the rela-tive stability of aggregate election figures over time conceals a good deal of wavering and change, and that this wavering is quite concentrated in a small part of the voting population. To be sure, this in turn means that a relatively small group of voters determines the "big" outcome of the election by means of the "little" outcomes of their processes of decision. But even despite this turn toward a more "final outcome" view of the election, the conclusions of the book emphasize the system's enormous long-run stability, arguing (315ff) that today's "long-term precommitted voters" on each side derive from the controversies of another era, and hence that "The vote is a kind of 'moving average' of reactions to the political past" (316). It is the millions of minor motions—the little processes of action and change and aging—that produce the aggregate stability.[6]

The Berelson and Lazarsfeld approach to elections differs considerably from that of their great competitors in election studies, the Michigan group led by Angus Campbell and others at the Institute for Survey Research (ISR). In their monumental *The American Voter*, which reports detailed compari-

5. Lazarsfeld was involved in two major voting studies: *The People's Choice* (Lazarsfeld and Gaudet 1948) and *Voting* (Berelson, Lazarsfeld, and McPhee 1954). I focus on the latter, which is the more fully developed. The SFT appears on p. 265 of that work.

6. It is clear, however, that Lazarsfeld believed that there were causally dominant factors (e.g., salience of class issues) that played a more important part in those processes than did other factors. These causal forces somehow pervaded the recurring, endless processes that fas-cinated him. In that sense, his disattention to outcome took him in the same direction in which other sociological methodologists were going (towards causality), but by a different path.

sons of the 1952 and 1956 elections, the Campbell group set forth a "funnel of causality" model for voting. The funnel model looks very much like the Kornhauser/Lazarsfeld purchase model, with the vote taking the place of purchase.

The funnel shape is a logical product of the explanatory task chosen. Most of the complex events in the funnel occur as a result of multiple prior causes. Each such event is, in its turn, responsible for multiple effects as well, but our focus of interest narrows as we approach the dependent behavior. We progressively eliminate those effects that do not continue to have relevance for the political act (Campbell et al. 1980:24).

Thus, while they are aware of "other effects"—the other grandchildren of the vote's causal grandparents—Campbell et al. explicitly set them aside as irrelevant. Nor do they seriously consider the election as a mere moment in the ongoing political life of the nation. Everything funnels into a particular moment of supreme importance, a particular election day, a final outcome.

Moreover, the funnel model embeds itself not in the real social process, but in what we might call "causal time." For despite the notion of a funnel channeling voters toward particular votes, the Michigan group did only one set of interviews before the election, whereas the Berelson-Lazarsfeld team had done four. In the thinking of the Michigan school, there was no real-time progress of individuals through the various moments of the campaign to the vote, but rather there was a causal structure starting with "big background factors" that set the stage, within which "smaller factors" then made minor adjustments.[7]

The contrast between the Lazarsfeld and the ISR approaches emphasizes

7. The book's exposition actually proceeds backwards in causal time, from "proximate" factors to "larger background" ones. It begins with "immediate psychological influences on the voting act" (e.g., popular perceptions of national politics, and individual sense of political commitment and efficacy). It then seeks "the roots of [these] proximal attitudes in either of two directions, moving deeper in time past or outward from the political core of the funnel" (118). Here the authors consider party attachment, issues and issue aggregation, and electoral laws and systems. Finally, the book turns to the social and economic origins of all these "more general" political factors: group memberships and their effects, class and its effect, SES effects, regional and sectoral effects, and so on. It is an easy and instructive exercise to create a narrative that rearranges this causal order, making the enduring political beliefs of individuals into a background that shapes party behavior, which then determines political structures and, thereby, the structure of SES and group membership. Note the similarity of this approach to Snook's analysis of the friendly fire shootdown in chapter 4.

Lazarsfeld's ambiguity on the outcome issue. While his work drifted at times towards a "funnel of causality" approach, he retained a fascination for turnover and process in themselves, a fascination for the mere flow of variables through time. Much more than the ISR group, Lazarsfeld saw an election as one sample in an ongoing sequence of samples that makes up the political life of the nation, and even that one sample as contaminated by long-gone issues and questions: "The people vote *in* the same election, but not all of them vote *on* it."[8]

Let me turn now to a third major Lazarsfeld work, *Personal Influence*, in which was reported the structure of personal influence in four issue areas (shopping, films, fashion, and public affairs) among eight hundred women in Decatur, Illinois.[9] Put simply, there is no outcome whatsoever in *Personal Influence*. There is nothing like the election: no concern with which appliance got bought, which movie was watched, which hairdo chosen, or which political view espoused. There is simply flow of influence itself: the network and nothing but the network. Katz and Lazarsfeld are quite explicit in positioning their argument against the emerging Michigan survey tradition:

> No longer can mass media research be content with a random sample of disconnected individuals as respondents. Respondents must be studied within the context of the group or groups to which they belong or which they have "in mind"—thus which may influence them—in their formation of opinions, attitudes, or decisions . . . (Katz and Lazarsfeld 1955:131).

8. The quote is at Berelson et al. 1954:316. The emphases are in the original. (We have seen this quote before, in chapter 1's examination of the historicality of individuals, which deals with some of the same issues.) To be sure, the Michiganders also saw this problem. Indeed, *The American Voter* was an attempt to move beyond the narrowly attitudinal conception of elections used by the first ISR report (on the 1952 election), *The Voter Decides*. But the "move beyond" was made by envisioning a broader causal structure, not by moving towards a study of attribute transition within individuals in real time.

9. The actual extent of Lazarsfeld's own contributions in his various books is unclear, although he was always careful to provide acknowledgements off the title page. Substantial parts of *Voting* were originally drafted by John Dean and Edward Suchman. Other parts began as dissertations, and Berelson attributed substantial portions of the ideas in chapter 14 to Edward Shils. The entire text of *Personal Influence* appears to have been drafted in three sections by (respectively) David Gleicher, Peter Rossi, and Leo Srole (see Katz and Lazarsfeld 1955:xiii). Given this corporate mode of production, one is reluctant to attribute ideas directly to Lazarsfeld. But for my purposes I assume him to be the presiding genius of this work, and attribute ideas to him on that basis.

The book thus focuses on flow itself. In retrospect, of course, this gives it what now seems an excessively "equilibrium" feel, in which it is taken for granted that there is a structure through which influence flows, and it is not expected that that structure will be recursive in any fashion—either self-activating, as networks would become in the social movements literature, or self-perpetuating, as they would be in the interlocking directorate literature. Networks are simply the medium through which social life flows.

In a sense, then, *Personal Influence* carries to its natural extreme the view of outcome implicit in *Voting*. Society is viewed as a more or less steady-state process, throwing off multitudes of temporary outcomes. There is no grand narrative with a final result, no smiling Harry Truman holding up the *Chicago Daily Tribune* with its "Dewey defeats Truman" headline. Rather, the book is almost completely descriptive.[10]

We see, then, that in much of Lazarsfeld's work there is a tendency to ignore final outcome or to treat it as something of little importance. Lazarsfeld saw outcome as something waving now this way, now that—a repeated and endless cycling around some value that never reached a decisive final result. By contrast, in *The American Voter* we have an analysis with clear outcomes, a type of analysis that became paradigmatic in sociology thereafter.

BEYOND LAZARSFELDIAN OUTCOME

The same division has characterized sociology since, although most of the discipline has followed the "final outcome" paradigm of the Michigan school. It is useful to examine some later examples.

Consider Blau and Duncan's justly celebrated *American Occupational Structure*. This book is the very paradigm of a "final outcome" study. Prestige of respondent's occupation in 1962 is the final point. To be sure, a variety of elegant models focus in on this variable; we are far from the simple funnel of causality. But like *The American Voter*, *The American Occupational Structure* comes to a sharp and final outcome. A stratification narrative is assumed in

---

10. Katz and Lazarsfeld defined themselves not only by contrast with emerging survey research, but also by contrast with the mass/disorganization view of public opinion, according to which the sudden expansion of media was creating a "global village." They traced this argument to Cooley's *Social Organization*, (Katz and Lazarsfeld 1955:16n1) and thought Louis Wirth and Herbert Blumer its current exponents. Ironically, then, the Columbia sociologists of the empirical tradition were arguing for location and grounding of social facts against two Chicago writers often thought to stand for precisely that location and grounding. (On the concept of location in the Chicago tradition, see *Department and Discipline*, ch. 7).

each life and is realized in the analysis by a path model, the same for every respondent. By contrast, when Berelson et al. mentioned path models in *Voting*, they were seen as models for long-term stabilities (and that was indeed the use to which they were generally put in economics). That is, they weren't models of ends, but of middles. But in Blau and Duncan they become metaphors for simple narrative; the funnel of causes was fashioned into the formal arrows of path analysis, shooting in towards the bull's-eye of occupation in 1962. Duncan himself tried to bring history back in by means of a synthetic cohort analysis, but the literature has taken from the book mainly its final outcome approach.[11]

It might seem that such a concept of "outcome-at-a-point" is confined to quantitative work. For it is a logical concomitant of a regression-based methodological framework. Yet the same view can easily be observed in the revolutions and social movements literatures, both known for their strong reliance on comparative and historical methods.

For example, Skocpol's classic book on social revolutions (1979) opens with two ringing questions: "How then are social revolutions to be explained? Where are we to turn for fruitful modes of analyzing their causes and differences?" (1979:5). Skocpol organizes her argument around comparisons of successful and unsuccessful social revolutions and their various qualities. The French, Russian, and Chinese revolutions preoccupy the book because they are successful revolutions; they made "fundamental and enduring structural transformations" (161). But the major outcome of interest—certainly in terms of the later literature—was not so much these transformations (that is, the further consequences of revolutions), but the success (or failure) of those revolutions themselves. When, the book asks, do revolutions succeed? Skocpol's book is of course filled with thoughtful historical argument and processual thinking. But its conception of outcome is closer to final outcome—outcome-at-a-point—than to Lazarsfeldian endless process. We see the same approach in work on social movements more generally. Much work on social movements

---

11. Interestingly, Berelson et al. cite Tinbergen—an economist modeling business cycles—as their source for path models (Berelson et al. 1954:281). Tinbergen had reinvented path analysis in the 1930s, not knowing about its prior invention by Sewall Wright in the early 1920s. Mike Hout has rightly pointed out to me that Duncan was in some senses more of an "historian" than was Lazarsfeld, having insisted that parameters would change as continuously as marginals. But I am here emphasizing not the actuality of Duncan's work, but the reading of it that became standard among his descendants, many of whom, after all, he eventually repudiated (in Duncan 1984).

in the 1970s reacted to and elaborated Gamson's (1975) study of the bases of successful movements that is, the bases of a certain kind of final outcome.

Yet the outcome-based social movements literature eventually produced a much more elaborated story of social movement formation and development by interpolating into the story of social movements such matters as political opportunity, authorities' response, and movement framing. This kind of narrative elaboration of a conception originally rooted in final outcomes has occurred throughout sociology. For example, the literature on stress evolved from a simple account of "what leads to stress" in the 1960s and 1970s to a more complex account of coping, social support, and the like in the 1980s. Yet in both literatures an implicit focus on final outcome (social movement success in the one case, stress in the other) remained in later literature, even though the complexities inherent in real social systems had led to an examination of intermediate outcomes or "stages." In the social movements literature, for example, interest gradually moved from successful final result to intermediate "successes" like increase of movement membership, securing of financial resources, and professionalization of movement personnel. But these were still seen as outcomes, even if now embedded as steps in a longer process moving towards a "larger" final result. There was thus a move from outcome-at-a-point towards a more flowing conception of intermediate, contingent point-outcomes. Yet it remains true that every concept of "social movement" inevitably involves the whiff of teleology; movements are still conceived to be trying to go somewhere, and in some sense are believed to stop when they get there.[12]

Final outcome conceptions remain strongest in the empirical mainstream. A quick scan of any recent journal reveals that the plurality or even a majority of articles in mainstream sociology look at individual level outcomes-at-a-point. When "larger trends" are analyzed, these are often decomposed into aggregates of such individual outcomes-at-a-point, inspected at successive points in time. But occasionally there are papers that—implicitly, at least—take a more Lazarsfeldian view, considering waves of successive outcomes.

For example, Paxton (2002) takes a processual view of the rise of democracy in countries. At the heart of the model (a reciprocal causation design) are two properties of countries: level of democracy (an interval measure) and level of associational life (here measured by numbers of international non-governmental organizations with an office in the country). Each dependent

---

12. On the stress literature, see Abbott 1990. The inevitably teleological qualities of narrative are discussed extensively in chapter 4.

variable is hypothesized to determine the lagged values both of itself and of the other. There are the usual exogenous variables in addition to these two endogenous ones—energy use, world system status, school enrollment rates, ethnic homogeneity, and so on. There are four time points, and hence three change equations are estimated.

The model thus takes an implicitly Markovian view of process; where a case goes next is a function of where it is now. From classical Markov theory, we know that such a design has a final outcome only in two cases. Final outcome can occur because the process has an "absorption state(s)," which, once entered, cannot be left. Second, if the stage-to-stage parameters never change, the process will have a final outcome in that the percentages of cases in the varying states will become stable. If neither of these two conditions holds, the (implicit) process will simply wander around according to the time-varying transition rules.

In such a design, then, we don't really have an outcome. We have rather, in the Lazarsfeldian sense, a process continuously generating new results. To be sure, the theoretical framing of the article implicitly takes democracy as a terminal, absorbing state. But the analysis does not in fact address the possibility of that absorption, rather thinking about each disaggregated step towards it in the traditional outcome-at-a-point framework. (Just so did Lazarsfeld bypass the transition-matrix character of his sixteenfold table.) With respect to long-term outcome, note also that rather than thinking about ultimate democratization (the paper's implicit long-run dependent variable—which is clearly hoped by the author to be an absorption state), one could in principle take as a dependent variable the percentage of time a country spends in a democratized state. Particularly if the parameters of the process change steadily, there is no reason to expect convergence and so the historical percentage of time spent by various cases in various democratic or nondemocratic states could be of far more interest than their "ultimate" status at some given point.[13]

---

13. The technically inclined will note that I have slipped into a discrete language for an article whose endogenous variables are continuous, although this is not a problem at so high a level of abstraction. Markov chains provide a useful formal way of thinking about the difference between "final outcomes" and "interim outcomes," both as facts and as frameworks for thinking about the world. In regular Markov chains, we envision interim outcomes. If the chain is irreducible, every state will be visited at some point, and indeed will be visited an infinite number of times, although the proportions of time spent in various states are determined by the transition probabilities and estimated by the row proportions of the multiplicative limit of the transition matrix. There are no final outcomes. In absorbing Markov chains, there is a final outcome or outcomes, and we are interested in the periods of time spent in various states

It is useful to pull together the various theoretical distinctions made among conceptions of outcome so far. The analysis of Lazarsfeld produced a contrast between imagining the social process to be a continuous sequence of interim results and imagining the social process to be a discontinuous sequence of final results. In literature since, it is common to move from the latter view towards the former by interpolating interim final results, but still to avoid the fully continuous concept of a social process with only interim outcomes. Note that the contrast between interim or process outcome and final (irrevocable) outcome is similar to that between short-term outcome and long-term outcome, but not quite identical. We usually think that interim outcomes involve short-term changes (however temporarily large they may be) within long-run stability, whereas irrevocable outcomes entail long-run changes that emerge from short-run instability. But there seems in fact to be a long and a short run for both types of outcome.

Mixed up in these distinctions is another, that of the social and the individual. Often we conceive of changing "final outcomes" at the individual level that produce processes of "interim outcomes" at the social one. Whether or not the social-level phenomenon is considered emergent, its outcome characteristics need not be the same as those of the individual processes coeval with it. It is easy to conflate the two levels.

Finally, recall that what I have called interim or process outcomes are long-run stabilities established by myriads of individual events: things like the particular unemployment episodes and voter transitions mentioned earlier. But these kinds of minor local outcomes do not necessarily lead to long-run stability. In between final point-outcomes and truly equilibristic outcomes lies a kind of outcome of which I have said little, but which is in fact implicit in many sociological articles. This is what I shall call "trend outcome." A trend conception of outcome is common for variables, like housing inequality and returns to education, for which the analyst does not expect a final outcome or an equilibrium of endless middles, but something in between, a steady movement in some direction.

---

before getting there. These will be a function partly of transitions between transient states (the interstate probabilities that would completely determine a regular chain), but also, to a critical degree, of the transition probabilities into the absorbing state or states. People who envision the world in terms of final outcome must focus on these, the probabilities of irrevocable change. In the current example, note that there is no particular mechanism explaining why the state of "democracy" should be absorbing, and there exist many empirical examples of departure from it.

Much of sociology today is concerned with trend outcomes, typically trends in inequality measures, as we shall see in chapter 8. Analysts usually don't worry much about a final outcome for variables like housing inequality or occupational segregation, but neither do they expect stable equilibria over time. In the main, they take a trend towards equality as "expected," obviously on a normative basis rather than an empirical one. As the late Bruce Mayhew (1990) found out from the incomprehending reception of his "baseline models for human inequality," most sociologists think persistent inequality and even the halting of trends towards equality are things to be explained. Trend outcomes are therefore centrally important in sociology today.

In summary, sociologists seem to have three broad conceptions of outcome: process (or interim or equilibristic) outcome, trend outcome, and point outcome. We consider these at the individual or the social level, and sometimes at both. We examine them over varying periods, from short to medium to long-term.

DISCOUNTING AND DECISION

Despite these internal variations, sociology's modal tradition studies final point outcomes, the results of an examined process at its end. We can contextualize this view of outcome by comparing it to the radically different conception of outcome that is common in economics. Economists also evaluate trajectories of value by referring to a single point in time. But for them, this is not the moment of final outcome, but the moment of decision. And unlike outcome, decision concerns not the past but the future; economists look ahead to potential rewards, not back to sunk costs. Note that this is precisely the reverse of the sociological ancestors plot, which looks back at the causes funneling into a final result. Economists focus not on the end of a period, but on its beginning; they study not the origins of an outcome, but the descendants of a decision. Economists accomplish this forward-looking trick by discounting potential future results, weighting them by their probability and bringing them back from the future into a single summation defined at a moment, the present.

This idea of discounting rests on the notion that all other things being equal, it is better to have a given amount now than at some moment in the future. There are two chief philosophical justifications for this belief. The first is that money in hand now can be invested to grow in the time between now and that future moment. Note that this "investment" justification for discounting naturally entails the view that we should discount using a negative exponential function, because of the implicit connection between discounting and investment at continuously compounded interest.[14] By contrast, the second major justification for discounting is precisely that uncertainties between the present and any future moment may reduce the value of future rewards. Our tastes may change, our health or even life may be lost, or a hundred contingencies may intervene before a future reward is enjoyed. Hence, that future reward is worth less to us at present than a certain reward of equivalent value that we can enjoy immediately. Note the assumption, in each of the two major justifications of discounting, that the decider is a finite individual rather than a social structure with a temporal duration of many human lifetimes. As we have already seen, social and individual outcome can be completely decoupled.[15]

The discounting approach to outcome is well illustrated by cost-effectiveness analysis of health outcomes. Rooted in 1960s business-school-based decision theory, this literature began with applications to clinical decision making and later moved into the allocation of scarce medical resources. By the mid-1970s it had converged on the concept of "quality-adjusted life years" (QALYs, in the standard abbreviation). QALYs rest on a formal estimation procedure that begins with ratings of the health-related quality of life (HRQL) for various disease states. Then, in standard decision analysis style, the various possible medical trajectories are arranged as a sequential tree of decisions, events, and contingencies (each with an associated probability).

14. Note that although the investment argument justifies our discounting now the value of resources in the future, it in fact judges the worth of an investment trajectory on the basis of its future outcome; the reason for wanting to invest now is to be better off later. To that extent discounting is still concerned with a final point outcome. For an extremely interesting discussion of discounting, see the splendid book of Colin Price (1993).

15. Both of these justifications of discounting are in fact more empirical than philosophical. That present resources can be invested to yield future profits (in some finite time) is not always true, and in any case the negative exponential justification presupposes continuous reinvestment of revenues, which is often impossible either in practice or in principle. As for time preference, the evidence is strong that individual time preferences are not exponential but hyperbolic, with more rapid value loss than the exponential early in the future, and slower value loss later. Studies of intertemporal choice are legion, going back to the celebrated prospect theory of Kahnemann and Tversky (1979). Probably the most comprehensive current writer on hyperbolic discounting is Ainslie (1992, 2001). Economists have considered a variety of interesting outcome problems, such as how current consumption decisions make the actor into a different person when he later enjoys the chosen utilities, and what happens when actors are no longer around to enjoy chosen future (social) utilities or disutilities. A few economists have turned to the question of evaluating whole sequences of consumption. It should be no surprise that the preferred sequence is one of gradual increase. (Loewenstein and Prelec 1991, 1992).

HRQLs are associated with each length of branch. Cost-effectiveness analysis consists of back-calculating along each branch from the leaves (death) to the original trunk, weighting HRQLs by their duration and likelihood, given the sequential probabilities of the eventualities producing them. This results in a sum of QALYs for each possible trajectory. Decision then proceeds by dividing the incremental cost of one intervention (more generally, one branch or trajectory) over another (or over no intervention) by the incremental total QALYs of that intervention (branch or trajectory) over the other (or no intervention.)[16]

At its outset, the health decision literature discounted only costs. There was doubt about discounting benefits, because it seemed worrisome "to assume that life years in the future are less valuable than life years today in any absolute utilitarian sense." Discounting future benefits was eventually urged on pure measurement grounds, however, since dollars were the instrument of measurement in cost-effectiveness analysis, and it was felt that anything measured in dollars must be discounted since dollars themselves are discounted. Today, the literature uniformly insists on discounting the benefits as well as the costs. Both are done at the same rate, which is typically 3 percent in American studies and 5 percent elsewhere.[17]

16. Cost-effectiveness analysis of health outcomes was standardized in the monumental Gold et al. 1996. On earlier decision theory, see Raiffa 1968. On clinical decision making, see Lusted 1968 and Weinstein and Feinberg 1980. On the debate about health related quality of life (HRQL), see Fitzpatrick 1996 and Nord 1999: ch. 2.

17. The quote is from Weinstein and Fineberg 1980:254. For the 3 and 5 percent discounting rates, see Muennig 2002:151. A 3 percent discount gives a net present value of about 75 percent at ten years, and about 54 percent at twenty. A 5 percent discount gives 61 percent at ten years, and 37 percent at twenty. Obviously, such discount rates ensure that governments are unwilling to invest much in long-term prevention of chronic diseases with late onset, a fact that has fed an intense political debate about fairness. For a discussion, see Tsuchiya 2000. QALYs have also been used for simple inequality measures; see Gerdtham and Johannesson 2000. Another important empirical discounting literature in social science is that on lifetime earnings. Here, too, early controversies about discounting seem to have settled into later conventions. Creedy's classic paper (1977) points out that variation in earnings profiles over the life cycle mean that differing discounting rates can produce differing rank orders of occupations in terms of lifetime earnings. But later literature (e.g., Dolton et al. 1989, Makepeace 1996, Johnson and Makepeace 1997) has usually assumed standard discounting. In an extremely cautious review, Creedy (1990) warns that any extending of the accounting period for earnings beyond instantaneous measure raises nearly insurmountable estimation difficulties. As a result, some work in this literature does not formally discount. For example Bosworth et al. (2002), working with American Social Security data, simply divide all wages by the average wage for the year, which

In summary, the economic view of temporal trajectories thus differs considerably from the sociological one. The usual view in sociology is to think of final outcome, the state of the trajectory at its end (in formal economic terms, the ordinate of utility at the end of the period). But economists do not think much about long run results, reduced as they are by discounting. The economic approach sees trajectories from the present forward. Economics lives in the now.[18]

Note that the now moves with time in a way that final outcome does not; the now gets steadily later as time passes. This dynamism implies a philosophical difference in conceptions of temporality. It turns out that philosophers have considered this difference extensively, in reaction to the famously controversial 1908 paper of J. M. E. McTaggart already mentioned in chapter 4 (note 26).

As we saw, McTaggart noted in that paper that there are two fundamentally different ways of thinking about time, which he called the A series and the B series. The A series involves thinking about time in terms of past, present, and future—thinking in terms of tense. The B series involves thinking about time simply as a transitive order relation, governed by the concepts "earlier than" and "later than." This is thinking in terms of dates. Thus, we might say that McTaggart wrote his paper 108 years ago, or we might say that McTaggart wrote in 1908. The first statement is indexical; we don't know what it means or whether it is true until we know when it was said. By contrast, the second statement is true no matter what.[19]

standardizes for temporal change without discounting. Economists seem more aware of the complexities of outcome conceptions than are sociologists; but, like the latter, they have settled into a fairly simple set of outcome conventions to avoid continuous debate.

18. For a forthright exposition of the "nowness" of economics, see the early chapters of Shackle 1960. Note that the sociological conception of outcome is implicitly like the Protestant one. The sociological aim of life—at least the aim that is implicit in books like Waite and Gallagher's (2000) *The Case for Marriage*—is to end up well. This is analogous to the Protestant aim to have lived righteously and to die ready to face a final tribunal that evaluates a whole life in order to send a soul to its eternally constant outcome. (Actually, as Weber and many others have pointed out, most Protestant theology doesn't recognize a quantitative final judgment.) Roman Catholicism, by contrast, focuses on dying in a "state of grace"; like the microeconomists, it focuses on the now—in this case, the "now" of death. I am grateful to Colm O'Muircheartaigh for pointing out this difference. Noting that by O'Muircheartaigh's argument, deathbed confession would ensure salvation for Catholics, Mike Hout ripostes that "planning a death-bed conversion would involve the sin of presumption." It is evident that religious traditions have given serious thought to conceptions of outcome.

19. McTaggart's paper set the problematic of the anglophone philosophy of time for the entire twentieth century. The continental tradition ignored it, preferring the phenomenologi-

The two series are not connected logically. They can be brought into alignment only empirically, with a statement of the form "2016 is now." But, given that they are logically distinct, it is quite difficult to sustain a coherent philosophy of time, a fact that led McTaggart to insist on the unreality of time itself.[20] But this philosophical worry is of less interest than is McTaggart's original distinction. Perhaps differences between the basic social scientific paradigms for appraising trajectories (i.e., paradigms for outcome broadly conceived) can best be understood in terms of McTaggart's different concepts of temporality: one tensed and emphasizing the passage of events from future into present into past, the other simply relative, emphasizing mere duration.

Microeconomics is a thoroughly A-series enterprise. It concerns the now, a tensed moment in which the future is guessable but uncertain, and the past known but unimportant. The now, this particular moment, is important because it is the present, in which we live and make choices. However, this present immediately becomes past. This fact was indeed the ground on which McTaggart found the A series incoherent; it assigns a property to events that changes, even though the events themselves do not change.

By contrast, mainstream empirical sociology is more or less a B-series enterprise. One reason why sociological ideas of outcome seem problematic is that most of the outcomes we study are not really endings at all, but arbitrary ends selected for some reason that is not very well understood. In Blau and Duncan, for example, why 1962? Why not 1960? Or 1963? The year 1962 is not a consequential moment, merely an arbitrary one. It simply happens to be

---

cal approach of Husserl and Heidegger, which I have ignored here. The McTaggart argument was restated, almost word for word, by the English heterodox economist G. L. S. Shackle, who does not seem to have been aware of McTaggart. "With this extended time seen from the outside by an extratemporal observer [i.e., the B series] we must contrast the time in which things happen to, and are perceived in their actuality by, an intratemporal observer, a living person in his act of living" (Shackle 1961:17). The distinction is also cognate with Bergson's time as duration (A series, in Bergson's view legitimate) versus time as extension (B series, in Bergson's view illegitimate). We have already encountered the issue of tenses in chapter 4's discussion of two types of tenses in European languages.

20. The details of this argument need not concern us here. Basically, once he has separated the two series, McTaggart shows that the B series cannot be a notion of time because it has no account of temporal direction, while the A series involves us in assigning to a single fact a property (futureness, presentness, pastness) that changes in a regular manner that we cannot specify without assuming the consequent: that time exists. (In McTaggart's proverbial example, [1908:460] the death of Queen Anne was the death of Queen Anne at the beginning of time and will be so at the end; its futureness has simply changed into pastness.) For a detailed modern exposition of the McTaggart position and its sequelae, see Mellor 1981.

the right-hand end of the period investigated. Men in Blau and Duncan's sample ranged from twenty to sixty-four years of age, and their fathers had been born as early as 1835 and as late as 1919. In dynamic, A-series terms, 1962 came at widely differing points in these men's lives. Yet all followed the same "narrative of variables"—from father's education and father's occupation to son's education and first job, to son's job in 1962, a standardization only partially escaped by Duncan's daring moves to cohort and synthetic cohort analysis.[21]

Mainstream sociology thus has a strong B-series character. It envisions a time line and slides a window of investigation along the line, cutting out a segment for investigation. Beginnings and endings are largely arbitrary, and separate time segments are surprisingly comparable (think again of Skocpol's three great revolutions—French, Russian, and Chinese—scaled into common, comparable trajectories). What gives this procedure its extraordinary rhetorical force is that once the temporal window of investigation is slid into a particular place, the familiar and powerful structure of narrative is implicitly invoked for the period involved. By the mere act of firmly defining a period of investigation, the period's beginning becomes a "real" beginning, its end a "real" end, and so on.[22]

It is difficult to analyze Lazarsfeld's process fascination in terms of the Mc-

21. On the ages of the senior generation, see Blau and Duncan 1967:83. Duncan would no doubt have justified his choice of 1962 by saying that there was no reason for 1962 other than convenience, but that the coefficients would probably be the same for any particular outcome moment, to a large degree. That sociologists' date periods are arbitrary is easily shown. A random sample of 1846 articles on the sociology of work listed in recent years of *Sociological Abstracts* (gathered for another paper) shows that about two-thirds of those with dates involve a decadal year at one end or the other. But of course there is no nonarbitrary reason why periods of investigation should start and finish with decadal years.

22. The outcome concept characteristic of most sociology thus draws its structure from the literary conventions of narrative (cf. *Time Matters*, ch. 2, 6, and chapter 4 of the present book). So we read in Aristotle:

Now a whole is that which has a beginning, middle, and end. A beginning is that which is not itself necessarily after anything else, and which has naturally something else after it; an end is that which is naturally after something itself, either as its necessary or usual consequent, and with nothing else after it; and a middle, that which is by nature after one thing and has also another after it. A well-constructed plot, therefore, cannot either begin or end at any point one likes; beginning and end in it must be of the forms just described
(Poetics 1450b26–33).

Taggart series. On the one hand, in B-series fashion Lazarsfeld's process work sought to look at an extended time interval, rather than privilege a particular now. But on the other hand, in A-series fashion it aimed to retain the "openness" of each moment in that extended interval, to insist on the moment's contingency. Lazarsfeld thus attempted to put McTaggart's Humpty-Dumpty back together again. Perhaps that is the task that faces us in developing new sociological conceptions of outcome.

EXISTING AND POSSIBLE CONCEPTS OF OUTCOME

With the concepts of tensed and untensed temporality in hand, we can review comprehensively the distinctions about outcome developed so far. Such a review shows how we have chosen different kinds of outcome conceptions for different kinds of questions, and forces us to ask how we might appraise outcomes differently. This is not an idle question, for, as I shall argue, our choices of outcome measurement are not innocent. Indeed, it is surprising that they cause so little conflict, given how value-laden they are.[23]

Location in Time: Point and Period Outcome

The first set of distinctions I have made has to do with the relation of outcome to the time interval studied. Imagine some raw measure of utility or well-being as a real-valued function defined continuously through some time interval. We can first distinguish between outcome at a particular in-

---

Moreover, Aristotle earlier says: "[In Narrative] the end is everywhere the chief thing" (1450a23), and "[Narrative] is an imitation of an action that is complete in itself" (1450b23–4). These passages identify the concept of narrative with the concept of final outcome. The (Lazarsfeld) process position is that, pace Aristotle, there is in social reality no end "with nothing else after it." (At the individual level, there is of course death.) Note too that there is no body of sociological methodology based on beginnings. One can think about time series in the ARIMA format as being about middles, as one can think about the standard regression model as an ancestors plot focused on ends. But there is surprisingly little thinking in terms of beginnings, even though the mathematics we call event history analysis began life as waiting-time-till-failure models in studies of industrial reliability, which are essentially beginning-focused models. Left-censoring—the question of beginnings—remains a central problem for event history analysis.

23. One immediately important consequence of this value-ladenness is that the universe of possible conceptions of outcome is only sparsely colonized by the social sciences. I shall therefore have occasion, in what follows, to refer often to normative or even literary models of outcome and outcome-based decision.

stant in that interval (what I have been calling outcome-at-a-point or point outcome, of which final outcome is one type) and outcome that cannot be located to a particular point (outcome with finite duration). In the first case, outcome is simply the value of the well-being function at a point: the ordinate. In the second, outcome is an integral or other weighted function of the curve over some finite time period. (This time period can be any finite period up to the entire interval with which we are concerned.) Note that the move to a duration or "period" conception could arise either because we think that point outcome is in principle a bad concept or because we think point outcome cannot be directly measured, but only approximated by some kind of average over a finite time interval. We should, however, treat the latter motivation as producing a version of point outcome rather than a true period outcome, since it arises merely out of measurement considerations, not conceptual ones.

I have so far presented only two of the many possible versions of period outcome: interim/equilibrium and trend. These are both patterns of expectations for processes—paradigmatic patterns—against which we measure results over time. It is plainly possible to have period outcome measures that do not involve paradigmatic comparison, what we might simply call "over-time measures of outcome." These require only some formal concept of aggregation to become equivalent to single-figure measures of outcome-at-a-point. This aggregation could, however, take several different forms. Integration is the obvious one, and it yields a single number that can be compared to other outcomes. One might also use maximum or minimum values in the interval. (A familiar nonsociological example would be heating degree days [an integration measure] versus mean monthly extreme maximum or minimum [single values defined by a criterion applied over an interval].) But one might also think that a "good duration" was one in which outcome did not fluctuate wildly, for example, in which case the proper measure would be some autoregression parameter or the range of variation. In such cases we are beginning to think more "paradigmatically" about outcome. Such measures are less simple values for comparison than general criteria for "good" patterns of the well-being function.

Conceptions like interim/equilibrium and trend are fully paradigmatic. They are general patterns against which trajectories of outcomes are assessed, expectations that we use to decide whether a trajectory must be explained or not. This last is by far the common use of trend conceptions of outcome in sociology, as I noted earlier (i.e., for many scholars "good" trends don't need to be explained, "bad" ones do).[24] The dual use of period outcomes (both as aggregated single-figure measures and as paradigms) differentiates them slightly from untensed point outcome—exemplified by the final outcome of the sociologists—which is almost always treated as a simple value for comparison, rather than as a paradigm. But taken together, these various measures—final point outcome, interim/equilibrium, trend, and the many other possible period measures (integration, range parameters, and so on)—give us a broad variety of outcome conceptions with respect to the time interval studied.[25]

Unit of Analysis: Individual and Social Outcome

A second basic distinction is that between the social and the individual levels of outcome. At the beginning, my examples seemed to suggest that social-level variables are often associated with interim outcomes, and individual ones with point outcomes. As later examples have shown, however, this is not necessarily true. Interim outcome patterns can be seen in individual lives, if only at short time intervals: purchase of goods, interaction habits, and so on. Conversely, revolution is an obvious point outcome at the social level. The crucial constraint here is that individuals do have finite life, and hence interim outcomes (equilibristic, trend, or some other process outcome) for them are constrained to a certain temporal duration, which we typically think is shorter than the duration over which we measure the "more important" individual point outcomes like marital duration, education, and so on. (These are, of course, more important precisely because they aren't interim outcomes, but irrevocable ones.)

Thus, all types of outcomes can be conceived at both individual and so-

24. The obvious example here is mobility studies, which has spent decades trying to explain departures from an outcome state of "pure chance" mobility. As chapter 8 will also note, pure-chance intergenerational mobility would have struck virtually all residents of nineteenth-century America or Europe as nonsensical: as either an empirical expectation or a paradigmatic standard. It was certainly not something they conceived to be the "natural state of affairs." For today's students of mobility, that their own children's life chances should be completely uninfluenced by any of their own personal input or qualities would no doubt seem equally bizarre. But that is the political position implicit in their work. On such "knowledge alienation," see chapter 9.

25. These are all untensed outcome conceptions; I turn to tensed conceptions below. But one could also conceive of tensed outcomes defined by a moving "now" that is an interval rather than a point.

cial levels. Take, for example, trend outcomes. At the individual level, education is always seen as an ordered outcome monotonically increasing over at least a substantial period of the life course, even though many a college senior knows less on departure than on arrival, net of maturational change, and even though we are ourselves losing education—forgetting things—all the time.[26] At the social level, economic growth has enjoyed since the 1930s a similar status as a trend both normative and empirical for nearly everyone in the society. As many have pointed out, there is no particular reason—normative or empirical—why the economy has to grow. The belief that it does and that it must—implicit in the notion that growth is the paradigm within which the economy must be understood—is a normative position, an outcome ideology, just like our outcome ideology about education.

Temporality: Tensed and Untensed Outcome

We have, then, a first set of distinctions about outcome measures, concerning their location in time: final point outcome on the one hand and the various period outcomes (equilibristic, trend, and other patterns) on the other. We then made a second set of distinctions about the unit that suffers (or enjoys) outcome: individual or social entities. The third fundamental distinction here made among conceptions of outcome is the one we get from McTaggart: outcome conceptions can be tensed or untensed. Some outcome conceptions take an A-series view of temporality. All that matters is the dynamic now, and results at other times must somehow be referred to that now. Other outcome conceptions take a B-series view. Time is a simple line of dates, and therefore understanding outcome does not require knowing temporal location in some contingent or dynamic sense. Any moment can be an end; any moment can be a beginning. Outcome is simply the state of affairs in some arbitrary time period or at some point.

---

26. The equivalent social level assumption—that it is somehow the natural state of affairs for the labor force to be getting more and more educated and skilled—is equally a normative rather than an "objective" judgment. It is because of this normative belief that we are already training far more college graduates (about 30 percent of a cohort of twenty-five- to twenty-nine-year-olds, according to the 2002 *Digest of Educational Statistics*, and rising steadily) than the labor force needs. About 22 percent of all jobs will require college degrees in 2010, according to "Occupational Employment Projections" in the *Monthly Labor Review* (124:11:57–84). (Chapter 8 will discuss this example in more detail.) And like the individual level conception, the social level one ignores our steady loss of skills no longer widely relevant: FORTRAN programming rather than JAVA programming, and so on.

But direction in time seems to matter in both the untensed and tensed conceptions of outcome. Nearly all the outcome conceptions considered so far disregard past well-being. Economists have no interest whatever in the past, as I noted earlier. Economics lives in the now. Sociologists are interested in the past, but only because of its causal implications for the present—in the sense of the point at which outcome is measured. Put another way, although sociologists occasionally consider trend or other period outcomes, they generally use an untensed, final, point-outcome measure, ignoring intermediate welfare.

That past well-being might live in memory to be enjoyed at later moments seems uninteresting to all concerned. (In the terms of chapter 1, memorial historicality is assumed away.) Nor is there much interest in the way in which past utilities can be changed, by later redefinition, into disutilities (and vice versa), despite the obvious occurrence of such redefinition in divorce, for example, or in rewritings of historical past experience (for example, the portrayal today of late nineteenth-century women—who thought themselves happy in their separate sphere—as oppressed victims of false consciousness).[27] Both memory and post hoc redefinition are thus essential parts of outcome. In order to bring them into the discussion, I shall distinguish outcome conceptions as prospective, momentary, retrospective, or pantemporal conceptions, depending on whether they look forward, to the present, backward, or in all temporal directions.

Untensed Outcome

The most familiar prospective outcome conception is the tensed concept of the economists. This is a prospective, tensed outcome (PTO) conception in which we guess the trajectory of future outcome in order to make decisions in the present. To be sure, even under the theory of discounting, the aim is to come out better (in consummatory terms) "in the end." But in the meantime, the idea is to imagine unconsummated outcome in order to make a decision. This is a fully tensed exercise.[28]

---

27. Tversky and Griffin (2000) point out that past welfare serves as a comparison standard for present welfare. On divorce, see Vaughan 1987:271ff.

28. I have here unpacked two distinctions run together by Kahnemann and Tversky (cf. Kahnemann and Tversky 2000:15 on "decision value" versus "experience value"). See also, on future outcomes, Shackle (1961:9): "It is hard to give a sufficiently arresting emphasis to the idea, and what is implied by it, that outcomes are figments and imaginations."

But we can also imagine a type of untensed prospective "outcome" in which a future outcome is established absolutely at a moment at the outset of a time period—a "point-outcome" measure, but one applied at the beginning rather than the end of the interval. In the simplest case, this is the sociological conception of ascription, which we generally consider both normatively wrong and scientifically somewhat uninteresting. Note that the equivalent situation (fixation of outcome very early in a period) arises for extreme hyperbolic discounters (like Tony Manero at the beginning of *Saturday Night Fever*). Hyperbolic discounting characterizes an interval's utility using an integral (as does exponential discounting), but in its case the discounting function is of the form $1/rt$, where t is time and r is a parameter. As r gets arbitrarily large, the value of the integral moves arbitrarily closer to a point outcome at time zero. Someone who is an extreme a hyperbolic discounter ascribes an enduring outcome to him- or herself at the outset of an interval because of an unwillingness to postpone any form of gratification.

But this kind of outcome conception—prospective, untensed, point-outcome—governs much more than Tony Manero and his blue shirt. The formal outcome theory of Calvinist theology was exactly this: predestinarianism, which is formally the reverse of what we might call the "last judgment" outcome concept characteristic of sociologists. Predestinarianism fixed the (ultimate) outcome of life at its beginning. And social systems that do this are in fact quite common. Some examples come from ascription systems. For example, aristocracies long justified the rule of elites on the ground that their financial preeminence (an outcome guaranteed prospectively at the outset) freed them to think about the interests of the nation as a whole. Educational systems like those of France and Japan stake much of life's outcome on a single examination taken very early in the career. These, too, justify themselves on arguments about freedom from careerist interests, in effect thereby justifying themselves on their success as self-fulfilling prophecies. Similar are concepts of term limits—for elective office, for scholarly fellowships, for punishment. They fix an outcome in advance, aiming to undercut the play of intermediate interests. Prospectively guaranteed outcome is thus surprisingly common in social life.[29]

29. One might ask whether Protestant predestination really fits this model: whether it was believed that people are predestined so that they are free of the cares of life, and can simply show forth God's grace in the manner they choose. We don't know the answer to this question, because Calvin believed it impious to pose the question of why God should have chosen to predestine (Constantin Fasolt, personal communication). An example of marriage limitations

Note that most of these forward-looking outcome structures aim to act or facilitate action. The tensed ones are an aid to decision. The untensed ones are often a way of creating social stabilities or undercutting negative social externalities. But note also that tensed prospective outcome conceptions are not in themselves consummatory; they appraise future outcome, but do not determine it. By contrast, the untensed forward-looking structures actually determine the limits of certain consummations in the future. That is why I have labeled them "predestination outcomes," by contrast to the "last judgment outcomes" that come at the end of untensed intervals.

Predestination is the last untensed form of outcome conception here considered. It is therefore useful to summarize the types of untensed outcome. We have discussed four particular types of untensed conceptions of outcome, each of which we have seen at the social and individual level. We have the two point outcomes: predestination at the beginning and last judgment at the end. We also have the two types of period outcome noted earlier: trend and equilibristic outcomes. All of these are general models for outcome, ways we have of imagining and paradigmatically measuring the nature of outcome. I have also suggested, but by no means explored, the enormous variety of aggregative period incomes—integrals and so on—that are possible as nonparadigmatic or semiparadigmatic versions of outcome over time. I have omitted momentary or retrospective untensed conceptions, however, preferring to focus on the tensed versions of those possibilities.

Tensed Outcome: Momentary and Retrospective

On the tensed side, I have devoted most of my attention so far to prospective tensed outcome (PTO), as exemplified by the classic discounted future of the economists. I now consider two other tensed possibilities.

There is, first, a truly "point" version of tensed outcome, which I shall call "momentary tensed outcome" (MTO). In one sense, of course, tensed outcome is always conceived in terms of a single point: the now. The very words

---

that were effectively term limits can be found in the Oneida Community (see Foster 1984, ch. 3), but of course there are also the familiar cultural images of "shipboard romance" and other such specifically limited dalliances. As for limited scholarly fellowships, the Rockefeller Center at Bellagio was famous for its one-month limit and ten-year waiting time till a return visit. Probably the oldest continuous example of a term-limit structure is the British Parliament, whose requirement of an election every seventh year (if not before) dates from 1716. (The requirement was for every third year from 1694 to 1716.)

"prospective" and "retrospective" are actually indexicals, lacking meaning until we know the now with respect to which they are prospective or retrospective. (In this sense, predestination is not really prospective, as we have seen.) But there are particular tensed conceptions of outcome that are purely instantaneous. The most familiar are philosophical. For example, in conceiving happiness, Aristotle (*Ethics* book 1, ch. 10, 1100a10–1101a20) explicitly rejects the idea of last judgment. Although condoling the sadness of Priam, whose happy life was at its end overshadowed by Troy's demise, he mocks Solon's advice to Croesus that no man count himself happy until he be dead and beyond misfortune. (That is, he mocks the idea that true outcome is how one is feeling at the exact moment of death, a truly final-point outcome.) Happiness, Aristotle tells us, comes from within. For happiness consists in "active exercise of our faculties in conformity with virtue" (1100b9–10). And "none of men's functions possess the quality of permanence so fully as activity in conformity with virtue" (1100b11–14). Only the most overwhelming of external misfortunes can challenge this, he thought. Thus, outcome is essentially a tensed constant unique to the individual, determined by who we have made ourselves to be, always produced in action in every now of our lives.[30]

It is not impossible to envision a social science concept of outcome of this kind. Csikszentmihalyi's celebrated theory of flow (1990) is essentially about a momentary type of experience that "is its own outcome." The flow experience is tensed, in that it presupposes the separation of a now from past and future. Unlike the PTO conception of the economists, however, flow does not bother looking beyond the now, either to past or future. It is a microstructure within the now that depends on a number of external and internal conditions. The external conditions are (1) completable tasks, (2) ability to concentrate

---

30. The Book of Job makes the same argument. Job's outcome in worldly matters results from God's judgment of his response to Lucifer's depredations. But Job's "outcome," in the sense of his own valuation of his experience, is that that experience is God-given, and therefore reasonable and "good." That is why its horrible content must be explained and justified, and why Job never ceases to address God even in his bitterest moments. This never-ceasing orientation to God, even in anger, is a quality that, like Aristotle's virtue, "comes from within," a momentary tensed outcome produced by the self. Of course it is also Job's ultimate justification before God, and thereby the cause of his return to riches, to the worldly outcome that it is the writer's aim to deprecate. Such MTO concepts of outcome are common. A similar sense that all of life is always at risk in every moment, and that outcome always depends on an instantaneous virtue in the now, is central to the Japanese samurai ethic and similar honor codes elsewhere.

and to control actions, and (3) immediate feedback. The internal conditions are (1) effortless involvement, (2) decrease of self-consciousness, and (3) deformation of temporal sense (Csikszentmihalyi, 1990:49). The deformation of temporal sense is what is important for us here. The change of time in flow is a certain kind of expansion: "Hours pass by in minutes, and minutes can stretch out to seem like hours." The former judgment seems to come from the outside. When one is not in flow, a prior experience of flow seems to have passed quickly. And the latter judgment is from the inside; when one is in flow, it seems to go on and on.[31]

Flow is clearly an outcome state, and one of the momentary tensed kind we have just seen in Aristotle. But it is not immediately clear how one would, in practice, operationalize flow as an outcome measure in actual studies, although there are some obvious possibilities. One could simply measure amount of Newtonian (as opposed to experienced) time spent "in flow," although this seems a problematic concept, given the deformation of time sense involved. Moreover, this approach simply treats flow as yet another kind of utility, rather than as a specific form of outcome conception. Such a measure would therefore fall under the class of untensed period outcome conceptions discussed above.

A more subtle way to operationalize flow as an outcome conception would be to treat it as a fractal—taking literally the idea that flow constitutes a way of expanding time. Think of time for the moment as a B-series line segment of a certain length or duration. Now imagine that we expand that line by replacing the middle third of it by the two sides of the equilateral triangle of which that middle third is the base. The segment is now a trajectory with a deviation in the middle, and is four-thirds as long as it was before, although its horizontal extension remains the same. Now do the same to each of the four segments of which the trajectory is currently composed. The total length is now sixteen-ninths of what it was to start with, although the horizontal extension remains exactly the same.

This construction—the Koch fractal—can, of course, be repeated end-

---

31. An interesting example of flow is expert speculation with money. Many extremely wealthy people continue to amass wealth not because they can in any way use it for consummatory pleasure (although one could try to save their behavior for standard utility theory by assuming that their "utility" lies in beating competitors). Rather, they do it simply to enjoy of the flow of the doing. It was perhaps for this reason that in the last pages of *The Protestant Ethic*, Weber berated capitalism for degenerating into sport.

lessly. We can think of it as an analogy for the expansion of time in flow. Linear time remains the same, but lived experience becomes much more than it was to start with. (It will pass twice the original length at the next iteration and is, in fact, infinite if we keep going.) The Koch fractal does not "fill a second dimension," but the degree to which it does so can be measured. This number—its fractal dimension—is 1.26. Other linear fractals of this type will of course have different fractal dimension. That is, although there is no linear way to measure the "time expansion" (because it involves another dimension not directly measurable), there is a monotonic scale (fractal dimensionality) directly related to that expansion, and that monotonic scale could be used in principle to measure a degree to which one's version of flow added extra lived-experience time to the fixed horizontal period of the line segment.[32]

How would we specify a measure of such "different types of fractal time expansion in flow?" Note that in a finite system there are two different parameters to this kind of time expansion: first, the one-step expansion induced by the fractal generator, and second, the number of times that generator is recursively applied. The first—how people make flow—could in principle be estimated directly from their flow experience. So, for example, "Koch people"—using the fractal expansion just discussed—would be people who broke up experience into a beginning, a flow-expanded middle, and an end. The second parameter—the depth to which people produce flow—would be more difficult to measure, although not to conceptualize. A "depth-two" Koch person would be one who takes the "ordinary time" before and after the "flow-middle" and expands it into a beginning, an ending, and a little flowlike middle part, rather like somebody who has a special set of rituals or exercises before a big sports competition and a special way of celebrating afterward. And so on, for depth three and higher. In principle, these two parameters of time expansion (the generator and its depth) could be measured. Such measures are no more fanciful than the "time-tradeoff" and "standard gamble" methods used to estimate HRQLs in the health outcomes literature. One can therefore imagine an empirically grounded program of research in which outcome is conceived as a momentary tensed phenomenon, of which each individual might have a characteristic version or type. This instantaneous aspect of outcome would have an enormous impact on "total experienced outcome over a lifetime," but would not be retrievable by simple survey measures of

32. Linear fractals like the Koch fractal are sometimes called meanders (Lauwerier 1991). A different meander might be one with a different generating rule.

"quantity of outcome over time," since it is concealed in the way that individuals experience the utilities that come to them.[33]

Note that this approach implies that flow as an outcome measure would be independent of social scales of valuation. It would not be a function of money, for example. Nothing about being rich makes flow more possible, with the possible exception of conferring freedom to control actions. Note also that because of flow's focus on the now, it is not at all clear how to aggregate it over the life course as an outcome or how to use its presence, absence, or possibility as a crucial criterion of decision. In a way, this is a problem with any tensed form of outcome conception. Referring everything to the now, they remake possibility perpetually, whether they are prospective or retrospective, momentary or pantemporal.

A final and most intriguing form of tensed outcome is not momentary, but retrospective. We have models for thinking about future outcome and present outcome. But there is little in the diverse social science literatures on outcome that really helps us conceive of the impact of past events on present outcome. (There is, to be sure, an increasing literature on psychic trauma.) Obviously, one could begin by recalling that untensed period outcomes essentially involve past outcome in a simple way. That is, if one considers the simple integral of utility as viewed from late in a duration, it obviously takes into account past as well as present welfare. One could move beyond this—towards a tensed conception of past outcome—by insisting that pleasant memory is itself part of present reward. To be sure, memories fade, and one might assume as a first rough approximation that memories fade exponentially, which leads one to a kind of reverse discount symmetric with the prospective discounting that is at the heart of standard microeconomic conceptions of outcome. This might be the simplest form of retrospective tensed outcome (RTO).[34]

---

33. For a review of the HRQL literature, see Torrance 1986. Note that I have dodged the problem that flow is very much tensed, and hence that flow's "time expansion" does not take place uniformly across any given duration but in some sense from left to right. This question would need to be addressed before flow could be used as an outcome conception.

34. The importance of memory in RTO suggests the reverse importance of anticipation in PTO, something that is ignored in the microeconomic version of PTO. The thing that is lost (q.v. note 20 above) when pleasure is consummated is the anticipation of pleasure, which ought to be recognized as having utility in and of itself, extended over the full period of anticipation. And the vaguest, most long-term anticipations are often the strongest and most sustaining. Just as memory should form the core of RTO, anticipation should not be ignored in PTO, as it currently is. The whole concept of "midlife crisis" is at root about the death of anticipation in consummation.

Whether it is measurable or not, RTO is quite commonly employed in life decisions. Some people choose to have children because they look forward to changing diapers a year hence (that is, they choose to have children on a PTO basis), and some simply because they see everyone else do it. But a not insubstantial number of people have children in order to avoid regretting, at some much later point in life, that they have not had children. This is an RTO decision, not a PTO one, because on standard prospective discounting rates, even quite massive regrets thirty years hence are of no substantial disutility today. But seen from the viewpoint of the end, with the diapers and wakeful nights successfully discounted (by selective memory, if by nothing else), this regret looms as a massive loss.

One difficulty with this way of thinking about RTO, however, is that it does not take account of the ways in which past utility remains "in question" even after the fact. Put more formally, it does not recognize the enduring historical vulnerability of consummation. The most obvious example of this has already been mentioned: divorce. It is well known that the process of divorce produces a variety of redefinitions of past events, inter alia of past consummatory outcome. Some of these are simple redefinitions of the "You know, I never really loved you" form, which suddenly eradicate the meaning (even the discounted meaning) of large bodies of past pleasure. Some are strategic. As Vaughan (1987: ch. 10) points out, these very redefinitions can be used as gambits and responses in the process of uncoupling itself. Others arise simply from the "placing into question" of all past interpretations—which have been protected by the secure, factitious quality of marriage.

But all of these mean that the past is not only discounted, but can also be revalued. This can be a literal redefinition, as we have seen. But it is more commonly a redefinition by a later act—as a marriage becomes merely a "first marriage" when the second occurs, or the brilliant early literary success becomes "merely a flash in the pan" when the second and third masterworks fail to appear. This indeed was at the heart of Aristotle's condolence for Priam, whose many apparently fully consumed years of success were redefined as "pride before a fall" by the Greeks' wasting of Troy. And it was this logic that led Solon to tell the fabulously wealthy Croesus not to count himself happy until dead (Plutarch n.d.:114).

A truly effective RTO outcome measure must take account of these redefinitions. Yet note that while in prospective discounting the uncertainty of the future is held to increase monotonically from the present, it is by no means clear that events in the past are systematically more susceptible to redefinition as we move further from them. Indeed, long literatures on Schutzian "sedimentation" and Freudian infantile sexuality assume that the reverse is true. Hence we are unlikely to handle the problem of redefinition by a simple negative exponential discount, even though the latter might seem the best way to deal with the easier problem of the forgetting of pleasures. Note too that at the social level such redefinition can work extraordinary transformations of past consummations good or bad, as the example of Peter Novick's brilliant book (1999) on the holocaust demonstrates in painstaking detail. At the social level, with its much longer time horizons and process outcome framework, the impact of such redefinition on present "outcome" is enormous.[35]

When we turn from retrospective tensed outcome to the possibility of pantemporal tensed outcome, we have reached what should be considered the ideal of possible outcome conceptions. That outcome conceptions should involve prospect, moment, and retrospect seems to me clear. We are not momentary creatures; we have pasts and futures, as do our social institutions. All parts of time are relevant to outcome at both levels—not perhaps equally so, but the balance of them is itself something we should explore, not simply make assumptions about. As for tense, it is clear that tensed outcome is at root preferable to untensed outcome because, as Bergson, Shackle, and dozens of others have argued, we live in a tensed world, not an untensed one. Action, deliberation, anticipation, and memory are all fundamentally tensed. Whether we think at the individual level of decision making (my implicit focus in these last few pages), or at the group level of "history moving forward," as in Lazarsfeld's studies of elections, we want our concepts to work in a tensed environment, because the people and social structures we study are always in that tensed environment. It may be that the move to untensed outcome is necessary because of the need to compare outcomes across agents—or because it is mathematically simpler and more tractable. But that should not blind us to its fundamental undesirability.

CONCLUSION

In this chapter I have tried to lay out a conceptual machinery for thinking about the results of individual and social life. In the ideas of tensed and untensed outcome, of retrospective, momentary, prospective, and pantemporal outcome, and in the various versions of untensed outcome here discussed, I

---

35. I lack the space here even to begin to touch the literature on collective memory and its individual-level equivalent, the literature on oral history. Both of these could have much to say to RTO conceptions of outcome.

have tried to provide us with terms for thinking about this complex and difficult issue.

I have borrowed concepts widely and ranged over quite disparate literatures because there was no other choice. For the problem is urgent. The vast majority of sociological inquiry aims to evaluate the "causes" of "what happens," even though it usually lacks a reflective concept of how to temporally conceptualize "what happens." More important, we often aim to figure out whether "what happens" to one kind of person is better than "what happens" to another kind of person. But every time we commit to a particular way of temporally envisioning these results, we make profound value decisions about which outcome is better—by deciding how we are going to conceptualize outcome in the first place. In particular, making decisions about how to think about the distribution of welfare over a trajectory—the life course of an individual or the history of a social formation—is a thoroughly value-based action. This is yet another way in which there can be no value-free sociology. It is only the existence of widely accepted, unreflective conventions about ways to envision outcome that shields us from this fact.

It may thus seem to make perfect sense that our articles about whether marriage is a good thing should rest on measures that emphasize how people end up after a spell of marriage rather than nonmarriage: having more money, living longer, being more satisfied with life and friends and children and so on. But such an emphasis imperceptibly but inexorably pushes us toward insisting that the ideal aim of erotic and family arrangements is to end up at sixty in reasonable health, with a paid-up mortgage, happy children who went to the right colleges, and ahead of us the pleasant vista of our life-table-promised 21.4 years of golf and merlot. But why not cut a broad swath and flame out at forty-five? A little calculus shows that Faust's discount rate—the rate at which twenty-four years of bliss starting now is worth the same thing as eternal bliss starting in twenty-four years—is a miniscule 2.89 percent, less than the 3 percent discount normally used in health evaluation studies in America. Faust was a cautious conservative for insisting on twenty-four years before damnation! On European health discounting rates, he would have accepted only fourteen.

The question of outcome is not simply another methodological difficulty. Most of sociology's outcome conceptions enforce on our data a view of life that is thoroughly and completely bourgeois; there is nothing "objective" about it. It is a conception organized around decency, circumspection, normality, and a certain kind of highly regulated aspiration. It is a conception that devalues strong experience and overvalues caution, It is a conception that enforces future calculation and disregards memory. It favors lives with nothing to regret and, perhaps, nothing to remember.

If I can return to my opening example from *Saturday Night Fever*, the final-outcome conception that has dominated sociology for decades seems to me a little Fusco-like. It has us standing in the hardware store, dutifully putting the paint up on the shelves, each in our allotted roles like the colorless, middle-aged analysts we are. But Lazarsfeld, like Tony Manero, realized that the essence of life was not so much about where you ended up as it was a commitment to the getting there. The opening of *Saturday Night Fever* consists of a five-minute closeup of John Travolta's feet, encased in red high-heeled imitation-crocodile boots, walking straight at the camera in heroic foreshortening: five minutes of walking, five minutes of tensed process, of past, present and future. We don't care about the final point-outcome—that Tony gets to the hardware store with the paint can. We want to watch him getting there—buying his slices of pizza, turning around to chase the beautiful girls who undulate past him, listening to the el overhead. It is the whole walk that is the outcome, and for us as sociologists, understanding that walk is the crucial matter, a matter—like the music Travolta walks to—of staying alive.

CHAPTER 7

Social Order and Process[1]

THE QUESTION OF SOCIAL ORDER

The preceding chapter distinguished between phenomena that have a final outcome and phenomena that can experience only an endless succession of interim outcomes. As I noted, the usual view is that individuals have final outcomes and social entities have successions of interim outcomes—although, as I also noted, if we look at shorter epochs within individual human lives we find many things that have interim outcome patterns (equilibria, trends, or some other form) for extended periods: grades in school, day-to-day happiness, and health, for example. And of course as I have noted in discussing serialism (chapter 5) and term limits (chapter 6), sometimes social entities have final outcomes as well. But we have generally envisioned outcomes for individuals but not for society, at least within the range of liberal social thought. Only the cyclical theorists like Ibn Khaldun and Hegel have held that every society or social group, like every individual, must inevitably come to an end. Rather, for social entities, we typically examine not outcome but social control or social order. These terms describe loosely measurable states of society that can be

1. This chapter was originally written at the kind invitation of Bernard Harcourt. An earlier version was published in *Cahiers Parisiennes* 2 (2006) 315–45, an occasional series from the University of Chicago Press. As the preceding chapter surveyed concepts of outcome with an eye to processual theory, this one surveys conceptions of order from the same point of view. It has been considerably revised, but it remains somewhat telegraphic. The problems it raises are, in reality, too much for chapter length.

considered, in the terms of chapter 6, to be interim momentary outcomes. They measure the quantity of organization of a society in a present of greater or lesser extent. Such control or order concepts are the focus of this chapter.

Historically, the concepts of social control and social order have been used in two ways. They sometimes mean simply a measurable variable. But more often they refer to the desirable level of that variable. Thus, social control often means strong or successful control (too much control, for many writers), and social order is normally opposed to social disorder. In what follows, the context should make the usage clear, but when ambiguity is possible I shall try to be specific about my intended meaning.

For the first Chicago School, social control meant those forms of social organization necessary to enable a society to accomplish what it desired to accomplish. The concept was a loose—not to say tautological—one, and was not articulated with any general theory of society. Morris Janowitz attempted to update it in the 1970s, but like his predecessors, he did not attach it to a general social or political theory. Moreover, both he and the earlier Chicagoans used the phrase "social control" to refer to processes as general as elections on the one hand, and as specific as the rules of a particular gang on the other. The term was quite unspecified. In addition, after the 1960s the phrase "social control" acquired pejorative connotations, being mainly deployed to label what were thought to be unjustified modes of domination of deviants by state agencies, and more broadly, to denote domination of subordinate individuals by elites. So the earlier nonpejorative usage has not survived, and I here use the more common term "social order."[2]

Social order is a much more evolved concept, one of the core concerns of social thinking since liberal political theory began in the seventeenth century. In the Anglo-American tradition, the most familiar presentation of the "problem of order" is that of *Leviathan*: How is it, Hobbes asks, that human beings with their conflicting aims and impulses can exist together in a society without destroying each other? This Hobbesian question continues to haunt sociology. Indeed, in *The Structure of Social Action*, Talcott Parsons argued that all post-Reformation social thought began with this question, first posed

---

2. Janowitz 1975 gives a brief history of the concept of social control. Carrier 2006 brings that history more up to date, and sketches the importance of the broader concept of social control that dominated early in the twentieth century. Note that the change may not be that the term acquired new pejorative connotations, but that the original connotations remained, but were now deemed to be pejorative.

by Hobbes and later modified in various ways by Locke, Malthus, and others down to Spencer.[3]

The logical layout of this problem of order is simple. It presupposes disconnected individuals who compete for gain, glory, and security (*Leviathan* 1:13). It then asks what is logically necessary for social life to exist among such individuals. This setup focuses our attention on the explanation of cooperation, and in particular on the extreme case of altruism, which is impossible *ex hypothesi* in the usual posing of the problem. And of course a variety of explanations have been given for the empirically widespread, if theoretically unexpected, phenomena of cooperation and altruism: explanations ranging from Hobbes's forceful Leviathan to Parsons's normative consensus. Like the concept of social control, these explanations have been accused of tautology.

But it is not my intention here to address the Hobbesian conundrum. Rather, I am concerned to envision what kinds of concepts of order might be appropriate under a different set of social premises: those of processualism. As the first two chapters of this book have argued, the processual ontology does not start with independent individuals trying to create a society. It starts with events. Social entities and individuals are made out of that ongoing flow of events. The question therefore arises of what concept of order would be necessary if we started out not with the usual state-of-nature ontology, but with this quite different processual one.

Of course, such a question has long been posed, although not in those stark terms. Rather, it is implicit in the long sweep of empirical and historical studies of social order that can be opposed to the abstract works of Hobbes and his descendants. This tradition has always realized that to consider the relation between individuals and society as a purely logical problem of order leads to an almost contentless analysis, one whose premises determine its results. To be sure, empirical examples are adduced by Hobbes, Locke, and Rousseau, but the foundations of their arguments are abstract and deductive. And in addition, social orders originate in actual societies, not in a state of nature that exists nowhere. The alternative tradition therefore rooted itself in empiricism, such as we find in Machiavelli, Vico, Montesquieu, and their heirs. Such writers filled their works with references to specific examples and cases—sometimes ancient, sometimes modern, sometimes both.

3. Parsons makes this argument at Parsons 1949:88. His view of Hobbes is somewhat idiosyncratic. My own view is that Hobbes represents the explicit statement of a theory of politics that had been developing implicitly in the common law. Most of his "laws of nature" in the final chapters of book 1 of *Leviathan* are actually common-law maxims.

But their empiricism matters less than their historicism. Machiavelli, Vico, and Montesquieu are all historical or genetic writers. Hobbes, Locke, and even to a great extent Rousseau are, by contrast, unconcerned with the flow of historical time; their societies live in an abstract universe of order and disorder. There is, we sense, no real time in that universe; indeed, there is very little particularity of any kind. Universal, contentless individuals band together in order to defend themselves against the equally unspecified horrors of the state of nature. To be sure, the problem-of-order tradition is not unaware of history. Rousseau recognizes that the succession of generations creates a fundamental problem for the social contract, and Locke often uses historical examples to justify his arguments. But their essential conception of social order is logical, not historical.[4]

In Machiavelli, Vico, and Montesquieu, by contrast, we are always in a historical world—a time and, indeed most often, a place. These writers give processualist theories of social life: theories that discuss order and disorder empirically, locally, within a flow of actual historical events. Such views place succession and process at the center. The social world is a world of events. Through the events, not only individuals but also institutions and rules and governments are always changing. Moreover, one empirical part of this social process can be ordered while another is not. This too contrasts with the problem-of-order tradition. In the latter, to be sure, most writers do separate a public and a private realm. But these are not empirical realities so much as analytic abstractions that pervade all empirical locations in the social process. The public realm is explicitly defined as universal in its orderliness.[5]

---

4. This is of course not to say that Hobbes and his followers were not motivated by very particular empirical situations and did not use very particular empirical facts as if they were abstractions. The use of common-law maxims as "laws of nature" is indeed an excellent best example of that deployment, as is Hobbes's definition of justice by the shopkeeper's rule of keeping one's contracts. But these definitions deployed quite particular, empirical things in abstract ways, claiming universalism for them. Similarly, Rousseau's "history" of inequality in the *Discourses* is purely hypothetical, which means that his argument must of necessity be tautological, although it does have the virtue of being a carefully reasoned hypothetical argument, unlike the arguments Rousseau was opposing. Similarly, the empirical passages of *The Social Contract* come after the abstract arguments of books 1 and 2, and qualify rather than motivate them.

5. Rousseau is the most celebrated exponent of this separation. Parsons, of course, did precisely the reverse of Rousseau's separation of the political and the civil, extending the Hobbesian model of order uniformly throughout all functional realms of society. David Lockwood (1992) has made an interesting argument that Durkheim did not do so, but rather regarded the

In processualist views, by contrast, the many internal boundaries of social life are perpetually changing. Institutions and social groups are not fixed beings that can succeed one another, but lineages of events strung together over time, to which new things are always being bound, and from which old things are always being detached. Nor are these lineages concentric structures, as in the familiar hierarchical list of individual, family, community, and society that echoes through the problem-of-order tradition right down to contemporary sociology textbooks. Rather, they crosscut and interpenetrate and divide and rejoin to make a web of structure as complex across the spaces of the present as it is interwoven over moments of time.

In such a world there is no possibility of a dynamically static order of the kind envisioned in the problem-of-order tradition; neither Hobbes's Leviathan nor Rousseau's Social Compact can exist. Yet we must nonetheless still pose a question of order. Even if we recognize the centrality of transition and contingency, we must still ask what concepts we can create within a processual scheme to be the empirical and normative equivalents of order as conceived in the classical tradition. How can we think of a contingent social process as being ordered in some quasi-Hobbesian sense?

To get to such concepts, however, we must first pass in review the various other concepts of social order, focusing on their degree of embeddedness in the flow of time. These concepts are a disparate lot, ranging from Hobbes's abstract "problem of order" analysis to workaday concepts in historiography like the ideas of periods and regimes, to general empirical descriptions like "reproduction" or "tradition," and eventually to the kinds of process norms that are most familiar in the idea of "due process." In order to subdue this diversity, I shall first define some criteria by which to analyze these various ideas of order. That task occupies the next section. Then I will turn to the diverse gallery of social-order concepts themselves.

PROCESSUALISM AND ORDER

Any concept of order faces a number of challenges, and these are made greater when we deny ourselves the simplifying assumptions about social ontology characteristic of contractarian tradition. From a processual point of view, there seem to be four particularly important issues for concepts of social

---

economic and status worlds as external disturbances to the core normative order of society. In that sense, Parsons went beyond his master.

order: substance, temporality, social distribution, and articulation of social order with individual outcome.

In the first instance, it is not clear that in a processually conceived world, a concept of order can avoid particular substantive content, as does the classical notion of order. In the problem-of-order tradition, the implicit model of order is a simple equilibrium; departures from order lead to corrective actions which make order return. Most often, the order involved is nonsubstantive. Order is simply the absence of conflict and of unpredictability, not some particular set of positive substantive attributes. In Hobbes, for example, injustice is defined as the failure to fulfill contract. Hobbes's individuals aim to be safe and free to do what they wish, but there is little discussion of what in particular they might wish to do. That is the realm of freedom. It is also the realm of inequality, a fact that will have important implications below.

In some writers of the liberal tradition, there is a more expansive concept of order. Durkheim's concept of regulation, for example, asserts that part of social order is a set of rules and models specifying the particular things that individuals ought to wish to do: the roles they should play, and the rewards accruing to those roles. And his notion of organic solidarity rests on the idea of socially patterned differences between individuals. But even Durkheim presumes wide variation (freedom) in the realm of individual experience. Social forces set the predispositions of action, but do not determine it. So there remains even in Durkheim a realm of freedom and action beyond the world established by social order. Thus, while there have been variations in the exact location of the line of separation, in practice contractarian liberalism always separates social practice into two realms: a purely formal realm of equality and a substantial world of particularity, difference, and inequality.[6]

---

6. That liberal bourgeois thought concerned form rather than content is a point made many times. A particularly elegant analysis is that of Mannheim in *Ideology and Utopia* (Mannheim 1936:197–206). Durkheim is particularly interesting because he did not make the separation zonally. Growing directly out of the common-law tradition, Hobbes makes the form/content separation by extending the concept of law to define social order itself, and therefore his world of universality and form is ultimately the world of things immediately subject to law. The private world is everything else. Although Durkheim seems to follow this scheme in *Division of Labor*, with its two solidarities based on two different kinds of law, his more extensive theory of order (in *Suicide*) separates general social forces (which establish predispositions) from particular individual wills (which somehow remain free to choose; e.g., to commit suicide or not). In effect, the Durkheimian model is a probabilistic one: forces of social order ordain general probabilities, but individual decision actually casts the die. I have discussed Durkheim's view of causality extensively in *Time Matters*, ch. 3.

It is not clear that this separation can work within processualism. For one thing, in a processual view, society is never in equilibrium. Conflict and un-predictability are the nature of social life, so social order cannot consist of their absence. More important, this "disequilibrium" is typically substantial, not purely formal. Some of the conflict is about particular things, not about a formal property of society like equality. This seems inevitable on both theo-retical and empirical grounds. From the point of view of theory, it seems logi-cally impossible that there could be a line of demarcation between a public (equal) and a private (potentially unequal) realm that did not privilege some groups (groups in the realm of substantive inequality) over others, if for no other reason than that people involved in running the realm of pure equal-ity (the political world, in the classical liberal model) inevitably enjoy certain advantages, as Plato noted. Empirically, we see social movements not only attacking substantive consensuses in their societies (that is, attacking substan-tive private inequalities that are supposedly "legitimate"), but also attacking the universal realm of formal equality that is supposed already to be adjudicat-ing such private inequalities: the voting system, the testing system, the regula-tory systems, and at times even the laws. These latter attacks are always made on formal grounds, but it is clear that most of them have largely substantive political purposes, which are associated with particular groups in the realm of inequality.[7]

In summary, for any concept of order there is a question as to whether it can be defined in a purely formal way or must also have some substantive content. Worrisome as this dilemma may be for the problem-of-order tradi-tion, it matters even more for processual approaches, with their grounding in empirical social reality.

Second, once we move away from a contentless concept of order, it be-comes difficult to say when society is ordered, for things valued at one point in time are not necessarily those valued at another. Given such perpetual motion of values, one cannot decide the time point from whose perspective order is to be judged. (Thus, social order has a "when" problem just as severe as does

---

7. The attack on the "culture-bound" nature of achievement tests is an obvious example. It arises because some people are upset that particular groups do badly on the current tests. But of course the tests are culture-bound in dozens of other ways about which the same people do not complain; it is the particular result, not the culture-boundedness, that matters for them. The same thing is observable (but on the political right) in the attack on banking regulation in the 1980s—conducted with high-minded talk about freedom, but actually aimed at raising particular profits.

individual outcome.) If, as in the problem-of-order tradition, we seek a notion of order that will somehow work transtemporally, we might have to imagine substantive orders that can not only envision but might actually embrace their own replacement by later orders.[8] That is, we might have to imagine different normative orders succeeding each other in a normative fashion. There is a trivial and unsatisfactory way to think about this, of course: the assumption that posterity is always right—an assumption just as common among highly educated and reflexive academics as among average people. But it seems silly to assume that later states of the social process are more ordered than earlier ones simply because they succeed them.[9] Such a tautological view of the temporality of order would indeed correspond to the notion of contentless, nonconflictual equilibrium in the problem-of-order tradition. But it seems almost wilfully ignorant, either as an empirical or a normative concept of order.

Third, the processualist view forces us to confront the issue of "order for whom?" I don't mean by this the changing relative order between two groups as time passes, for those groups may themselves have been reassembled into new groups, perhaps on a completely different basis. The steady process of succession reweaves lineages over time; classes divide and recombine, criteria of differentiation shift, standards of consumption or behavior are constantly rearranged. The very units of society shift into each other from moment to moment. In such a view, thinking of the succession of orders in terms of society-wide trends such as "permissiveness" or "puritanism" becomes impossible. But even at a given moment there may be wide local variation in types of order.

8. This sense of an order that envisions its own disappearance pervades E. P. Thompson's *The Making of the English Working Class* (1963), as we saw in chapter 4. It also pervades Lampedusa's brilliant portrayal of the death of an aristocracy in *The Leopard* (1960) and Lessing's *The Making of the Representative from Planet Eight* (1983).

9. Hence Thompson's effort to rescue the losers from "the enormous condescension of posterity" (1963:13), already discussed in chapter 4. The professional world is littered with failed professions: railway surgeons, conveyancers, electrotherapists, and so on. The governmental past is littered with reorganized agencies, the commercial past with failed companies and even failed company forms. Even historians all too commonly side with the winners. It is centrally important that there have been periods in history in which the dominant opinion has been that the present represents a decline from past glories. Although this is often believed to be simply a form of conservative, even reactionary politics, there are often periods in which views of decline are widespread even on the left: Germany in the late 1930s, China during the warlord era, the United States during the Progressive era. The easy acceptance of "present is best" (or "present is the best so far") is a profound danger.

Fourth, and perhaps most important, a processualist view of social life presents us with a new conflict between collective order and individual outcome. In the problem-of-order tradition, this difference takes concrete shape as the issue of personal freedom, the ability of a particular individual at a particular moment to pursue an order that is different from the dominant, collective one, perhaps because he prefers an order that gives him a better outcome. That is, in this tradition the difference is really between the dominant social order and an individual's preferred outcome, thereby threatening the separation of public equality and private inequality at the heart of the liberal solution to the problem of order. This difference is a substantive one (in the private realm) that is suppressed by the political (or other) formal system of equality. The literature on the tyranny of the majority addresses this question, of course, as does that on proportional representation.

Such conflicts are located at some abstract instant of time.[10] Political theory generally conceptualizes problems of freedom as issues in particular instances, in part because that is how freedom is adjudged in the law, from which our political theory has grown. But a processual account of individual freedom requires a concept of freedom over time, not simply at a moment. For individuals have a limited term of life, while most social structures do not.[11] So concepts of order for individual and group may differ profoundly. A social structure can redeem itself and return to order, but it cannot thereby revoke for finite-lived individuals the wounds its disorder has made on them in the meantime. Moreover, freedom of an individual (in the general sense of the "free" articulation of the individual life course with the world of social order) must in a processual approach be defined not at an instant, but over time. This idea is implicit in the assumption, universal in the social sciences, that rich people are "more free" than poor ones because they can use opportunities to gain access to more opportunities, and so on.

Yet that assumption leads most analysts of the individual level back to concepts not of social order, but of individual outcome, precisely because the indi-

10. Individual/society conflicts are also conceived in fractal terms. In the literature on the tyranny of the majority, for example, the issue of individual freedom is usually conceived within a concentric and fractal framework. Thus, the libertarian claim that drove the Pilgrims to Plymouth Rock is regarded as simply a larger version of what led Roger Williams to leave that very Pilgrim colony for Rhode Island fifteen years later. The problems facing the idiosyncratic individual and the minority social group are identical. Although this point is not used in the sequel, it is an important issue in rethinking the individual/society articulation.

11. As noted in chapter 1, only social structures immediately dependent on the lives of individuals—like marriages and other personal contracts—have a term of life as do individuals.

vidual's experience of order and disorder is ultimately time-limited. In processual thinking, then, the reconciliation of individual and group interests must face the fact that individuals' claims for a reasonable future outcome before too much time has passed may place enormous constraints on the present nature of a social system that has itself a much longer period in which to find a possibly preferable order.[12] Moreover, because the various groups into which an individual's life is bound are both nonconcentric and perpetually changing, the nature of those constraints changes kaleidoscopically, as does the level and quality of the conflict between an individual and the various social orders in which he is involved. The question of "individual freedom" is completely dynamic.

These four issues provide a framework for my discussion of concepts of processual order below. I evaluate order concepts in terms of their degree of substantive content, their distribution of order in time, their handling of the complex interweaving of social lineages, and their relation of the different types of orders appropriate to social groups and individuals. My core terms are thus substance, timing, interweaving (of lineages), and articulation (of "levels").

There are two important caveats before beginning the analysis. First, this discussion of criteria for examining concepts of order leaves untouched the question of whether we shall take order here to mean empirical regularities or moral rules. This difficulty arises whether we take the classical or the processualist approach. Under either framework, writing about the concept of order seems invariably to join the empirical and the normative. Indeed, the power of the concept of order in political theory may well derive from its forcible union of these two opposing fields of meaning. Nonetheless, in what follows, I shall attempt to maintain consistent terminology by using "regularity" and "regularities" to refer to the order we see when society behaves in a routinely repeated manner, and "norms" to refer to rules that have some kind of moral authority.[13]

---

12. It is ironic that even though processualists generally view both individual and social entities as simple lineages of events, and hence resolve a priori such thorny issues as the structure and agency problem, they still must face a conflict between individual and social orders because of the association of the former with particular human bodies, which have limited terms of existence. In classical liberalism, the problem of simultaneously realizing maximal individual and social benefits is solved by the Benthamite—and thoroughly ahistorical—market-based realization of the greatest good of the greatest number, later transformed into the tautological "welfare" of the neoclassical economists. Here, however, I am concerned only with social order, not with levels of benefits.

13. Order is thus what I have elsewhere called a *syncresis*, a term deliberately constituted of ambiguity (*Chaos of Disciplines*, p. 43). Contemporary usage usually blurs my attempted

I should note second that in political thinking, the liberal distinction of the public and the private is usually conflated with the distinction of the universal and the particular. (We see this in Durkheim's linking of the collective consciousness to mechanical solidarity and particular consciousnesses to organic solidarity.) Indeed, in everyday discourse, the distinction of public and private is often conflated with the distinction between the empirical and the moral, on the ground that the public world is universally accepted and hence is de facto an empirical reality. This confusion was a major problem in the reception of the work of Durkheim and Parsons, both of whom believed, in effect, that normative matters could be studied empirically, even though a lawyer would argue that they can be "studied" (i.e., rigorously examined, understood, analyzed) only in their own normative terms: as law, governed by rules of legal, not scientific, rightness. In the sequel, when I use the word "normative," I mean it in this legal sense. (Chapter 9 takes up these issues in more detail.)

CONCEPTS OF PROCESSUAL ORDER

This section—the main body of the chapter—examines a number of concepts for social order over time, from the simplest equilibrium forms to more elaborate normative order structures like trusteeship. It studies how they are structured internally and how they address the four process criteria of substance, timing, lineage, and articulation. I have ordered the examined concepts roughly in terms of their departure from the simplest concept of order—the classical Hobbesian model with its contentless, atemporal, and uniform approach to order.[14] There are four subsections. The first concerns the equilibrium concepts of order that arise from the problem-of-order tradition. The second discusses the various elaborations of equilibrium that arise when we relax its assumptions about uniformity of order across social time and social space. Here I consider concepts like period order and cohort order. My first

---

distinction between rules and norms, since computer science regularly uses the word "rules" to denote the reproducible commands that create process regularities, while Parsons and many sociologists who have followed him have allowed themselves to speak of norms—at least in some contexts—as merely empirical aspects of the social system. To maintain clarity, I shall use "regularities" and "norms" to refer to the empirical and the normative aspects of "order" respectively. In chapter 9, I shall begin to sketch a preliminary concept of normative reality in processual thinking.

14. Interestingly, this ordering finds a parallel in an increasing emphasis on the normative over the empirical. We apparently perceive the processual as normative, and vice versa.

two subsections thus address order concepts that are ultimately static rather than truly historical (in order to see how processes fare in them). The third and fourth subsections then turn to fully processual conceptions of order. The third treats empirical concepts of historical order, like reproduction and tradition. The fourth considers normative concepts of historical order, like due process and trusteeship.

Equilibrium Concepts of Process Order

I begin with the classical problem-of-order model, viewed from the side of its processual implications. This gives us a basis for later comparison.

In the classical model, order is the absence of conflict. One defines indicators of conflict or disorder, and order lies in whatever social institutions minimize these indicators. Under such a view, we do not imagine that social order consists of having a certain array of roles, a certain set of ideal life courses, and a certain set of social institutions as in, say, More's Utopia or Durkheim's "regulation." That is, there is no real substance to social order. Order is simply the absence of disorder. As I noted earlier, Hobbes is explicit about this in *Leviathan* 1:15; justice is defined simply as the absence of injustice, and injustice is previously defined as failure to fulfill contract. Social order is largely formal.

In the liberal theory of society more generally, social order consists of the absence of some relatively minimal set of bad things, the most common name for these being "crimes," and the most common minimal set of them having to do with the physical safety of individuals and their property. The liberal state is also, of course, imagined to have some minimal set of shared institutions for making collective decisions. Hobbes, Locke, and Rousseau lay these institutions out in varying detail, but they are not really the focus of their respective social order concepts. It is, rather, the crimes and delicts that are that focus, and the great debate between Hobbes and Locke, on the one hand, and Rousseau and Marx, on the other, is over the kinds and extents of property whose violation should be regarded as social disorder (in particular, whether private property is something that can be countenanced as part of the universal or public realm versus the private realm, and hence can be protected by public order mechanisms).[15]

15. Logically, there is no necessity that the minimal sets of bad things should involve physical safety, property, and enforceability of contracts. Our notion that these things are not substantive and that they leave us free to construct personal orders—that is, differing real lives with

By virtue of this definition of order in terms of the minimization of some small set of disorders, the implicit process concept becomes one of equilibrium. Order in this model returns because disorder (the outbreak of the bad things in the minimal set) invokes some sort of control mechanism that removes the causes of disorder. This is the model of negative feedback formalized by Norbert Wiener and others.[16] One can imagine such a system having localized problems of divergence and oscillation, but in a stable system these are all transient states on the way to renewed equilibrium. This concept of order is thus dynamic, but only in a limited sense. At heart, the negative feedback idea captures the entire model of temporal order implicit in the Hobbesian conception of order and its direct descendants.

Even in the Durkheimian formulation, where external crises can disturb the larger and more substantive content that Durkheim finds in the universal and public versus the particular and private realm, the concept is still one of equilibrium. Durkheim's focus on occupational integration and regulation as replacements for the declining force of religion and family simply provides a more specified example of negative feedback. The loss of equilibrium forces us to create a new mechanism guaranteeing a return to order; Durkheim thinks that occupational integration will provide that mechanism.

The equilibrium version of process order generalizes naturally to the related concept of an evolutionary order, which involves random, undirected proliferation (or division) in an ongoing system, followed by equilibrium-like

---

differing real contents—is simply a restatement of this view's division of the social process into two kinds of things, one of which is guaranteed, consensual, and minimal, and thus seems contentless, while the other is malleable, differenced, and extensive, and thus seems substantial. The placing of one or another attribute of the social process into one or the other category is arbitrary. One could, for example, imagine a society in which physical safety was not guaranteed, but universal education to a very high level was guaranteed. In such a society there would be lots of assassination, to be sure, but education would seem contentless (because it was the same for all), and the many and no doubt creatively complex forms of self-protective behavior imagined by these highly educated people would be the source of diversity in social life and, in most people's eyes, the main location of its substantive content. That is, it may be simply definitional that whatever is placed in the category of the universal cannot seem substantive because it cannot sustain difference and (in)equality.

16. Interestingly, Wiener ([1948]1962:163) at first thought that social life could not support such models because "social time series" change too rapidly to produce governing parameters that could be used to guide the invocation of negative feedback. He later modified this position somewhat (Wiener 1954).

convergence within the newly differentiated suborders. In social theory we usually call this process differentiation rather than evolution, and usually underplay the problem of convergence within the suborders. But as a form of order, evolution/differentiation is like dynamic equilibrium in that it is simply a description of certain kinds of regularity. It contains no normative content, as does, for example, the logically similar idea of progress. It merely adds to the idea of equilibrium the ideas of proliferation and differentiation. Theorists of differentiation, like Spencer, have such implicit concepts of evolutionary order.

Within these two frameworks, equilibrium and evolution, there are a variety of actual feedback mechanisms that maintain order. There is the concept of social control; disorder produces a correcting response. (Evolution differs from simple equilibrium in allowing this process to go on in differentiated subunits, as well as across the whole society.) There are also more complex, cyclical reinforcement mechanisms such as those whereby advertisers give people what they want and people reciprocally want what they are told to want. Convergence to equilibrium does not necessarily require feedback between a large process and a small governor, as in the Wiener model. It can reflect other kinds of circular relations that become self-governing. All the same, equilibrium processes can drift. Various forms of misunderstanding—indexical meanings, misattribution, and so on—can produce considerable drift even in an enforced or emergent equilibrium. This means that equilibrium models are better than they seem as empirical conceptions of order in societies.

In terms of my four criteria of substance, temporal distribution, lineage, and individual/social order relation, equilibrium and its subchild, evolution, are relatively simple. Neither involves much substantive content. They guarantee only regularity, not any particular content. They can thus make no substantive determinations of the future, and over time equilibrium thus becomes a kind of dynamic stability. There is no long-run change other than drift, and so there is no immediate problem of determining the proper temporal point from which to determine order. Similarly, since the concept of order here is global equilibrium, there is no question of order varying through different parts of the social process at a given time. Such local differences are merely incidental to the larger stability. In empirical practice, of course, all this means that the major controversies in such conceptions of order have to do with changes in the collection of "disorders" that must be minimized. Politics takes the form of putting social problems into that category or taking them out of it. The politics of victimization is a classic example of this kind of politics:

the assertion that harm to this or that particular group involves some form of universal disorder, and thus requires redress.

As for my final criterion—the matter of levels—the equilibrium/evolution family of order concepts resolves the conflict of individual and social orders *ex ante* by assuming that no personal order is achievable without social order. This is indeed the core assumption of these ideas of order (as it was of Hobbes). They imagine exceptions to it only in highly formal terms—conscientious objection, liberty of the individual, and so on—but ultimately the social order is always primary; residence within it gives consent, as Rousseau and Locke both argue.

My first pair of order concepts are thus equilibrium and evolution. They are usually contentless models of an abstract order, specified in abstract time, largely ignoring local variation in substance, but with quite specific mechanisms that produce the regularities observed: in the one case, simple feedback, and in the other, simple feedback within subdividing lines. It is well known that these concepts are sometimes invested with normative qualities. But conceptually, both forms are at root purely abstract structures in which any particular empirical substance could be arbitrarily embedded.

Complexifications of the Equilibrium Concept of Order

Other important empirical concepts of order arise by moving away from the eternal and pervasive quality of these general models. By allowing temporal variation, we get ideas of order in terms of periods and cohorts; by allowing sociospatial variation, we get ideas of order in terms of regions and dominance.

I begin with the idea of order in terms of templates or snapshots. This is the idea of order implicit in the historians' view of successive "periods." Periodization is itself a purely empirical concept, designating successive sets of social worlds (and I have noted its worrisome qualities in chapter 1). When we see these successive worlds as successive systems of social order, we often call them regimes. Thus we say that Fordism is succeeded by post-Fordism, or that the Progressive Era is succeeded by the Roaring Twenties. In that sense, snapshots improve on the conception of equilibrium order by giving us a way of thinking about change in global order over time. But that improvement is merely arbitrary. For there remains a crucial difficulty; the idea of regimes leaves us with the problem of explaining transition between them, a problem that fatally wounded Foucault's concept of epistemes, for example. The same question arises for successive social orders, whether we take them in the empirical or the normative sense. They are a useful analytic convenience, but we have no very effective way of thinking about succession between them.

The snapshot approach to thinking about the order of processes thus offers only a limited advance on the equilibrium view. It accepts the possibility of changing orders, but has no particular idea for how that change happens either empirically or normatively. Nor does it make allowance for the weaving of lineages through the social system and for possible diversity of orders throughout that system. On the other hand, snapshots do focus on the actual substance of order—the content of the regularities themselves—in a way that equilibrium does not. The heart of the equilibrium model is simply the measure of disorder, which is usually taken to be an unchanging scale. At least with snapshots we allow the possibility of successive substantive contents to order, which will in turn define different criteria for our measures of disorder as time passes. Moreover, the snapshot approach to temporal order can at least represent a succession of different relations of individual and society, as for example in Simmel's notion of the differences of typical characterology between different periods (Simmel 1950:58–84). And thinking in snapshots is clearly behind the Durkheimian analysis of social change, with its two snapshots of past and present, softened in the analysis into a (purported) trend.

Moreover, combining the notion of generations with the snapshot conception produces the notion of cohort order. This allows us to think much more effectively about the relation of orders for individual and for society. One of the obvious problems with snapshot order is that individuals live across regime boundaries. As I noted in chapter 1, most of the people of the Roaring Twenties lived the Great Depression as well, and well over half of them lived the Second World War into the bargain. These periods had fundamentally different social orders in some sense, yet we must seek to define orderly life courses—empirically and/or normatively—for people who lived them at quite different life stages. The life course defined by young adulthood in the 1920s, family building under terrible conditions in the 1930s, and war dislocation in the 1940s at the prime of life is quite different from the life course of one who spent young adulthood in the shadows of the 1930s, experienced the war as liberation from the personal dislocation of childhood, and finally reached adulthood during the salad years of the 1950s. Yet each life course must have (at least in principle) its "orderly" version, both an empirically ordered typical biography and a normatively ordered "satisfactory life course." Such a cohort concept of order might not solve the explanatory issues of empirical succession. Nor can it deal with what we might call the issue of moral succession: how it could be that (a) one life history should be normative for one generation, (b) a different life history should be normative for the next, and yet (c) the two generations might live their overlapping lives side by side in some normatively just way. But it would at least enable us to represent such problems of succession to ourselves, and thereby to open them to analysis.

The snapshot (and cohort) approaches to order complexify the equilibrium notion by relaxing the assumption of an equilibrium fixed over time. By contrast, another family of order concepts relaxes the assumption of an equilibrium fixed over social space. In the simplest version, these are concepts of regional orders. The most familiar of them come from the long-standing tradition of slum studies showing that slums, which appear to be disorderly in terms of "general" social norms, are nonetheless characterized by their own particular types of social orders. Such regional orders do permit a practical resolution of the individual /social conflict (in its tyranny-of-the-majority version), since they create the possibility of interregional mobility; the Roger Williams example shows this well (see footnote 10; regional orders are often fractals, as the Williams example also shows). But studies of regional orders have tended to focus on their temporal frailty. Because the boundaries of regional orders are precarious, regional orders decay and interpenetrate with time, forcing us towards fully processual accounts of order that would be based not on the assumption of regional separation, but on normative models for the processes by which regional boundaries change (or ought to change). That is a quite different business, as legions of studies of imperialism show.

Thus, a more advanced regional conception combines regionalism and snapshots into an order model in which successive regional differences embody power differentials. In this approach, the more powerful regions are able to determine the overall social order, leading to comprehensive regime change. Marx's dialectical materialism is the most famous version of this type of conception, although one finds such arguments made in many places. Joseph Ben-David, for example, noted the clear succession of dominant nations in the history of science since the seventeenth century—from England to France to Germany to the United States, a quite literally regional change—and attributed this succession to the competitive power of different (regional) normative systems for science and scientific communication (Ben-David 1971).

This regional/snapshot view of social order does not, however, really leave the realm of equilibrium temporality. That is, it does not take processualism to the level of social entities themselves. Rather, it talks about the relative competitive power or social authority of the various regions of order at a moment and asks empirical questions about how and why they might succeed each other. The concept of temporality implicit in such an argument is not really a dynamic one in which every new present raises new possibilities. Rather, there is a fixed narrative to history, which we can watch again and again, as we would a film, always getting the same result. Historical materialism, with its grand inevitability, is again the best example of this quality of many regional dominance and succession models. As we shall see, the truly processual approaches to order avoid this inevitability and focus on the process of succession itself.

We can specify this "fixed narrative" problem by relating these forms of order with their quasi-equilibrium temporality to the tensed and untensed temporalities of the preceding chapter. Although cohort orders, regional snapshots, and the like are not simple date orderings, neither are they truly dynamic tensed orders. They are not anchored in an explicitly open present. Rather, they tend to tell narratives that have an internal, almost teleological dynamic. For all its optimism and utopianism, the Marxist analysis in its scientific guise is quite deterministic. Its predictions are ineluctable, and if they have failed of realization, it is not thought to be the theory's fault, but it can be explained by the epicycles of hegemony and false consciousness. Another way of putting this is that Marx's analysis—at least as it has been deployed in the twentieth and twenty-first centuries—is surprisingly vague about its genuinely normative content. The main focus has been less on the rightness of the proletarian utopia than on its inevitability (and hence on the "puzzle" of its failure to arrive).

The second broad class of order concepts thus derives from relaxing the assumptions of the equilibrium model. This buys us some differentiation of orders in time and social space, but does not move us out of the fundamentally static approach to temporality implicit in equilibrium orders. In most cases it brings us much closer to comprehending and certainly to representing the actual content of social orders than do the equilibrium models with their second-order measure of regularity as mere absence of conflict. It also allows us to see how cohort difference and interregional migration serve as mechanisms to mitigate the conflicts between individual and social orders that become so visible once we start thinking processually. But, as I have noted, none of these ways of thinking about order in the social process really engages with the specifically historical nature of that process.

Empirical Concepts of Process Order

I turn therefore to a third major family of concepts of order: those focused more directly on the process by which social moments—and by implication, social orders—succeed themselves. These are largely empirical concepts (I turn to normative ones in the next section), and thus are concepts trying to explain the succession of social regularities. Since these views find the origins of order in orderly processes, they are rooted in the dynamism of the present. Each grounds order in a certain property of the social process. Thus order is not a state of society, but a state of the process by which the actual present makes the potential future into the new actual present. I begin with those focusing on the short-term present, and move towards views with longer time horizons. There are three main notions of empirical process order: habituation, reproduction, and tradition.

An important conception of purely processual order a century ago, although less discussed today, is unconscious reproduction—what used to be called habit. Much of social order happens because we simply keep doing the same things over and over, both as individuals and as social groups. Put another way, that is orderly which is habitual. Moreover, the relative looseness of most forms of social control means that an enormous amount of practical variation can be embraced within a system of habits without producing any overall sense that there is change. There are no real rules, for example, about how college classes are supposed to be taught, and there is an astonishing lack of formal controls over them. But classes wander along staying much the same because of habits, and because the variation that might lead to serious differentiation is simply ignored and thus often peters out without having much permanent effect. Habitual order is compatible with enormous local variation. It is only when that variation becomes systematic or is systematically selected that habitual order is threatened.

Like the equilibrium concept, the notion of habit does not involve any particular content. Habits can be any sort of thing. And like equilibrium order, habitual order is compatible with a substantial amount of drift. Since we do not think of unconscious reproduction as being directed one way or another (at least outside the Freudian theory of the personality), the concept of order as habit does entail the possibility of random temporal variation. As for spatial variation, habits can apply at many different social levels, and of course could in principle vary across social regions. Although logically there seems little difference between habits and equilibria in this quality—one could, for example, easily imagine local equilibria—we usually imagine unregulated, habitual reproduction as considerably more chaotic than we do equilibrium. (There is no negative feedback to govern it.) Finally, habits do not involve any novel relation between the individual and the social. Habits exist at both levels, and could be either reinforcing or contradictory.

Things are somewhat different with conscious reproduction or, as functionalists call it, "socialization." Socialization is basically the functionalists' name for the training of young people in the rules of a society. (The French version of this concept, in many logical ways equivalent to the functionalists' socialization, is "*la reproduction*," as we find it in Bourdieu and Passeron 1977.) Socialization is essentially a reification of the functional "fact" (it is actually a purely logical necessity) that if the rules of society endure over time, there must be a way in which these rules are "taught" to young people. Unfortunately, this assumption is mistaken. Rules can persist for many other reasons besides their inculcation in the young. They could persist because there is no pressure to change them, or because it is structurally impossible to behave otherwise, or because new generations discover similar solutions to common problems on their own, and so on. Nonetheless, conscious reproduction of social rules is often pursued, whether it works or not, and so we must consider such reproduction as a possible conception of how order emerges in the social process.

Note that this form of order presupposes a flow of control from the social to the individual level. Unlike any other concept of order besides Hobbesian equilibrium—of which it is a logical corollary—socialization assumes a specific flow of determination between individual and social. That flow is devoid of any particular content—we can speak even of "socialization" into the criminal lifestyle as opposed to into bourgeois life—but it nonetheless does have a content, unlike the mere "disorder" of the equilibrium view. That content presumably comes from the core of the social world involved, which, as my crime example suggests, can be at any one of a number of levels or extents. As for its temporality, socialization is usually imagined as taking place over a substantial duration, rather than in an instant. In terms of spatial differentiation, while it can be envisioned as differing in different regions of the social process, it is not usually imagined as itself complex and internally differentiated. The metaphorical model for socialization is mechanical reproduction, and failures are imagined (at least within the functionalist literature where this concept is common) to occur as mechanical failures of socialization agencies (schools, prisons, etc.) rather than as conflicts between different forms and contents of socialization.

The third and most general empirical model for process order is tradition: that society is orderly which has working traditions. Serious theorizations of tradition are rare, because our literature about tradition is dominated by caricatures. Struggling with the new absolutism, the Enlightenment rejected tradition virtually on principle. And the nineteenth century's immense changes

in labor, family, and governance eventually led thinkers from Ferdinand Tönnies to Emile Durkheim to Robert Park to believe that the enormous transformation in their time was a unidirectional, perpetually accelerating process
of tradition destruction. We now know that this view of tradition—as a huge,
placid reservoir ever more rapidly draining as the floodgates open—is wrong;
the reservoir seems as full as ever. Not only are traditions continually being
created both consciously and unconsciously, but also the dramatic social
changes of the late nineteenth century have slowed, at least in the First World.
Indeed, to preserve what is for us the familiar world of social change, we now
must label smaller and smaller things as "social change."[17]

A first step towards a better conception of tradition is the recognition that
tradition is to a considerable extent relational, as I argued in part 1. The various lineages of society change at varying rates. In any given society, there is
generally one lineage or type of lineages that changes more slowly than the
others, and this inevitably becomes identified as the bearer of "tradition." In
our society at present, for most purposes this means that tradition is located
in "personal lineages"; that is, in people.[18] Individuals in fact change more
slowly than most social entities, so individuals become themselves the locus
of tradition. Hence our increasing sense of "rapid social change," since society changes faster than we do. In a society where individuals died faster,
this of course was not the case. There, social institutions often lasted longer
relative to individuals, who did not live long enough to see so many of them
change. So the longest lasting of those social institutions got labeled as traditions. Now we live so long that few if any social structures appear constant and
hence traditional.

This is by no means to suggest that what "is" tradition is not contested and
so on. Rather, it is to suggest that the notion of tradition—the idea that there is

17. I have elsewhere analyzed this process to some extent (*Chaos of Disciplines*, pp. 195ff).
On the slowing of change, note Fischer's (1992) discussion of the telephone. People used the
new communications device to do the old things faster. The same seems to some extent true
of the Internet. It must be recalled that communications media have been "revolutionized"
about every fifty years since the late nineteenth century. Mass education and newspapers were
followed shortly by mass radio around the First World War, television immediately after the
Second, and the Internet around 2000. It may well be that the main effect of these revolutions,
which diffuse over considerable time periods, has been to increase the generational separation
originally created by mass education. Most people can probably manage only one of these
transitions in a lifetime. That is, the real issue is articulation of change between social entities
and the individual.

18. This paragraph summarizes parts of chapter 1.

some part of the social process that changes more slowly than the rest—arises naturally even if we ignore the cultural construction of the past. If we begin with this simple relativist notion of tradition, we can then see how various other things—properties both normative and empirical—get added to it.

Even in this simple, relational sense, however, tradition has a particular design with respect to my basic criteria. First, traditions have real content. They are about some particular thing. Second, they take temporal duration seriously; indeed, the whole concept is based on a notion of long duration. Third, since the concept of tradition presupposes relative difference in temporality, it also presumes differentiation in social space. The definitional fact that tradition changes more slowly than other lineages might seem to imply that it would be increasingly shared as the more rapidly changing lineages of events redefined social groups and institution around it, retaining it as a common theme. But precisely because of those redefinitions, a given tradition occurs in more and more different contexts, and so takes on more and more different meanings. Rock music is now "traditional" in modern societies, but both generationally and spatially this tradition means vastly different things to different groups of people.

Finally, as we have seen, the idea of tradition can embrace a quite complex relation between individuals and social structures. Thus, to mention an example used throughout the book, one can find societies in which individual beings are in effect the longest-lasting entities in the social process. In First World societies in the twentieth century, for example, labor markets, family patterns, and educational and training regimes all changed faster than did the people in them. But at other times and places, very much the reverse is true.

The relational concept of tradition is not the only one, however. Tradition is something much broader than simply our label for whatever parts of the social process change slowly relative to others. It can refer also to the cross-cutting and interweaving of lineages that characterize that process in general. It is thus the richest empirical concept of processual order. At the same time, it is often made an explicitly normative concept, as we shall see below in the concept of conservatism.

Habit, socialization, and tradition are thus three microprocessual and empirical conceptions of how order obtains in the social processes. Of these three, habit is a kind of null hypothesis, an image of social inertia and of mechanisms leading to it. Socialization is the conception corresponding to the equilibrium notion of non-process order, a relatively mechanical and abstract model for the reproduction of social order. Tradition is a more contentful and differentiated idea of processually induced order. Unlike the others, it makes a direct and empirical connection with the temporal and spatial variations of the social process. Above all, it invokes a much more richly empirical concept of the ways in which the individual/collectivity relation can vary over time.

Note that all three of these concepts are fundamentally tensed, in the terms of chapter 6. That is, their temporality rests on a notion of past, present, and future, rather than simply on dates or order. Habit always starts from a present in which action is fully intended and not habitual. Socialization always starts with a (relatively) blank slate. Tradition always starts with a present in which some things are traditional and some not. All three are fundamentally tied to a present of a particular kind, and describe concepts of order that are always indexical relative to a moving present. New presents mean new possibilities.

It is important also to remember that I am here viewing habit, socialization, and tradition not as mechanisms of some other social order, which order is then conceptualized in the Hobbesian sense as the absence of some list of evils or disorders. Rather, they are themselves orders: things, which, if properly practiced, *constitute* order. They are not means to some order otherwise conceived. In the usual view, these are means because they are mechanisms by which we aim to reduce the number of "disorderly things," whose absence is held to define the existence of social order. But in the processual view, there is no such list of things; the social process is simply itself. Tradition (or socialization) is itself a concept of an ideal form of that process, not a means to some social order measured in another way.

Order in Process: Normative Concepts

This reading of habit, socialization, and tradition as definitions for order, rather than as mechanisms conducing to an order that is otherwise defined, leads us naturally into explicitly normative concepts of order in social processes, concepts not customarily used in social sciences but in other realms: law, ethics, and the like. They are nonetheless important, in part because, as I argued earlier, the normative and the empirical are in practice often combined in order concepts, either by choice or through carelessness. And they are also important because, as I shall argue more strongly in part 4, the social process is in any case inevitably a moral process *ab initio*. Therefore, we must consider these other concepts of order in social processes.

The normative order concepts can be categorized by the direction they look in time, much the same as were categorized the outcome concepts investigated in the previous chapter. I consider first a concept that looks only at the current instant: due process. I then turn to two views which look out from a dynamically moving present: the idea of progress, with its vista of perpetual future improvement, and the idea of conservatism, with its equally great fascination for the past. I then close with a pantemporal model for order: trusteeship. These forms of social order are directly analogous to the momentary, prospective, retrospective, and pantemporal orders of the preceding chapter.

I should note that I am not here discussing any of these views as they are actually argued; they are too complex and multilayered for such cursory analysis. Rather, I am considering them—like my earlier models—simply as abstract models for the ways we discern (and/or normatively define) order in social life viewed as a process.

It is a crucial fact that all of these concepts involve a dynamically moving present. The content of conservatism or progress, to take the two most obvious cases, changes steadily as the present moves forward. This is not because of internal drift, but simply, in the first instance, because the now moves: the present becomes past and is hence accessible to conservatism but lost to progress, which is now looking further forward. Similarly, due process means due process now, in the present. All three are tensed concepts. Their dynamism follows directly from the normative quality of these order concepts. Choices for behavior exist only in the present, and hence norms to govern those choices must move with that present. By contrast, most other accounts of order in social processes can view time "from outside," either as a complete trajectory (as in Marxian historiography of capitalism) or as an ultimately stable dynamic system, as in the equilibrium view. Even the socialization view of order to some extent partakes of this contentless, dynamic stability. Of all the empirical process orders, only the tradition concept involves a truly dynamic and historical concept of the present. But the normative orders are all dynamic in this way.

I begin with the concept of due process. Due process is the notion that normative order exists if certain procedures are faithfully followed in the now. It can even, as in the amendment process for the US Constitution, claim to be fully recursive—that is, able to change itself. (Ermakoff 2008 investigates interesting cases where due process votes itself out of existence.) Due process is in many senses the normative analogue of the equilibrium concept of the problem-of-order theorists. It is contentless, referring only to the following of normative procedures; it thus entails no notion of equity, of substantial justice. (Indeed, the claim that due process simply perpetuates substantive inequities has been central to meliorist critiques of classic liberalism.) In temporal terms, due process is momentaneous; it concerns nothing more than enforcing a type of action in the current moment, just as the equilibrium model requires only the evaluation of present disorder and consequent invoking of present social controls. Due process has little room for temporal succession or change, as is illustrated by the twin facts that the majority of amendments to the US Constitution concern individual rights rather than governmental forms, and that conversely, most changes to American governmental forms—the creation of large and powerful bureaucracies, for example—have happened with nothing more than metaphorical constitutional approval. As for variation throughout society, due process as an order is always intended to be universal and uniformly distributed in the social world, partaking as it does of the liberal faith in a universal political realm set apart from the inequalities and regional variations of the civil society. Finally, due process has in practice been conceived mainly at the individual level, although there is no inherent reason why it should not be a model for purely social order as well. This individual emphasis of due process reflects its origins as a remedy for the tyrannies of Leviathan. Due process is thus the normative expression of the problems that arise when the equilibrium model for social order is taken as a normative model for government, and a guarantee is required against the tyranny of the majority.

By contrast with due process, the normative order concepts of progress and conservatism look away from the present moment—in the one case ahead, in the other behind. Both of them involve substantive content, generated by a selective imagination of the future in the one case, and by a selective memory of the past in the other. Obviously, both of them also involve a real flow of time, and treat that time dynamically. Yet neither one pays much attention to the differentiation of orders throughout the various regions of society. Quite the contrary, both emphasize a coherence and uniformity that is in fact not present in the social process as we actually experience it.

The idea of progress is without question the dominant conception of process order in the contemporary world, at both the social and the individual level. At the social level it provides the general framework for beliefs in everything from scientific cumulation to socialist liberalization, globalization, the new information economy, melioration of economic inequalities, feminism, and so on. At the individual level it provides the core of the idea of "realizing one's potential," whether that be through occupational achievement, successful psychotherapy, happy marriage, or whatever. The idea of progress has, in many senses, no limits and no denials. At the individual level it eventually runs afoul of death, to be sure, which few people still imagine as the rebirth (progress) that their religions say it is, but it is still the case that much of Americans' personal self-understanding is framed around "realizing potential," even if only potential pleasure. At the social level, the ideology of progress lives a completely charmed life, unimpugned by the manifold evidence of social stability and even social degeneration.

At least in theory, there is no deep connection between the individual and social instantiations of progress. Optimists like John Dewey run them together—believing that social and individual progress moved hand in hand—but there is no necessary connection. It is well also to recall (see the discussion of cohort conceptions of order above) that social progress often involves personal regress for some part of the population; after all, that is what redistributive taxes accomplish. In short, the connection between the two levels is undertheorized by the idea of social progress. It is also worth noting that the two levels are explicitly decoupled in areas like athletics, modeling, and musical performance (although not academics), where absolute meritocracy (sometimes coupled with faddism) automatically trumps purely personal progress. More commonly, the two levels are coupled by the rule of seniority, which automatically guarantees an ascending life course for those subject to it. Michael Young's original book on meritocracy (it coined the word) imagines what a frightening world it would be if not seniority but absolute momentary meritocracy were the general rule (e.g., if professors lost their faculty jobs when younger people started doing better work [Young 1958]).

Like the idea of progress, conservatism too leads a charmed life, although it has in many ways been on the defensive in the last century. Conservative Americans are today actively promoting a "lost way of life" that in fact never existed, just as feminists have spent the last forty years revolting against a "traditional" family form that became normative at most a century and a half ago and (then at least) only for a small portion of the population. But the relative recency of many valued or detested traditions does not stop conservatives from accepting them or meliorists—who usually have a strong faith in the (undesirable) endurance of the past—from rejecting them.

In its most general sense, conservatism is simply the normative version of tradition as an order concept. In this normative use of tradition as a conception of order, two separate things are combined. One is a purely retrospective account of a dynamic past, a past rich in interwoven complexity, leading to the present moment. The other is a teleological understanding of that past as having culminated in a present beyond which no change is envisaged, at least for oneself. That is, we have on the one hand a concept of order in the social process and on the other hand a concept of largely individual outcome. Even a reflective conservative usually forgets that had he been forced to live through some of the changes that he retrospectively characterizes as "the rich diversity of the tradition," he would have hated them, just as many conserva-tives conveniently forget that they are themselves the beneficiaries of recent modifications in yet older traditions of whose destruction they are unaware. Conservatism in that sense is a form of what in Chapter Six I called retro-spective tensed outcome. It accepts as legitimate all changes up to a moving present, but none thereafter. It thus combines a view of social order and a view of personal outcome in very particular way. As we shall see, this kind of combination is characteristic of normative order conceptions.[19]

Note that although historically the idea of conservatism has been on the political right, there has evolved in the last fifty years a considerable interest in a similarly retrospective meliorism, encapsulated in the idea of reparations (or other exchange) for past social delicts. This is conservative in my techni-cal sense, because it imagines the present in terms of the past, but it is not conservative in the usual sense because it does not involve preservation of past inequities via the preservation of past institutions. Viewing a concept of process order in terms of its temporal assumptions can thus make for strange bedfellows.[20]

Both conservatism and progress have a fundamental flaw as normative ac-counts of the working of order in the social process. Each not only ignores one whole direction of the social process, but each also takes a one-sided view of the direction it does choose. Conservatives forget that an enormous amount of "tradition" takes the form of destroying things that were highly valued by some yet earlier group. Progressives forget that much change consists of re-discovery (the history of social science is quite instructive here, see *Chaos of Disciplines*, C. 1) and of the destruction of existing valued things, both social and individual. Most especially, progressives tend to forget that only winners write history, which inevitably biases our image of the past towards the vacu-ous assumption (discussed several times earlier) that posterity is always right.

19. For a profoundly reflective analysis of an extended tradition see Dix 1945. But even Dix's enormously persuasive analysis of the richness of the Christian liturgical tradition some-times forgets that the building of so rich a heritage required enormous quantities of Schumpe-terian "creative destruction," not to mention perhaps even larger quantities of quite deliberate, wanton destruction. Real individuals and their lives were the victims of both kinds of destruc-tion. Melioristic liberalism salves its conscience about that destruction with the comforting thought that all the destroyed things were unjust or otherwise evil in the first place. But this is just another version of Thompson's "condescension of posterity."

20. Of course with the decline of the welfare state, meliorism is becoming defined as con-servative in the lay sense. It looks back to a rosier past.

This brings me to my last normative concepts of process order, which might be called pantemporal. Pantemporal concepts explicitly involve the taking of several temporal positions. The most common examples of these are legal concepts like trusteeship, stewardship, and entail that either directly or indirectly bind the present holder of some good in the interest of protecting the rights of those not temporally present. Such concepts attempt to maintain in the present the rights of other times. Legally, of course, the rights of the past can be maintained into the present by various forms of inheritance law and trusteeship. The rights of the future in the present, by contrast, have been the subject of fairly systematic assaults in Western law since the Middle Ages. We see them very clearly in the development of Anglo-American law, from the destruction of strict entail and of limits on enclosure of common land down to the sale of future interests in the present that is implicit in the legal structure of futures markets and secondary mortgage markets.

At first glance it seems that societies in which pantemporal conceptions of process order have dominated are societies in which there was relatively little social change. Indeed, it seems clear from the historical record that the destruction of general, long-term legal safeguards of future interests was necessary to the evolution of capitalism in the West. Yet it does not seem necessary that trusteeship, for example, should involve immobility. In the United States, universities and churches are examples of institutions governed in large measure by trusteeship models of normative process order, and both have changed quite steadily over any historical period we could choose to evaluate. The central issues with trusteeship, as with any pantemporal conception of order, concern how far into past and future the trustees should consider their obligations to reach and how rapid is the transition they feel can be tolerated between the one and the other. A central concept in such a system is thus the concept of toleration over time.[21]

As for my basic criteria, trusteeship is clearly content-based, though it involves making decisions about the future substantive content of a lineage when that content is unknown and potentially unknowable. (Imagine planning for

---

21. The concept of toleration is profoundly interesting and important, not least because the mathematical relation called a tolerance (reflexive and symmetric but not transitive) describes most social relations far better than do the equivalence relations (reflexive, symmetric, and transitive) that we use to define our variables. Unfortunately, examining the formal concept of tolerance would quickly take us beyond present topic. We shall, however, encounter it again in Chapter 8.

the future of university libraries in the present moment, for example.) Yet the unknowability of the future leads trusteeship in many cases to maximize retention of highly generalized future resources—that is, of money—which results in precisely the reverse of content-based decision-making. Temporally, trusteeship is obviously a very sophisticated notion, anchored in the present but reaching out to both past and future. Its recognition of diverse social orders in that present moment, however, seems in practice much less subtle than its temporal breadth, although its broader temporal perspective surely provides a great ability to embrace the more complex over-time relations of groups that may seem all too simply opposed to one another in the immediate present. The same seems true for its potential to reconcile the abilities of the individual and the collectivity. By taking a longer view, trusteeship provides more diverse ways to reconcile the interweaving interests of these two levels.[22]

With trusteeship, I come to the end of this brief review of normative concepts that specifically locate order in the nature of how we conduct the social process. These four concepts—due process, progress, conservatism, and trusteeship—all rest on a dynamic conception of the present and build out in various directions from that. All involve placing explicitly normative values on particular parts of the social process.

In the past two chapters, I have discussed the broad range of concepts and measures we can bring to the measurement of individual outcomes and social orders. As both chapters show, our typical approaches to these questions in the social sciences are rather limited and unreflective. When one takes seriously the question of process—whether in the evolving life course or in the perpetual changings of society—it is clear that a whole range of issues opens up for theory, both empirical theory about the nature of the social process and normative theory about the ideals of that process. There is much more to thinking about outcome than the contrast between the final point outcome characteristic of the sociologists and the tensed "present value of future out-

22. One can imagine a definition of pantemporal order in terms of a categorical imperative: Act so that any person from some time period larger than the present would do your action, assuming some kind of reasonable translation of the situation. This, for example, would require people to foresee possible changes of order such that their own currently moral actions might become defined as immoral. (This is the standard we implicitly invoke in judging retrospectively those who deprived Native Americans of what are now thought to be their rights, and so on. The question is how far ahead—or behind—we are expecting people to look.) This, by the way, is an individual-level conception of order. It isn't clear to me whether there is an equivalent social-level one.

comes" characteristic of the economists. There is much more to thinking about order than the contrast between the functionalists' order as equilibrium and the meliorists' order as progress. The world is far more complicated than these simple oppositions imagine. By thinking seriously about process, we can begin to tame that normative complexity.

* Part 4 *

The two chapters in this final section continue the normative move of the chapters on outcome and order. But here the normative lens is turned on sociology itself.

The processual approach raises the long-vexed question of "value-free inquiry" in a particularly pressing manner. Processual ontology makes it evident that all the "empirical realities" of social life are in fact congealed values of one sort or another. "The family" is not a "social institution" in some transcendent analytic space. It is a current pattern of groupings of related individuals that has grown out of an ongoing process of evolution and transformation. It is driven by the actual choices, actions, and values of the people who are now making families daily out of materials that include not only a certain group of relatives, but also encoded (but still in lineage form—that is, at risk) cultural symbols and ideologies of a dozen kinds, as well as free moral commitments.

To be sure, one could see these complexities mainly as a methodological inconvenience. *Faute de mieux*, our quantitative analyses must treat "the family" or "juvenile delinquency" or "racism" as if they are solid, measurable empirical realities. There's little else we can do. For our political life requires some kind of "measure" of such things, even when they are in principle not measurable. Such commensuration—erroneous in principle as it often is—remains an underlying presupposition of liberal democracy, as I noted in chapter 5.

But in the actual lifeworld, things like the family, juvenile delinquency, and racism are all also in part defined by values and normative judgments. For example, the notion of racism almost always contains the value that racism is wrong, just as the idea of juvenile delinquency contains the idea that it is wrong to mug someone, but for some reason not wrong to use student activities funds to take yourself and your fellow student government leaders out to a well-deserved dinner at the end of the year. As for "the family," it is surely one of the most hotly contested concepts in social science. E. Franklin Frazier's (1939) book about problems with the black family ignited a controversy that has raged ever since, much of which has concerned what kinds of social arrangements are or can be referred to by the phrase "the family." No one can have the slightest doubt that the main burden of that long controversy is normative rather than empirical. There is much less disagreement about the trends in living arrangements and kin relations among African Americans than there is about whether the current forms are normatively good and about who is to blame for the various ways in which they may (or may not) play a role in the less than optimal outcomes observed in African American life courses.

As with the family, so with everything else. Because the processual view emphasizes the perpetually remade character of social life, and indeed even of apparently rigid and enduring social structures, it emphasizes potential for action and the openness of the present to genuine choice. Actors—both individuals and social entities—are not the mere expressions of giant social forces beyond them: of various group identities, of traditions. Those things structure the decisional present, to be sure; they are the stuff of constraint, facility, and location. But they are themselves just as exposed to risk and change as any other entity in the present—our actions can change them—and they structure a world in which we envision the possibility of actor choice, and indeed judge that choice on moral grounds. Thus, the processual view openly recognizes the mixedly empirical and normative quality of the social world. These two chapters begin to explore the implications of that mixture for sociology as a form of analysis.

The first of the two investigates the main topic of contemporary American sociology: inequality. It begins with a simple demonstration that our inequality concept is inherently normative. The ostensibly empirical character of "inequality" is merely a local coloring driven by the exigencies of the societal politics that is one of the many ecological constraints that surround us. Following the outline of chapter 6, the chapter then discusses certain problems in the measurement of inequality, showing how these are not merely methodological issues, but often normative ones as well. The argument then turns specifically to problems raised for the concept of inequality by its failure to recognize the processual character of the lifeworld: an inability to speak coherently about inequality over the life course; an equal opportunity concept that is at variance with everything we know about how individual selves develop through time; a failure to confront the normative problem of articulating social order and individual outcome. The chapter closes with a short illustrative example.

Chapter 9 addresses the issue of value freedom more formally, by examining it within the life of the social analyst. Here I focus on the issue of what I call knowledge alienation: publishing one theory of the world while running your life on the basis of another. We social scientists all publish articles about inequality and the fact that certain children are advantaged over others by family background, cultural capital, and the like. But almost all of us also do as much as possible to give our own children those very advantages. Very few of us, I imagine, would want to live in a world where the social status and achievements of our children would be completely independent of any input from ourselves. Yet this is in fact the implicit null hypothesis of the inequality literature, as chapter 8 notes. Chapter 9 addresses this inconsistency on the turf of my own expertise: the professions. I begin from the problem that I have written one theory of the professions, but then have lived my professional life according to a quite different one. The chapter then considers the various literatures on the morality of professions, both inside sociology and beyond it. It also notes the problems with Weber's position on value freedom. It then turns to an examination of Durkheim's sociological analysis of morality, which leads into a similar examination of Talcott Parsons's application of the Durkheimian analysis to the professions. Finding this analysis ineffective, I set forth a pragmatist account of professional morality, one in which we recognize the simultaneously empirical and moral quality of the social process itself.

The book closes with a short epilogue, reprising the topic of humanist sociology first introduced in chapter 4. By humanist sociology I do not mean a particular method or substantive topic or normative position or politics. I mean, rather, a stance of investigation that, whatever our disciplines of method and theory, places first the obligation to understand on its own terms the social reality we study, whether it is close to us in social time and space or far away. The core of sociology as an enterprise—whether quantitative or qualitative, historical or contemporary, public or professional—should be humane sympathy with our subjects of analysis. We too will be studied in our time, and it behooves us to study others as we would be studied.

CHAPTER 8

Inequality as Process[1]

Chapters 6 and 7 confronted what are clearly the crucial normative questions about social processes: How do they turn out for individuals, and how do they turn out for the social world itself? But both chapters were actually motivated by simpler questions about everyday sociological practices: How do we think about outcome? How do we think about social order? In the end, however, both of these questions kept producing problematic answers and contradictory results until we dug down to the everflowing foundations of the social process. The present chapter has the same design. It starts out from the familiar and widely used concept of inequality. But contradictions and inconsistencies about that concept appear almost immediately. Reflection about problems of measurement begins to resolve some of these, but leaves in their place other, worse problems. Again we find it necessary to turn to processual thinking. And by the end of the chapter, we arrive at an empirical posing of the implicit question left by the unresolved pairing of chapters 6

1. This chapter is the most recently written in this volume. It was originally written at the request of the Pedagogical Institute of the University of Halle for their annual conference on matters related to instruction. The original version was delivered in early October 2014. I thank the conference participants for their comments, and also thank commenters at the Collège de France and the universities of Oxford, Warwick, and Pennsylvania, who also made useful points about the piece. A version is in press in the conference volume, to be published by Springer Verlag. This chapter is of very recent vintage, and unlike some of the other chapters in this book, it may not have had its rough edges smoothed by years in the bottle. But my concern for the matters discussed here is of long standing, and perhaps the issues were the readier for writing.

and 7: How can we think about a social world that is simultaneously optimal for individuals and for the social process itself? Without the crutch of the simplistic ontology of utilitarianism and the happy resolution it permits of the contradictions between individual and social welfare, we seem condemned to a perpetual searching.

Like several of the earlier chapters, then, this one begins with an apparently nonprocessual question that leads us almost unerringly to the central themes of the book. It begins with the ambiguity of the inequality concept as customarily deployed in American sociology, arguing that when we say "inequality," we usually mean "injustice." The chapter thus begins with the now familiar step from the empirical to the normative. It then outlines some problems in sociological thinking about injustice, beginning with measurement issues. These raise general questions about the measurability of normative things, and indeed the chapter suggests that some version of immeasurability may in fact be the identifying mark of the normative. But even so, questions still remain, and these turn us inevitably towards the processual ontology: How can we think about "inequality" at some given point in the life course when inequality, like everything else, evolves across and through the life course, moreover deriving much of its meaning from the ecology of others around us? The social theories of the Enlightenment—which at present silently undergird our reflection about inequality—prove much too limited for this discussion, and so I invoke the processual social ontology, which emphasizes certain central problematics for sociological concepts of injustice. The chapter closes with a simple example that effectively captures these problematics, offering that example as a puzzle for further reflection.

THE INEQUALITY CONCEPT IN AMERICAN SOCIOLOGY

Let me begin by discussing the concept of inequality as it is deployed today in a typical part of the American stratification literature: intergenerational class mobility. Journals annually publish many articles examining the probabilistic advantages enjoyed in intergenerational transition by families of high socioeconomic status, education, ancestry, race, and so on. While these articles never substantively define "inequality," its operational meaning is quite specific. "Inequality" means that in linear models predicting social outcomes in the second generation, the coefficients on such things as socioeconomic status, ancestry, and race are significantly different from zero. By implication, equality is the state of affairs in which these coefficients are not significantly different from zero.

While this implicit definition of equality can be logically inferred from our quantitative practices, it is not very useful. First, we know that inequality is built cumulatively from the very beginning of the life course. The most deprived classes in liberal societies suffer enough damage even in the first six years of life as to be marked by virtually unbridgeable deficits. To guarantee at midlife insignificant coefficients in intergenerational predictions of outcomes, we would have to take children from parents at birth and raise them under arbitrary conditions. This is a social intervention that no large-scale society has ever attempted and that has almost uniformly been seen as dystopic by writers of literature, science fiction, and social science.

Second, the very things that sociologists of inequality typically wish to see preserved in the face of intergenerational stratification—minority group cultures, alternative social practices, subaltern languages or religions, different tastes and desires—are maintained largely through parental influence. For example, when American sociologists of inequality argue that children of English-speaking parents have an unjust advantage over children of Spanish-speakers, what they really mean is that they believe it to be normatively preferable that immigrants be able to preserve their language and culture. Yet the main causal underpinning of this preservation is the family, which, as has just been noted, also has the socially undesirable quality of reproducing inequality.

Thus, while nearly everyone in American sociology is upset about inequality, most of us think about it in a somewhat inconsistent manner. We decry inequality, but do not actually believe in the radical egalitarianism that our usage of the word "inequality" implies in the limit.

In practice, of course, we disregard this limiting case of insignificant intergenerational class transmission, and focus on the question of decline in the transmission coefficients. That is, we evaluate whether class status or some other measure of personal outcome in the second generation becomes, over time, more and more independent of class status and personal outcome in the first generation. We thus speak of "improvement in these coefficients over time." (This is an example of chapter 6's "trend outcome.") This approach makes good sense. When incomes in a society vary by a dozen orders of magnitude, we need not worry about the impossibility of absolute equality. Similarly, the old Schumpeterian argument (1950) that socialism will fatally weaken motivation does not apply when we have income distinctions that are thousands of times as large as those necessary to avoid such a lack of motivation. In sum, our societies are so far from equal outcome that the limiting case does not matter. Any progress towards equality is welcome. So I am not by any means rejecting here the study of inequality, which remains as politically important as ever. Rather, I am suggesting ways in which we must make our inequality concepts more realistic, both empirically and normatively.

Some of the difficulties with our inequality concept reflect a simple issue of language. In most American sociology, the word "inequality" doesn't actually mean "inequality" in a literal sense. Rather, the word "inequality" in American sociology is usually a euphemism for the stronger and more general word "injustice." This fact of euphemism becomes clear when we think about the different interpretations put on intergenerational prediction coefficients by economists and sociologists. What is "inequality" for the sociologist is "investing in human capital" for the economist. Their analyses may be exactly the same, but the interpretations differ precisely in whether the analyst thinks the identified disparity is a bad thing or a good thing. Moreover, interpretations of nonfindings differ as well. For most American sociologists, a failure to find significant effects of class or gender or race on intergenerational outcomes would indicate a failure of measurement or specification. By contrast, many American economists might take such a failure as evidence of justice.

One can see the historical emergence of sociologists' euphemistic preference for "inequality" over "injustice" by considering the frequency of the words "inequality" and "injustice" over time. The longest continuous and consistent data series we have is the articles published in the *American Journal of Sociology* (*AJS*). Table 1 gives by decade the number of articles containing the indicated word for the century from 1895 to 1995.

In the first thirty years of the *AJS*, editor Albion Small made it a mouthpiece for Progressivism. As a result, both inequality and injustice were important topics, but injustice was the more important. From 1926 to 1965, American

TABLE 1.

	Inequality	Injustice
1895–1905	38	59
1906–15	20	48
1916–25	30	46
1926–35	13	10
1936–45	9	17
1946–55	14	9
1956–65	15	6
1966–75	57	13
1976–85	153	18
1986–95	168	15

sociology scientized, and both words disappeared. Indeed, a reading of the actual articles including the word "inequality" in those years shows that the word appeared often in formal mathematical expositions, not in discussions of social inequality. After the political upheavals of the 1960s, however, the word "inequality" rapidly increased, particularly in relation to "injustice." The AJS published about thirty-five papers a year in the final decade shown here, so the word "inequality" appeared in roughly half the articles in that period. (It has surpassed 50 percent in recent years.) Indeed, one can infer that "inequality"—primarily in the meaning of "injustice"—constitutes the principal topic of American sociology.

This usage parallels the evolution of American politics. The civil rights agitations of the 1960s established the victimization model of politics, which married America's long-standing politics of interest groups with a new basis of interest: discrimination. Almost by definition, social science was central to that political model. The employment of social science in the 1954 *Brown v. Board of Education* decision showed the Supreme Court's willingness to allow injustice to be measured as an empirical fact in addition to its traditional assertion through purely legal argument. When groups such as women, Hispanics, the aged, and the handicapped followed the African American innovation, their levels of social equality also required ongoing "scientific evaluations." On the one hand, such evaluations would reveal whether America had "equal opportunity," and on the other, they could be used to appraise such controversial egalitarianist policies as affirmative action. Moreover, the Equal Employment Opportunity Commission and other government agencies made it clear in the 1973 *ATT* consent decree (on wage discrimination by gender) that purely statistical evidence of discrimination would be accepted as creating a right of redress. There was now no need to demonstrate intent, which had previously been the standard (legal) test for harmful discrimination. In effect, the US legal system declared that identification of injustice was an empirical rather than a normative problem.

In summary, the word "inequality" in sociology usually conveys a political judgment rather than an empirical one. It thereby enables people in sociology and the kindred social sciences to talk about that thing which, a century ago, our Progressive predecessors would not have hesitated to call "injustice." But it enables us to discuss "injustice" in a way that sounds scientific rather than moral or political. And by so sounding, it evades the immediate surveillance of the dominant forces of society, which are often interested in perpetuating precisely that social situation that many sociologists think is unjust.

THE MEASUREMENT OF INJUSTICE

Once we recognize that "inequality" in American sociology actually means "injustice," we can ignore the problems that arise from defining equality simply as the absence of all inequality. Injustice is a more general concept than inequality, and justice can involve forms of inequality in the literal sense. (For example, few people think the status difference between parents and children is unjust *tout court*.) In practice, the next important question might concern which kinds of inequalities of status are incompatible with justice. But this is a political question I wish to set aside. Rather, I am interested in asking about the sociological requirements of a concept of justice per se. Although I have already noted the failure of the "no inequality" concept in the limit, I have not specified other issues that might affect the sociological soundness of various concepts of justice, equality among them. In the remainder of this chapter I shall address two broad sets of such issues. The first and simpler issues are measurement problems. We are familiar with some of these, and for that reason they provide a useful beginning. The second and more difficult issues are ontological, particularly those ontological issues concerned with the embedding of social life in time, in the flow of changes in the social process.

I shall begin my consideration of measurement problems with questions that are already somewhat familiar from debates about existing measures and indices. They concern the normative implications of assumptions about "measuring" justice: questions of linearity, combination of scales, and creation of general measures. Note that here I am interested not in the scientific problems of these aspects of the measurement of injustice, but in the normative implications and assumptions of that measurement. This parallels the approach I took thirty years ago in my paper on "general linear reality" (Abbott 1988b reprinted as chapter 1 of *Time Matters*), which focused not on the scientific problems of modeling (as many readers thought), but on the ontological and philosophical assumptions made by the general strategy of linear modeling. The present situation is similar. There is a distinguished literature on the scientific problems in the measurement of inequality, and the reader is well advised to read it. But I want here to view those measurement problems in a normative light.

I begin with the simplest matter. Imagine for the moment that we have well-defined units (people, societies, social groups). Injustice among these units is logically a comparative concept; we say the relation of two groups is unjust because we have compared them and found differences. (Thus, I am not discussing here acts of injustice, such as enslavement, oppression, or swindling. That branch of the theory of justice does not usually involve the word "inequality," but something much stronger.) Such comparison implies the existence of pairwise data specifying whether the relation of group A and group B is just or unjust. This is a very general data form—a "justice matrix" of pairwise comparisons between groups. In most of our practical applications, however, injustice is expressed in a much more specific form: a linear scale measuring things like income, well-being, probability of advancement, returns to education, and so on. The enticing power of inferential statistics leads us to make the strong assumption of linear order for our indicators, and, by implication, for the unmeasured underlying concepts as well. Implicit in these practices are two assumptions about the normative world. The first is that the "justice matrix" can have its rows and columns simultaneously permuted until most or all of the "just" comparisons lie close to the main diagonal and the "unjust" ones are far away from that diagonal. The justice matrix can be "partially ordered," in formal terms. Second, linearizing justice assumes that we can define a quantity metric on justice such that we can consistently "measure" distance between positions in the order provided by the permutation just noted. That is, we can create not just an order, but an order with difference measured on some linear scale.

But there is no theoretical reason to think that most types of injustice have these properties. The second assumption is very strong, and is made simply because it seems implicit in the existence of linear scales of things like income, which are often our measures of injustice (inequality). But, for example, since a given income will purchase different amounts in different places, assuming a linear order to income has major problems; what we are really trying to measure is individual well-being once income is deployed, not the wherewithal to seek that well-being in an unspecified place. Moreover, the justice matrix may fail to meet even the first criterion of partial order. The proper response to these problems, of course, is not a statistical fix-up to turn something inherently nonlinear into a linear approximation that we then treat as a sufficient measure. A wiser choice would be to avail ourselves of the arcane but quite highly developed body of algebraic tools for talking about nonlinear orders. The majority of what we regard as linear scales of inequality are in fact a type of semiorder: relations of the form "A is about as rich as B." Such relations—formally called tolerances—are reflexive and symmetric, but not transitive. Applied to things like income data, they give rise to loose, overlapping sets in an acyclic order, but do not permit the powers of our customary statistical models. If we are to be more creative about a formal approach to theories of injustice, we need an inference system for such tolerance orders, not simply ways to linearize things that are not inherently linear.

A second familiar measurement problem arises not in conceptualizing a single scale, but in mixing scales together. We often create our measures of injustice by mixing different kinds of comparisons into composite measures— typically via additive scale construction, factor analysis, or some other means. But no more than linearizing are such techniques normatively innocent procedures. Factor analysis, for example, treats the core of injustice across a set of measures quite specifically as the line maximizing captured variance across the measures in N-space. But this procedure assumes that there is a conceptual "weighting" of the various measures being synthesized, such that all the measures are of equal conceptual importance and, furthermore, that they possess in some sense variances that are "conceptually of the same weight," since variance capturing is the essence of factor analysis. That we can "standardize" our variables (and their variances) does not mean that we have somehow escaped normative choices about our data. We have simply refused to make those choices consciously, and have let our (quite possibly unconscious) choice of relative scales of measurement make the normative choices on our behalf, but on unexamined grounds. The algorithm itself weights variables in terms of "information," which means that in effect it imposes its own weighting, privileging variables that are largely orthogonal to others. Nor is there any reason other than convention for treating standard deviation as a normatively neutral unit of spread, since we could have used any of the even-numbered Minkowski metrics for that purpose. Thus, combination of scales of inequality or injustice makes a host of assumptions, all with normative as well as empirical roots and consequences.

A third problem arises with summary measures of injustice across a whole society. For this purpose we don't create pairwise measures of injustice, but composite ones; the Gini index is the most familiar. But summary measures have their own assumptions about what is just and unjust, as we see from debates over measures like the Atkinson index, which can weight inequality differently in different portions of the income distribution. These debates are indeed a healthy sign of normative theorizing in social science. But we should be conducting such debates not as if the stakes were simply "scientific," but as if the stakes were themselves normative. We should be reflecting on why justice requires that we focus on inequality in a particular part of the distribution, what that degree of focus should be, and how to implement it.

The familiar problems of linearity, additivity, and generality are thus not only practical issues about the measurement of injustice, but also normative questions. But beyond these familiar issues lies a second level of measurement questions: issues that arise in the very project of measuring justice and that are perhaps less familiar.

First, to the extent that we place equality at the center of our concept of injustice, we must recognize that in most probabilistic systems, equality is a very unusual event. Suppose we have one hundred equivalent and indistinguishable bits of welfare, and we distribute them at random among twenty different people. The probability that all the people have exactly five bits of welfare is about one in ten to the 13.7th power. Even the number of arrangements in which no unit contains more than six or less than four bits of welfare is only a tiny fraction of this heroic total. Since this extremely rare perfect equality is our usual null hypothesis, it is not surprising that we find inequality everywhere (although it is important to note that what we find is patterned inequality rather than random inequality). To be sure, there are physical conditions under which equality naturally arises. Gas pressure in a closed volume is equal at every point, for example. But this happens because kinetic forces lead randomly moving molecules immediately to fill any relatively empty part of the volume. By contrast, bits of welfare do not move rapidly and randomly through a largely vacant social space. Moreover, they are consumed, not indestructible. Even more important, the kinetic energies of individual gas molecules vary widely; it is only in the average—the pressure measure—that there is equality. Only in rigid systems like crystals is there actual uniformity and equality. And the human social system is not by any means rigid, as we have seen throughout this book. So there is no escaping the disturbing fact that the typical random state of affairs is inequality, and that equality is not a sensible baseline for statistical inference about the normative character of a particular social situation.

The second, more general measurement problem returns us to the broader focus on injustice. It is not clear what is entailed by the assumption that injustice can be measured, and whether those entailments are conformable with the usual rules of normative argument. Measure requires a metric, and mathematically, a metric is a quite specific form of ternary relation, associating with any two points in a set a real number that is subject to three requirements: that metrically indiscernable points be identical (metric zero from each other), that the metric be symmetrical between points, and that it obey the triangle inequality.

But it is by no means clear that all or even most aspects of justice (or even of social life generally) are measurable and metric in this sense. Do we think, for example, that a relation of justice must be symmetric? Louis Dumont (1970) argued that the inclusion relationship was the foundation of the traditional Indian hierarchy, which Indian traditional society took to be just and legitimate (at least in his view), and which he contrasted with Western concepts of "stratification" as a linear order. Yet "A includes B" is not a symmetric relationship, although it is a transitive one.

Or again, do we think that injustice obeys the triangle inequality—that the degree of A's injustice under C must be less than or equal to the sum of A's injustice under B and B's injustice under C? Yet many stratification systems have intermediate brokers who are thought to maintain relatively just relations with subordinates on the one hand and with superordinates on the other, even while the distance of those sub- and superordinates from each other is virtually infinite. Of course, when we impose linear scales on these relationships—as has been done with occupational prestige and many other scales, for example—they automatically become metric scales. But that we usually think about justice using inequality measures that presume metricity is not a reason for assuming that metricity exists for the normative aspects of the actual social world.

Another version of this problem is the old question of whether there is not one form of injustice that matters more than all the others. At many times and places, various dimensions of human life—typically religious, but also nationalistic or racial—have been regarded as infinitely important. Yet such unbounded importance cannot be measured, and in effect it divides the social world into completely separated equivalence classes, with a trivial metric of membership versus nonmembership separating each class from all the others.

This issue of metrizability is a profound one. It could be that the central idea of normativity is nonmetrizability. What makes something normative in character might be precisely its inability to be measured. As Duncan (1984), Desrosières (1998), and many others have argued, modern culture has in general assumed that all social aspects of social life can be measured. This assumption is implicit in early concepts like life insurance, but was later generally diffused through the spread of operations research into political decision making in the 1940s and 1950s, and the use of discounting to bring into our current social accounts such unknowabilities as the welfare of future generations. This universal possibility of measure was made explicit in the daring work of Gary Becker (e.g., 1976), which rests on the idea that we can always measure the value of something for an individual by the price of the measured resources that individual is willing to sacrifice for it. With Becker's argument, however, we have come dangerously close to tautology. On the definition of value that is standard in modern economics, his claim cannot possibly be false.

But such an operational definition of value remains only an assumption, an ideology. Even David Ricardo thought value had two sources—not just scarcity in exchange, but also labor. And Ricardo's ambivalence remains. Most of us in sociology assume that true value is not defined operationally, as "whatever results from the act of measurement." Rather, most of us assume that measurement must always be considered an indirect and incomplete approach to justice, which is itself something elusive and in the last analysis not perfectly capturable. More important, it may be that that infinite fertility of justice—the ability to find new dimensions and aspects of it—is what marks it as a concept. Perhaps it is, in Maine's terms, a matter of status rather than contract: open rather than specified. And if that is the case, if justice is in principle immeasurable and indeed not finally determinable at a moment, then we can no longer trust the approach—mathematical and operational—that we have taken to injustice in the guise of inequality.

In summary, the two abstract problems of measurement are: first, that equality itself is an extremely rare condition and, second, that normativity may definitionally entail immeasurability, or at least, that any measure of it must be inherently insufficient because of the infinite novelty of potential justice claims. Our practice witnesses a certain recognition of the second problem, for we typically believe numerical equality to be a legitimate measurement approach to some aspects of justice, but not to all. The obvious justice "measures" are things like income, wealth, and mortality, which are already expressed in measures common across all people—recognizable commensurations that we have all come to accept, at least in advanced liberal societies. Yet there remains the desire to measure justice in other, less obviously measurable things: success, feeling of accomplishment, life satisfaction.

However, once we move beyond the simple problem of measure itself, there is a third issue. These less measurable arenas of justice are subject to variation between individuals. Success for person X must be success in something that person X wants to accomplish, and satisfaction for person Y must be satisfaction in terms of the good life as conceived by person Y. Thinking about injustice, then, requires us to be able to compare years of person A as a janitor with years of person B as a salesman—a comparison that may or may not take account of personal preference and character, skill match, and other such factors. Even worse, these "personal" qualities of the individual whose inequalities we seek to know may change over the life course. And they may also be subject to "false consciousness" in the sense that an individual's desires may stem from external forces—advertising and hegemonic ideology, for example. We feel that we should define his "success" in the terms in which he would define it if he were free of those external forces. But what are those terms?

When we reach these kinds of questions, we are beginning to challenge not so much our idea of measuring injustice as the nature of the social world as we imagine it. For by distinguishing personal qualities, we start to move away from the political theory of independent and identical abstract citizens that emerged from the Enlightenment, and from which grows our ideology of justice as pure equality. More specifically, we must question the basic social ontology on which those political theories were built.

ONTOLOGICAL PRELIMINARIES OF JUSTICE

A useful way to understand the social ontology implicit in our debates about injustice is to reflect about the problem of equality of opportunity. As this phrase suggests, there are two basic ways to think about how equality/justice might be achieved. One way is simply to equalize rewards to any position in society, creating what the French would call equality of places (Dubet 2010), or what might in English be called equality of result. Equality of result means the lessening (across all positions) of positional differences in salaries, conditions of life, and access to services and security. By contrast, equality of opportunity means that everyone in the society has an equal chance at all forms of achievement, but that achievement means achievement in a system of unequal positions. If equality of opportunity holds, then in a situation of true equality every social subgroup would be represented in the various unequal positions of society in proportion to its population proportions. But under equality of result, we would have equal rewards not only across subgroups, but within them as well, because there is no difference between rewards across positions. So mobility between positions does not matter.

Of course, it has been argued, against equality of result, that under it there would be no motivation to strive—the Schumpeterian argument noted earlier. John Rawls's idea of the "original position" attempts to resolve this problem. People agree ahead of time (the "original position") on a level of societal inequality (level of difference of result) without having any information on what will be their place in it. They thus choose a level of inequality they are willing to endure (Rawls 1971). Most sociologists would consider this to be another just-so state-of-nature story in the Hobbes/Rousseau tradition, rather than an analysis useful for thinking about inequality in actual societies.

But in fact, our own result/opportunity debate involves a similarly unrealistic ontology. First and most important, the result/opportunity debate in our social mobility literature takes the social structure to be a given structure, with more or less fixed positions. The main rewards of society are allocated through these fixed positions, which are usually understood to be occupational positions. These enduring positions will be occupied by individuals (rather than families, as in the "family wage" position of the nineteenth-century English labor movement and in its continuation as the male-breadwinner concept of the twentieth century). And the chief comparisons giving rise to judgments of justice and injustice are comparisons between the rewards associated permanently with these fixed positions. As the results/opportunity debate is usually posed, these comparisons are cross-sectional. From the viewpoint of equality of result, one focuses on positional comparison: one measures the oppression of waiters by comparing their daily wage with that of the yuppies whose tables they clear. From the viewpoint of equality of opportunity, one studies—at a given moment—the relation of parental qualities (and occupation) to the current generation's occupational achievement. In either case, everything takes place at a moment, the moment of survey. The social world of positions does not have a history, nor do the individuals moving in it have life histories. Rather, we find ourselves in the timelessly abstract social ontology of classical liberalism, where freestanding and identical individuals choose whether or not to form a society, and under which rules. To this classical abstract world, the returns/opportunity debate in fact adds only one other abstract concept: a fixed division of occupational labor, as first theorized by Adam Smith. In the usual inequality debate, otherwise identical individuals are located in this schematic division of social labor, which is subdivided into positions with certain rewards. These individuals are thus eternal specialists in a division of labor that does not change.

This simple and static ontology remains a presupposition in the present debate between equality of result and equality of opportunity. But on both sides it creates fundamental problems. On the equality of results side, positions are contrasted statically, even though the relative incomes of, say, American factory operatives have changed radically by comparison with those of American craft workers in the last thirty years. More generally, this stability assumption is obviously problematic because of the steady and radical change in the division of labor since the eighteenth century. Moreover, the diverse sources of well-being are not canvassed; only wage or wealth is considered. But this limitation creates obvious difficulties because different individuals have different conceptions of well-being, and, even more problematically, those conceptions of well-being are to a large extent socially generated.

On the equality of opportunity side, however, the problem is less ahistoricality than incoherence. Equality of opportunity presumes an inner, true self that can achieve whatever it wants, given the proper opportunity. But when in the life course does this true inner self actually exist to get such a proper opportunity? Fifty years of empirical social science tells us that no matter how early we look in the life course, social differences will already have been etched into the self by life experience. But it follows from this fact that there is no meaningful time at which equal opportunity could be said to occur, and therefore that there is ultimately no way even to conceive of equal opportunity, much less to bring it about. Indeed, given that the self is a social construct built in interaction (rather than a utilitarian homunculus that is present from conception), the whole idea of a true inner self capable of showing its worth if given an opportunity is sociologically senseless. There is no inner, independent true self. The self is built in interaction from its earliest moments, and those interactions cannot but communicate difference—and advantage or disadvantage—if they are there to be communicated. Moreover, even if the homunculi existed, differences between them that would justify different rewards would violate the underlying contractarian assumption of the equality of all, in effect condemning people for their genetic endowments.

We see, then, that the whole debate between equality of results and equality of opportunity rests on a social ontology that none of us actually believes, and that has been decisively rejected by a century of theoretical and empirical work. Individuals are not timeless beings, but actual humans in various life stages. There is no point at which they are independent of social life. Their inner beings are populated with ideas, languages, models, and values, all of which come from the various social environments around them. There is no pure self, no homunculus who "deserves" to succeed because of his unique personal virtues, because there is no such thing as a uniquely personal person. Personalities are made up of shreds of social life.

So also is social life itself merely the interaction of shreds of persons. And it too has a real history. Its positions and in particular its occupations change at a dizzying pace, much faster in fact than change in individual personalities, as we saw in chapter 1. After all, a person who lived in the United States from 1911 to 2007 would have experienced two world wars, wild swings in levels of immigration, the rise and demise of a centralized manufacturing system, three or four different employment regimes, a complete transformation in the social roles of women, and politics swinging to the right, then the left, then the right, then the left, and then the right again. So there is no constant structure in which certain positions get certain rewards, just as there is no constant placement of individuals in social positions, given that the latter are themselves changing all the time. The social world is a world of events, and the lives of both social groups and individual persons are navigated as complex trajectories across this heaving sea of happenings. If we are to think about injustice, it must be within this real framework of how social life actually happens, not in some never-never land borrowed from the liberal theory of another time.

Thus, the central problems with the normative social ontology that undergirds our arguments about justice arise in its failure to recognize the processual nature of social life, at both individual and societal levels. We must therefore create concepts of justice that are processual, trajectory-based. For example, during their twenties, most university students in the United States are poorer than those who have dropped out of the educational system and entered employment in skilled crafts. In fact, the latter are likely to have stronger economic status for quite a few years. But eventually, of course, many of the university students will enter professions and surpass the craft workers in income, and eventually in wealth. Even in a society with a stable division of labor, this relationship would obtain. More generally, different life courses of education and employment inevitably have different income and wealth signatures over time, both because of life course occupational patterns and because of social change in occupations and the world of consumption itself.

How should we think about the justice of these signatures? There are many possibilities. One could imagine a standard that all people should have equal present value of expected lifetime earnings at age twenty-one, but while this could be set as a standard, it is hard to see how it could be permanently enforced as a measure of justice, because it would be prospective and subject to moral hazard: one could gamble that others would take care of one if early consumption left one destitute. And why should we use twenty-one as the point of reference? In the modern labor force, the twenties are actually a life stage of work exploration, of trying out this occupation and that occupation, this employer and that employer, as a way of searching out employment that is available and acceptable before making a firm commitment to some kind of work. Perhaps age thirty-one is a better anchor point.

But, as Frank Knight noted almost a century ago, there is uncertainty throughout the life course. And that uncertainty could easily turn a just life course unjust. To have experienced fairness for much of a lifetime is no recompense to ending one's life hurt and oppressed, and to have had a stable factory job for twenty years does not prepare one for the shock when the factory moves to Mexico. Yet this possibility suggests that perhaps we should evaluate whole trajectories of lives in terms of justice or welfare: that it is direction that matters, not actual result. Such a position has been the solace of many on the right, who argue that an ever-expanding economy allows everyone to experience an increasing trajectory. But it is obvious that everyone can be moving in a positive direction at a time when injustice—at least in the simple sense of literal inequality of the Gini index type—is rapidly increasing.

Moreover, this analysis presumes that the experiencing person does not change in terms of his experience of justice or injustice. But of course this, too, is false. People whose ambitions are thwarted do often find new ambitions, and the closure of a factory can be a surprising boon to some workers who retrain and then find new and more rewarding work, even while it is the expected catastrophe for others (see., e.g., Broughton 2015).

It is useful to summarize these individual-level ontological problems of thinking about injustice. First, individuals live actual lives in a dynamically changing society. Therefore, we should be trying to theorize a just life, not a just treatment at a moment. It is, in fact, clear—as my craft worker/student example suggests—that trajectories of welfare may cross over the life course, and that this could in some cases be (justly?) reconciled with the existing personalities of individuals as of the moments when they make the choice of one trajectory over another. (Note too that the fact of differing trajectories means that cross-sectional comparisons will always find injustice, but that this injustice may actually be a poor or even erroneous measure of injustice over a lifetime and of injustice at the end of life.)

Second, as is suggested by the distinction just made between injustice at twenty-one, injustice over a whole lifetime, and injustice at the end of life, it is not clear how to theorize outcome or result when we speak of the entire life course. Indeed, chapter 6 has already shown in some detail how extraordinarily complex this problem is.

Third, because people change throughout their lives not only in what work they have and what else they do in their lives, but also in the actual things they come to desire, and perhaps even in their preferences for welfare "now" over welfare "later," there is an almost imponderably dynamic relation between experience, desire, and reward. Economics has written about aspects of this complexity in topics like free riding, moral hazard, and sour grapes, but there are many other such phenomena: retrospective rationalization, remorse, and so on. It is not at all clear how best to think about these things in terms of justice. Should we, for example, try to imagine a world in which there could be no remorse?

At the social level, the ontological issues are similarly complex. First of all, it is clearly the case that the social world, for all its power over the individual, actually changes much faster than does the individual, as I have already argued several times in this book. This is the central meaning of my earlier summary of the astounding changes observed for a lifetime running from 1911 to 2007 (my father's lifetime). Contrary to the Enlightenment ontology employed in the results/opportunity debate, there is no stable social structure from which people will take positionally dictated rewards. Factories close. Expertise is commodified. Markets change. Skills move offshore. It was for that reason that the great welfare states were conceived in terms of individual citizenship rights, which are more enduring than employment possibilities or even, in many cases, than families. It is not sensible to think about social injustice (or even the specific injustice-concept of equality) within the framework of stability, but only within a society of perpetual and often quite random change.

But the second and more difficult problem at the social level is how to reconcile social achievement (what Adam Smith called the "wealth of nations," and what is now typically called "economic efficacy") with individual achievement (or equality or justice). In the classical liberal model, this reconciliation was realized by the invisible hand of the market. Adam Smith's subtle argument, hardened into dogma by Bentham, was that the market enables simultaneous maximization of the realization of the desires of individuals and of the output of society as a whole. But if we believe that individuals have full and complex life cycles, and that society changes rapidly within those life cycles, this kind of cross-sectional, equilibrium-theorized maximization makes no sense. If we must think about injustice in life course terms, then we must think about social efficiency and output in historical terms as well.

Thus, the fundamental challenge is whether one can imagine just life courses for all individuals, and simultaneously a society that achieves maximum output under those circumstances. This is clearly an iterative problem, without the analytic solution possible in the simpleminded utilitarian case of equilibrium. It is comparable to scheduling college registration for courses when students have sequences of courses they would like to take, but professors are offering a fixed set of courses, of fixed sizes, at fixed times of day, and sometimes get replaced, go on leave, or take up new interests. This is an extremely complex problem. And it is not, in fact, solvable even by an iterative algorithm, because the conditions of the problem are continually changing as the algorithm executes. It will inevitably turn out that some students end up disappointed, and that some faculty have to change the times of their course offerings. And thus perhaps the only possible justice criterion in such a system is to set an upper bound on the amount of injustice a particular individual must suffer. But this familiar and everyday example is just one simple version of the larger problem of reconciling individually rewarding work life courses with the actual structure of employment in the world.

As I have just noted, such simultaneous optimizations require much local adjustment. Indeed, there is in practice already a considerable amount of adjustment of this kind. Modern societies have an enormous need for restaurant staff, for example; yet this is not a very rewarding occupation. The same thing is true of in-home child care. As a result, in the US these occupations have become largely life-course occupations. Over half the total annual workforce effort of Americans between seventeen and twenty-two (ten million person-years of work) is delivered in the restaurant occupations (both genders working as counter staff, busboys, waiters, and short-order cooks) or as private child care workers (mostly girls doing babysitting; for these figures see Abbott 2005:316). The mean duration in these positions (adding all spells together) is a little over two years. Thus, junk work becomes part of the long-term labor experience even of individuals who will ultimately reach very high status in the society. More broadly, the example shows that our economies are already trying to resolve the constantly iterating problem of fitting rewarding work life courses together with a socially functional economy.

A CLOSING EXAMPLE

I close with an obvious current example of such adjustment, one of great practical importance, which allows us to consider ontologically sensible theories of justice. Consider the following two facts about the American labor force. First, the skill level of the labor force demand in the United States has not changed substantially in the last twenty years. (The data can easily be found in the biennial Employment Outlook issues of the *Monthly Labor Review*.) Despite the continually optimistic forecasts of some economists, the observed demand for employment in the United States requiring a bachelor's degree has stayed flat at about 22 percent of the labor force since at least 1996. Jobs requiring only one month of on-the-job training are today about 40 percent of the United States labor force, exactly what they were eighteen years ago, and expansion of some skilled occupations has been offset by the export of others. In reality, the high-tech, high-change, high-skill economy is a myth. The second fact is equally interesting. Given the high return to education, more and more Americans are, quite sensibly, seeking the BA degree. So the level of BAs in the labor force has risen steadily, from about 29 percent of the labor force in 1996 to about 36 percent in 2012 (*Statistical Abstract of the United States* for the relevant years). The ratio of supply to demand has thus risen from 1.3 to 1.6 in about twenty years.

These numbers mean, by simple algebra, that returns to higher education must decline in the United States over the next decades. But, more important, these numbers provide a useful puzzle for our thinking about inequality or injustice in the labor force. Suppose for the moment that all these BA degrees were in some sense equivalent, and that all their possessors were of equal ability. Given this, it is obvious at once that some group of individuals—a larger and larger one as time passes—must be underemployed. There is in fact no way to guarantee equity between individuals once the BA supply has surpassed the BA demand. This factor is to some extent concealed while the two figures are rising simultaneously, because older generations are less educated, and so employment in the newly skilled jobs that do exist can be concentrated at the bottom of the age distribution of the labor force. But gradually the BA level creeps up the age distribution, and this mitigating factor disappears.

How could we allocate work so that individuals in this labor force had equitable results? Let us again assume that individuals are exactly alike in terms of talent, preferences, and other such things, and that there are far more educated people than our labor force needs, simply because it is obvious at the margin that having an education is advantageous. The only resolution of this equity problem is to get away from the notion that there is a simple and fixed lifetime mapping between individuals and jobs. No such mapping can be equitable in the specified conditions. So the person/job mapping must vary over time. It seems logical to think of this variation as taking place at two different time scales, each of which has advantages and disadvantages.

We could, for example, switch off on a weekly basis. Since demand is three-fifths of supply, if the people with BAs worked at BA-level jobs only three out of five work days, the system could absorb the extra people with BAs. So I could be a professor three days a week and clean our offices the other two days, and that would work as an equity policy. This may seem silly. But in fact, this is precisely the change that has occurred, for faculty now do most of the clerical work that would have been done by secretaries fifty years ago. Of course there are no such brilliant secretaries today as there were fifty years ago—smart young women with BAs from top colleges and universities. Women with those qualities are now faculty themselves, and the price of that gender equity, in fact, has been that we all—men and women faculty alike—do our own clerical work. Of course the personal computer made the change possible, but it was gender equity concerns that in effect drove the shift, and it remains a fact that college faculty do far more clerical work than they did fifty years ago, and that in many ways this change has occurred via the reallocation of work that made yesterday's faculty secretaries into today's faculty colleagues.

On a much longer time scale, we could resolve the overeducation problem by shortening the period of the life course in which one does education-appropriate work. This clearly is also one of the major mechanisms for handling the injustice that arises through overeducation. Mandatory retirement constitutes a policy of this kind in rapidly aging societies, and indeed it was first used in the United States as a policy to generate employment, not as a social insurance program. It may well be that the turning of the life stage of the twenties into a longer and longer period of training and exploration is also an example of this form of adjustment.

We see, then, that with the necessary rejection of the Enlightenment ontology, we approach a more processual and complex situation with respect to injustice. Our central problem is to theorize the joint realization of individually just life courses and socially effective (although constantly adjusting) divisions of labor. This is not an easy question. But it is the only sensible one.

CHAPTER 9

Professionalism Empirical and Moral[1]

The preceding chapter shows that there is no normatively naive ontology within which we can effectively understand modern inequality. Any social ontology we choose has distinctive implications for what we will find empirically when we investigate normative issues like inequality or injustice, just as chapter 6 showed that any outcome conception we choose will have similar implications for the empirical investigation of normative matters like the quality of human lives. These conclusions about normativity and our criteria of "goodness" or justice are, in the broadest sense, methodological reasons why commitment to a processual ontology makes more evident the necessity of explicit normative reflection about social life.

In the present chapter, I turn to an even more profound reason that processualism requires a commitment to normative reflection. That is the fact—mentioned at various points earlier in this book—that to a large extent the social process consists of the congealing of values into social things, the gradual weaving of choices and actions into the stable lineages of events that we call social entities. Value is central to this process, and so there is no escape from value in sociology. I investigate this problem in detail by looking at a particular aspect of our work—professionalism—that is well understood empirically, but that is not as politically controversial as is (for example) the problem of inequality investigated in the preceding chapter. By studying a less politically loaded question, we can theorize more clearly the exact interplay of the moral

1. This paper has never been published. It was originally given to a doctoral seminar at the Free University of Brussels, 20 October 2011.

and the empirical, both in the social process and in our work commenting on that process. A less controversial topic allows us to see the contradictions involved, but without the reactions born of political bias one way or another.[2]

The chapter begins with the questions of political controversy and value freedom in academic life, using professionalism as a case for reflection. It then examines the relation of the empirical and the normative in Durkheim, seeking the roots of our current approach to this dichotomy. It then traces the application of that Durkheimian position to the professions by Durkheim's successor, Talcott Parsons. As that application makes clear, however, the Parsonian and Durkheimian accounts simply ignore the normative nature of most sociological reflection as well as the real problems presented by the centrality of values in the social process itself. The chapter closes with an analysis of that centrality, couched in the terms of a processual ontology and the pragmatist theories that grow from it.

INTRODUCTION: THE PUZZLE OF PROFESSIONALISM

Is professionalism an empirical concept or a moral one? Is it both? These are hard questions, but they provide a useful, constrained framework for thinking about the broader question of the relation of empirical and moral knowing, or—to put it in another terminology—the relation of theory and practice.

My choice of the professions as a site for investigating these questions is arbitrary. One could raise the same issue about gender equality or stratification or whatever. However, the professions are a good example for two reasons. First, as just noted, debates about the professions are not highly politicized. Second, while the professions are well studied as social phenomena, there is much less written about the professions as moral communities.

2. Responding to this challenge also forces me to address the obvious counter-question with which a colleague like Michael Burawoy could challenge the "humane sympathy" argument gradually built throughout the latter part of this book: Are there conditions under which I would myself become an explicitly political, activist sociologist? There are such conditions, and indeed they have occurred in the past decade. I spent much of that decade defending libraries and humanistic knowledge from a variety of threats (see, e.g., the preface to the book *Digital Paper*, Abbott 2014a.) I have become the public sociologist against whom I seemed to inveigh when I wrote the paper that has become the epilogue of this book. But, as the present chapter will make clear, the more worrisome case is of much longer standing: my failure to undertake any public sociology with respect to the professions, an area in which I have some expertise, not to mention the inspiring example of the great Eliot Freidson, who combined public and professional approaches to the professions with such rare grace.

This gap is obvious in my own experience. Although I have written an influential book on the subject of the professions, I have never addressed a professional association on the subject of how that profession ought to behave. I have explained professional history to social workers and librarians. I have given strategic advice to librarians and occupational therapists. I have predicted the future to information scientists and the army. But I have never addressed a professional association about the moral obligations and duties of professions. Indeed, the only talk I have ever given about professional ethics debunked professional ethics as a largely symbolic purity ritual (See Abbott 1983a).

Yet this is not because I do not myself believe in professionalism as a moral phenomenon. Far from it. I not only believe in professionalism, but live it on a daily basis. At the *American Journal of Sociology* I expect my reviewers to tell me if they have read a submission before, if they know its author, or if they gave him advice on the paper. When supervising students, I make them undertake detailed researches that will never appear in print, merely to teach them that their readers must be able to trust them to have done such things. When I submit my own work to journals, I expect my colleagues to set aside their personal prejudices about my work, as I do when I read theirs. All these are moral aspects of professionalism that I not only expect in others but undertake for myself. I don't think them symbolic purity rituals at all. They are not only the way I expect my professional world to work, they are also the way I think that professional world ought to work.

Elsewhere, I have named this situation "knowledge alienation." By this I mean the situation of saying one thing and living another. We all seem to do this. As social scientists, we are in the business of explaining other people's behavior. But as humans, we live our own lives as if we were free moral beings, Kantian individuals. We don't explain our own lives, we live them: it is other people's lives that we explain.[3] Explanation plays no role in our own living except in the Machiavellian sense: we use our skill at explanation to predict what may result from this or that act that we plan. But those predictions do not determine whether we feel we should do such an act or not. For most of us, this latter question belongs to the realms of politics or morals or whatever else—all of them areas we have agreed to separate from academic inquiry. Political science—with its subdiscipline of political theory—is the lone excep-

---

3. To paraphrase Oscar Wilde (on fashion in *An Ideal Husband*, act 3) "Freedom is what one does oneself. What is determined is what other people are doing."

tion to this isolation of morality in American academia. The rest of us make a sharp separation of objectivity and advocacy.

I should note, parenthetically, that there is an equivalent divergence on the other side of this empirical/moral divide. If I open recent books about professionalism as an ethical system (e.g., Kultgen 1988, Koehn 1994), I find in them no reference whatever to my own work. There is only the most grudging reference to the "conflict school" in the sociology of professions—to Eliot Freidson and Magali Larson, for example, who are dismissed as unworthy cynics. "Changes in university disciplines," Koehn tells us, "especially [in] history and sociology, also have played a part in displacing the notion that professional practice serves the public interest." In the views of such scholars, she tells us:

> Professions have no inherent legitimacy. They are only a dominant ideology to be replaced, one infers, by institutions or practices that truly aim at the public good (1994:2).

Koehn aims to displace all this writing.

> This book is an attempt to confront and rebut this challenge to the authority and ethics of professions by showing that [their] authority rests upon a secure and morally legitimating ground (1994:1).

And she says—somewhat in agreement with the position I will ultimately take here—that

> it is a normative matter to assert that a profession has no inner meaning, but rather consists of the sum total of what all or a majority of its members happen to be doing at a certain point in time (1994:7).

Thus, analytic historical and sociological work about the professions largely disappears in moral analysis of them, and vice versa. I shall come back to this point later.

But for the moment, let me put aside this interesting duality. I want to return here to the sharp separation of objectivity and advocacy that we make in the social sciences. Many of us, at least in the United States, have often bemoaned the politicization of academia. We feel that many of our colleagues pursue more or less explicit political agendas in their scholarship: sometimes feminism, sometimes liberalism, sometimes this or that religion or ideology or whatever. Those of us who have decried this politicization have had good reason, for we have seen what politicized academias can do. Marxist social science in the Soviet Union, Lysenkoist biology, Nazi race studies, counter-insurgency studies: the list is a long one.

Yet a large group even of those sociologists who oppose politicization—probably the majority of them—have themselves pursued what we might call politics *à la contrebande*.[4] They import their politics quietly rather than openly. To mention the example considered in chapter 8, many of us study inequality. But there is no purely empirical reason why inequality needs to be taken as something to be explained. Quite the contrary, as we just saw: distribution theory tells us that probabilistically, pure equality is an extremely unusual result. It is therefore a strikingly political act to assume that equality is the default value for social life, that equality is the value from which deviations must be explained. Yet certainly the majority of articles written in American sociology make just that assumption. I could proliferate such examples ad infinitum: intensive study of homosexuals when they are in fact a trivial portion of modern populations, collection of data in terms of politicized and probably nonsensical racial definitions, and so on. All of these indicate the continuous presence of a politics *à la contrebande*.

Compared with these other areas of inquiry, however, the literature on the professions does not suffer from a major problem of politicization, or even from a politics *à la contrebande*. The professions are not a major political issue in most societies. To be sure, people care about the privileges of professions—their high incomes, their self-governance, their power over other occupations. And they worry about whether those privileges are in some sense deserved. That is clearly a political issue, and it was openly debated in the early sociology of the professions. Parsons and the functionalists thought that the professions' privileges were deserved, while the conflict school exemplified by Freidson and Larson just as clearly implied that they were not. But this issue has largely disappeared from the sociology of professions since the 1970s. To be sure, many occupations still worry about whether they "really are" or "really aren't" professions, and that is clearly a political matter. But the sociological literature on professions hasn't worried about that issue for at least fifty years, even while writers in the professions themselves are wildly passionate about it.[5]

4. The phrase "politics *à la contrebande*" was coined by the French sociologist Etienne Ollion, with whom I have discussed these issues.

5. Indeed most invitations I have received to speak to professional groups have come with the implicit invitation to reassure my hosts that they "really are a profession."

So the professions literature is a good setting within which to examine the question of the relation between empirical facts and moral ones, because it is not a conspicuously politicized literature. But more important, we are all of us professionals ourselves, and so must live in practice the contradiction between professionalism as explained and professionalism as experienced, between professionalism as empirical fact and professionalism as moral obligation. It is plain that we ought to practice the objectivity that we preach. It is just as plain that we don't.

To engage this topic is to cross the moral Rubicon. For once we acknowledge that professions have some kind of moral being, we must begin to judge them under the sign of morality: that is, in moral and political terms of right and wrong, rather than—or perhaps in addition to—judging them in the cognitive terms of truth and falsehood. But by doing this, we turn our backs on Weber's celebrated argument in "Science as a Vocation (Weber 1946)." We have turned our backs on value-free science.

There is, to be sure, good reason for that. Weber's position is indefensible, for two reasons. The first and more important is that—as I have noted throughout this book—the social process itself consists mainly of things that are congealed values. "Juvenile delinquency" may sound like a scientific term, and of course it may be specificable in terms of various particular offenses at any given place and time. We can create a scale of empirical items defining a "measure" of juvenile delinquency. But we know perfectly well that including some things in that category while omitting others is a value process, not a scientific one. The grafitti artists who claim that their work is art rather than vandalism are certainly correct that the word "vandalism" denotes a socially produced value category, not a scientific reality. The same holds throughout the social process. Most of what appears to be solid social structure is just the hardened remains of some past value judgment, and those judgments can always be made to come back to life. They can made again contingent and open to issues of value.

This fact does not obliterate the possibility of social science, as some have claimed. For there are differences of degree. Some things are more value-laden than others. This can be true in several senses, it seems to me. Sometimes to say that something is "value-laden" is simply to make the empirical remark that there is more current controversy about it than about other things. At other times, to call something "value-laden" is to say that it is morally absolute—the rule not to kill others, for example. At still other times, calling something "value-laden" may mean simply that it is not easily measurable or is in principle unmeasurable, as when we say that one cannot set a value on life, and that it "has a unique value of its own." But even given these differences of degree, the Weberian position cannot stand, because of the centrality of value in all parts of the social process.

Yet there is another reason why the position fails. Weber's argument is, in fact, internally contradictory, because of Weber's own knowledge alienation. In the body of his famous essay on science as a vocation, Weber preached a value-free *Wissenschaft* to be applied to the social world around us. Yet he closed the essay with a paean to the values of the professional scholar. Did he actually think those values were themselves subject to a "value-free" analysis? That they could be "explained" by the interests of the scholar, or by other mechanical social forces? Clearly not. He thought they were transcendent, free. Weber's essay was an *apologia pro vita sua* pronounced in one of Germany's darkest hours: a moment of death, defeat, and destruction. Weber believed very profoundly in scholarship, and his belief was moral and normative. He believed that *Wissenschaft* was right and good, not simply that what it discovered was true. In this essay, he sought to enact that scholarly ideal by speaking it, by promulgating it, by literally naming it into existence. There is no more moral an act. And of course, in the essay's closing pages, his hymn to the "plain intellectual integrity" (p. 156) of the scholar must be regarded as the same kind of illusion as those illusions held by the (religious) people whom he gently mocked, saying that they "cannot bear the fate of the times like a man." His own position was every bit as religious a credo as those of the "traditional churches" he quietly scorns in these closing words.

Thus far I have proposed the problem: How are we to understand professionalism as a moral as well as an empirical fact? I have argued that scholars of professions all experience professionalism in two ways: once in the way we explain it in the professions we study, once in the way we practice it in our own professional lives. And I have argued that the imbrication of facts and values in the social world is inevitable in any case, because the social process itself consists in large measure of congealed social values, which are liable to "come to life" at any moment.

In the rest of this chapter, I shall set forth a new analysis of this problem. I shall first study the Durkheimian position on facts and values, which seems to me to undergird most sociological thinking on the matter. I shall then consider the adumbration of this position by Parsons in his work on the professions. Having rejected the Parsonian position, I shall then turn to a more abstract approach to the general problem of facts and values in sociology, from which I shall then try to sketch a pragmatist, processual theory of professionalism as a simultaneously empirical and moral enterprise. Like chapter 3, this chapter thus uses the case of the professions as a site for examining what is in fact a general question in social theory.

DEFINITIONS AND DURKHEIM

Before I go on, I wish to make give some specific definitions. Theoretical confusion is common in this area; indeed, sometimes obscurity is deliberately sought. We need to avoid this. Thus, some definitions:

1. By "profession," in this paper, I shall mean an expert occupation that looks more or less like American medicine or law. For most research purposes, that's a worthless definition. But it will be enough for us here.

2. By "empirical fact" I shall mean a fact that is commonly agreed to be ascertainable via surveys, interviews, or other forms of social data gathering. Empirical facts are judged by the criterion of truth or falsehood. I am not particularly worried that some empirical facts are more clearly so judgeable than others. That goes without saying. In a materialist culture, such as the one in which we find ourselves, the notion of empirical facts is not controversial in the slightest. Indeed, the majority of serious materialists think that empirical facts are the only kind of facts that there are.

3. By "morality" and "moral facts" I shall refer to a body of human phenomena that, in the phenomenology of experience, are taken to be rooted in a notion of "oughtness," and that are judged in that experience not by the criterion of truth or falsehood, but by that of right and wrong. I take it as primitive that humans have moral experience and understand some intentions as moral. Of course in a materialist culture such as ours, the existence of moral facts is generally an embarrassment to rigorous philosophies, but that doesn't stop materialist philosophers from themselves making in their personal lives all sorts of judgments that are moral in my sense. So they, in effect, admit the existence of moral judgments in their practice of living. That their theories sometimes say otherwise (e.g., by trying to "explain" morality) is of no interest here.

4. I shall use the word "normative" as an opposite to "empirical." Thus, I speak of "empirical sociology" versus "normative sociology." That is, normative things are for me under the criterion of oughtness *tout court*. They are not, as they were for Parsons, a projection of moral factors in my sense into the empirical world. They are radically moral: right or wrong, not true or false.

5. I shall use the word "value" to refer to the arbitrary assignment of oughtness or desirability to some quality or aspect of experience by human actors. The arbitrariness of this assignment is not something we identify from the

outside, as analysts, but rather refers to an aspect of the experience of the actor: a girl falls in love and comes to "value" a certain boy; a painter decides that "photographic" painting is not interesting, and that he will paint in little glints of light; and so on. It will be a question of theory and research whether such "value setting" in the phenomenology of experience is "real" in some ontological sense.

These definitions are not meant to be strong positions of any kind. They exist simply to prevent misunderstanding. Such misunderstandings arise because of the way these words—particularly the words "moral" and "normative" —are used in certain classics of sociology. The chief producer of these misunderstandings is Durkheim, who persuaded himself that he had resolved the great issue of facts and values. So let us examine his position.

Durkheim attacks the fact/moral issue from the beginning, in the introduction to the *Division du travail.*[6] He starts by treating the division of labor as a purely empirical fact. He chronicles its spread as an empirical phenomenon and as an interest of economists, biologists, and other writers. He then slides into a discussion of specialization, which is not exactly the same thing as the division of labor. (The latter concept assumes interdependence, but the former does not.) He accepts the biologists' seemingly evaluative notion of a "scale" of animals, and asserts that an organism's level on that scale is determined by the elaborateness of the division of labor within it. He underscores that the division of labor is not simply a social institution originating in the intelligence and will of humans (p. 3), but a general biological phenomenon. He refers to it as a law, as a condition of existence. All of this seems an attempt to make the division of labor seem to be a purely empirical reality, a matter of science, a thing of truth or falsehood.

But then suddenly, on page 4, he wonders whether such a fact must not shape our "moral constitution." This term comes from nowhere. Durkheim has not yet invoked the moral, nor indeed shown or speculated that such a thing as a "moral constitution" might exist. But he goes ahead and wonders whether we have a duty to follow the division of labor or resist it. This is, of course, a moral statement in my terms. But Durkheim does not answer this moral question directly, with a moral analysis of some sort: a study of legal theory, for example, or a jurisprudential reflection, or a theory of justice, or maybe a normative concept of personal growth. He does nothing like that. Rather, he notes that there is diversity of public opinion about whether to

6. All page references are to the French edition (Durkheim 1998), a relic of the chapter's origin as a talk to a French-speaking audience. The translations are mine.

accept or resist the division of labor. That is, he notes the empirical fact that there are differences of opinion about this moral issue. And he tries to lull us into thinking that such a discussion itself concerns morality (always, in my sense), by invoking the Kantian phrase "categorical imperative" (p. 6) to summarize the view of the division of labor that takes it as a good and positive thing. Throughout this analysis, he uses the obvious empirical fact that there is disagreement about moral matters to reject the notion that morality could be a disciplined or rigorous (in his word "scientific") form of apprehension of the world. (I avoid the word "knowledge" here deliberately.) He dismisses all generalizing theories of morality for their failure to be fully consistent, and all empirical theories of morality for their failure to be general.

It is essential to see what has happened here. Durkheim has looked only at empirical differences about moral matters, and has dismissed without mention long traditions of rigorous argument in fields like jurisprudence, legal theory, normative politics, and so on. His rejection of morality as an independent realm of apprehension rests completely on the fact that it does not conform to his own model of positive science (which he is, implicitly, defining as the only valid form of apprehension, an argument that we would partially admit were we to use the word "knowledge" here instead of "apprehension"). For morality to be real knowledge would require deductive regularity, Durkheim says, and as he says, the summary statements of the great moral theorists

> ne nous donnent donc pas un resumé des caractères essentiels que presentent réelement les règles morales dans telles sociétées ou tel type social determiné. . . . Rien n'autorise à voir dans les aspirations person- nelles ressenties par un penseur, si réelles qu'elles puissent être, une expression adéquate de le realité morale (p. 7).

> (. . . really don't give us a summary of the essential traits that moral rules actually present in such and such a society or type of society. . . . . Noth- ing allows us to see in the personal aspirations felt by some individual moralist, however real they might be, an adequate expression of moral reality.)

That is, morality is not a nonempirical fact (that is, it is nothing more than an empirical fact like any other) for three reasons: (a) because Durkheim doesn't think it consensual enough, (b) because we can't measure it using measures that measure only empirical facts, and (c) because there are differences among moralists (as if there were not among scientists?!). The only reality Durkheim concedes to morality is its empirical traces in people's views of their duties, their obligations, their righteousness. These are what he "measures"—the disagreements over moral issues—and these appear to lack the consistency Durkheim requires of a "science."

Of course, this entire argument applies to scientific positions as easily as it does to moral ones, and while there is a community discipline that adjudicates scientific debates, there is a similar community for the law, which Durkheim simply ignores. His entire argument is specious. By its logic, there is no empirical difference between morals and science. Both are subject to extensive debate, neither can be fully deductivized, neither evinces uniform consensus. Durkheim assumes that this single type of knowledge is "science," by which argument he means to assert both that there is only one kind of knowledge and that it is, as it happens, closer to the specific cognitive activity currently called "science" than to anything else. He also assumes that this (one) kind of knowledge is founded on material reality. In fact, these are simply assumptions of his argument, not conclusions from it.

Thus from the start, Durkheim redefines moral experience as empirical experience. He will use this argument, both here and throughout the book, to apply scientific measures to moral rules. To put this more precisely, he will apply empirical measures to behavior he defines—empirically—as "moral" and then assume that he has thereby achieved a rigorous and adequate representation of morality as it exists in the lifeworld and the phenomenology of experience. Note that I say a rigorous representation, not a scientific representation. For the word scientific, in Durkheim, actually means "materialist." Durkheim takes pains throughout these passages to insist that the entire moral realm of experience is merely an empirical thing, that it does not differ in any essential way from any other form of activity. And he concludes this great introductory passage by begging the question, as he so often does:

Si nous trouvons que [la division du travail] joue un rôle similaire à quelque autre pratique dont le caractère moral et normal est indiscuté, que, si dans certains cas elle ne remploit pas ce rôle, c'est par suite de déviations anormales; que les causes qui la déterminent sont aussi les conditions déterminantes d'autres règles morales, nous pourrons conclure qu'elle doit etre classé parmi ces dernières (p. 8).

(If we find that the division of labor plays a role similar to some other practice whose normal and moral character is indisputable; that if in certain cases it does not play this role, that [failure] follows from abnormal deviations; that the causes which determine it are also the determining causes of other moral rules; we will be able to conclude that it ought to be classed among those rules.)

That is, he will treat the division of labor as a moral fact (a) because it is like other things that are indubitably moral (things he never defines), (b) because it has a social function, and (c) because when it doesn't have that function, it looks abnormal (something that follows a priori). The entire passage simply ignores the phenomenological experience of moral life, including its author's experience of his own moral life, which by all accounts was certainly very considerable, since he was a passionate anticlerical and Dreyfusard.

Thus with Durkheim, moral facts, as I have defined them, disappear. Like Plato's forms, they exist only in terms of the shadows they cast in the empirical world. A Durkheimian analysis of professionalism follows immediately from this. For Durkheim, as indeed for most sociologists writing about professions, professionalism is simply a measurable empirical phenomenon in professional life. For example, we measure the existence of ethics codes. We categorize their contents. We create vignettes of moral dilemmas and administer them to professionals to derive scales of personal professionalism. Most important, we treat all of those measures as simply one more thing to explain. They are empirical facts in the great chain of empirical facts that is the materialist conception of the social process. Themselves explained by things like self-interest and conflict, they will in turn determine and therefore explain things like professional social status by the structural outcomes of the closure they produce.

Thus, thirty years ago I wrote an article on professional ethics deriving from empirical examples five basic properties of professional ethics activities: universal distribution, correlation with intraprofessional status, enforcement dependent on visibility, individual level of enforcement, and emphasis on collegial obligation. And I explained these five by a signed causal graph involving five variables: professional ethics activities, extraprofessional status, status threats, new skills, and control of skills. There was nothing whatever in the article about the moral (in my sense here) character of professional ethics, although there was to be sure a politics *à la contrebande*: I chided medicine for treating ethics as a purely individual matter, noting the problem of the rates and scheduling of caesarean sections, a kind of delict evident only in aggregate statistics, just like the Durkheimian "moral" regularities in the division of labor or national suicide rates. But aside from that, I looked only at the shadows that professionalism cast on the empirical wall. I looked carefully, to be sure, but only at the wall.

Thus, in the Durkheimian approach, professionalism is an empirical fact, and because of that fact, it is subject to "explanation," in the sense that it can be "caused" by antecedent variables. This fact of causation, of course, violates a fundamental rule of most ethical or moral systems, which is that the concept of duty should involve the free ability to perform that duty, St. Augustine's *non posse non peccare* notwithstanding. We find it hard to accept an ethical system in which certain people are, for various "causal" reasons, more able to be ethical than others, although the minute one writes that sentence, one realizes that Hindu ethics clearly involved such a system, and that the notion that a rule of morality must be universal may simply be an ideological prejudice of Western law.

PARSONS AND THE FUNCTIONALIST ANALYSIS OF PROFESSIONS

The Parsonian analysis of professions accepted the Durkheimian empiricization of morality, but concealed it under the abstractions of functionalism. This move made Parsons's analysis appealing to the professions themselves, even as it seemed in the long run unanalytic and politically conservative to Parsons's peers in sociology. In effect, Parsons took the professions' own assertions of their morality at face value; he took them as moral (in my sense) facts, representing truly nonempirical, willed commitments, ultimately subject to criteria of right and wrong, at least in the sense of "socially beneficial" or "not socially beneficial." Moreover, he justified his acceptance of professions' moralities with a functional argument that was, in fact, little different from that of the professions themselves: because professions served important social functions, their members deserved special rights and privileges. From the point of view of later theorists of the professions, Parsons simply accepted the professions' accounts of themselves as eleemosynary bodies who reaped the benefits of social closure only because of their *ex ante* dedication to the service of the society.

The two most important of Parsons's writings on the professions are the 1939 paper "Professions and Social Structure" and the essay on professions in the second edition of the *International Encyclopedia of the Social Sciences* (*IESS*). In the first of these, Parsons tries to undercut the notion that individual professionals are altruistic by arguing that the altruism of professionals is guaranteed by the "institutionalized moral order" of the profession itself. Translated into English, this means that individual doctors strive for success and achievement just as do other achievement-oriented modern social actors, but that their success is measured by scales that include moral (in my sense) order as part of their content. That is, doctors try to achieve excellence as doctors, in part to be financially rewarded, but part of the excellence they must display in order to get this financial reward is behaving in a properly moral manner. Of course this view simply pushes the problem up to the group level, for the professional rules that establish these scales-that-include-moral-requirements themselves require explanation, and in Parsons that comes from the social function of the professions as eleemosynary institutions—that is, as institutions committed to public welfare.

This commitment is, of course, just a functionalist assumption. It was itself a kind of moral idealization of what a pure empiricist would say "is really going on in society." At worst—and this would later be the argument of the conflict school—the whole functionalist story was simply a cover for the social closure projects of the professions, which the conflict school believed aimed purely at power and resources. But at best, the Parsonian analysis could pass for a truly moral analysis of the standing of professions.

Read in such a manner, this moral analysis is what Parsons gives in his *IESS* article. In his definition of professions, he follows the then-dominant "traits" view, arguing that a profession must have an intellectual basis and applicable skills. But he also insists that "a full-fledged profession must have some institutional means of making sure that such competence will be put to socially responsible uses." Note the meaning of "must" here. There are three possible English parsings of this sentence, and Parsons seems to mean one of them in particular. By the word "must," Parsons does not mean that "a full-fledged profession is required definitionally to have such institutional means," in the sense that some legitimating authority will take away its charter as a profession unless those means exist; for, after all, neither such an authority nor such a charter exists, although of course various levels of legal recognition do exist. Nor does Parsons mean that "the antecedent social causes that create professions also have as another of their consequences the result that every full-fledged profession will, by virtue of determining causes, have such institutional means." No, Parsons means that "a full-fledged profession *ought* to have some institutional means of guaranteeing socially responsible use of its competence, and an expert group without that is a morally bad profession." That is, Parsons's argument here is plainly normative in my sense. It is not an empirical statement of any sort.

But when we take Parsons's writing in a purely empirical sense, as many of his readers did, it is just a labeling of whatever exists as a "normative order," along the lines of Alexander Pope's "Whatever is, is right." Thus universities were said to be "institution complexes," and so on. Underneath the jargon, Parsons seemed to be simply idealizing a particular empirical order, saying quite literally that whatever is must, by that very fact, be right. (This problem is analogous to the problem raised by the position that posterity is always right, which has been noted several times before.) Thus (p. 540), he says, "Law is specifically social, being concerned with the intellectual grounding and systematization of the normative bases of social order." In essence, that is true tautologically. If one thinks that the law is that which serves a social function (rather than that the law is a group of people, or a set of organizations, or whatever) then this is probably the best definition of what law "is." If we already have some vague idea of what law is in terms of ideal functions, then we can use a definition like this (as opposed to one based on people, or groups, or texts, etc.) to embody that definition and to identify for us a set of activities as "law," of which we describe the boundaries and limits by giving this definition.

But doing that is very close to undertaking prescriptive social theory, as Parsons's many critics argued. Parsons's mistake—directly traceable to Durkheim—was that rather than thinking he was doing prescriptive social theory, he thought he was doing empirical social theory. Camic has emphasized this slide in his analysis of Parsons's very flexible usage of the word "normative" (Camic 1989:66), which in Parsons sometimes means "morally good," and at other times means "typical," and at still other times means "sensed by actors as dictated by a certain kind of social rule." And Parsons tended to embed "norms" in "larger normative orders" which in turn embodied "values" and even "ultimate values." This brought him quite obviously to the realm of the purely moral or religious, which he nonetheless insisted on treating as a purely empirical world.

If we can summarize the discussion to this point, then, I began by posing the question of how we are to understand professionalism as an empirical and as a moral fact. I insisted that scholars of professions experience professionalism one way in our explanations of the professions we study, and a different way in our living of our own professional lives. I argued that this contradiction—or "knowledge alienation," as I called it—is inevitable because the social process itself consists in large measure of congealed social values, which are liable to "come to life" at any moment. It cannot be studied by pure empiricism.

After some definitions differentiating the moral and empirical realms, I showed that Durkheim handled moral facts by looking only at whatever shadows they cast in the empirical world—quantities of "moral" acts, texts of laws, and so on—and by treating those shadows as explicable social facts like any other. The Durkhemian claim that this constituted an analysis of morality in the nonempirical sense is false: Durkheim simply ignores or dismisses rigorous traditions of purely moral (in my sense) inquiry.

Parsons continues this Durkheimian claim that empirical analysis suffices for moral analysis, although his analysis of the professions can be read as a purely moral one, and may very well be excellent as such. (For example, it certainly correlates very closely with the proposals of the ethicist Koehn, quoted at the outset.) That is, we could think about the Parsonian analysis of professions as the proper foundation for a book on what professions and professionals "ought" to do, and that might be a worthwhile book to write. But as it stands, the Parsonian analysis is, like Durkheim's, an empirical analysis claiming to "account for" phenomena of morality whose origin it in fact simply ignores.

A PRAGMATIST VIEW

I wish now to address the problem that Durkheim ignored: the presence in the social process of a kind of activity and consciousness that is, quite simply, moral.[7] I continue to use professionalism as my example.

---

7. I should note that I could just as easily use the word "political" here, since my argument applies to both the moral and the political, in terms of the preceding chapter. I would actually prefer to use the word "normative" (which embraces the moral and the political), but I am afraid of the confusions that plague Parsons's use of that word. I considered the differences between the moral and the political at length in *Chaos of Disciplines*, ch. 7. That analysis focuses on the difference between two kinds of sociological encounters with the normative side of the social process: the political one, which emphasizes attempts to change a social process perceived as unjust, and the moral or humanist one, which emphasizes the attempt to understand the complexities and varieties of the social "for themselves," as they are. Most of that argument was dedicated to what I viewed and still view as the normative inconsistencies of the political position. The "normative" chapters of the present book try to elaborate the moral/humanist position that was merely sketched in *Chaos of Disciplines*. But the opposition between the politicians and moralists there noted lies within a larger opposition that pits both groups against the pure empiricists who fail altogether to see the inherently valued nature of the social process. Both the politicians and the moralists find something fundamentally erroneous in the Durkheimian position and the knowledge alienation it entails.

The puzzle remains the following. We can measure professionalism "empirically," just as Durkheim measured suicide empirically. We can develop scales of moral behavior among professionals: the vignettes and measures mentioned earlier. We can find variables that measure past professional behavior, the relative status of professions and professionals, threats to that status, and on and on. And we can create a model showing how these things "cause" each other in some sequence and indeed how they "cause" professionalism (and/or social closure) as our final dependent variable. We can probably "explain" a good deal of variance with this model.

But this doesn't somehow get rid of the fact that, if viewed in phenomenological terms, thousands of professionals—ourselves among them—experience complex dilemmas of professionalism and try to resolve them in terms which they understand to be moral terms. Even the fact that those decisions may turn out in ways that we can to some extent predict does not make all that experience into some kind of noise or meaninglessness.

Once again, Durkheim offers an instructive example. In *Le suicide*, he is at pains, in a famous footnote at the end of book 3, chapter 1, to announce that his demonstration of the regularity of certain social patterns in suicide, and indeed his hypostatization of those regularities into the things he calls "social forces," do not impugn free will. As he tells us, his demonstrations only guarantee that a certain proportion of a certain group commit suicide, not which ones do so in particular (Durkheim 1951:325).

Of course his argument here is trivial or, at best, not worked out. He should have argued that social determination is one of several factors—along with the immediate contextual situation, moral rules, and peer pressures—that weigh on the deciding individual. The problem of theorizing morality then comes down to theorizing how a self confronts such a mix of influences. But in effect, Durkheim argues that actual, willed behavior is essentially noise, in the modern sense; it is simply the error variance against which we test the "real forces," the social ones. Durkheim was in this sense merely one of the many pioneers of probabilistic conceptions of causality.

But of course the willed behavior of human beings is only noise when analysts choose to view it as such, and the fact that we can always—no matter how tiny a portion of it we consider—show that willed behavior has some social origins, or even more generally some determining origins (in Durkheim's sense), does not rid us of the problem that much of willed behavior is, in any experiential sense, "moral" and to be judged right or wrong, not true or false or explained versus unexplained. After all, we must believe this if we acknowledge the legitimate existence of a law presuming individual responsibility, an acknowledgement that is virtually universal among sociologists, so far as I can tell.

A metaphor may make my point clearer. Durkheim's procedure—and indeed the dominant procedure of modern "explanatory" sociology—is rather like looking at a given child and attending only to its male ancestors. Every child has two grandfathers, four great grandfathers, and so on, back to 128 great-great-great-great-great-grandfathers. And we can explain a good deal about the child by looking at all of those grandfathers, even the ones way over on the "maternal" side: the father of the mother of the mother of the mother, and so on, down to the child. But just because we can create an account of some things about the child in terms of grandfathers, we aren't any less obliged to understand the contribution of the grandmothers. Nor should we regard that contribution as "noise," as do our current statistical methods. Phenomenologically, moral experience disappears in Durkheim's analysis only because he refuses to look at it, not because it is inherently unreal. But the Durkheimian approach is very seductive because every "family unit" in such an array leading to the present act is, in fact, represented in the Durkheimian approach, always by its "causal" portion: the male of the pair. Thus it can be argued that we "see some piece of" every antecedent act. The problem is that it is always the same type of piece.

Moreover, Durkheim makes this "causal" piece seem like the only one by focusing his analysis completely on determination. In my metaphor, the male ancestors affect the child through determining him (or her), whereas the female ones—the moralities, in this metaphor—relate to the child as a kind of moral ancestry, whatever that might be. That is, it is in part the very notion of causality itself—and the promotion of causality to the position of centrality in our attempt to apprehend the social world—that makes moral experience disappear. That the measurable and the determined are the only things we can rigorously apprehend about social life is an ideology, as indeed Koehn pointed out in the book quoted at the outset of this chapter. It is one of our core ideas as sociologists, to be sure, but it is clearly an ideology, in the sense of being a value position about which we are not willing or able to entertain negative evidence.

It should be remembered that we have many ways indeed of relegating the moral dimensions of things like professionalism to invisibility. We can, like Durkheim, simply regard the conflict of moral ideas as prima facie voiding the validity of moral inquiry. Or we can, like him, simply regard morality as unmeasurable, and then measure something related to it, and announce that we have thereby measured the original unmeasurable thing. Or we can define professionalism as a tacit skill, or we can say that professionalism is "something that can be taught only by apprenticeship." We really do have many ways of not seeing the inherently moral quality of the social process that we analyze, even though we wouldn't for a minute live our own lives simply as if we were living out the causal plan established for us by our determining causal ancestors, whether real grandparents or Durkheimian social forces.

Thus far, then, I have argued that acts have two lines of ancestry: one of them causal, the other moral. Moreover, I have argued that these lines of ancestry have different quality: both are means of apprehension and connection, but one of them involves causality while the other involves moral descent, a concept as yet unelaborated.

It will help elaborate that concept if we examine the literature of law and jurisprudence. In that literature, the "causal" analysis characteristic of Durkheim appears, to be sure, but in a position quite literally reversed. In legal analysis it is assumed that people do what they do out of a will free to choose. In extreme cases, one may consider the "causal origins" of an act. In juvenile courts, for example, the home situation might be treated as a factor "explaining" a criminal action that would otherwise be treated as originating in moral choice. Just as in the social sciences free will becomes the distant penumbra around the core facts of determinism—the noise around the reality of social determination—so in legal theory causal determination can become at times the residual explanation that allows a modification of formal rules of responsibility, the "noise" around the reality of free will.

Note too that the analysis to this point fits very closely with the pragmatist theory of the self adumbrated by James, Cooley, and Mead. In the Meadean formulation, the "I" is the independently acting self, an originator free of social causation. This is the moral actor of my analysis so far, and the moral professional of the ethical professionalism literature. By contrast, the Meadean "me" is the socially constrained self, built of social experience and thereby "caused" in its approach to action.

At the same time, the distinction is not exactly parallel. Mead himself always held that activity originated with the "I," even if the "me" immediately changed, modified, or reinterpreted that action. And Mead would have argued that moral rules would have been part of the "generalized other," and hence part of the "me" rather than the "I." So the parallel is not exact. On this logic, however, Mead would have been treating moral rules as somewhat empirical things: actual specifications of empirical duties. But he might have held that the type of obligation attached to them was different from the obligation that governs purely empirical prescriptions: thus, a moral prescription would be, "You should behave as a responsible professional because that is the right thing to do," while the purely empirical prescription would be, "You should behave as a responsible professional because if you don't, you will be disbarred" (personal consequence) or "because the profession will be brought into disrepute and other professions will seize our areas of work" (social consequence). In this example, that is moral which is done for its own sake, while the same thing done for a further end is simple instrumentalism.

This analysis seems to imply that descent, result, and consequence are the indicators of empirical connection, while value immediately contained in a moment is the indicator of moral status. Yet the pragmatist theory of ethics quite specifically defined duty as having to do with the future, and in particular with the concept of growth or elaboration into the future. Causality, by contrast, involves the past. In *Human Nature and Conduct*, Dewey is explicit:

> The moral issue concerns the future: it is prospective. . . . The moral problem is that of modifying the factors which now influence future results (1922:18).

> Questions of causation are physical, not moral, except when they concern future consequences. It is as causes of future actions that excuses and accusations must alike be considered (1922:17).

Or, as Dewey and Tufts put it in *Ethics*:

> Duty is what is owed by a partial isolated self embodied in established, facile, and urgent tendencies, to that ideal self which is presented in aspirations which, since they are not yet formed into habits, have no organized hold upon the self and which can get organized hold upon the self only by a more or less painful and difficult reconstruction of the habitual self (1908:362).

As Dewey and Tufts note, this constitutes a relativizing of Kant's antithesis between the self of desire and the self of reason. Morals in such a context are always relative to a point in the trajectory of the individual (or, to take the example at hand, in that of the profession). More important, they are also always relative to time and place. The great variety of "moralities" in the world does not testify, as Durkheim thought, to the incoherent quality of morality in itself, but rather to its extraordinary fecundity and imagination. Indeed, the heart of morality, in Dewey's view here and elsewhere, is the notion of aspiration. Although he viewed habit in a much more optimistic way than did Weber, Dewey knew well that pure habit was a deadening of the human spirit. No profession, he might have argued, could ever achieve true professionalism. Professionalism for Dewey, quite the contrary, would lie in a perpetual aspiration towards improvement, towards broadening of experience, towards breadth of sympathy, and so on.

Now to be sure, the pragmatists did admit that meaningful moral action could degenerate into mere routines, gestures that lost moral significance. Dewey was inclined to deny to such routines what was for him the positive name of "habit." For example, he argued that "the essence of habit is an acquired predisposition to ways or modes of response, not to particular acts except as, under special conditions, these express a way of behaving" (1922:32). Later in the same book, however, he admits to dead habits of the Weberian "routinization" type: There are "two kinds of habit; intelligent and routine. All life has its élan, but only the prevalence of dead habits deflects life into mere élan" (p. 51). A dead habit was a habit no longer in the service of a larger aspiration. The true professional, for Dewey, would undertake the most routine interview or service with an aspiration of making it more alive, more serviceable, more real. Professionalism would not be one given thing: an ethics code, a typical stance towards clients, a set of secure if routine habits. Rather it should be a dynamic, growing experience of professional work, always bringing new kinds of work under the moral discipline of a willed professionalism, a continuous adjustment to changes in professional techniques, in professional organizations, in professional relationships.

For Dewey was quite explicit that these environing relations, like everything else, could change. The social process was a perpetual adaptation of actors and groups to each other. There was for him nothing absolutely individual (rather than partly social) about professionalism or any other form of moral action. Thus, on the subject of criminal punishment, he remarked:

> By killing an evil-doer or shutting him up behind stone walls, we are enabled to forget both him and our part in creating him. Society excuses itself by laying the blame on the criminal: he retorts by putting the blame on bad early surroundings, the temptations of others, lack of opportunities, and the persecutions of the officers of the law. Both are right, except in the wholesale character of their recriminations. But the effect on both sides is to throw the whole matter back to antecedent causation, a method which refuses to bring the matter to truly moral

judgment. For morals has to do with acts still within our control, acts still to be performed (1922:17/18).

So here we have again the notion of morals as related to the future (not the past), but also the insistence that moral responsibility pervades society, because it involves all the conditions of an act.

> Honesty, chastity, malice, peevishness, courage, triviality, industry, irresponsibility are not private possessions of a person. They are working adaptations of personal capacities with environing forces. All virtues and vices are habits which incorporate objective forces. They are interactions of elements contributed by the make-up of an individual with elements supplied by the out-door world (1922:16).

Thus, for Dewey an increase in professionalism would be an improvement of both the profession and its clients, since society and individual are produced by the same things. As a reality, professionalism is not the property of an individual professional or profession, but a relation between the habits of individual professionals and professions and the changing world around them. It is, like everything else, a process.

It seems possible, then, to create a view of professionalism that merges the causal approach of the sociologists following Durkheim and the moral approach we might develop from Dewey and the pragmatists. Professions and their members evolve steadily through time. They are, like all else in the social process, lineages of events unfolding in a process of perpetual re-creation and change. Their stability as social entities—the social structures we call professions on the one hand, and the individual ones we call personalities on the other—is built steadily through event after event, as action weaves together the threads of determination that come to it from the past in the face of the possibilities of the present and in light of the moral potentialities of the future.

That's a very abstract statement. But what it means is that at any given moment, a professional comprises all of his characteristics and past experiences, professional and otherwise, and must make himself again in his coming actions. These actions are open because the present is ever-changing; because there are, as we have noted, new techniques, new colleagues, and new clients, as well as a hundred irrelevant novelties in his life as family member, social figure, and so on. The same is true for the profession as a whole, which is a more distributed kind of actor, concretized, perhaps, in the formal reality and structure of a professional association, but also embodied in professional schools, textbooks, and professionals themselves. It too has present characteristics and past experiences, all of which can shape its behavior, and it too faces a present situation that is largely defined not so much by the logic of its own past as by the environment of competing professions, of new ideas and new possible jurisdictions, of changing larger conditions, and all the vast ecology of the system of professions.

It is action that in its progress from situation to situation knots off these possibilities into defined events that themselves send on determinant forces to later events. That action can obey various logics, but one of them is the logic of moral professionalism. In keeping with Dewey, I will define that professionalism as an attempt consciously to shape the situation in light of a particular set of idealized rules which are familiar enough to all of us. Those rules can be studied for their own sake, and indeed can sustain a literature that, contra Durkheim, can have both rigor and tradition. In a longer work one could develop several aspects of this argument. But the most important is that professionalism is not so much a particular content as it is a particular way of doing the activity of being a professional. This is not to say that contents of professionalism do not exist. Quite the contrary, professionals produce such contents all the time and embody them in texts, in ethics codes, in vignettes, and in all the things that I earlier noted that we could measure. But none of these things contains professionalism. Dewey said in *Democracy and Education* that it is not possible to tell another person an idea. It is impossible for the other to hear the idea as other than a fact, a dead thing. That is what happens to the contents of (moral) professionalism. They become dead facts, which may or may not stimulate this or that professional to the real thinking that is professionalism, or, put more properly, to the aspiration that is professionalism.

At the same time, however, these dead contents do have causal effects, and, as many people have shown, one of the obvious consequences of ethics codes, for example, is social closure and, ultimately, rise of professional status. These are in some sense an unintended consequence of moral professionalism. They are also, of course, very often the intended consequence of other people—and of some professionals—who may very well desire the rewards of social closure rather than the moral practice that is professionalism. Thus, we can see that this approach allows us to believe in the fact that there are obvious causal regularities that will appear in the histories of professions, such as are noted by the conflict school. These can arise both intentionally and unintentionally. But the approach also allows for truly moral action as a professional: that is, for professionalism, although this is not a particular content but a way of acting, and as such cannot be taught directly. We therefore allow the possibility of a developing historical tradition of theories of (moral) professionalism.

This evolving tradition of professionalism not only might include the usual ethics codes, personal rules, and so on, but might also grapple with the kinds of corporate delicts that I mentioned in my long-ago paper on professional ethics: the volume and scheduling of caesarean sections. That is, one of the inputs to this moral literature on the professions needs to be the sociological detection of potential moral and ethical problems at the professional level.

This last suggestion points me to a closing question: How ought we to pursue the social study of professions once we have recognized the interpenetration of the moral and the causal in the unfolding of the histories of professions and the lives of professionals? I think the way forward on this topic lies in considering the fractal nature of action, and indeed of situations. Professionalism, like any moral type of acting, must be scaled to meet many different kinds of situations, and to govern the action of people who vary widely in antecedents, education, desires, interests, even moral quality. So our concept of it must embrace that complexity, which I think involves a kind of fractalizing of Kantian ethics, as I have argued elsewhere (in *Chaos of Disciplines*, ch. 7). But that is yet another topic.

Epilogue

In this epilogue, I want to argue that sociology has its deepest roots in the humanities, even though in pursuit of its humanistic aims it must often employ scientific forms of knowing, like inferential statistics and pattern search, in addition to those forms of knowing that are traditionally seen as more humanistic, like ethnography and archival analysis. To understand what is meant by this assertion requires some extended reflection.[1]

As I noted in the preface, the opening chapters of this book are written in what might be called the abstract style of theory. The "historicality" of chapter 1, the "processual human nature" of chapter 2, the "linked ecologies" of chapter 3, and the "excess" of chapter 5 are presented from outside the processes they discuss. These chapters could have been written by a sociological theorist from another planet. Only chapter 4, on lyrical sociology, takes for granted—in its insistence on an author's emotions and in particular on the

---

1. This epilogue draws in part on a paper written at the request of Robert Zussman, as a contribution to a collection of pieces on Michael Burawoy's concept of "public sociology" ("On Humanistic Sociology," in D. Clawson et al., *Public Sociology* [Berkeley: University of California Press, 2007], pp. 195–209). But it repurposes completely what it takes from that earlier piece. Note also that while I speak throughout this epilogue about "sociology," in keeping with the language of the present book, the argument here generalizes to all social science. And the apparent distinction between "scientific" and "humanistic" knowledge, both in this paragraph and later on, should be understood within the fractal conception of knowledge (both empirical and normative) laid out in *Chaos of Disciplines*, especially chapters 1 and 7. As I argued there, no such distinction is ever complete; there is always science within humanism, and vice versa.

concept of humane sympathy—the idea that the sociologist is necessarily part of the picture of social life that he or she creates.

Leaving this outsider stance, the four closing chapters follow chapter 4's lead in locating the sociologist irremovably within that created picture—not, in their case, treating the analyst as an emotional being, but as a moralist and an actor. Choosing an outcome measure, choosing a concept of social order, conceptualizing types of inequality, imagining a truly professional life: these are not purely theoretical perceptions of the social world, but practical acts towards it. In many ways, they are moralizing acts, and we should be conscious of them as such. Moreover, their moral judgment can be seen as a way station towards an explicitly political desire to turn the social process in some new direction.

It might then seem that there are two separable types of theorizing, one dispassionate and external to the social process, the other committed and internal to it (just as there are two temporalities, one outside the process, one within it). This is indeed the position of Michael Burawoy (2005) in his celebrated paper on public sociology, where he labels these two approaches as "professional" and "critical" sociology respectively. (For Burawoy, professional sociology means maximizing precision in methods and science, while critical sociology means addressing the philosophical and normative foundations of the discipline.) But I shall argue that these are not separable practices, but only two interpenetrating parts of a unified practice that unfolds as we do sociological work.

To understand why a unified practice is necessary, it is helpful first to state three themes that underlie parts 3 and 4 of this book. First, all humans believe themselves capable of free action. Partial explanation of their activity by "determining causes" of the Durkheimian statistical sort does not prove that they are not so capable, and the openness of all social entities to action in the present provides an obvious possible location for free action governed by moral values rather than by causality. These things being the case, we must treat normative action as something that is "real" in precisely the same senses that "explained" action is real. Determination and freedom are both expressed in the social process; neither is residual to the other.

Second, the social process is local. Sympathies, acts, meanings: all three are always located in a particular time and (social) space, and the strategy of universalism—either as politics or as science—cannot ultimately escape this particularity, because it ends up thereby ignoring one of the defining aspects of human experience—being a particular someone, somewhere, sometime. This is as true of social "science" as of any other activity that attempts a project of universalism; "obvious" measures of outcome and "obvious" ideas about inequality turn out to be loaded with particular normative and value assumptions. But all the same, the first of my three themes implies that our particularity (and, therefore, that of our explanations) is only partial. We are particular, but we possess some means of struggling with that particularity.

Third, as emphasized throughout, the social process is largely constituted of "things" that are essentially congealed values: social entities, phenomena, and personality attributes that have been preferentially encoded or enacted or "lineagized" because of value concerns that vary across the regions of the process. One can pretend—for good political reasons associated with the admirable heritage of classical liberalism—that things like "social mobility" and "the family" and "bureaucracy" and "feminism" can be regarded as fixed social things like molecules of water. Our political system creates powerful incentives to behave as if this were true. But that doesn't make it true. The astounding variety of human societies both over time and across space reveals that the social entities and abstractions within those societies are and were the ongoing concretizations of social values that have their ultimate origin not in causes, but in the endless conversation among humans about the particular nature of what has value, what should happen, and what is good. The implication of this fact for social science is that even a purely arbitrary or random choice of explanandum will involve taking something as natural—as not needing explanation—and will hence necessarily entail implicit value-choices, even if investigators themselves were magically universalist.

These three themes place a certain absolute limit on the abstract universalist project that lies behind the kind of thinking characteristic of chapters 1, 2, 3, and 5, and that is familiar to any working social scientist trained since the turn of the twentieth century: the ideal of a progressive, cumulative social science that will explain or predict more and more human behavior. Ultimately, there cannot be such an abstract account of social life independent of any form of value commitments. One can claim to have such a thing: economics is the classic modern example. But one makes such a claim only by ignoring everything that doesn't fit into one's view and—to take the case of economics in particular—relegating everything important (and indeed everything actually determining) in human life to the unparsable realms of "utility" and chance, and simultaneously creating—indeed enforcing—a world in which behavior that doesn't follow economists' rules is severely penalized. The end result is not universal truth, but only performative ideology masquerading as truth. There is no escape from either the value-nature of the social process or from the corollary that any absolutely universalizing strategy for understanding that process has inherent limits.

If we must forego the possibility of universal abstract knowledge of the social process, this by no means implies a simple surrender to particular values. Rather, we must create forms of unified practice that simultaneously pursue both universal and particular understandings, subject to the limits each places on the other.

To understand this unified practice, it is helpful to consider in some detail Burawoy's argument mentioned earlier, but to begin not with the empirical/normative distinction already noted but with a second distinction Burawoy makes, that between the two audiences for sociology. Burawoy's first audience for sociology is the discipline itself, and it is within that audience that he locates the contrast between professional (empirical) and critical (normative) sociology. His second audience is the world beyond the discipline. Here, the contrast between professional and critical sociology becomes that between "policy sociology" (the empirical evaluation of actual policies chosen by the legitimated political system) and "public sociology" (the sustaining of general political positions within civil society, and possibly the critique of the legitimated political system itself).

It is hardly surprising that there is a difference in sophistication and style between social science whose audience is other professionals and social science whose audiences are politicians and public. But the more important difference between inside and outside arises from the fact that most modern societies are not very interested in having (or paying for) deep knowledge about themselves, while the social science disciplines assemble precisely those who are most interested in that deep knowledge. It is therefore all the more important to state why social scientists are committed to deep knowledge of social life.

Deep knowledge about society is worthwhile for two reasons. First, it is worthwhile for its own sake. Burawoy (2005:10) and many others hold that the only reason for knowing anything about society is to change society. This is wrong. Knowledge of all kinds—social, memorial, artistic, craft, genealogical, whatever—is one of the great projects of humanity. Saying that there is no noninstrumental reason for good knowledge of society is like saying there is no noninstrumental reason for good knowledge of how to play the mbira, how to follow cricket, how to apply makeup, or how to understand relativity. Making knowledge of things—even of passing or unimportant things—is one of the principal activities of our species, and all forms of knowledge other than deliberately evil knowledge (e.g., how to torture and kill) are good things. And improving that knowledge—where the direction of "improvement" itself constitutes a subject of organized debate and investigation by committed groups and individuals—is an equally essential human pursuit.

But deep knowledge of society is important for a second and perhaps greater reason. As Burawoy argues, it can help guide the social process. And a social science discipline like sociology can and should play a crucial role in that guidance, precisely because it has a moral obligation to view itself—following the terms of chapter 7—as one of several trustees of the long-run project to understand society, one that tries to reach beyond the specific interests and concerns of a particular social place and a particular moment in time. Such trusteeship doesn't involve a universal view from nowhere. That doesn't exist. But it does mean recognizing that the present moment—together with its ideals and criteria for living—is a moment of passage, which must always be seen as part of the endless flow of things. A trustee must use terms and criteria that strive to reach beyond those of the current moment and the current society. A trustee must try to imagine modes of addressing difference across social space and time that are normatively just even though they cannot be perfectly universal (and of course they wouldn't mean anything if they were). Creating such connection across time is even more difficult than doing it across social space at a moment. But the discipline must follow E. P. Thompson's advice to provincialize the present.

It is, of course, difficult to persuade society to provincialize itself. It is hard to make sacrifices in the present on behalf of the future or the past, particularly because the sacrificing of the interests of all other time periods to the interests of the present is one of the essential elements of the dominant idea of our age, that of capitalism. But sociology cannot be so narrow. It must broaden its temporal range of vision, just as it must broaden its social range beyond its local region in the present. Neither of these can occur through pure universalization. For stripping oneself of particular content denies that it is the universal human experience to be particular. No, a sociologist must be a traveler, across time as well as across social space. Only as a company of travelers can we become in effect trustees of the larger process through and across which we travel. What we must discover—or, rather, imagine—are humane, just, and creative rules for that travel.[2]

---

2. An interesting fictional investigation of the question of travel and trusteeship can be found in Doris Lessing's novel, *The Making of the Representative of Planet Eight* (Lessing 1982). The careful reader will note that my own position can be used to show that the trusteeship argument just made is in principle unrealizable. Even trusteeship is ultimately located in time and social space, and cannot escape that location. Put another way, even conceiving

The practical implications of Burawoy's inside/outside distinction seem clear. The discipline should preserve its most secure resources for this disciplinary project of trusteeship, and should use as many as possible of its fungible resources for specific subprojects related to that trusteeship: subprojects that the discipline itself finds truly important, but that governmental or other funders may find unimportant or even threatening. This is all the more essential because of pressing changes in higher education, which has long been the main fungible resource base of sociology. On the one hand, teaching is being pushed towards occupational training, and research is being pushed towards purely applied work, even in elite universities. On the other, the disciplines themselves are surrendering to heteronomy under deans pursuing the chimera of innovation as "measured" by meaningless metrics. Such changes mean that the disciplines themselves are under major threat, much less the trusteeship project of moving our encounter with the social process beyond the here and now.

The issues raised by Burawoy's inside/outside distinction thus provide a first glance at the importance of thinking processually about the combined empirical/normative role of sociology. But more complex issues are raised by the other distinction, that between the two types of thinking with which I began: external/empirical/means-based thinking and internal/normative/ends-based thinking.

In the processual view, the means/ends distinction falls apart. It can be made at any given time, but it is meaningless across time. Every end is both a moment of consummation and a starting point for new projects. Every present becomes past, so every end disappears. No end can be permanently secured, because even the past is being perpetually rewritten in line with the present, and will be again rewritten in the future. In any case, there is no unchanging self with respect to which means/end status can be decided. The whole means/ends distinction comes apart when viewed diachronically.

But the means/ends distinction actually creates problems even as an approach to a single moment, for it enforces a curious inversion. We normally expect the ends to be more important, but in the synchronic application of the distinction, this expectation does not necessarily hold.

At any given moment, aspects of society can serve as means to particular

---

of ideal action as some form of "ideal participation in the inevitable process of change" is ultimately something that could ultimately disappear from the social process, as indeed many forms of trusteeship have done under the dominance of capitalist reasoning, where discounting deliberately devalues the future, and deliberate ignorance disregards the past.

ends only if they are stable, fixed, and given. Such social means will be based on those individual and social entities that are most taken for granted in the social process at the moment and in the social region at issue: those aspects of the social process that are "most congealed," and in which the value content of the process is least evident. These can then be treated as "objective facts" to be understood with "scientific methods," supporting "expected policy implications," and so on. An example in modern societies would be things like the "laws of economics" or the "institutions of democracy." Both are almost completely fixed and lawlike systems in the present moment. But both are in fact long-run accretions of socially constructed values; both are in part continuously encoded only by the expenditure of hundreds of billions of dollars spent teaching them as objective truth; and both could, like so many such accretions before them, be destroyed by any number of potential turnings of the social process. Nonetheless, for the moment, one may for most explanatory purposes treat them as materially real and hence ignore the values congealed in them, even though those values are, for this very reason, the most consequential values of society.

Because such momentarily absolute values are relatively uncontested, they can serve as means for other values that are contested. Thus, the unquestioned ideals and machineries of democracy are used as the means by which to achieve gay marriage or the advancement of women or the right to worship God in one's own way or the shrinkage of government or whatever. In such everyday experience, "ends" are differences in value about those things which are not specified already in the value structure of the taken-for-granted core. That core is "means," because it is fixed for the moment; it is "human nature"; it is "the universal." Thus, paradoxically, the strongest value constructions in the social process act by virtue of their very strength simply as means to other values, about which there is "legitimate conflict."

Such means/ends reasoning is characteristic of Burawoy's "professional sociology" (for the inside) and "policy sociology" (for the outside). For example, sociologists need to get the science right about what causes inequality (professional sociology). Then, they can participate in democratic politics (a means) to decide what to do about the situation (acting as public sociologists), and can evaluate that doing (as policy sociologists). This is the exact equivalent of having debates in a legislature about issues of private difference (valued ends) and then deciding what to do about them on the basis of (that is, by means of) "due process," "constitutional rules," and so on, which are not contested. We have already seen this model in chapter 7 in its guise as the liberal resolution of the problem of order.

But as the Burawoy distinctions suggest, there will also exist a critical periphery that is interested in raising even the "hidden" (congealed, temporarily fixed) social values to visibility. This is the group that thinks that what are currently regarded as universal "means" in society are in fact simply a version of a particular valued end, to which one can in fact conceive viable alternatives. Obviously, this line of argument will appeal to those whose particular desired ends are not realized by whatever is presently the universally accepted public means of decision.

An example in sociology would be critical sociologists' arguing that the whole idea of control variables is political because by using sufficient controls in highly detailed employment data on modern societies, one can show that men and women do in fact receive very nearly equal pay for equal work. In the critical view, that is, if our "science" doesn't find the expected (and by this group politically preferred) answer (that women suffer discrimination), then something is the matter with the science. In this case, for example, the argument concerns controls for choice of occupation, hours per week of employment, and degree of experience, since those controls assume implicitly that women freely choose occupation, hours, and experience, whereas the feminist critics would argue either that women have been forced into low positions on occupations, hours, and experience, or that they should not be penalized for choosing to assume family obligations that indirectly but inevitably push them into such low positions. To the "professional sociologists," critical work that so denies the usefulness of "obvious controls" will look like non-science or non-knowledge when the work is directed inside the profession, and like politicization when it is directed to the outside. But to its authors it will seem to be penetrating criticism; that is, it will be (Burawoy's) "critical sociology" when directed inside, and "public sociology" when directed outside. Again the analogy to liberal politics is exact. Any absolute critique of the values enshrined in the usual forms of conflict resolution in liberal societies (parliaments, laws, rules, and regulations) appears to classical liberals to be an attack on the very nature of due process or constitutional forms. But it appears to its authors to be the only means of having any political input at all, since their own desires are automatically silenced by "normal procedures." As readers of the *Federalist Papers* will remember, this can be a fear on the conservative side as well as on the democratic one.

Thus, there is always an internal contradiction in the means/ends distinction. For one group, the most congealed, stable values have become mere means to settle disputes about (lesser) ends. For another, the stable, congealed core values are not means but simply the legitimated permanent rejection of their own ends.

It should be noted that this relationship is structural, not substantive. It is given in the nature of such temporary stability as emerges in the social process. Neither the orthodox nor the heterodox side of this relation has any necessary particular content. In particular, there is no necessity that the "means" side (the professional sociologists) should be (as Burawoy assumes it to be) conservative, nor that the "ends" side be left-leaning (in the usual sense of extending minority rights in terms both of liberty of action and of support from the state). In a strong and successful socialist state, for example, heterodoxy would surely take the form of attacking excessive and imposed equality: its lack of aspiration and motivation, its quelling of passions intellectual, artistic, and spiritual, its inability to imagine great new meanings for the future, the potential for corruption inherent in its inevitably large bureaucracy. These were major themes in the critique of democracy in Tocqueville's *Democracy in America*, as in the critique of mass society in Ortega y Gasset's *The Revolt of the Masses* (1932), and in Schumpeter's case against socialism in *Capitalism, Socialism, and Democracy* (1950). They were also the central burden of many of the internal critiques of the Soviet Union. In any everyday sense, all this work is (was) "critical sociology," even though it disagrees with the content of Burawoy's politics. Heterodoxy is simply heterodoxy, not any one particular set of values.

That the heterodoxy/orthodoxy relationship is structural means that the contents of each side change with the social process itself. This in turn vitiates Burawoy's approach to the problem of reconciling the external/empirical/means-based world of scientific sociology with the internal/normative/ends-based world of critical sociology. Essentially, Burawoy proposes a division of labor. The cognitive and the value strands of the sociological enterprise are to be carried on by largely different groups of people—a "mainstream" of professional sociology and a "loyal opposition" of critical sociologists—as long as they are in a continuous dialogue.

But in practice this cannot work. When a "professional sociologist" ignores the value content of the social process, what happens is what happens to anyone who misspecifies a regression equation. The value-ladenness of the underlying enterprise finds its way out into the results under the guise of something else. Chapters 6 and 8 showed this at length. But this problem also arises in routine positivist analysis. By coding people into reified categories of race, ethnicity, occupation, and socioeconomic status, sociological analysis inevitably fostered the reification of those categories, with large consequences for modern societies. By ignoring values, sociology hides them, transforms them, presents ideology as fact, and so on. To do research on delinquency is to accept the funders' definition of delinquency, and what may have begun as a known and conscious sacrifice may quickly become a deadening habit and even an overtly political act.

One might, of course, justifiably retort that if such seduction by the current world of power is the pathology of instrumental, means-based sociology, then dogmatism and faddishness are the pathologies of reflexive, ends-based sociology. But this "plague on both your houses" response suggests that the real problem lies in the mistaken decision to separate ourselves in terms of means and ends, orthodoxy and heterodoxy, internal and external. To become purely one kind of sociologist, instrumental or reflexive, is to face at once the overwhelming pressures that conduce automatically to the pathologies just noted: servility on the one side, dogmatism on the other.

But if division of labor is not an option, can we—alternatively—articulate these different activities with the professional life cycle? Perhaps we might do professional sociology as young people, then reflect as we grow older. Age does, after all, bring the salutary experience of irrelevance, and with it recognition of the restless nature of the social process. But this cannot work either. Often it is the young who have the greatest ambition for critique (because of its high status and, within limits, its high payoff) and perhaps the greatest ability for it (because of the daring that comes with youth). Life-course models are not practicable; any sociologist must be at all times both means-focused and ends focused, both professional and critical.

In seeking the right way to enact this duality in practice, it seems again best to return to basics. As I have implied at various points in the preceding chapters, it is useful to think about the social process in terms of three kinds of relation: emotion, action, and meaning.[3] Emotion captures our own sense of being and our direct sympathy with other beings of all kinds. (Sympathy here has the literal sense of "feeling with" another, not the common modern one of "providing emotional support for" another. The latter is a form of action.) Action captures our desire to act upon the other and be acted upon in return. Meaning captures our ability to abstract from action itself, and to represent it

3. The immediate roots of this threefold division are in Charles Peirce's Firstness, Secondness, and Thirdness. But parts of it can be equally traced to Adam Smith's *Theory of Moral Sentiments*, to Meadean social psychology, and many other sources. I am employing it here largely as an organizing device, although I am elsewhere developing it more formally.

in a transferrable symbol of some kind that can engage a third party. In this triad action requires emotion, in the sense that we can envision action only with respect to other beings whom we understand (in some immediate sense) to be beings. Similarly, we can create abstract meanings only on the basis of acting, and, indeed the creation of abstractions is itself a special form of action, the creation of something striving away from particularity. (This last is the standard Peircean theory of symbols: indexes are still completely embedded in action and particularity, symbols aim to escape from it.)

On this argument, sociology must begin with sympathy, with immediate understanding of others and their particularity, rather than with symbolic representation of them as universal abstractions endowed with particular properties. I mean "sociology must begin with immediate understanding" in a fractal manner, at various levels. At the most abstract level, a sociological vocation must begin with a broad personal desire for such immediate understanding, but at a more particular level, a given research project should begin with immediate understanding of its objects, and at the most particular level, a given act of reading or statistical analysis should begin with immediate understanding of—sympathy with—the material at hand. The social process is made by human beings, and our analysis of them must begin with humane sympathy and its consequence of some partial degree of immediate understanding.

Such humanism does not mean, for example, that we can't code variables trying to describe people. (That is, positivism could be humane in my sense.) But it does mean that we have to ask ourselves about the ways in which our doing such coding does violence to the nature of these people as moral beings in the value and meaning space that is inevitably theirs by virtue of their humanity. And we have to modify our practice continuously, not in the direction of making it more and more "scientific" or "clean," which simply ignores more and more important aspects of particularity, but in the direction of making it more and more humane. This does not necessarily mean vaguer, more fuzzy, or more ethnographic, as is usually assumed. For example, it might mean having completely alternative forms of coding that reify alternative particularities. (Actually, we have these already but don't see them for what they are; we usually think them to be purely "cognitive" alternatives.) It also means "giving voice to the subject"—not necessarily by the quaint but absurd procedure of quoting him or her at length out of context, but by figuring out how to translate the being and moral activity of that subject into our own ways of imagining what happens in the social process.

This project of humane translation can, I think, avoid the Scylla of self-referential disengagement (pure meaning in the Peircean triad) and the

Charybdis of dogmatic politicization (pure action). It avoids these because it starts with sympathy, which is prior to both pure action and universalist disengagement. Any subject I study is a human being, deserving of the same dignity and care I would take in understanding myself. Yet all are other to me in various ways and at various levels, and can be reached only by a continuing effort at translation.

There are great challenges involved. As a humanist, I have to accept whatever it is that I am trying to translate into my world in order to understand it. As a scholar rooted to a particular social position I will inevitably have major problems with that task. Moreover, if I set myself Terence's rule that nothing human will be alien to me, I am going to be translating into my own universe of meaning not only some wonderful and comprehensible and excellent things whose acquaintance will broaden and develop me, but also some horrible and strange and frightening things, which may well terrify me. These last will include not only things to which I am politically opposed, but also immoral and evil things that are nonetheless the products of the social process and that must, at the least, be humanely understood in order to be avoided.[4]

In summary, I am making a case for sociology as a humanistic, inherently moral enterprise. I do not think that this obliges us to some particular methodology. There is no reason why we should not conceive of a positivism that is humanistic by relaxing some of the more philosophically inane assumptions of classical positivism. Indeed, this was my own aim two decades ago in creating a "narrative positivism" that introduced real history—rather than simple waiting time—into positivistic sociological methods in the first place: to make a space in positivist methods for the sequential framework through which

---

4. Avoidance in a processual view would mean imagining a way of living the social process that has guarantees against producing such horrors. This does not mean that one simply declares "the following things shall not occur." That is the solution of classical liberalism again: to make a list of forbidden (or protected) things and to then let all politics take the form of putting things on that list or taking them off it. No, a successful processualist rule would simply be a rule for living each particular moment that had the effect, when iterated forever, of perpetually avoiding—or minimizing the time in—in such negative values. If we think in Markovian terms, this means rules for "making the next moment" that maximize the exit probabilities for evil states of affairs rather than attempting the in-principle impossible task of never arriving in them. It could, however, be the case that the defining mark of what is evil is that it cannot be translated by a humane effort; although if I admit that, we are perhaps almost back to the identity of politics and morals that I am trying to escape. All too much of our sociology of evil takes a fairly unrealistic and domesticated view of it, as a question of merely finding "good guys" and "bad guys." Unfortunately, we are all both, in various ways and to various others.

we actually experience our lives (see *Time Matters*, ch. 6). Nor does use of nonpositivist methods guarantee our humanism. In the last twenty years, the practice of nonpositivistic methodologies like ethnography and archival work has drifted a long ways towards explicit politicization without any first passage through humane sympathy. Thus, the belief that humanism as a moral stance obliges us to be nonpositivistic, or the belief that that nonpositivism somehow guarantees our humanism, is yet more of the bizarre conflation that has so damaged the sociological imagination in the last forty years.[5]

Sociology must thus always begin with humane sympathy. Some of us will find this the most important phase of disciplinary work—I am one such person. Such a humanist is first and foremost interested in understanding the social world (as a value enterprise) rather than in changing it. The humanist thinks it may be presumptuous of the sociologist to judge the rights and wrongs of others. He or she starts from the presumption that the other is a version of humanity, to be granted the dignity of being taken seriously on his or her own terms, to be understood or translated by whatever methodology into something recognizable both in its original world and in that of the analyst. A humanist sociologist is hesitant—although not absolutely unwilling—to decide that others "have false consciousness"; that is, that we the sociologists know their own needs better than do they themselves. It is in this latter sense—understanding the other in terms of (definitionally imperfect) translation into our own world—that sociology does indeed constitute, in my view, the pursuit of knowledge for knowledge's sake. Burawoy's mistake in dismissing this position flows from his belief that the only form of moral behavior is political behavior in the broadest sense. That is, he thinks that a moral person who understands the moral nature of the social process must of necessity want to change it. I disagree. The project of understanding the social process—which is in itself a moral process and cannot be otherwise analyzed—seems to me inherently a moral project, whether we go on to exercise our undoubted political right to urge change or not.

Either way, sociological analysis must always begin with the aim of immediate understanding, itself based on humane sympathy, and not on any particular judgment, political or otherwise. Only then can it move on to the project of analysis, possibly with the aim of action, recognizing, however, that any analysis aimed at action must necessarily entail a particularity in the analyst

---

5. The problems with conflation are set out at length in *Chaos of Disciplines*, ch. 1. On the problems with contemporary archival research, see the passages in my text on library research that discuss the morals of research (Abbott 2014a 143–48, 246–47).

that is in some sense inherently judgmental—moral or political. Another way of putting this is that one is not really qualified to begin the normative judgment of human affairs until one has first extended sympathy to the other one studies, until one has shown oneself humble about one's own particularities and taken on the (unfillable) obligations of a trustee. Otherwise, one is simply a politician masquerading as a scientist.

It seems to me very clear that a central and ongoing part of this preparation for analysis, both in career terms and on a yearly, monthly, even daily basis, is the reaffirming encounter with the astonishing variation of the social world. We must begin with that, and with forcing ourselves to see it. We must also force ourselves to confront the continuous process in which new differences are being created and old ones being crushed. A consciously prescriptive stance can only be taken after a renewed encounter with this diversity. That is an exercise that goes well beyond the arguments presented in these chapters, which are mainly designed to show that our earlier approaches to thinking about the normative in social science have profound limitations. I am elsewhere pursuing this idea of specific and diverse encounter with diversity, through my long-standing collaboration with Professor Barbara Celarent.

But Burawoy is right that humane sympathy is not enough. We do in fact do research. And that research constitutes moral action whether we like it or not. Moreover, many sociologists affirmatively wish, as Burawoy saw well, to deploy sociology in political action. For me, the problem here lies not in the intent of political action, which is the right of sociologists as of anyone else, but in its manner of execution. The discipline's positivist apparatus is far more developed than its normative one. We have distinguished literatures on all kinds of methodologies. But we do not pursue a systematic inquiry into normative reasoning, and so, in fact, our proposed political actions are usually simpleminded in the extreme. They draw minimally on the formal literature of political theory, with the sole possible exception of Marxist theory. We draw almost nothing from historical jurisprudence, even though that field long antedates sociology (it provided the vast majority of Max Weber's theoretical ideas) and for many centuries has discussed issues that we paper over with a few references to our canonical writers. Moreover, we draw surprisingly little even from the mainstream of liberal political theory, and of course we pay almost no attention at all to normative traditions outside the Western canon. (Islamic banking has a critique of capitalist economics every bit as thoroughgoing as that of Marx, for example.) Chapter 8's analysis of the concept of inequality shows how much work there is to be done in making our political contributions worthy of the discipline's ambitions.

It seems, then, that sociology—and social science more broadly—needs a much larger and more diverse normative subdiscipline: one that is rigorous in its normative reflection, as is the law, for example. Such a subdiscipline would resemble political theory, the subdiscipline of political science dedicated to normative argument. But it would need to reach beyond that narrow subdiscipline into the realms of other social sciences. Political theory—in the United States, at least—is at present almost completely contained within the confines of liberal thought and of the Enlightenment ontology that undergirds it. As the four last chapters of this book have shown, in their several ways, such a limited ontology is simply insufficient for a serious normative approach to the world. Liberalism of the "universal characterless citizen" type was a historical necessity at one time, and, indeed, I certainly cannot envision a practicable and preferable alternative to it, as a practical basis for politics. Nor would I myself want to live in a nonliberal society. But I can realize that billions of people have done so and do today do so. A normative account of human social life that is unwilling to recognize that fact is therefore unwilling even to think about normative rules that will make some kind of sense in all forms of society, and could therefore easily end up proving irrelevant to an enormous portion of the human race.

Such a normative subdiscipline must be founded on a full engagement with the astounding diversity of human societies. By this I do not mean diversity in what they eat and what they wear and how they speak, although of course those diversities exist as well. Rather, I mean diversity in how they imagine human life, in what they value, and in what future seems ideal to them. This is the often painful diversity of cultural misrecognition, not the facile fatuity of multiculturalism. People will continue to live in fundamentally different ways in fundamentally different societies. They will make up different worlds, because it is the nature of humans to do that. Once you start to live in the airy castles of symbolic imagination, you will never stop doing so.

Processualism is no doubt one of those castles. Like all general approaches to the social world, it is subject to Russell's paradox—in this case, by claiming to be right but claiming at the same time that all views (including itself) are ultimately changed. But in the current world it seems a viable response to the problems of the other major approaches to thinking about society. It means acceptance of the fact that differences will continue to be created at all levels of our symbolic machinery—that there can be no escape from process. Not through the liberal theory of independent identical citizens or market-exchangers, where ultimate difference disappears behind grand universals in exchange for some possibly large but ultimately limited core of diversity. Not through Durkheimian absolutism, which fails to recognize the inevitable future splitting and recombining of the very solidarities that are to save us from what Durkheim wisely saw was a declining universal framework. Not through Marxian conflict theory, otherwise so historicist, which does not recognize that new differences would arise within the state of socialism, including meta-differences that might transform it completely. Not through the labyrinthine neverland of pure symbols—since humans are not only symbolists, but also actors who do things. As I noted on this book's first page, these are all distinguished traditions and they have their distinguished intellectual monuments. Processualism is simply another alternative: a world of actors but without reification of individuals and groups, a world of large forces but forces that must replicate themselves perpetually or waste away, an historicism without the dead hand of overarching historical determination, a symbolic analysis that does not forget the centrality of sympathy and action.

As for me, it is ironically appropriate that my processual views should never seem finished. This is the second collection that I have issued instead of finishing my long-overdue treatise on the social process. Four hundred pages of chapter drafts exist for that book: originally written in 1997, then modified, rewritten, and edited at various times in subsequent years. Perhaps my own writing illustrates the processual approach all too well. I cannot freeze my thinking long enough to write. Rather, as in chapter 4, I feel I must tell my readers the thought of the moment, the emotion of insight that comes with each piece, lest I give them a giant dead tome. Perhaps these little theoretical lyrics matter more than some great epic no one will read.

Abbott, A. 1982. "The Emergence of American Psychiatry, 1880–1930." Unpublished PhD dissertation, University of Chicago.

———. 1983a. "Professional Ethics." *American Journal of Sociology* 88:855–85.

———. 1983b. "Sequences of Social Events." *Historical Methods* 16:129–47.

———. 1988a. *The System of Professions*. Chicago: University of Chicago Press.

———. 1988b. "Transcending General Linear Reality." *Sociological Theory* 6:169–86.

———. 1990. "Positivism and Interpretation in Sociology" *Sociological Forum* 5:435–58.

———. 1992. "From Causes to Events." *Sociological Methods and Research* 20:428–55.

———. 1997. "Of Time and Place." *Social Forces* 75:1149–82.

———. 1999. *Department and Discipline*. Chicago: University of Chicago Press.

———. 2001a. *Chaos of Disciplines*. Chicago: University of Chicago Press.

———. 2001b. *Time Matters*. Chicago: University of Chicago Press.

———. 2005. "The Sociology of Work and Occupations," in N. J. Smelser and R. Swedberg, eds., *Handbook of Economic Sociology*. New York and Princeton, NJ: Russell Sage Foundation and Princeton University Press, pp. 307–30.

———. 2006. "Mobility: What? When? How?" in S. L. Morgan, D. Grusky, and G. Fields, *Mobility and Inequality*. Stanford, CA: Stanford University Press, pp. 137–61.

———. 2014a. *Digital Paper*. Chicago: University of Chicago Press.

———. 2014b. "The Excellence of IT," in M. Herbst, ed., *The Institution of Science and the Science of Institutions*. Dordrecht: Springer, pp. 147–65.

Abbott, A., and A. Tsay. 2000. "Sequence Analysis and Optimal Matching Analysis in Sociology." *Sociological Methods and Research* 29:3–33.

Abell, P. 1989. "Games in Networks." *Rationality and Society* 1:259–82.

Adorno, T. 1989. "Lyric Poetry and Society," in S. E. Bronner and D. M. Kellner, eds. *Critical Theory and Society*. New York: Routledge, pp. 155–71.

Ainslie, G. 1992. *Picoeconomics*. Cambridge: Cambridge University Press.

——. 2001. *Breakdown of Will*. Cambridge: Cambridge University Press.

Alihan, M. 1938. *Social Ecology*. New York: Columbia University Press.

Art, R. J., V. Davis, and S. Huntington, eds. 1985. *Reorganizing America's Defense*. Washington: Pergamon.

Auerbach, E. 1953. *Mimesis*, tr. W. R. Trask. Princeton, NJ: Princeton University Press.

Austing, R. H., B. H. Barnes, and G. L. Engel. 1977. "A Survey of the Literature in Computer Science Education Since Curriculum '68." *Communications of the ACM* 20:13–21.

Bachelard, G. 1957. *La poétique de l'espace*. Paris: PUF.

Barthes, R. [1966] 1981. "Introduction à l'analyse structurale du récit," *Communications*, 8:7–33.

——. [1953]1972. *Le degré zéro de l'écriture*. Paris: Seuil.

——. 1974. *S/Z*. New York: Hill and Wang.

Bataille, G. 1991. *The Accursed Share*. New York: Zone Books.

Becker, G. S. 1965. "A Theory of the Allocation of Time." *Economic Journal* 75:493–517.

——. 1976. *The Economic Approach to Human Behavior*. Chicago: University of Chicago Press.

Bell, M. M. 1994. *Childerly*. Chicago: University of Chicago Press.

Ben-David, J. 1971. *The Scientist's Role in Society*. Englewood Cliffs, NJ: Prentice Hall.

Benveniste, E. 1971. "Correlation of Tense and the French Verb," in *Problems in General Linguistics*. Coral Gables, FL: University of Miami Press, pp. 205–15.

Berelson, B. R., P. F. Lazarsfeld, and W. N. McPhee. 1954. *Voting*. Chicago: University of Chicago Press.

Berger, P. L., and T. Luckmann. 1967. *The Social Construction of Reality*. New York: Doubleday.

Bergson, H. [1889]1910. *Time and Free Will*, tr. F. L. Pogson. London: Allen Unwin. Original title: *Essai sur les données immédiates de la conscience*.

Berlant, J. 1975. *Profession and Monopoly*. Berkeley: University of California Press.

Berman, E. P. 2002. "Creating a National Medical Field." Unpublished paper, Department of Sociology, University of California, Berkeley.

Blake, E. V. 1901. *History of the Tammany Society*. New York: Souvenir Press.

Bosworth, B., G. Burtless, and E. Steuerle. 2000. "Lifetime Earnings Patterns, the Distribution of Future Social Security Benefits, and the Impact of Pensions Reform." *Social Security Bulletin* 63:4:74–98.

Bourdieu, P., and J-C Passeron. 1977. *Reproduction in Education, Society, and Culture*, tr. R. Nice. Beverly Hills, CA: Sage.

Breslau, D. 1997a. "Contract Shop Epistemology." *Social Studies of Science* 27:363–94.

———. 1997b. "The Political Power of Research Methods." *Theory and Society* 26:869–902.

Brint, S., and J. Karabel. 1989. *The Diverted Dream*. New York: Oxford University Press.

Broughton, C. E. 2001. *Reforming Poor Women*. Unpublished PhD dissertation, University of Chicago.

———. 2015. *Boom, Bust, Exodus*. Oxford: Oxford University Press.

Brown, R. C. E. 1922. *History of the State of New York: Political and Governmental, Vol III: 1865–1896*. Syracuse, NY: Syracuse Press.

Brown, R. H. 1977. *A Poetic for Sociology*. Cambridge: Cambridge University Press.

Bryk, A. S., and S. W. Raudenbush. 1992. *Hierarchical Linear Models*. Newbury Park, CA: Sage.

Burawoy, M. 1979. *Manufacturing Consent*. Chicago: University of Chicago Press.

———. 1998. "The Extended Case Method." *Sociological Theory* 16:4–33.

———. 2005. "For Public Sociology." *American Sociological Review* 70:4–28.

Burton, J. W. 1988. "Shadows at Twilight." *Proceedings of the American Philosophical Society* 132:420–33.

Camic, C. 1989. "Structure after Fifty Years." *American Journal of Sociology* 95:38–107.

Campbell, A., G. Gurin, and W. E. Miller. 1954. *The Voter Decides*. Chicago: Row-Peterson.

Campbell, A., P. E. Converse, W. E. Miller, and D. E. Stokes. [1960]1980. *The American Voter*. Chicago: University of Chicago Press.

Capetti, C. 1993. *Writing Chicago*. New York: Columbia University Press.

Capshew, J. H. 1999. *Psychologists on the March*. Cambridge: Cambridge University Press.

Carrier, N. "La depression problematique du concept de contrôle sociale." *Deviance et société* 30: 3–20.

Carson, R. 1962. *Silent Spring*. Greenwich, CN: Fawcett.

Castells, M. 1968. "Y a-t-il une sociologie urbaine?" *Sociologie du travail* 10:72–90.

Chambliss, D. F. 1989. "The Mundanity of Excellence." *Sociological Theory* 7:70–86.

Chandler, J. 1998. *England in 1819*. Chicago: University of Chicago Press.

Chateaubriand, F-R. [1802] 1926. *Atala* and *René*. New York: Oxford University Press.

Christakis, N. A. 1999. *Death Foretold*. Chicago: University of Chicago Press.

Clifford, J. 1986. Introduction to J. Clifford and G. F. Marcus, eds., *Writing Cultures*. Berkeley: University of California Press, pp. 7–26.

Cockton, P. 1988. *Subject Catalogue of the House of Commons Parliamentary Papers, 1801–1900*. Cambridge: Chadwyck Healey.

Comstock, T. G. 1868. "Experience in the Late Epidemic of Cholera in St. Louis." *Transactions of the Twentieth Session of the American Institute of Homeopathy* 3:34–47.

Creedy, J. 1977. "The Distribution of Lifetime Earnings." *Oxford Economic Papers* 29:412–29.

———. 1990. "Lifetime Earnings and Inequality." *Economic Record* 67:46–58.

Crosby, T. L. 1976. *Sir Robert Peel's Administration*. Newton Abbot, UK: David and Charles.

Csikszentmihalyi, M. 1990. *Flow*. New York: Harper and Row.

Dahl, R. A. 1961. *Who Governs?* New Haven: Yale University Press.

Danto, A. C. 1985. *Narration and Knowledge*. New York: Columbia University Press.

Davis, V. 1985. "The Evolution of Central U.S. Defense Management," in R. J. Art, V. Davis, and S. Huntington, eds., *Reorganizing America's Defense*. Washington: Pergamon, 149–67.

Dear, M. 2002. "Los Angeles and the Chicago School." *City and Community* 1:5–32.

De Man, Paul. 1983. *Blindness and Insight*, 2nd ed. Minneapolis: University of Minnesota Press.

———. 1984. *The Rhetoric of Romanticism*. New York: Columbia University Press.

———. 1993. *Romanticism and Contemporary Criticism*. Baltimore: Johns Hopkins University Press.

Demeny, P., and G. McNicoll. 2006. "World Population 1950–2000." *Population and Development Review* 32:Supp:1–51.

Desrosières, A. 1998. *The Politics of Large Numbers*. Cambridge, MA: Harvard University Press.

Dewey, J. [1922] 1988. *Human Nature and Conduct*. Carbondale: Southern Illinois University Press.

———. 1927. *The Public and Its Problems*. New York: Henry Holt.

Dewey, J., and J. H. Tufts. 1909. *Ethics*. New York: Henry Holt.

Dix, G. 1945. *The Shape of the Liturgy*. London: Dacre.

Dolton, P. J., G. H. Makepeace, and W. Van der Klaauw. 1989. "Occupational Choice and Earnings Determination." *Oxford Economic Papers* 411:573–94.

Dubet, F. 2010. *Les places et les chances*. Paris: Seuil.

Duffy, J. 1968. *A History of Public Health in New York City, 1625–1866*. New York: Russell Sage.

———. 1974. *A History of Public Health in New York City, 1866–1966*. New York: Russell Sage.

Dumont, L. 1970. *Homo Hierarchicus*. London: Paladin.

Duncan, O. D. 1984. *Notes on Social Measurement*. New York: Russell Sage.

Durkheim, E. [1893] 1998. *De la division du travail social*. Paris: Quadrige/Presses Universitaires de France.

———. [1897] 1951. *Suicide*. New York: Free Press.

Einhorn, R. 1991. *Property Rules*. Chicago: University of Chicago Press.

Ekman, P. 1972. *Emotions in the Human Face*. New York: Pergamon.

Eliot, T. S. [1919] 1975a. "Hamlet," in *Selected Prose of T. S. Eliot*. New York: Harcourt /Farrar, pp. 45–49.

———. [1920] 1975b. "The Perfect Critic." in *Selected Prose Of T. S. Eliot*. New York: Harcourt /Farrar, pp. 50–58.

Erickson, A. B. 1952. *The Public Career of Sir James Graham*. Oxford: Basil Blackwell.

Evans-Pritchard, E. E. [1937] 1976. *Withcraft, Oracles, and Magic Among the Azande*. Oxford: Clarendon Press.

Fabian, J. 1983. *Time and the Other*. New York: Columbia Univresity Press.

Fabiani, J-L. 1999. "Les règles du champ," in B. Lahire, ed., *Le travail sociologique de Pierre Bourdieu*. Paris: La Découverte, pp. 75–91.

Finer, S. E. 1952. *The Life and Times of Sir Edwin Chadwick*. London: Methuen.

Fischer, C. 1992. *America Calling*. Berkeley: University of California Press.

Fitzpatrick, R. 1996. "Alternative Approaches to the Assessment of Health-Related Quality of Life," in A. Offer, ed., *In Pursuit of the Quality of Life*. Oxford: Oxford University Press, pp. 140–62.

Fleck, L. [1935] 1979. *The Genesis and Development of a Scientific Fact*. Chicago: University of Chicago Press.

Foster, L. 1984. *Religion and Sexuality*. Urbana: University of Illinois Press.

Fox, D. M. 1967. *The Discovery of Abundance*. Ithaca, NY: Cornell University Press.

Frazier, E. Franklin. 1939. *The Negro Family in the United States*. Chicago: University of Chicago Press.

Freidson, Eliot. 1970. *Professional Dominance*. New York: Atherton.

———. 1986. *Professional Powers*. Chicago: University of Chicago Press.

———. 2001. *Professionalism: The Third Logic*. Chicago: University of Chicago Press.

Friedman, M. 1953. "The Methodology of Positive Economics," in M. Friedman, *Essays in Positive Economics*. Chicago: University of Chicago Press, pp. 3–43.

Frye, N. 1966. *Anatomy of Criticism*. New York: Atheneum.

Furner, Mary O. 1975. *Advocacy and Objectivity*. Lexington: University Press of Kentucky.

Gal, S. 2011. "Polyglot Nationalism." *Langage et société* 136:31–51.

Galbraith, J. K. 1958. *The Affluent Society*. Boston: Houghton Mifflin.

Gamson, W. A. 1975. *The Strategy of Social Protest*. Homewood, IL: Dorsey.

Gans, H. J. 1962. *The Urban Villagers*. New York: Free Press.

———. 1967. *The Levittowners*. New York: Vintage.

———. 1997. "Bestsellers by Sociologists." *Contemporary Sociology* 26:131–35.

Gash, N. 1953. *Politics in the Age of Peel*. London: Longmans.

———. 1965. *Reaction and Reconstruction in English Politics, 1832–1852*. Oxford: Clarendon Press.

——. 1972. *Sir Robert Peel*. Totowa, NJ: Rowman and Littlefield.

Gellner, E. 1988. "'Zeno of Cracow' or 'Revolution at Nemi' or 'The Polish Revenge: A Drama in Three Acts,'" in R. Ellen, E. Gellner, G. Kubica, and J. Mucha, eds., *Malinowski Between Two Worlds*. Cambridge: Cambridge University Press, pp. 164–94.

Genette, G. [1972] 1980. *Narrative Discourse*. Ithaca, NY: Cornell University Press.

Gerdtham, U-G., and M. Johannesson. 2000. "Income-Related Inequality in Life-Years and Quality-Adjusted Life-Years." *Journal of Health Economics* 19:1007–26.

Gigerenzer, G. 2000. *Adaptive Thinking*. New York: Oxford University Press.

Ginzburg, C. 2000. *No Island Is an Island*. New York: Columbia University Press.

Gluckman, M. 1967. Introduction to A. L. Epstein, ed., *The Craft of Social Anthropology*. London: Tavistock, pp. xi–xx.

——. 1947a. "Malinowski's 'Functional' Analaysis of Social Change." *Africa* 17:103–1.

——. 1947b. "Malinowski's Contribution to Social Anthropology." *African Studies* 6:41–46.

——. 1955. *Custom and Conflict in Africa*. Glencoe, IL: Free Press.

——. 1958. "Analysis of a Social Situation in Modern Zululand." *Rhodes-Livingston Institute Papers*, #28. Manchester, UK: Manchester University Press for the Rhodes-Livingston Institute.

——. 1963. Introduction to *Order and Rebellion in Tribal Africa*. London: Cohen and West, pp. 1–49.

Goethe, J. W. [1774] 1984. *The Sorrows of Young Werther and Novella*. New York: Modern Library.

Goffman, E. 1963. *Behavior in Public Places*. New York: Free Press.

Gold, M. R., J. E. Siegel, L. B. Russell, and M. C. Weinstein. 1996. *Cost-Effectiveness in Health and Medicine*. New York: Oxford University Press.

Johnson, D. H., and G. H. Makepeace. 1997. "Occupational Advantage in the Eighties." *Work, Employment, and Society* 11:401–11.

Goldman, J. A. 1997. *Building New York's Sewers*. West Lafayette, IN: Purdue University Press.

Gouldner, A. 1968. "The Sociologist as Partisan." *American Sociologist* 3:103–16.

Halperin, M. H. 1974. *Bureaucratic Politics and Foreign Policy*. Washington: Brookings.

Halperin, M. H., and D. Halperin. 1985. "Rewriting the Key West Accord," in R. J. Art, V. Davis, and S. Huntington, eds., *Reorganizing America's Defense*. Washington: Pergamon, pp. 344–58.

Hamlin, C. 1998. *Public Health and Social Justice in the Age of Chadwick*. Cambridge: Cambridge University Press.

Hammack, D. C. 1982. *Power and Society*. New York: Russell Sage.

Hammond, J. D. 1848. *The History of Political Parties in the State of New York.* Syracuse, NY: L. W. Hall.

Hannan, M. T., and J. Freeman. 1977. "The Population Ecology of Organizations." *American Journal of Sociology* 82:929–64.

Hawley, A. H. 1950. *Human Ecology.* New York: Ronald Press.

Hoffman, F. 1999. "Goldwater-Nichols after a Decade," in W. Murray, ed., *The Emerging Strategic Environment.* Wesport CN: Praeger, pp. 156–82.

Hsiung, C. 2010. "Young Women and Dress: A Study of Intellectual Life." Unpublished MA paper, MAPSS Program, University of Chicago.

Hughes, E. C. 1971. *The Sociological Eye.* Part III: Work and Self. Chicago: Aldine.

Huot, S. 1987. *From Song to Book.* Ithaca, NY: Cornell University Press.

Janowitz, M. 1975. "Sociological Theory and Social Control." *American Journal of Sociology* 81:82–108.

Jenkins, J. S. 1846. *History of Political Parties in the State of New York.* Auburn, NY: Alden and Markham.

Jenkins, T. A. 1996. *Parliament, Party and Politics in Victorian Britain.* Manchester, UK: Manchester University Press.

Johnson, S. [1765] 1958. "Preface to Shakespeare," in *Rasselas, Poems, and Selected Prose.* New York: Holt, Rinehart and Winston, pp. 239–87.

Johnson, W. F. 1922. *History of the State of New York: Political and Governmental, Vol II: 1822–1864.* Syracuse, NY: Syracuse Press.

Johnson, W. R. 1982. "On the Absence of Ancient Lyric Theory," in *The Idea of Lyric.* Berkeley: University of California Press, pp. 76–95.

Kahnemann, D., and A. Tversky. 1984. "Prospect Theory." *Econometrica* 47:263–91.

———. 2000. "Choices, Values, and Frames," in D. Kahnemann and A. Tversky, eds., *Choices, Values, and Frames.* Cambridge: Cambridge University Press. New York: Russell Sage, pp. 1–16.

Katz, E., and P. F. Lazarsfeld. 1955. *Personal Influence.* New York: Free Press.

Kaufman, M. *Homeopathy.* Baltimore: Johns Hopkins University Press.

Keynes, J. M. 1923. *A Tract on Monetary Reform.* London: Macmillan.

———. [1930] 1963. "Economic Possibilitities for Our Grandchildren," in *Essays in Persuasion.* New York: Norton, pp. 358–73.

Koehn, D. 1994. *The Ground of Professional Ethics.* New York: Routledge.

Kokinshu: A Collection of Poems Ancient and Modern [ca. 905], tr. and annotated by L. R. Rodd and M. C. Henkenius. Boston: Cheng and Tsui.

Kornhauser, A., and P. F. Lazarsfeld. [1935] 1955. "The Analysis of Consumer Actions," in Lazarsfeld and M. Rosenberg, eds., *The Language of Social Research.* Glencoe, IL: Free Press, pp. 392–404.

Krugman, P. 1994. *Peddling Prosperity.* New York: Norton.

Kultgen, J. H. 1988. *Ethics and Professionalism.* Philadelphia: University of Pennsylvania Press.

Di Lampedusa, G. T. 1960. *The Leopard*, tr. A. Colquhoun. New York: Pantheon.

Larson, M. S. 1977. *The Rise of Professionalism*. Berkeley: University of California Press.

Laumann, E. O., and D. Knoke. 1987. *The Organizational State*. Madison: University of Wisconsin Press.

Lauwerier, H. 1991. *Fractals*. Princeton, NJ: Princeton University Press.

Lazarsfeld, P. F., and H. Gaudet. 1948. *The People's Choice*. New York: Columbia University Press.

Leach, E. R. 1954. *Political Systems of Highland Burma*. Boston: Beacon.

Leifer, E. 1988. "Interaction Preludes to Role Setting." *American Sociological Review* 53:865–78.

Levi-Strauss, C. 1955. *Tristes Tropiques*. Paris: Plon.

Levine, G. 1981. *The Realistic Imagination*. Chicago: University of Chicago Press.

Levrault, L. 1902. *La poésie lyrique*. Paris: Librairie Paul Delaplane.

Lewis, R. A. 1952. *Edwin Chadwick and the Public Health Movement*. London: Methuen.

Lindner, R. 1996. *The Reportage of Urban Culture*. New York: Cambridge University Press.

Lockwood, D. 1992. *Solidarity and Schism*. Clarendon, UK: Oxford.

Logan, J. R., and H. L. Molotch. 1987. *Urban Fortunes*. Berkeley: University of California Press.

Long, N. 1958. "The Local Community as an Ecology of Games." *American Journal of Sociology* 64:251–61.

Loudon, I. 1986. *Medical Care and the General Practitioner*. Oxford: Clarendon Press.

Lovejoy, A. O. 1936. *The Great Chain of Being*. Cambridge, MA: Harvard University Press.

Loewenstein, G., and D. Prelec. 1991. "Negative Time Preference." *American Economic Review* 81:347–52.

——. 1992. "Anomalies in Intertemporal Choice," in G. Loewenstein and J. Elster, eds., *Choice over Time*. New York: Russell Sage, pp. 119–45.

Lusted, L. B. 1968. *Introduction to Medical Decisionmaking*. Springfield, IL: C. C. Thomas.

Maclean, N. F. 1940. "Theory of Lyric Poetry in England from the Renaissance to Coleridge." Unpublished PhD dissertation, University of Chicago.

Makepeace, G. H. 1996. "Lifetime Earnings and the Training of Young Men in Britain." *Applied Economics* 28:725–35.

Malinowski, B. [1922] 1961. *Argonauts of the Western Pacific*. New York: Dutton.

——. 1935. *Coral Gardens and Their Magic*. London: Allen Unwin.

——. 1938. "The Anthropology of Changing African Cultures," in *Methods of Study of Culture Contact in Africa*. International African Institute, Memorandum

XV. London: Oxford University Press for the International African Institute, pp. vii–xxxviii.

———. 1945. *The Dynamics of Cultural Change*, ed. P. M. Kaberry. New Haven: Yale University Press.

———. 1989. *A Diary in the Strict Sense of the Term*. Stanford, CA: Stanford University Press.

Malthus, T. R. [1798] 2008. *An Essay on the Principle of Population*. New York: Oxford University Press.

Mandelbaum, S. J. 1965. *Boss Tweed's New York*. New York: Wiley.

Mandeville, B. [1724] 1989. *The Fable of the Bees*. New York: Penguin.

Marx, K. [1852] 1963. *The Eighteenth Brumaire of Louis Bonaparte*. New York: International Publishers.

———. [1887] 1967. *Capital*. New York: International Publishers.

Massey, D., and N. Denton. *American Apartheid*. Cambridge, MA: Harvard University Press.

Maulpoix, J-M. 2000. *Du lyrisme*. Paris: José Curti.

Mayhew, B. 1990. *Researches in Structural Sociology*, ed. John Skvoretz. Columbia, SC: Department of Sociology, University of South Carolina.

McAdam, D. 1982. *Political Process and the Development of Black Insurgency*. Chicago: University of Chicago Press.

McCormick, R. L. 1981. *From Realignment to Reform*. Ithaca, NY: Cornell University Press.

McDonald, T. J. *The Parameters of Urban Fiscal Policy*. Berkeley: University of California Press.

McDonald, T. J., ed. *The Historic Turn in the Human Sciences*. Ann Arbor: University of Michigan Press.

McNamee, L. F. 1968 *Dissertations in English and American Literature*. New York: Bowker.

———. 1969 *Dissertations in English and American Literature*, Supplement 1964–68. New York: Bowker.

McTaggart, J. M. E. 1908. "The Unreality of Time." *Mind* 17:457–54.

Mellor, D. H. 1981. *Real Time*. Cambridge: Cambridge University Press.

Miles, J. 1942. "Wordsworth and the Vocabulary of Emotion." *University of California Publications in English* 12, no. 1.

Mills, C. W. 1959. *The Sociological Imagination*. New York: Oxford.

Miner, E., H. Odagiri, and R. E. Morrell. 1985. *Princeton Companion to Classical Japanese Literature*. Princeton, NJ: Princeton University Press.

Monkkonen, E. H. 1995. *The Local State*. Stanford, CA: Stanford University Press.

Morris, A. 1975. "The American Society of Criminology: A History 1941–1974." *Criminology* 13:123–67.

Muennig, P. 2002. *Designing and Conducting Cost-Effectiveness Analyses in Medicine and Health Care*. San Francisco: Jossey-Bass.

National Academy of Sciences 1971. *Rapid Population Growth*. Baltimore: Johns Hopkins University Press.

New York, Secretary of State, various years. *Legislative Manual*.

Newbould, I. 1990. *Whiggery and Reform, 1830–1841*. Stanford, CA: Stanford University Press.

Newman, C. 1957. *The Evolution of Medical Education in the Nineteenth Century*. London: Oxford University Press.

Nord, E. 1999. *Cost-Value Analysis in Health Care*. Cambridge: Cambridge University Press.

Novick, P. 1999. *The Holocaust in American Life*. Boston: Houghton Mifflin.

Nussbaum, M. 1988. "Narrative Emotions." *Ethics* 98:225–54.

Ortega y Gasset, J. 1932. *The Revolt of the Masses*. New York: Norton.

Padgett, J. F., and C. K. Ansell. 1993. "Robust Action and the Rise of the Medici." *American Journal of Sociology* 98:1259–1319.

Paine, H. M. 1867. "Epidemic Cholera." *Proceedings of the Nineteenth Session of the American Institute of Homeopathy* pp. 126–41.

Park, R. E., E. W. Burgess, and R. D. Mackenzie. 1925. *The City*. Chicago: University of Chicago Press.

Parris, H. 1969. *Constitutional Bureaucracy*. London: Allen Unwin.

Parry, J. 1993. *The Rise and Fall of Liberal Government in England*. New Haven: Yale University Press.

Parsons, T. 1939. "Professions and Social Structure." *Social Forces* 17:457–67.

———. 1968. "Professions." *International Encyclopedia of the Social Sciences*. 12:536–47.

———. 1949. *The Structure of Social Action*. New York: Free Press.

Patten, S. N. 1902. *The Theory of Prosperity*. New York: Macmillan.

Paxton, P. 2002. "Social Capital and Democracy." *American Sociological Review* 67:254–77.

Perrow, C. 1984. *Normal Accidents*. New York: Basic.

Piven, H., and A. Alcabes. 1968. "Education and Training for Criminal Justice." *USDHEW, Office of Juvenile Delinquency and Youth Development. JD Pub* #78. Washington: Government Printing Office.

Plutarch. n.d. *Lives*. New York: Modern Library.

Price, C. 1993. *Time, Discounting and Value*. Oxford: Blackwell.

Propp, V. A. 1968. *Morphology of the Folktale*. Austin: University of Texas Press.

Raiffa, H. 1968. *Decision Analysis*. Reading, MA: Addison Wesley.

Rawls, J. 1971. *A Theory of Justice*. Cambridge, MA: Harvard University Press.

Reader, W. J. 1966. *Professional Men*. New York: Basic.

Reay, M. 2004. "Economic Experts and Economic Knowledge." Unpublished PhD dissertation, University of Chicago.

Richards, A. I. 1939. *Land, Labour and Diet in Northern Rhodesia*. London: Oxford University Press for the International African Institute.

Richards, I. A. 1929. *Practical Criticism*. New York: Harcourt.

Rieder, J. 1985. *Canarsie*. Cambridge, MA: Harvard University Press.

Riesman, D. 1950. *The Lonely Crowd*. With N. Glazer and R. Denney. New Haven: Yale University Press.

Riesman, J. M. 1991. *A History of Clinical Psychology*. New York: Hemisphere.

Rosen, S. 1981. "The Economics of Superstars." *American Economic Review* 71:845–58.

Rosenberg, C. E. 1962. *The Cholera Years*. Chicago: University of Chicago Press.

Rosenfeld, P. 1984. "Protecting the Public or Promoting the Profession?" Unpublished PhD thesis, State University of New York at Stony Brook.

Rothstein, W. G. 1972. *American Physicians in the Nineteenth Century*. Baltimore: Johns Hopkins University Press.

Rotolo, T., and J. M. McPherson. 2001. "The System of Occupations." *Social Forces* 79:1095–1130.

Routh, D. K. 1994. *Clinical Psychology Since 1917*. New York: Plenum.

Russell, C. A., N. G. Coley, and G. K. Roberts. 1977. *Chemists by Profession*. Milton Keynes, UK: Open University Press.

Ryder, N. B. 1965. "The Cohort as a Concept in the Study of Social Change." *American Sociological Review* 30:843–61.

Sahlins, M. 1972. *Stone Age Economics*. New York: Aldine.

Saiedian, H. 2002. "Bridging Academic Software Engineering Education and Industrial Needs." *Computer Science Education* 12:5–9.

Sanjek R. 1991. "The Ethnographic Present." *Man* NS 26:609–28.

Schumpeter, J. A. 1950. *Capitalism, Socialism, and Democracy*. New York: Harper and Row..

Shackle, G. L. S. 1961. *Decision, Order, and Time in Human Affairs*. Cambridge: Cambridge University Press.

Simmel, G. 1950. *The Sociology of Georg Simmel*, tr. K. Wolff. New York: Free Press.

———. [1922] 1955. "The Web of Group Affiliations," in G. Simmel, *"Conflict" and "The Web of Group Affiliations."* New York: Free Press, pp. 125–95.

Singh, J. V., and C. J. Lumsden. 1990. "Theory and Research in Organizational Ecology." *Annual Review of Sociology* 16:161–95.

Skocpol. T. 1979. *States and Social Revolutions*. Cambridge: Cambridge University Press.

Small, A. E. 1876. *Manual of Homeopathic Practice*. New York: Boericke and Tafel.

Snook, S. A. 2000. *Friendly Fire*. Princeton, NJ: Princeton University Press.

Spann, E. K. 1981. *The New Metropolis*. New York: Columbia University Press.

Stinchcombe, A. L. 1968. *Constructing Social Theories*. New York: Harcourt, Brace, and World.

Strawson, G. 2004. "Against Narrativity." *Ratio* 17:428–52.

Suttles, G. D. 1990. *The Man-Made City*. Chicago: University of Chicago Press.

Teaford, J. C. 1984. *The Unheralded Triumph*. Baltimore: Johns Hopkins University Press.

Thompson, E. P. 1963. *The Making of the English Working Class*. New York: Vintage.

Todorov, T. 1969. *Grammaire du décameron*. The Hague: Mouton.

Toffler, A. 1970. *Future Shock*. New York: Random House.

Torrance, G. W. 1986. "Measurement of Health State Utilities for Economic Appraisal." *Journal of Health Economics* 5:1–30.

Tsuchiya, A. 2000. "QALYS and Ageism." *Health Economics* 9:57–68.

Turner, J., and S. Turner. 1990. *The Impossible Science*. Newbury Park, CA: Sage.

Tversky, A., and D. Griffin. 2000. "Endowment and Contrast Judgments," in D. Kahnemann and A. Tversky, eds., *Choices, Values, and Frames*. Cambridge: Cambridge University Press. New York: Russell Sage, pp. 702–25.

Uberoi, J. P. S. 1962. *The Politics of the Kula Ring*. Manchester, UK: Manchester University Press.

Van Velsen, J. 1967. "The Extended-Case Method and Situational Analysis," in A. L. Epstein, ed., *The Craft of Social Anthropology*. London: Tavistock, pp. 129–49.

———. 1964. *The Politics of Kinship*. Manchester, UK: Manchester University Press.

Van Ingen, P. 1949. *The New York Academy of Medicine*. New York: Columbia University Press.

Vaughan, D. 1987. *Uncoupling*. New York: Vintage.

Venturi, R., D. S. Brown, and S. Izenour. 1972. *Learning from Las Vegas*. Cambridge, MA: MIT Press.

Verdery, K. 1983. *Transylvanian Villagers*. Berkeley: University of California Press.

Vieillard-Baron, M. 2001. *Fujiwara no Teika et la notion d'excéllence en poésie*. Paris: Institut des Hautes Etudes Japonaises, Collège de France.

Waite, L. J., and M. Gallagher. 2000. *The Case for Marriage*. New York: Doubleday.

Walsh, J. J. 1907. *History of the Medical Society of the State of New York*. Brooklyn, NY: New York State Medical Society.

Wallerstein, I. 1976. *The Modern World-System*. New York: Academic.

Warner, N. H. 1858. "On Epidemic Cholera." *Proceedings of the Fifteenth Annual Meeting of the American Institute of Homeopathy*, pp. 102–19.

Warner, S. B. 1968. *The Private City*. Philadelphia: University of Pennsylvania Press.

Weber, M. [1919] 1946. "Science as a Vocation," in H. Gerth and C. W. Mills, eds., *From Max Weber*. New York: Oxford, pp. 129–56.

Weinrich, H. 1973. *Le Temps*, tr. M. Lacoste. Paris: Seuil.

Weinstein, M. C., and H. V. Fineberg. 1980. *Clinical Decision Analysis*. Philadelphia: Saunders.

Werner, M. R. 1928. *Tammany Hall*. Garden City, NY: Doubleday.

White, H. 1973. *Metahistory*. Baltimore: Johns Hopkins University Press.

———. 1987. "The Value of Narrativity in Representations of Reality," in *The Content of the Form*. Baltimore: Johns Hopkins University Press, pp. 1–25.

Whyte, W. F. 1958 "Urban Sprawl," in *The Exploding Metropolis*, ed. by the editors of *Fortune*. New York: Doubleday, pp. 115–39.

Wiener, N. [1948] 1962. *Cybernetics*. Cambridge, MA: MIT Press.

———. 1954. *The Human Use of Human Beings*. New York: Anchor.

Williams-Ellis, C. 1928. *England and the Octopus*. London: Geoffrey Bles.

Williamson, G. E. 1935. "Mutability, Decay, and Seventeenth-Century Melancholy." *ELH: A Journal of English Literary History* 2:121–50.

Wordsworth, W. [1801] 1965. "Preface to the Second Edition of Lyrical Ballads," in J. Stillinger, ed., *William Wordsworth, Selected Poems and Prefaces*. Boston: Houghton Mifflin, pp. 445–64.

Young, M. 1958. *The Rise of the Meritocracy*. London: Thames and Hudson.

Young, M., and P. Willmott. 1957. *Family and Kinship in East London*. Harmondsworth: Penguin.

Zorbaugh, H. 1929. *The Gold Coast and the Slum*. Chicago: University of Chicago Press.

INDEX